INDEPENDENT SECTOR

INDEPENDENT SECTOR is a coalition of 830 corporations, foundations, and voluntary organizations with national interests in and impact on philanthropy, voluntary action, and other activities related to the educational, scientific, cultural, and religious life, as well as the health and welfare, of the nation.

INDEPENDENT SECTOR is a meeting ground where diverse elements in and related to the sector can come together and learn how to improve their performance and effectiveness.

INDEPENDENT SECTOR is serving the sector through

- education, to improve the public's understanding of the independent sector
- research, to develop a comprehensive store of knowledge about the sector
- government relations, to coordinate the multitude of interconnections between the sector and the various levels of government
- encouragement of effective sector leadership and management, to maximize service to individuals and society, by promoting educational programs for managers and practitioners
- communication within the sector, to identify shared problems and opportunities

The impact of INDEPENDENT SECTOR's effort can be measured by the growth in support of the sector, as manifested by increased giving and volunteering.

For additional information, please contact

INDEPENDENT
SECTOR

1828 L Street, N.W.
Washington, DC 20036
(202) 223-8100

Care and Community in Modern Society

Paul G. Schervish,
Virginia A. Hodgkinson,
Margaret Gates, and Associates

Care and Community in Modern Society

Passing On the Tradition of Service to Future Generations

Jossey-Bass Publishers • San Francisco

TCF Manufactured in the United States of America on Lyons Falls Pathfinder Tradebook. This paper is acid-free and 100 percent totally chlorine-free.

Library of Congress Cataloging-in-Publication Data

Care and community in modern society : passing on the tradition of service to future generations / Paul G. Schervish, Virginia A. Hodgkinson, Margaret Gates, [editors]. — 1st ed.
p. cm. — (The Jossey-Bass nonprofit sector series)
Includes bibliographical references and index.
ISBN 0-7879-0109-1 (alk. paper)
1. Public welfare—Philosophy. 2. Social service—Philosophy. 3. Voluntarism. 4. Caregivers. I. Schervish, Paul G. II. Hodgkinson, Virginia Ann. III. Gates, Margaret Jane. IV. Series.
HV13.C37 1995 95-13733
361.2—dc20 CIP

HB Printing 10 9 8 7 6 5 4 3 2 1 FIRST EDITION

The Jossey-Bass Nonprofit Sector Series

Contents

Preface

When we conjure up images of a caring society, we think of caring families, helpful neighbors, kindness to strangers, and active citizens in communities. We also think of institutions that support caring behavior and traditions, such as religious institutions, voluntary associations, schools, private enterprises, and government agencies. We could also think about public policies that encourage and support caring—for example, policies that reflect commitments to the social welfare of citizens through education, pensions, health care, and the care of population groups with special needs. These groups might include people who are unemployed, or who are single parents, or who suffer from physical and/or mental handicaps. Programs that encourage people to engage in public service, volunteering, and giving also come to mind as evidence of a caring society.

But how do caring societies come about, and how are the traditions of a caring society transmitted to future generations? These questions indicate the theme of this volume. Many research studies have focused on the characteristics of healthy families or the characteristics and values of caring individuals. There are libraries full of information on how different governments and their programs provide social welfare to their citizens. There are numerous studies about the transfer of knowledge and culture through schools and colleges. But little attention has been paid to the transfer of caring traditions—evidenced in concern and service to others—to future generations.

While the means of transmitting the traditions of a caring society seem obvious to many, many national youth groups and educational associations spent more than a decade to revitalize teaching the tradition of public and community services to their students, and to make such a tradition a public policy priority, as reflected in the passage of the National and Community Service Act. These efforts were made when volunteering among young people dropped dramatically during the early 1980s and when educators began to grapple with why the traditions of public and community service were dropped from the curriculum of most schools and colleges.

The questions that need to be addressed fall into six broad categories. First, we need to know what we mean by *care*. Second, we need to know how family upbringing relates to the development of individuals who care about strangers or provide service to their communities or nation. What kinds of activities do caring individuals engage in when providing service to others, as exemplified in giving and volunteering for public purposes? Third, we need to know about the kinds of institutions that are most likely to teach and transmit caring traditions and how they do it. Fourth, we need to identify the characteristics of government programs that exemplify caring for the welfare of citizens. Fifth, we need to explore the types of public policies that promote caring, service, and generosity to others. And sixth, we need to know whether the transmission of caring values in the context of a pluralistic society like the United States provides special challenges not found in nations whose populations are more homogeneous. Finally, both practitioners and scholars need to think about how all these elements fit together and affect the ability of society to transmit caring traditions.

The contributors to this book include both scholars and practitioners, and the chapters attempt to strike a balance between the insights of the two groups. The research presented in these chapters comes from a variety of disciplinary perspectives and research methodologies. The transmission of the values of caring and service covers a broad terrain of research extending from psychology to history, and from religious studies to public policy studies. Practice ranges across a number of institutions—from small youth groups to schools, from community organizations to national governments. The populations concerned range from the unborn to the elderly; they include children, parents, and grandparents as well as the generations that precede and those that follow.

The Organization of the Book

Care and Community in Modern Society: Passing On the Tradition of Service to Future Generations seeks to address the major questions discussed above to increase our understanding of the complex set of relationships that lead to caring societies. The introduction attempts to outline the philosophical, religious, and social dimensions of *care* in both its private and public senses. Part One focuses on the transmission of care by families, schools, communities, and society as a whole. It is concerned with ways of theorizing about the various dimensions of care—that is, about ways of defining this term. Chapter One explores how the traditions of giving and volunteering are transmitted to the next generation. Chapter Two is devoted to the development of prosocial orientations in children. Chapter Three is a historical case study that explores how a particular communal orientation within a set of families devoted to a socialistic way of life is transmitted to children within a society that has other beliefs. The final chapter in this section explores the motivations for philanthropy and the transmission of such values to their children by wealthy individuals.

Part Two looks at the theme of children as both receivers and transmitters of care. In each of the chapters, the authors address the need for nurturing children as well as for their full participation in the community. The three chapters in this section explore the impact of children's participation in various types of charitable and service activities on their personal development, on their relationships with adults, and in promoting caring communities. Chapter Five explores the importance of engaging young children in charitable activities in their community. Chapter Six looks at two groups working at a local library—one a group of Camp Fire children and the other a group of adults who work with them—and discusses the collaborative relationships developed in these groups. Chapter Seven reports on the impact of Boys and Girls Clubs in promoting caring in public housing developments.

Part Three explores civic and religious traditions of care. Chapter Eight addresses how the humanitarian ethos of leadership education promoted both citizenship and voluntarism in a historical context in the United States. Chapters Nine to Eleven focus on Jewish, Islamic, and Catholic traditions of care and service, respectively.

Part Four is devoted to the institutional and governmental environment of care. In several chapters in this section, the authors criticize institutions, governments, and citizens for showing a lack of caring in philanthropy, citizen involvement, and government programs for low-income citizens. Chapter Twelve attempts to address the meaning of caring institutions and explores what type of institutions promote or inhibit the development of caring societies. Chapter Thirteen is devoted to the need to encourage a more active citizenry that takes responsibility for its future and suggests that many institutions—both inside and outside government—have made citizens dependent rather than responsible. Chapter Fourteen explores corporate philanthropy, and especially corporate support for racial and ethnic populations, and attempts to determine what kinds of corporate philanthropy help to build caring societies. Chapter Fifteen examines the public charity of government in terms of its care for poor families, looking in particular at whether citizens exhibit a caring society through their support of income-transfer programs. Chapter Sixteen presents the results of a comparative study of several nations and their traditions of service and care, both through government and through an array of charitable, nongovernmental institutions.

Part Five looks at the mobilization of care and mutual aid and the kinds of caring values such organizations develop. Chapter Seventeen establishes the context for the section with a review of the literature on self-help groups. Chapter Eighteen presents an analysis of the emergence of voluntary initiatives to help refugees from Bosnia and Herzegovina help one another. Chapter Nineteen reports on the motives that induce individuals to become active volunteers in their communities and includes research across several countries. Chapter Twenty surveys the characteristics of communities by levels of generosity throughout the United States. The conclusion of the book reflects on the relevance of the volume and its relationship to practice.

Audience

Care and Community in Modern Society: Passing On the Tradition of Service to Future Generations is directed to several major audiences. First, in exploring a broad range of theoretical questions and presenting new research that addresses a set of questions about the complex array of people, institutions, and governments that transmit caring traditions, this volume should be of interest to scholars and students in the areas of history, sociology, psychology, cultural and religious studies, political science, policy studies, and international and comparative studies. Second, because we attempt to discuss the distinctive characteristics of caring traditions and service to communities, the book should be of interest to educators, educational administrators, religious leaders, leaders of voluntary institutions, leaders of youth development organizations, and others who are primarily responsible for transmitting these caring traditions. Third, foundation and corporate leaders should be interested in the programs that work. Fourth, policy makers also should be interested in the impact of government programs and policies that impede or promote a caring and active citizenry. Fifth, we believe that this book should be of interest to parents, to volunteers, and to contributors who are actively engaged in transmitting the traditions of care and community service.

July 1995

Paul G. Schervish
Belmont, Massachusetts

Virginia A. Hodgkinson
Alexandria, Virginia

Margaret Gates
Washington, D.C.

The Contributors

Jennifer Alstad is a 1992 graduate of the University of Minnesota, where she studied political science and Chinese. While at Minnesota, she served as the student legislative liaison to the Minnesota State Legislature and Minnesota's Congressional Delegation and was elected student body president. She also staffed the Legislative Commission on Public Education for two years. In 1992–93, Alstad was the Robert Chollar Research Fellow at the Charles F. Kettering Foundation in Dayton, Ohio. She is planning to pursue graduate study in political science.

Helmut K. Anheier is associate professor in the Department of Sociology at Rutgers University, senior research associate at the Johns Hopkins University Institute for Policy Studies, and visiting associate professor in sociology at Johns Hopkins University. Prior to this, he was Social Affairs Officer at the United Nations International Narcotics Control Board. He graduated from the University of Trier in Germany. His primary areas of interest are organizational studies, and structural and comparative analysis. He is the author of *The Third Sector: Comparative Studies of Nonprofit Organizations* and *The Emerging Sector*, and editor of *Voluntas*.

John Bell is senior research manager at ECOTEC Research and Consulting, based in Birmingham, England. He was previously head of research at the Community Development Foundation and has also worked for disability and health organizations. His particular areas of interest include analysis and policy work around the nature and roles of the voluntary and community sectors. His published works include *Community Development Teamwork: Measuring the Impact—CDF, Social Change and Local Action in an Urban Area*, and *A Framework for Evaluation in the Voluntary and Community Sector.*

Thomasina Borkman is professor of sociology at George Mason University. Formerly she was associate professor of sociology and president of the Association for Research on Nonprofit Organizations and Voluntary Action (ARNOVA). Her primary areas of interest are research on self-help groups, voluntary associations, and health and social services. Her published works include "An Organizational Typology for Self-Help Groups" in the *American Journal of Community Psychology* (with Marsha Schubert), "Experiential, Professional, and Lay Frames of Reference" in *Working with Self-Help*, and *A Social-Experiential Model in Programs for Alcoholism Recovery.*

Robert O. Bothwell is executive director at the National Committee for Responsive Philanthropy. Previously, he was director of the School Finance Reform Project at the National Urban Coalition. He is the author of *United Way's Donor Choice: Who Benefits?* (with Beth Baker and Kevin Ronnie), *Burgeoning Conservative Think Tanks* (with Beth Baker), and *At the Margin of Change: Unrealized Potential for the Disadvantaged.*

Michael K. Briand was a program officer at the Charles F. Kettering Foundation when his chapter was prepared. Currently, he serves as director of the Community Self-Leadership Project, a community civic development program that he conceived and implemented for the Colorado Community College and Occupational Education System. Briand graduated from the University of Michigan and studied law at Stanford University. In 1988, he conducted the first-ever face-to-face meeting between representatives of the South African government, white conservatives, and black opponents of the South African regime. He is currently working on a book with the title *Practical Politics: A Citizens' Guide to Effective Public Problem Solving*.

Emmett D. Carson is president and CEO of the Minneapolis Foundation, the second oldest and thirteenth largest of the nation's 411 community foundations. Previously, he was a program officer at the Ford Foundation, first in the area of social justice and then in governance and public policy. During his five years with Ford, he managed foundation grants supporting black citizens' rights and opportunities, and implemented national and international grantmaking programs promoting philanthropy and the nonprofit sector. Prior to that, he served as project director of the Study on Black Philanthropy at the Joint Center for Political and Economic Studies in Washington, D.C.; as an adjunct professor in the Afro-American Studies program at the University of Maryland; and as a social legislation analyst at the Library of Congress. Currently, he is chair of the Association of Black Foundation Executives. He has received several national awards and published over thirty papers and articles. His published works include *A Hand Up: Black Philanthropy and Self-Help in America* and *The Charitable Appeals Fact Book: How Black and White Americans Respond to Different Fund-Raising Appeals*.

Margaret Gates is a consultant to nonprofit organizations. As national executive director of Girls Incorporated, she was an advocate for girls and introduced programs to meet the special challenges of girls in contemporary society. A lawyer by training, Gates was Deputy Inspector General of the U.S. Department of Agriculture from 1979 to 1981. In 1972, she co-founded the Center for Women Policy Studies. She is a graduate of the University of Maryland.

Silvia Blitzer Golombek is coordinator of Leadership Development Programs at the Congressional Hispanic Caucus Institute in Washington, D.C. She is the founder of KIDS IN ACTION, a program that involves young children as leaders in volunteer community projects. Golombek's publications include *A Sociological Image of the City: Through Children's Eyes*.

Peter Dobkin Hall is a research scientist at the Program on Nonprofit Organizations at Yale University. Hall has been associated with Yale's Nonprofit Program since 1978. His primary area of interest is the history of nonprofit and for-profit organizations. He is author of *Inventing the Non-profit Sector*, *Lives in Trust*, and *The Organization of American Culture*.

Martin Halpern is associate professor of history at Henderson State University in Arkadelphia, Arkansas. Formerly, he was a research analyst and project director at the Michigan Department of Public Health and an instructor at Wayne State University. His primary areas of interest are social, labor, and minority history; public policy and political history; gender studies; and women's and family history. His published works include *UAW Politics in the Cold War Era*, *Minority Health in Michigan: Closing the Gap*, and "The 1939 UAW Convention: Turning Point for Communist Power in the Auto Union?" in *Labor History*.

Heidi Hartmann is the co-founder, president, and director of the Washington-based Institute for Women's Policy Research, a scientific research organization that focuses on policy issues affecting women. In 1994, Hartmann received a MacArthur fellowship. In the spring of 1988, she was the director of the Women's Studies program at Rutgers University. Her published works include the IWPR reports (coauthored) "Unnecessary Losses: Costs to Americans of the Lack of Family and Medical Leave," "The Rhetoric of Self-Interest and the Ideology of Gender," and "Internal Labor Markets and Gender: A Case Study of Promotion."

Virginia A. Hodgkinson is currently vice president for research at INDEPENDENT SECTOR and executive director of the National

Center of Charitable Statistics. Her most recent publications include *Giving and Volunteering in the United States*; the *Nonprofit Almanac, 1992–93: Dimensions of the* INDEPENDENT SECTOR (coedited with Murray S. Weitzman, Christopher M. Toppe, and Stephen M. Noga); *Governing, Leading, and Managing Nonprofit Organizations: New Insights from Research and Practice* (with Dennis R. Young, Robert M. Hollister, and Associates); and *The Nonprofit Sector in the Global Community: Voices from Many Nations* (with Kathleen D. McCarthy, Russy D. Sumariwalla, and Associates). Hodgkinson is an adjunct professor at the Georgetown University Graduate Public Policy Program.

Eliezer David Jaffe is professor of social work at the Hebrew University of Jerusalem and is chair of the Israel Free Loan Association. Formerly he was director of the Jerusalem Municipal Department of Welfare. His primary areas of interest are nonprofit organizations and private philanthropy, child welfare policy and services, and ethnic relationships. He is author of *Child Welfare in Israel, Giving Wisely: Nonprofit Organizations in Israel*, and "Israel: State, Religion, and the Third Sector."

Amani Kandil is Expert on Public Policy Analysis at the National Center for Social and Criminological Research in Cairo. Formerly she was United Nations Consultant on Social Policies in the Arab World (Economic and Social Commission for Western Asia). Her primary areas of interest include public policy analysis, interest groups and associate life in Egypt and the Arab world, and public opinion polls. Her published works include *Education Policy in Egypt*, *Public Opinion Poll on Political Parties and the Democratization Process in Egypt*, *Nonprofit Organizations in Egypt*, and *Status of the Third Sector in the Arab World*.

Anica Mikuš Kos is a consultant child psychiatrist at the Counseling Center in Ljubljana, Slovenia. Formerly she was director of the

Counseling Center in Ljubljana and senior fellow at the Institute for Policy Studies at Johns Hopkins University. Her primary area of interest is the contribution of volunteers to mental health protection. She is the author of "Volunteers in the Field of Child Mental Health Protection," *Mental Health in School*, and numerous articles on volunteer work in the field of child mental health protection.

Steven L. Paprocki is acting director of research at the National Committee for Responsive Philanthropy. Formerly he was president of Impact Giving, Inc. His primary area of interest is philanthropic giving to the disadvantaged. His published works include "The Why and How of Personal Giving Plans," "The Effects of Multiple Charity Campaigns on United Ways and Total Workplace Giving Contributions," and "Marin County: Reflections on a Troubled Relationship."

Maria Parisi is a research assistant in the Research and Evaluation Division of KRA Corporation. Formerly she was a research assistant at George Mason University and an intern at the General Accounting Office (GAO). Her primary area of interest is applied research on children, youth, and family issues.

Lester M. Salamon is professor at Johns Hopkins University and director of the Johns Hopkins Institute for Policy Studies. Prior to this he was director of the Center for Governance and Management Research and of the Nonprofit Sector Project at the Urban Institute. His primary areas of interest are economic-structural change, alternative instruments of government action, and the processes of policy formulation and implementation. He is the author of *America's Nonprofit Sector: A Primer* and *Government and the Third Sector: Emerging Relationships in Welfare States* (edited with Benjamin Gidron and Ralph Kramer).

Paul G. Schervish is associate professor of sociology and director of the Social Welfare Research Institute at Boston College. His primary areas of interest are the sociology of religion, cultural studies, social theory, philanthropy, and the sociology of money and wealth. His published works include *Empowerment and Beneficence: Strategies of Living and Giving Among the Wealthy* (1988, coauthored with Andrew Herman), "Adoption and Altruism: Those with Whom I Want to Share a Dream" in *Nonprofit & Voluntary Sector Quarterly*, (winter 1992) and "The Dependent Variable of the Independent Sector: A Research Agenda for Improving the Definition and Measurement of Giving and Volunteering" in *Voluntas: International Journal of Voluntary and Nonprofit Organizations* (August 1993).

Steven Schinke is professor in the School of Social Work at Columbia University and serves as a consulting editor to *Addictive Behaviors*, *Behavioral Medicine Abstracts*, *Children and Youth Services Review*, *Journal of Adolescent Research*, *Journal of Family Violence*, *Journal of Social Service Research*, and *Research on Social Work Practice*. His research interests center on prevention training, with a special focus on substance abuse and minority-culture adolescents. He has published over 170 articles on preventive interventions and skills training for adolescents.

Roberta Spalter-Roth is research director at the Institute for Women's Policy Research. She is also a researcher in the Sociology Department at American University. Her primary areas of interest are work/family issues, welfare policy, and social and economic inequalities and restructuring. Her published articles include "Combining Work and Welfare: An Alternative Anti-Poverty Strategy," "Science and Politics and the Dual Vision of Feminist Policy Research: The Example of Family and Medical Leave," and "Mothers, Children, and Low-Wage Work."

Roxanne Spillett is assistant national director at the Boys and Girls Clubs of America. Formerly she was director of program services at the Boys and Girls Clubs of America. Her graduate work was in guidance and counseling as well as health administration. Her primary area of interest relates to children from disadvantaged circumstances. Her published works include "Commitment to Quality" and a *School Age Child Care Manual*.

Ervin Staub is professor of psychology at the University of Massachusetts, Amherst. He has taught at Harvard University and has been visiting professor at Stanford, the University of Hawaii, and the London School of Economics and Political Science. Since the late 1960s, he has been conducting research on and developing a theory about the personal and social determinants and development of helping and altruism, and about passivity in the face of others' need. In addition to many articles and book chapters, he has written a two-volume book on the topic *Positive Social Behavior and Morality*, Vol. 1: *Social and Personal Influences*, 1978, and Vol. 2: *Socialization and Development*, 1979. He has also coedited two other volumes, *Development and Maintenance of Prosocial Behavior* and *International Perspectives on Positive Morality*.

John E. Tropman is professor in the School of Social Work/School of Business at the University of Michigan. His primary areas of interest are American values, religious values, charity and social welfare, the policy-making process, and policy decision making. His published works include *American Values and Social Welfare*, *Committee Management in the Human Services*, and *Entrepreneurial Systems for the 1990's*.

Virginia A. Walter is assistant professor at the UCLA Graduate School of Library & Information Science. Formerly she was Children's Services Coordinator, Los Angeles Public Library. Her primary areas of interest are social construction of childhood reality, children's access to information, and children's participation in their community. Her published works include *War and Peace Literature for Children and Young Adults: A Resource Guide*, *Output Measures for Public Library Service to Children*, and "Children as Citizens-in-Training: Political Socialization for a Strong Democracy" in *Nonprofit and Voluntary Action Quarterly*.

Julian Wolpert has been the Henry G. Bryant Professor of Geography, Public Affairs, and Urban Planning at Princeton University's Woodrow Wilson School for the past twenty years. He previously taught at the University of Pennsylvania. He was elected to the National Academy of Sciences and has been a fellow of the American Association for the Advancement of Science, the Guggenheim Foundation, the Smithsonian's Wilson Center, the Center for Advanced Studies in the Behavioral Sciences, and the Rockefeller Foundation's Bellagio Center. His current teaching and research are focused on U.S. domestic policy relating to land use and service provision in metropolitan areas. His most recent study, *Patterns of Generosity in America: Who's Holding the Safety Net?* was published by the Twentieth Century Fund in 1994.

Care and Community in Modern Society

Gentle as Doves and Wise as Serpents: The Philosophy of Care and the Sociology of Transmission

Paul G. Schervish

The subject of this book—passing on the tradition of care to the next generation—has various subtopics that we treat in the five main parts of the book. These include an examination of how individuals become dedicated to care, the importance of civic, ethical, and spiritual traditions, the involvement of children and youth as providers of care, the institutions, here and abroad, that infuse care into daily life, and the productive role of self-interest properly understood in mobilizing care and service to the community.

In the pages introducing the specific parts of the book, we will speak more about these topics and how the contributors address them. In the conclusion, Margaret Gates also takes up several of these topics, elaborating the important practical implications of what our contributors have written. In my comments that follow here, I want to say a few words about the two central themes of this volume—care and its transmission. I am aware of the rich literature on both these topics that has fashioned our Western intellectual heritage. It is not my intention, however, to review this legacy even in a rudimentary way. Rather my purpose is to present what I have learned from my teachers, colleagues, and research about the meaning of care and about the social-psychological processes that teach us to care. In speaking about care and its transmission, I invoke Jesus' injunction in the Gospel of Matthew (10:16): "I am sending you out like sheep among wolves. Therefore be wise as serpents and gentle as doves." If caring requires us to be gentle as doves, teaching people to care requires us to be wise as serpents.

Gentle as Doves: The Virtue of Care and the Ethics of Identification

I believe there is something profoundly mistaken in the way many people think about philanthropy. The mistake is to conceive of philanthropy as an act that must be spurred on because it is not something people would naturally desire to do and find rewarding. Such a notion is not without precedent or intellectual authority. In fact, it originates—at least in its modern form—in Immanuel Kant, one of the giants of Western intellectual history. In an essay on Hegel's philosophy of history, Frederick Copleston (1965) points out an important distinction between Kantian and Hegelian ethics. In the Kantian tradition, an act loses its moral value if performed from inclination—that is, if it is something that people naturally want to do. But in the Hegelian tradition, says Copleston, morality does not require "a constant warfare against inclinations and natural impulses" (p. 250). Rather, a moral act can be inspired just as much as an immoral one from what people find pleasing and satisfying. This does not mean that morality consists in whatever someone feels like doing. It does mean that morality derives from choices people make from among competing inclinations rather than from choices between immoral inclinations and moral disinclinations. Now it seems to me that much of our current thinking about philanthropy is quite Kantian. By this I mean that otherwise genteel and wise advocates tend to idealize a morality that is foreign to human inclinations—that is, a morality of selflessness.

How did Kant come to fashion his ethics of disinclination, or what we have come to know as his duty principle? Kant's starting point is that human senses are unreliable. Principles of morality must be derived from deductive logic rather than from inductive experience. Thus Kant justified his categorical imperative—that we should act in a way that it would be beneficial if everyone acted in the same way—by its correspondence to reason rather than to experience. Of course I have no objection to elevating duty to its rightful prominence. Indeed, it is a salutary antidote to the relativism that spans the political spectrum. From my point of view, however, the Kantian perspective is problematic because its proper emphasis on duty is undermined by an unfounded ideal of selfless altruism. To be fair, I should point out that those who advocate a Kantian perspective rarely, if ever, claim that all efforts to care for others require pure intentions. Still, the notion prevails that for philanthropy to be moral it should, at least in some minimal way, embrace the counterinclination of selflessness. Why, one may ask, am I so resistant to the Kantian viewpoint? After all, how much damage can be done by selfless intentions? A lot, suggests the Sufi story told by Idries Shah about the philanthropist who turns out to be just a well-meaning meddler (see Dervish, 1982, pp. 29–30).

One day a dervish discovers a poor family that, despite his persistence, refuses his charity. To make his gift more acceptable, he disguises himself as a carpet merchant and returns to the woman of the house, offering 100 pieces of gold to buy a dirty rug that an ancestor had left them. The woman says she will have to discuss the offer with her husband and asks the merchant to return the next evening. Suspicious of the merchant's intentions, the family has the rug appraised and discovers it is worth ten times more than the merchant offered. When the holy man returns to the house, the police arrest and convict him on "what seemed to everybody but him the clearest possible evidence that he was trying to steal from a poor family by a mean trick."

Does the fate of this well-intentioned but unenlightened holy man imply that we should abandon the ideals of duty and care? Certainly not! It does mean that high intentions are no substitute for careful attention. It also means that we should look somewhere other than selfless altruism to locate the principle of duty and the ideal of care. It is one of the ironies of philanthropy that cherishing altruism does so little to advance our cherishing of each other.

So can we do any better if we put aside the Kantian perspective? Can we find an ethic of care that corresponds more closely to our natural inclinations, helps us avoid the pitfalls of pure intention, and offers a productive practical strategy for teaching others the duties of care? I believe we can, and at least implicitly, so do the contributors to this book.

As an alternative to the Kantian ethic of *selfless engagement*, I propose the Thomistic ethic of *dutiful identification*. As we will see, Thomas Aquinas advances a morality in which people extend to others rather than curtail their love of self. Three considerations are important to establish a motivating principle for philanthropy that is based on natural inclinations and the potential for those inclinations to mature over the course of one's life.

Philanthropy as a Social Relation

The first consideration is the somewhat obvious but often-neglected fact that philanthropy is a social relation (see Ostrander and Schervish, 1990). It is a form of human interaction in which donors respond to the needs of others as valuable in their own right. In the commercial realm, firms generally respond to needs to the extent that those needs are expressed by dollars to be spent. In the political realm, politicians generally respond to needs to the extent that they are expressed by votes and campaign contributions. In philanthropy, however, donors respond to needs to the extent that these needs are felt to be important to the donors. If in commerce and politics there is a material basis for responding to needs, in philanthropy there is a moral basis. This does not deny that some aspects of commerce and politics move toward philanthropy to the extent that they honor needs expressed nonmaterially. Nor does it deny that philanthropy can move toward politics and commerce to the extent that it responds to material incentives. Still, the point is that the heart of philanthropy is a relationship between donor and recipient ultimately mobilized and regulated by moral incentives. Since the philanthropic donor is in a superior material position, the donor must embody a high level of moral sensitivity if a materially adequate philanthropic relationship is to exist.

Caritas: Meeting the True Needs of Others

The second consideration concerns the nature of this moral sensitivity. What rudimentary disposition is substantial enough to be the basis for duty and yet familiar enough to be a natural inclination? It is the virtue of *care*. The term *care* derives, of course, from the Latin *caritas*. It is usually translated as "love" or "charity"—two words with profound meanings despite a tendency to be taken superficially. In the realm of philanthropy, love is sometimes seen as too soft, ambiguous, pretentious, or private. Charity, for its part, is viewed as too reminiscent of guilt-assuaging remedial intervention or entailing the paternalistic attitude of noblesse oblige. Let us put aside these two terms and concentrate instead on the fundamental dimension of *caritas* encompassed by the attribute of care.

Philosopher Jules Toner (1968) goes to great pains to formulate a notion of care grounded in a phenomenological analysis of love. For Toner, care is love focused on meeting the true needs of others. Care is the practical implementation of *radical love*, which he defines as the affection by which a lover "affirms the beloved for the beloved's self (as a radical end) . . . [and] by which the lover affectively identifies with the loved one's personal being, by which in some sense the lover is the beloved affectively" (p. 183). Therefore, according to Toner, radical care

> is an affirmative affection toward someone precisely as in need. It is not the need nor what is needed that is the object of radical care; radical care is of the one who has the need, under the aspect of needing. For example, I have an affection of care toward one who needs

> food or friendly words or a listener or instruction. As a consequence of care, I desire food for him, or friendly words and so on. If I have a care or concern for the food or words or instruction, etc. it is only . . . relative and derivative care [p. 75].

The implication for philanthropy of Toner's definition of care is to elevate care as the cardinal moral characteristic defining the relation between donor and recipient. The philanthropist is first and foremost a caregiver, not a giver of time and money. Time and money are the medium by which care is expressed. But the fundamental moral standard to which philanthropists should dedicate themselves is caring for others in need. While Toner cannot tell us what caring will mean in any particular situation, he does point us in the right direction. First, he emphasizes that care for another person is a radical end. Certainly people speak of caring for education or for the Boston Symphony. But Toner is clear that such concerns are derivative care, not to be confused with or substituted for radical care directed toward the only worthy object—other human beings, the so-called "ultimate recipients" or "ultimate beneficiaries" of philanthropy. Second, Toner insists that care, as the practical implementation of love, is an affective involvement in meeting others' *true needs*. Again, we can never know in the abstract what another's true needs are; nor does simply setting out to attend to someone's true needs exempt us from critical scrutiny. Yet by emphasizing the notion of *true* needs, Toner places front and center the obligation not just to respond to others but to respond effectively. According to him, taking the effort to figure out how to respond in a way that accomplishes a beneficial end (even if not always viewed as such by others or even by the recipient) is a crucial test of how much we care in the first place.

Thomas and Tocqueville: The Ethics of Identification

Along with understanding philanthropy as a social relation and as a disposition of radical care, the third step in establishing the moral imperative of philanthropy is to recall the Western religious emphasis on the identity between love of neighbor and love of self. Toner's notion of care explicitly makes this connection, as we saw earlier: "The lover affectively identifies with the loved one's personal being, by which in some sense the lover is the beloved affectively." Notice two things, about which I will say more in a moment. First, a true act of care is an act of identification with another. It is recognizing a radical affinity connecting the destinies of self and neighbor. Second, a true act of care is actually an act of self-love. We have now arrived at the point where it is possible to specify a morality of natural inclination that is substantial and familiar enough to ground the duties and ideals of philanthropy. I call this morality an *ethic of identification*.

If the essence of philanthropy is a social relation, and the essence of such a relation is radical care, the essence of radical care is identification. In modern discourse, self-identity revolves around the awareness of oneself as a distinctive personality. However, such a notion was not always prevalent. If our contemporary emphasis is on the notion of *self*-identity, the more classical emphasis of Thomas Aquinas, for instance, was on self-*identity*. To be clear, I should stress that not only did Aquinas not share our modern conception of identity, he did not even use the term. But he did speak eloquently about *identification* as the basic condition of *caritas*—what Toner refers to as radical care. As Aquinas puts it, "by the fact that love transforms the lover into the beloved, it makes the lover enter inside the beloved, and conversely, so that there is nothing of the beloved that is not united to the lover, just as the form attains the innermost recesses of that which it informs, and conversely" (*III Sent.*, d 27, q. 1, a. 1, ad 4; cited in Gilleman, 1959, p. 126).

It is not stretching things too far to suggest that what Aquinas describes in scholastic terms as the fundamental mutuality of love is akin to what Tocqueville enunciates in civic terms as "self-interest properly understood." As Tocqueville ([1835] 1966, p. 526) says, Americans "enjoy explaining almost every act of their lives on the principle of self-interest properly understood. It gives them great pleasure to point out how an enlightened self-love continually leads them to help one another and disposes them freely to give part of their time and wealth for the good of the state." Harriet Martineau ([1838] 1989, p. 218), a contemporary of Tocqueville who wrote six volumes on her travels in America, is equally persuaded about the need for a sense of identification to make a society a place where "charity has gone deep as well as spread wide." According to Martineau, the spirit of charity becomes one with "the spirit of justice" only in those societies with a full-fledged "spirit of fraternity." Such a spirit of fraternity, she maintains, arises "from the movers feeling it their own concern that any are depressed and endangered as they would themselves refuse to be" (p. 218).

An obvious objection is that the above formulations too easily permit self-interest to masquerade as mutual self-interest. But having to confront this prospect turns out to be one of those proverbial "good problems." Having to be vigilant about the dangers of specious mutuality is a small risk compared to the potential benefits of an ethic that predicates duty on the mutual inclinations of identification. In his treatise on charity, Gerard Gilleman (1959) acknowledges that Aquinas properly recognizes the possibility that in the name of love one may end up being egocentric. It is always appropriate to ask whether a professed intention of charity actually accomplishes its desired end. Still, holding individuals accountable for objective outcomes makes the most sense from the point of view of an ethic of identification that from the outset requires us to scrutinize actions as well as intentions. In the end, to accept an ethic of identification is to accept a rigorous (though nondogmatic) criterion for judging practical affairs, namely, whether I have loved my neighbor as myself. Even though the morality of *caritas* does not enable us to make *ultimate* judgments about another person's moral status, it does establish the primacy of charity as an ethical standard, supports the notion of philanthropy as a social relation, and provides the basis for us tentatively to appraise our own and others' behavior. In the long run, the most important implication of moving charity to center stage is that it avoids the distracting debate about the contaminating influence of self-love and shifts attention to the quality of one's identifications.

From my point of view, then, it is woefully inadequate to offer an ethic of altruistic selflessness precisely in that area of human dedication in which the self is most involved. When it comes to *caritas*, what matters is the quality of the self and not the absence of self, the quality of what we do in the name of identification and not the absence of identification, the horizon of our interests and not the absence of interests. Aquinas recognizes and even extols this seemingly paradoxical unity of duty and pleasure in the implemental aspects of *caritas*. As Gilleman (1959, p. 125) says, "For St. Thomas there is no place in a morally good act of will for an absolute disjunction between love referred to self and love referred to another. The proper effect of love is to associate self with the other."

Relation, care, and identification, then, are three pillars of philanthropy because they are three pillars of morality. To repeat, neither philanthropy nor the nonprofit sector has a corner on virtue. But because the charitable sector must rely on the moral sensitivity of those in command of resources, it is crucial to be clear about the meaning of care and about the human inclination toward identification that motivates that care. Fortunately, care and identification are not foreign endeavors. By inclination we identify our fate with the fate of others, even if these others are at first just family and close friends. Experience imbues us at least with embryonic sentiments of radical love and radical care. Although we may tend to ignore these sentiments or limit their application to those in our immediate environment, we are also constantly invited to expand our horizons.

Wise as Serpents: The Social Psychology of Socialization

To say that care and identification are natural proclivities does not mean they are uneducated virtues or easily applied outside our familiar frontiers. The ethic of identification requires moral instruction if we are to care effectively and identify with souls beyond our immediate habitat. For this reason, we must devote a comparable amount of attention to the transmission as we do to the understanding of care. We must care about the transmission of care. That is, we must be wise as serpents in addition to being gentle as doves. The second theme of this book is the mechanisms by which parents and institutions transmit to their charges a dedication to care. While as a practical matter transmitting care is never easy or automatic, it is theoretically something as simple as moral education or socialization. Just as there is nothing more central to the philosophy of philanthropy than love and identification, there is nothing more central to the conduct of philanthropy than setting and socialization.

My own research on charitable giving among the wealthy (Schervish and Herman, 1988) and the population at large (Schervish and Havens, 1994) reveals a specific array of important motivating factors. Our eyes tend to glaze over when we hear social scientists speak of "multivariate analysis." Nevertheless, researchers who apply sophisticated statistical techniques to ferret out causal forces are simply being systematic about a notion that is a matter of common sense for any thinking person—that every outcome stems from several overlapping and interacting forces. Indeed, it is generally not the multidimensionality so much as the unidimensionality of an explanation that undermines its credibility.

I have found six factors especially important for inculcating a moral identity of care. Of course others may wish to add or subtract variables from this list. But for now, the following may serve as a preliminary working model of the six mobilizing factors that appear to induce charitable engagement across levels of income: (1) groups and organizations in which we participate, (2) frameworks of consciousness that shape values and priorities, (3) persons or organizations that directly invite participation in philanthropy, (4) discretionary resources, (5) people or experiences from our youth that serve as positive inspirations for our adult engagements, and (6) the intrinsic and extrinsic rewards of engagement that draw us deeper into a philanthropic identity. The first five variables work to induce charitable involvement in the first place and then to increase our level of commitment. The sixth variable—reinforcing rewards—is by definition relevant, since rewards reinforce the participation of those who have already become involved. For a particular individual, any one of the first five factors may be enough to induce at least a minimal level of philanthropic care; but in most cases the path to philanthropic care is via the influence of several if not all the factors.

Communities of participation—the first factor—comprise the entire range of informal and formal organizations in which individuals participate as a result of circumstances or choice. For instance, people with children are drawn into a number of school, extracurricular, and sports programs that offer opportunities to volunteer time and contribute money. The same is true if we belong to a church, alumni association, work-based professional association, union, or social club. Affiliation with a political party, social movement, political candidate, or neighborhood cause are other avenues for engagement. As I will discuss in a moment, these communities of participation often directly request assistance from the participants. But simply becoming involved in such organizations ends up creating a familiar setting in which we are spontaneously made aware of needs to which we may choose to respond.

Frameworks of consciousness—the second of the six factors—are the ways of thinking and feeling that are rooted deeply enough in our awareness to make us committed to a cause. These ways of thinking and feeling can have to do with religious beliefs, political ideology, or social concerns. An awareness of the redemptive value of Alcoholics Anonymous's twelve-step program in our own or a family member's life is one example. Equally common are the deeply felt convictions about political prisoners that lead concerned citizens to join Amnesty International, about the homeless or battered women that lead volunteers to work at a shelter, about community violence that lead parents to patrol the streets as part of a neighborhood watch, about the value of religious faith that lead church members to work in a food bank or a program for racial justice. The list of motivating concerns is, of course, as long as the list of cherished beliefs. Just as there are different types of organizations in which we may participate, there are different types of beliefs. Some mobilizing beliefs are better described as general values, other beliefs are really fundamental orientations, while still other beliefs involve causes we are dedicated to. Again, there are no impermeable boundaries separating these kinds of beliefs, any more than there is a sharp demarcation between what we do because of heartfelt feelings, on the one hand, and communities of participation, on the other. Communities of participation and frameworks of consciousness almost always occur together.

The third mobilizing factor entails *direct requests* for contributions of time and money. Many of these invitations arise as a result of our participation in an organization. Multivariate analysis of the biennial INDEPENDENT SECTOR Survey on Giving and Volunteering being carried out by Virginia A. Hodgkinson and her associates and by our research team at Boston College has begun to produce a set of consistent findings. In addition to being connected to the level of involvement in communities of participation (for example, the frequency of attendance at religious services), the most important factor leading to involvement is simply being asked for assistance. Certainly, some people volunteer their time and money without being asked. But the majority of givers cite being asked as a major reason for their charitable efforts. Of course, we are all asked through telephone and mail solicitations. But there is every reason to believe (as Hodgkinson points out in Chapter One) that people in all income groups follow what I found among wealthy contributors, namely, that being asked by someone we know personally or by a representative of an organization we participate in is a major mobilizer. Again, a multivariate model makes sense. Being asked to contribute occurs from within existing communities of participation and appeals to existing frameworks of consciousness.

The presence of *discretionary resources* is a fourth factor leading to charitable commitment. The level of our discretionary resources of time and money is of course a mixture of objective and subjective considerations. For instance, the amount of discretionary time available to retired people with children out of the house may seem greater than that available to members of the labor force who are still raising children. Similarly, a family of four with a household income of $75,000 presumably enjoys more discretionary spending than a family of four with an income of $25,000. But there are a number of complicating factors, including the amount of time needed to care for a sick spouse and the amount of money devoted to necessary expenditures such as college tuition and taxes. One family's necessity is another family's luxury, which highlights the fact that the amount of discretionary resources is also a matter of subjective disposition. Although difficult to measure, the amount of resources people are ready to give is in large part a function of how much they identify with and care for others in need. As is true with the previous three variables, disposable resources, while an important variable in its own right, also reflects the fundamental quality of our moral identity. The organizations in which we participate, the cultural frameworks we embrace, the pleas to which we are attuned, and the resources we feel we are able to give are all inextricably linked to each other and to our moral identity as caring individuals.

The same is true for the fifth determinant: the positive *models and experiences from our youth* that encourage adult philanthropy. By speaking of models from our youth, I do not mean to neglect models from our adult life that we emulate. But for the sake of clarity, I include such adult models (be they friends, business associates, or colleagues on a board of directors) as part of our community of participation. Emphasized here are the activities and lives that we are more or less drawn into in the course of growing up. To some extent, we voluntarily choose such contacts. But the majority of them are likely to have been unavoidable, put in our path by our parents, grandparents, churches, youth groups, and schools. As such, they are forms of initiatory training in identification and care. They are part of a moral education that molds our lives in a period when we are less guarded about our priorities and more apt to accrue at least a feel for the charitable impulse.

As I have said, a sixth variable influences the intensity of people's philanthropic commitment. This is the set of *intrinsic and extrinsic rewards* that accrue to individuals who are already active in philanthropy. The source and intensity of such satisfactions are connected to the additional communities of participation and frameworks of consciousness that philanthropists encounter in the course of carrying out their commitments. Such reinforcing factors will include getting to know other givers, formal and informal expressions of gratitude, public recognition of various sorts, and direct material benefits such as preferred seating at the symphony and decision-making clout at a welfare agency. But most important among such reinforcing rewards is the personal satisfaction from helping others and from seeing one's money and time used as an effective investment to accomplish cherished goals. In this regard, less involved philanthropists might take a hint from Hull House founder Jane Addams and from those who work directly with the beneficiaries of their philanthropy. One of the richest sources of reinforcing satisfaction is to witness firsthand the positive effect of care on the lives of others and to be able to more fully identify with one's beneficiaries as radical ends.

Conclusion

Although we have assigned the chapters of this book to specific sections, each chapter makes some original contribution to the themes of care and the transmission of care that I have just presented. Together with the preceding comments and Margaret Gates's conclusion, these chapters suggest several propositions about care and the generation of a caring society. First, care entails not just a willingness to assist others. It also involves an inner disposition that regards those in need as ends in themselves. As such, care requires that caregivers concentrate on discovering just what in fact is needed and how to provide it. Care is loving others in their true needs. Becoming informed about the lives of those for whom we care, especially through direct contact, may be one of the most important yet least practiced aspects of contemporary philanthropy. Where such contact does occur, we find both an extraordinary dedication of resources and exceptionally fruitful outcomes.

Second, the disposition of care is a matter of moral identity. Caring individuals come to view themselves and not just others in a different light. To exhibit a caring orientation toward others in a consistent and dedicated fashion is to assume a self-definition in which one does not so much become selfless as self-expansive. A caring person is one who becomes profoundly self-concerned about what happens to others by identifying with their fate. When self-interest properly understood *is* properly understood, it is the noblest—not the basest—motivation. In this way, all help of others is self-help and all true self-help is help of others.

Third, participation in organizations from church and school to social movements and political efforts is the breeding ground for philanthropic commitment. While not automatic or inevitable, initial engagement tends to spawn deeper engagement. Participation opens our eyes to where we are needed and places us in circumstances where we will be invited to commence or expand our dedication.

Fourth, extraordinary commitment requires extraordinary inspiration. Heartfelt civic, political, and humanistic values are one such source of motivation. Perhaps even more profoundly influential are spiritualities in which one discerns the inextricable affinity between love of God, love of neighbor, and love of self. In either case, however, such frameworks of consciousness induce care by guiding people to first taste and later embrace the ancient wisdom in which duty becomes an attractive path. Virtue, says Aquinas, is the habit of doing good. Transmitting the tradition of care means awakening people to more habitually encounter and more readily bear that *munus suavissimum* ("most agreeable burden") of *caritas*.

References

Copleston, F. A *History of Philosophy*. Vol. 7. Garden City, N.Y.: Image Books, 1965.

Dervish, H.B.M. *Journeys with a Sufi Master*. London: Octagon Press, 1982.

Gilleman, G. *The Primacy of Charity in Moral Theology*. Westminster, Md.: Newman Press, 1959.

Martineau, H. *How to Observe Morals and Manners*. New Brunswick, N.J.: Transaction Books, 1989. (Originally published 1838.)

Ostrander, S. A., and Schervish, P. G. "Giving and Getting: Philanthropy as a Social Relation." In J. Van Til and Associates, *Critical Issues in American Philanthropy: Strengthening Theory and Practice*. San Francisco: Jossey-Bass, 1990.

Schervish, P. G., and Havens, J. J. "The Greening of the Yuppies: The Factors Behind the Findings of Increased Giving and Volunteering." Paper presented at the 1st annual meeting of International Society for Third-Sector Research, Pécs, Hungary, July 1994.

Schervish, P. G., and Herman, A. *Empowerment and Beneficence: Strategies of Living and Giving Among the Wealthy*. Final Report on the Study on Wealth and Philanthropy. Chestnut Hill, Mass.: Social Welfare Research Institute, Boston College, 1988.

Tocqueville, A. de. *Democracy in America* (G. Lawrence, trans.; J. P. Mayer, ed.). New York: HarperCollins, 1966. (Originally published 1835.)

Toner, J. *The Experience of Love*. Washington, D.C.: Corpus Books, 1968.

Part One

The Role of Family and Community in Transmitting the Tradition of Care

Part One contains four chapters addressing how families, schools, and society communicate their traditions of caring and service to those in their custody. In many ways, these are the most theoretical chapters in the book. Each explores the meaning of care and the social-psychological processes by which it gets passed on to others. At the same time, each derives its theoretical analysis from a close scrutiny of one or another aspect of the empirical world. Taken together, these chapters provide an important first step in developing a general theory of the transmission of care that can direct future research and provide a practical guide for those who strive to teach others to care.

Virginia A. Hodgkinson's chapter on the determinants of giving and volunteering among teenagers and adults (Chapter One) provides an overview of the factors that generate a charitable commitment. Hodgkinson bases the bulk of her analysis on the 1992 INDEPENDENT SECTOR Survey of Giving and Volunteering among adults and its 1992 survey of teenagers twelve to seventeen years of age. She finds a number of strong positive forces that encourage philanthropic behavior. For both teens and adults, events and experiences from their youth such as volunteer experience or having parents who volunteer positively influence philanthropic commitment. Participation in organizations such as schools and youth groups and especially attendance at religious services also positively influence levels of giving and volunteering. Moreover, there is strong evidence that participation by teens and adults in volunteer activity provides a variety of rewards that encourage further commitment. Importantly, the kinds of benefits reported by teens are not so much instrumental rewards (such as learning new skills) as communal ones (such as learning to respect others and deriving satisfaction from their involvement). In addition, feeling a moral duty to help others and being concerned about the welfare of others are highly associated for both teens and adults with philanthropic participation. Consistent with what was said in the introduction about the importance of communities of participation is Hodgkinson's finding that teens and adults are far more likely to give money and volunteer time when they are linked to a social network in which they are explicitly asked or expected to contribute. On a practical level, Hodgkinson's findings on the importance of organizational participation, role models, youth experience, values development, and simply being asked to contribute indicate the kind of initiatives that those seeking to create a more caring society in this and future generations may take.

In Chapter Two, Ervin Staub summarizes what he and his colleagues have learned from years of research on what enhances the transmission of a prosocial orientation to children. What is crucial in the home also proves important for schools and society. Staub's central insight is that care is inculcated by care. By this he means something far more profound than striving to communicate an amorphous sense of love. First, care itself is a sense of empathy that entails a positive evaluation of human nature, a concern for others' welfare, a sense of responsibility, a realization of one's capacity to help, and the experience of actually helping. Teaching children to care begins with nurturance and affection but must at the practical level go beyond the realm of sentiment. At home, in school, and in society, children require guidance and positive discipline. They learn to internalize a caring disposition by actively helping others. Early childhood experiences are crucial, especially those that reduce the tendency to separate the world into "we" and "them." Ultimately, becoming a caring person is to learn a moral identity, what Staub refers to as coming to think of oneself "as the kind of person who will help other people."

In Chapter Three, Martin Halpern also helps identify the key variables that make so much difference in transmitting care to children. Halpern studies the efforts by parents in the left-wing movement in the twentieth century to transmit their aspirations for social justice to their children. The left is a caring subculture with a particular concept of care that is continuously undermined by conventional influences. Historically, says Halpern, the left's notion of care is distinguished by what it includes, not by what it excludes. Despite popular misconceptions, the left has always been concerned with spiritual transformation, family, and neighborhood. The crucial ingredient it adds is the importance of including in our realm of care the downtrodden outside our immediate purview and a commitment to transformative rather than remedial solutions "through the medium of political and social activism." Halpern presents a series of accounts from the writings of leftists describing the socialization of red diaper babies. The common elements in the communication of the left-wing version of care include a firm emphasis on education as the basis for securing a livelihood, the importance of acting for justice to defend the economic and political rights of the oppressed, and the need for hands-on participation in communal organizational settings intended to train children in these values.

Paul G. Schervish's chapter on the intergenerational transmission of financial care by the wealthy—Chapter Four—also charts a set of variables by which parents communicate care. While Halpern discusses the distinctive attributes surrounding what could be called political care, Schervish discusses the notion of financial care. He defines financial care as the attempt to link the empowerment of wealth to an appropriate sense of public and private responsibility. From interviews with 130 millionaires, he found parents citing five factors that affect their ability to transmit financial care to their children: (1) social forces that shape the contemporary moral environment, (2) effect of the family's life-style, (3) role of parental modeling around life-style and philanthropy; (4) direct involvement of children in business and charity, and (5) explicit verbalization of beliefs, principles, and values. In addition to these five factors there are an array of extrafamilial influences revolving around school, work, friends, travel, and volunteer service that transmit a commitment to financial care. The factors that affect the transmission of financial care by the wealthy are, with only minor adjustments, relevant for the transmission of financial care by parents from across the economic spectrum.

Chapter One

Key Factors Influencing Caring, Involvement, and Community

Virginia A. Hodgkinson

Building caring communities has long been a concern in the United States. As a country composed of people of diverse national, ethnic, and religious backgrounds, we have faced major challenges in building community throughout our history. Part of the response to such challenges has been the highly developed cultural tradition of membership in organizations, and the voluntary contribution of time and money for a variety of causes. The great majority of Americans give, and about half of the population volunteers. Another 40 percent of the half of the population that currently does not volunteer has volunteered in the past, indicating that over a lifetime, about 70 percent of American adults volunteer time. From a special analysis of various surveys of giving and volunteering among adults and teens, this chapter addresses the following questions: How do such traditions get transmitted? Which people and which institutions are most responsible for teaching the traditions? What childhood experiences are most important in developing traditions of caring, citizen involvement, and community?

One of the priorities of the INDEPENDENT SECTOR research program has been to explore motivations for giving, volunteering, and community participation. In 1988, it launched its biennial series of national surveys of the giving and volunteering behavior of adults eighteen years of age or older. In 1990, it added an experimental survey exploring such behavior in teens fourteen to seventeen, and in 1992, expanded the teen survey to include young people twelve to seventeen. Each of these surveys is designed by a national advisory committee of scholars and practitioners, who attempt to test findings from research and practice relating to giving and volunteering.

The sample size of the adult surveys is over 2,500, with oversampling of African American, Hispanic, and affluent households. The surveys are conducted through in-home personal interviews. The 1992 survey of teens included in-home personal interviews with 1,400 young people (Hodgkinson and Weitzman, 1988, 1990; Hodgkinson and Weitzman, with Noga and Gorski, 1992a, 1992b). Several new questions were added in the 1992 surveys that have emerged from research on prosocial behavior, as Ervin Staub describes in Chapter Two of this volume.

One of the purposes of the INDEPENDENT SECTOR research has been to identify the kinds of experiences, values, and background influences that increase caring behavior and active participation. If such characteristics could be identified, strategies could be developed to preserve and increase those experiences to build a more caring society in future generations. This special analysis of various surveys is designed to test some of these basic assumptions. Unless otherwise noted, all references to the data come from the 1992 national surveys of *Giving and Volunteering in the United States* (Hodgkinson and Weitzman, with Noga and Gorski, 1992a) and *Volunteering and Giving Among American Teenagers 12 to 17 Years of Age* (Hodgkinson and Weitzman, with Noga and Gorski, 1992b).

From our research, we know that individuals have multiple motives for engaging in many behaviors. For example, people may join a small theater group because they have a personal interest in some aspect of theatrical production, but they also may hope to provide theater to their community and believe they have an obligation to contribute to that effort. This example involves a mixture of personal interest, caring for the quality of life in the community, and personal responsibility or obligation. In terms of motives, there is a motive to serve others as well as to participate in an activity of personal interest.

Motives for involvement generally include both personal interests and concerns for others or for whole communities, because individuals share membership in those communities. This type of caring or concern that serves multiple motives is most typical of people's behavior. Pure altruism is rare as a sole motive for caring or is unusual and occurs in crisis situations. Saving a drowning child or pulling victims from a fire without thought of one's own safety is unusual. What we are examining here are the kinds of caring behaviors that allow for the better functioning of communities, and for shared responsibility in accomplishing the work of communities.

Even within this construct, some individuals are more active and more generous than others. About 19 percent of adults reported household donations of 2 percent or more of average U.S. household income. About 9 percent of contributing adults reported household contributions of 5 percent or more. The pattern is similar for volunteering. Approximately 14 percent of adults reported volunteering five or more hours per week. Determining the characteristics of this active group could help us to better understand how to increase such participation and generosity.

The meaning of *caring* in this chapter is quite broad. It includes individually caring for and helping others, but it also includes helping others or society through active gifts of time and money to and through organizations, communities, and causes. Our question then becomes what characteristics, personal experiences, and values lead individuals to actively engage in behaviors that serve others or communities or causes beyond, but not necessarily exclusive of, their self-interest.

Influence of Childhood Experiences on Giving and Volunteering

Both teens and adults were given a series of events and asked if any of these events had happened to them when they were young (Table 1.1). Their responses were then compared to their current

Table 1.1. Influence of Childhood Experiences on Giving and Volunteering (Percentage of Respondents[a]).

	Adults					
Event	*Event occurred*	*Contributors*	*Volunteers*	*Event did not occur*	*Contributors*	*Volunteers*
You saw someone in your family help others.	57.6	80.9	61.2	42.4	60.3	37.4
A close friend/relative became seriously ill or died.	59.6	76.4	54.9	40.4	65.9	45.5
You often dreamed about being wealthy and famous.	33.8	74.1	52.9	66.2	71.2	50.2
You belonged to a youth group or something similar.	49.5	84.2	66.4	50.5	60.4	36.2
You personally saw someone you admire (not a family member) helping others.	45.6	83.6	66.6	54.4	62.6	38.1
You were helped in the past by others.	44.2	77.8	60.0	55.8	67.7	44.1
You did some kind of volunteer work.	43.3	85.6	69.0	56.7	61.9	37.4
You have always wanted to make a significant change in society.	24.3	84.4	67.2	75.7	68.3	45.9
You went door to door to raise money for a cause or organization.	28.1	86.1	68.3	71.9	66.8	44.4
You saw, in person, people living in extreme poverty.	42.8	75.5	56.6	57.2	69.7	47.0
You were seriously ill.	17.5	73.5	53.0	82.5	71.9	50.7
You were active in student government.	17.4	87.4	79.6	82.6	68.9	45.1
You, yourself, grew up in poverty.	20.0	64.1	44.3	80.0	74.2	52.8

Teens

You saw someone in your family help others.	75.8	53.6	65.2	19.6	36.1	43.0
A close friend/relative became seriously ill or died.	69.0	53.4	63.5	27.2	39.4	53.4
You often dreamed about being wealthy and famous.	68.1	50.9	61.2	26.9	44.5	56.5
You belonged to a youth group or something similar.	65.4	58.1	71.9	30.5	32.2	37.2
You personally saw someone you admire (not a family member) helping others.	62.2	55.4	66.3	31.7	38.9	49.3
You were helped in the past by others.	59.9	54.7	65.8	32.8	40.9	50.8
You did some kind of volunteer work.	57.9	59.1	83.5	38.2	35.3	27.0
You have always wanted to make a significant change in society.	50.7	57.8	68.1	39.4	38.9	51.4
You went door to door to raise money for a cause or organization.	49.9	57.9	71.9	44.9	39.8	46.9
You saw, in person, people living in extreme poverty.	46.4	56.7	67.4	47.1	42.0	53.3
You were seriously ill.	26.0	58.4	68.6	66.7	45.4	56.7
You were active in student government.	19.7	64.5	76.7	72.4	45.3	55.4
You, yourself, grew up in poverty.	6.0	32.8	52.6	85.3	50.3	60.1

[a]Respondents could give multiple responses.

Source: Data from Hodgkinson and Weitzman, with Noga and Gorski, 1992a, 1992b.

giving and volunteer behavior. The list of events included activities such as membership in a youth group or student government; life conditions, including whether they grew up in poverty or saw others living in poverty; specific experiences such as engaging in volunteer work or going door to door to raise money for a cause; or having been very ill or having had a close friend or relative who either was very ill or died. The list also included personal observations, such as seeing others helped by a family member or another adult they admired, or having been helped themselves by others; and aspirations and dreams, such as wanting to be wealthy or wanting to make significant changes in society.

Certain events experienced during youth have an impact on adult behavior, both positively and negatively. Over 80 percent of adult respondents who reported that they were members of a youth group, did some volunteer work, went door to door to raise money for a cause, saw a family member help others, saw an adult they admired help others, or were active in student government reported household contributions, and over 60 percent of these groups reported volunteering. A significantly smaller percentage of adults who did not have such experiences reported household contributions and volunteering. Rates for this latter group were far below the national rates of reported household contributions and volunteering. (Seventy-two percent of respondents reported household contributions, and 51 percent reported volunteering in 1991.)

The teen responses to this question followed the same pattern. Between 66 and 84 percent of teens who reported having had these experiences as children reported volunteering, while 27 to 39 percent of those who reported that they had not had such experiences reported volunteering. Two particular events that did or did not occur during youth had a powerful impact on later rates of volunteering. Nearly seven out of ten adults who reported that they had done some volunteer work when they were young currently volunteered as adults. Among those who had not done some volunteer work when they were young, slightly more than one out of three currently volunteered. Over eight out of ten teens who reported that they had done some volunteer work when they were children currently volunteered. Among those who did not have the experience, only slightly more than one out of four currently volunteered. Among the 50 percent of adults who reported that they had belonged to a young group, two-thirds currently volunteered as adults. Among those who had not belonged to a youth group, slightly more than one out of three currently volunteered. Over seven out of ten teens who reported belonging to a youth group as children currently volunteered. Among those who had not, only slightly more than one out of three currently volunteered.

Responses to the occurrence of events when young were put through a statistical procedure to test which events experienced during youth had a strong relationship with adult behavior. Among teens, the events occurring during childhood that had the strongest relationship to and the strongest predictive values for later volunteer behavior were having done some volunteer work and having gone door to door to raise money for a cause. In fact, prediction of volunteering by teens can be improved by 48 percent if one knows whether this person volunteered as a child. Knowing whether teens went door to door to raise money for a cause increases prediction of volunteering by 22 percent. No other event in youth has that predictive power. Other events during childhood that had a moderate to strong relationship to later volunteering were membership in a youth group and wanting to make a significant change in society. These findings suggest that actual experience volunteering is the strongest predictor of later volunteering. Membership in a particular group had a moderate to strong relationship with volunteer behavior, as did wanting to make a significant change in society. Clearly, however, there is no substitute for direct experience—at least for young children.

Statistical analyses of adult responses to events occurring during youth produced somewhat different results than analyses of teen responses. The events experienced in youth that both had a strong relationship with and were strong predictors of adult volunteering were membership in a youth group, having done volunteer work, and having gone door to door to raise money for a cause. Events that had a moderate to strong relationship to adult volunteering were having seen a family member help others, having been active in student government, and having seen someone they admired help others. Of these, the events with the capacity to better predict volunteering among a group of a hundred adults are knowing whether members of the group had done the following: belonged to a youth group (29 percent), saw someone in their family help others (21 percent), did volunteer work (20 percent), and saw another adult they admired help others (10 percent).

Volunteering, or the contribution of time for a cause or organization, is crucial in the transmission of this tradition for both teens and adults. Assuming these are positive experiences, and nine out of ten teens rated their volunteer experience positively, actual volunteering experiences when young are very important to future volunteering. The findings from the teen survey reveal that teens who had volunteered as children were more than three times more likely to volunteer as adolescents than those who had not volunteered as children. The same pattern was evident among adults: adults who reported volunteering when they were young volunteered at nearly twice the rate of those who did not have the experience.

Several correlations with events during youth and later volunteering were stronger for adults than teens, suggesting that certain events in youth gain in influence with the passage of time. These include membership in a youth organization and having had role models—for instance, seeing family members and other respected adults help others. While the correlation to current volunteering was not as strong among teens, the rate of volunteering among teens who reported such experiences was similar. These findings suggest that membership in a youth organization is important to future behavior. Youth groups can transmit values, provide a community experience, and teach sharing and concern for members as well as the larger community.

Over time, role models are important. Six out of ten adults who reported that they saw members of their family help others when they were young currently volunteered, compared with slightly more than one-third among those who did not. Less than six out of ten adults remembered seeing a family member help others when they were young, yet among this group, two-thirds currently volunteered compared with four out of ten among those who did not have the experience. Less than half of adults reported that they had such an experience when they were young. These events—membership in a youth group, having done volunteer work, and having seen someone they admired help others—were among the most important variables that distinguished generous volunteers from nonvolunteers (Hodgkinson and others, 1993).

Role models also had an impact on the rate of volunteering among teens. However, the importance of role models seems to increase over time. Three out of four teens reported having seen someone in their family help others when they were children. Among this group, nearly two-thirds currently volunteered. Among the group that did not report seeing such helping behavior, slightly more than four out of ten currently volunteered. Approximately six out of ten teens reported seeing someone they admired who was not a relative helping others. Among this group, two-thirds currently volunteered. Among those who did not report this experience, one out of two volunteered.

We explored the transmission of the tradition of giving voluntary time through another question with both adults and teens. We asked both groups whether both parents or only their mother or father volunteered and compared this response with their volunteer rates, as shown in Table 1.2. We found that parents' example had a strong impact on volunteering among both adults and teens.

Among the one out of four adults who reported that both parents volunteered when they were young, three out of four currently

Table 1.2. Volunteer Status of Parents and Actual Volunteer Behavior (Percentage of Respondents).

	Adults		Teens	
Parent volunteers	*All*	*Volunteers*	*All*	*Volunteers*
Total	100.0	51.1	100.0	60.6
Yes, both mother and father	25.2	74.9	19.6	87.4
Yes, mother only	16.2	59.9	15.5	76.3
Yes, father	3.2	61.5	5.9	55.9
No, neither	45.6	38.6	54.5	47.5
Don't know/no answer	9.8	30.4	4.5	55.2

[a]Respondents could give multiple responses.

Source: Data from Hodgkinson and Weitzman, with Noga and Gorski, 1992a, 1992b.

volunteered as adults. Six out of ten adults also currently volunteered if either their mother or father volunteered. Among adults whose parents did not volunteer, fewer than one out of four volunteered as adults.

Only one out of five teens reported that both of their parents had volunteered, but among this group, nearly nine out of ten teens currently volunteered. Having a mother who volunteered had a greater impact on teens' volunteering rate than having a father who volunteered. Three out of four who reported that only their mother volunteered also currently volunteered. Over half of the teens who reported that only their father volunteered currently volunteered. Among teens who reported that neither parent had volunteered, about one out of two currently volunteered. These findings suggest that volunteering by parents is very important in transmitting the tradition of volunteering within the family structure.

Influence of Membership in Organizations on Voluntary Behavior

Institutions and organizations have a strong influence beyond the family in transmitting the tradition of voluntary service and giving.

In our survey of teens, we looked at the influence of religious organizations, schools, youth organizations, and other voluntary organizations on rates of volunteering and giving. In adults, we explored the influence of membership in various types of organizations, ranging from religious institutions to work-related organizations. We also examined the impact of membership in these organizations on the rate of giving and volunteering and the level of generosity among adults. As shown above, direct experience with volunteering, good role models, and membership in youth groups were influential in determining later volunteering in adolescents and adults. The question of the influence of various types of institutions on voluntary behavior is also very important. All young people are exposed to schools, the predominant institution in their lives throughout their youth. The next most important institution is their religious institution: nearly 75 percent of teens reported membership in a religious institution. Membership in a youth group for 65 percent of teens was the most common experience with a voluntary organization.

Findings from the giving and volunteering surveys have consistently shown that membership in religious institutions, and particularly frequency of attendance at religious services, is a strong predictor of giving and volunteering. Part of the reason for this influence is that churches are voluntary institutions and must be totally supported by the membership; in other words, they would not survive without contributions and voluntary service. They are in essence the first shared community beyond the family for a majority of young people. Individuals who are active members of religious institutions may spend a considerable amount of time at these organizations. In a recent survey of religious congregations, it was found that 85 percent of all the workers at congregations were volunteers and that over nine out of ten congregations engaged in activities other than religious services. Approximately 73 percent of congregations had youth programs. Out of the 92 percent of congregations that reported engaging in one or more human service programs (such as programs for youth), nearly half also reported that they ran these programs both within the congregation and in affiliation with other programs outside the congregation. Therefore, for many individuals, the congregation provides the first connection with the outside community while providing practice in community living (Hodgkinson and Weitzman, 1988; Hodgkinson and others, 1993; Hodgkinson, 1990; Hodgkinson, Weitzman, and Kirsch, 1988, 1990). Experience in a congregation includes sharing in a tradition of faith, practicing obligation to the community, providing time and resources to ensure support of the community, and participating as part of the congregation in meeting the needs of the larger society. Thus, congregations provide primary and long-term experience for a majority of Americans in learning to care and to share responsibility within a community.

Membership and participation in religious organizations is equally important for young people and for adults (Table 1.3). Three-quarters of the teen sample population reported membership in a religious organization, as did 70 percent of the adult sample population. Among teens, nearly half reported attending religious services nearly every week; more than one out of three adults reported such attendance. Two-thirds of teens reporting membership volunteered, and nearly six out of ten contributed. Among teens who were not members of religious organizations, four out of ten volunteered and three out of ten contributed. Nearly six out of ten adults who reported membership volunteered and nearly eight out of ten reported household contributions. Among adult non-members, slightly more than one out of three reported volunteering and approximately six out of ten reported household contributions. In both groups, the rate of giving and volunteering increased by frequency of attendance at religious services. For example, teens who reported attending religious services nearly every week volunteered at more than three times the rate of those who never attended. Adults who attended religious services volunteered at four times the rate of those who never attended.

Table 1.3. Membership in Religious Organizations and Giving and Volunteering (Percentage of Respondents).

	Adults			Teens		
Membership and attendance	*All*	*Contributors*	*Volunteers*	*All*	*Contributors*	*Volunteers*
All respondents	100.0	72.2	51.1	100.0	49.9	60.6
Members	69.7	78.4	58.3	74.1	57.2	66.7
Not a member	30.3	57.8	34.5	24.5	29.1	41.5
Attend church	74.5	77.4	56.0	84.0	54.1	63.5
Weekly or nearly every week	35.5	88.4	69.0	46.8	66.0	70.0
Once or twice a month	15.4	73.4	51.0	18.0	45.6	63.3
Only a few times a year	23.6	63.6	39.6	19.2	33.3	47.7
Do not attend church	24.4	57.3	36.3	15.2	26.4	45.1

Source: Data from Hodgkinson and Weitzman, with Noga and Gorski, 1992a, 1992b.

How does membership in religious organizations affect membership in as well as volunteering and contributing to other charitable organizations? Members of religious organizations are also more likely to join other voluntary, service, and professional organizations. Among the 33 percent of adults who reported membership in these organizations, over three-quarters were also members of religious organizations; among the two-thirds of adults who reported nonmembership in other organizations, two-thirds reported membership in religious organizations. Certain types of organizations were likely to have a high percentage of their members who were also members of religious organizations: sororities and fraternities and fraternal associations (88 percent), alumni organizations (79 percent), and service clubs (78 percent). Members of these organizations reported extraordinary participation in contributions and volunteering: nine out of ten respondents reporting membership in these organizations reported household contributions and three out of four volunteered.

The respondents who joined organizations other than religious organizations did tend to have a higher level of household income and education than the rest of the population. But the association between religious membership and high participation in giving and volunteering suggests that membership in religious and other voluntary and service organizations provides more situations to encourage individuals to share their time and resources with other organizations. These findings suggest that participating as members of a community in such organizations increases opportunities for sharing of personal resources and greatly increases the level of donations of time to charitable organizations. In all of these organizations, the individual is given an opportunity to participate as a member of a group and to share both the benefits and the responsibilities of membership. Members experience working together to achieve the goals of the organization. In the United States, religious and other voluntary organizations are important institutions for the transmission of the values of service and sharing of resources for charitable and community causes.

Institutions That Transmit Traditions of Caring and Service

In the 1992 national survey, teens were asked whether their schools encouraged community service, and their responses were compared with reported volunteering. Among the 55 percent of teen respondents who reported that their schools did encourage voluntary service, 75 percent volunteered. Among the 36 percent of teens who reported that their schools did not support such service, 44 percent volunteered.

Schools, religious institutions, and voluntary associations are the primary organizations where teens reported finding their voluntary assignments. Across a variety of possible voluntary assignments ranging from the arts and cultural activities to religious activities, teens were asked whether they had become involved in that activity through their school, their church or synagogue, or other types of organizations. Since the typical teen volunteer had almost three volunteer assignments, they could give multiple answers. When their responses were aggregated, 78 percent of teens reported that they found their voluntary assignments through their school, 56 percent through their church or synagogue, 26 percent through a youth organization, and 20 percent through community groups.

Volunteer assignments most likely to be found through the schools included assignments in the arts and cultural events, the environment, human services, political organizations, and health. Assignments through religious institutions primarily included voluntary assignments to religious institutions and in youth development. About 25 percent of voluntary assignments at schools were done through extracurricular activities, but the other three-quarters of assignments were in the community.

Churches and schools are comprehensive institutions. While school attendance is not voluntary, young people are exposed to many clubs and groups at school that are voluntary. They also are exposed to many activities in their community through the school. Religious congregations and religious membership are voluntary in the United States. About 40 percent of all volunteer hours contributed were in activities other than religious services and education. Rather, these hours were contributed to a variety of activities run by the congregation in health, human services, public and societal benefit activities, and artistic and cultural activities, among others. For example, over nine out of ten congregations reported one or more activities in the area of human services, and over eight out of ten congregations reported one or more programs for youth, including recreation programs or other youth groups (including scouts programs or 4-H programs or congregational youth groups). Furthermore, in addition to running their own programs in these areas, three out of four congregations reported that they participated in, supported, or were affiliated with similar programs in other organizations in their community or in their denomination (Hodgkinson and others, 1993).

The major institutions that teens come in contact with transmit the traditions of voluntary service and giving. Schools and religious institutions that encourage and provide such opportunities for young people greatly increase the incidence of volunteering among the young. They also provide the opportunity to inculcate such behaviors as habits, since young people have an extensive association with both schools and religious institutions. Such early experiences, as discussed above, last throughout adulthood.

Values, Attitudes About Life, and Volunteering and Giving

Not only do institutions have a direct influence on transmitting the traditions of voluntary service, but young people also learn values related to caring about others and about the responsibilities of citizenship in a pluralistic, democratic society. What is learned from volunteering? Does the experience of volunteering lead to more caring and citizen responsibility? Which values lead to higher levels of service and generosity to the community?

When teens were asked what benefits they derived from their volunteer service, the results were somewhat surprising, because some scholars assumed that the primary benefits would be self-serving, such as learning new skills or getting one's foot in the door for a future job. In fact, teens reported that the primary benefits they derived from their volunteering were learning to respect others, gaining satisfaction from helping others, learning to be helpful and kind, and learning to get along with and relate to others. Finally, in order of frequency, they reported that the benefits they derived from volunteering were that they learned new skills, and that they learned to understand people who were different from themselves. If we were to provide a list of learning outcomes to be derived from volunteering, we could not come up with a better list.

A whole series of questions was asked in both the teen and adult surveys about personal life goals, goals to accomplish from giving and volunteering, and attitudes toward life in general (Table 1.4). When responses to these questions are compared with actual behavior, certain personal goals, attitudes, and values are associated with higher rates of volunteering and contributions. In each of the three surveys, certain major personal life goals were associated with extraordinary levels of giving and volunteering. These goals were making a strong commitment to their religion or spiritual life, making financial contributions to religious institutions and other charitable organizations or causes, or giving time to religious and other charitable institutions or causes. These responses were also selected in a discriminate function analysis to separate generous givers from nongivers, and generous volunteers from nonvolunteers (Hodgkinson and Weitzman, 1990; Hodgkinson and Weitzman, with Noga and Gorski, 1992b). Teens who rated these personal goals as essential also had the highest proportion of volunteers. These findings suggest that having certain personal life goals involving spiritual commitment and a commitment to give

Table 1.4. Benefits Teens Gained from Their Volunteering (Percentage of Volunteers[a]).

Statement of volunteer experience[b]	*A very important benefit to me*	*A somewhat important benefit to me*	*Not too much/not a benefit to me*
I learned to respect others.	48.3	26.4	8.0
I gained satisfaction from helping others.	46.0	28.2	8.5
I learned to be helpful and kind.	44.5	30.5	8.2
I learned how to get along with and relate to others.	40.1	33.8	9.4
I learned new skills.	37.2	31.6	13.8
I learned to understand people who are different than me.	34.6	32.1	15.6
I learned how to relate to children.	34.6	26.9	21.0
I developed leadership skills.	34.1	33.1	15.2
I'm a better person now.	32.7	34.1	15.4
I'm more patient with others.	32.7	33.2	16.2
I understand more about good citizenship.	29.7	37.1	15.7
I understand more about how voluntary organizations work.	25.1	38.7	18.5
I'm more aware about programs in my community.	21.4	34.6	26.6
I explored or learned about career options.	21.0	31.8	29.4
I've developed new career goals.	20.3	23.3	37.6
I did better in school/my grades improved.	16.6	25.2	39.6
I learned how to help solve community problems.	16.2	30.9	34.5
I understand more about how government works.	11.4	24.2	45.6

[a]Data from the 60.6 percent of respondents who volunteered in the past year.

[b]Statements are ranked by the percentage of respondents stating that a specific experience was a "very important benefit to me." Excludes those who did not respond or were not sure of their answer.

Source: Hodgkinson and Weitzman, with Noga and Gorski, 1992b.

time and money is evidenced by higher levels of volunteering and giving.

Certain attitudes about life in general also were associated with more giving and volunteering among both adults and teens. Other personal attitudes led to less participation. Three personal attitudes led to particularly high levels of giving and volunteering. Among adults who strongly agreed that it was their moral duty to help those who suffer (22 percent), eight out of ten reported household contributions and over six out of ten volunteered; among adults who disagreed with this statement (11 percent), six out of ten reported household contributions and one out of three volunteered. Among teens who strongly agreed with this statement (27 percent), over seven out of ten volunteered. Among those who disagreed (9 percent), slightly more than one out of three volunteered.

Among adults who strongly agreed that it was in their power to improve the welfare of others (13 percent), eight out of ten reported household contributions and two out of three volunteered. Among adults who disagreed with this statement (21 percent), six out of ten reported household contributions and three out of ten volunteered. Among teens who strongly agreed with this statement (15 percent), three out of four volunteered. Among those who disagreed (18 percent), four out of ten volunteered.

Among adults who disagreed with the statement (23 percent) that we have a right to be concerned first with our own goals rather than others' problems, over eight out of ten reported household contributions and two out of three volunteered. Among adults who strongly agreed with this statement (22 percent), six out of ten reported household contributions and four out of ten volunteered. Among teens who disagreed with this statement (27 percent), seven out of ten volunteered. Among those who strongly agreed (16 percent), nearly six out of ten volunteered.

Other personal attitudes that led to significantly higher levels of household contributions and volunteering were disagreement with the statement that individuals can do little to alleviate suffering in the world. Those adults who strongly agreed with the statement reported significantly lower rates of household contributions and volunteering. One personal attitude had a significant impact on the percentage of adults who reported contributions but did not have as strong an impact on the level of volunteering. Among adults who disagreed with the statement that most people with serious problems brought those problems on themselves (52 percent), three out of four reported contributions. Among those who strongly agreed with the statement (5 percent), two out of three reported contributions.

Another personal attitude led to significantly higher levels of volunteering but not contributions. Among adults who strongly agreed that if we all volunteer time and effort, social problems can be overcome (14 percent), two out of three volunteered. Among adults who disagreed with the statement (24 percent), fewer than one out of two volunteered. This pattern was similar among teens. Among teens who strongly agreed with this statement (31 percent), over seven out of ten volunteered. Among those who disagreed (11 percent), four out of ten volunteered.

While holding certain personal attitudes is not predictive of volunteering, a higher percentage of contributors and volunteers had positive social attitudes than nongivers and nonvolunteers. Volunteers and givers were also far more likely to have strong moral values about helping those who suffer. They were far less likely to think that their goals are more important than the goals of other people. In other words, they were more other-oriented.

Factors That Increase Involvement in Giving and Volunteering

Membership, parents, institutions, and personal values and attitudes all influence the level of participation in giving and volunteering to a variety of causes. The question addressed in this section, given all of these factors, is the following: What are the factors or situations that get individuals to move from motive to action—the act of making a contribution or a commitment to volunteer time? In all of the adult and teen surveys, we have explored in various ways how and why people get involved. We have also explored the levels of participation among certain groups—African Americans, Hispanics, single people, and young people—how they get involved and the impediments to their involvement. Emphasis was placed on trying to understand these groups because volunteering among young people eighteen to twenty-four years of age and among single people declined between 1980 and 1985. We also wanted to explore why volunteer participation among blacks, Hispanics, and adults in low-income households is lower than among whites and among households in other income groups. Over the past decade, all of these groups have increased their participation in both giving and volunteering, with African Americans showing the greatest increases.

To explore how people get involved in volunteer activities, we developed a series of questions. Primary among these questions were: How did you first learn about your volunteer activities? Were you asked to volunteer in the past year? Were you asked to give in the past year? The findings here are from the 1992 surveys, but responses reported were similar for the same questions on previous surveys.

As Table 1.5 shows, the most frequently cited ways that adults and teens first learned about their volunteer activities were: they were asked by someone; through participation in an organization; or they had a family member or friend in the activity or benefiting from the activity. (Respondents could choose multiple answers for this question.) It should also be noted that only 18 percent of teens and adults reported that they sought out a volunteer activity on their own. Thus, volunteer participation is most likely to occur through personal contacts or institutional membership rather than individuals finding the activity on their own.

Teens and adults who reported that they were asked by someone were then asked: Who asked you? Teens most frequently

Table 1.5. How Teens and Adults First Learned About Their Volunteer Activities (Percentage of Volunteers).

	1992	
Method	*Teens*[a]	*Adults*
How did you first learn about your volunteer activities?[b]		
Asked by someone	40.7	35.9
Through participation in an organization or group (including a religious group) or through my workplace	31.3	36.1
Had a family member or a friend in the activity or benefiting from the activity	31.3	25.9
Sought out activity on own	18.0	18.1
Saw an advertisement or request—radio, TV, or printed source	5.7	3.8
School	1.7	c
Other	2.6	2.1
Who asked you?[d]		
Friend	47.6	57.1
Teacher or other school personnel	31.2	c
Family member or other relative	30.6	21.6
Someone at church or synagogue	21.5	33.0
Someone at work (not employer)	0.8	15.0
My employer	0.4	8.0
Other	8.1	11.0[e]
Which organization?[f]		
Church/synagogue/temple	62.4	61.7
School/college	34.3	18.5
Another voluntary organization	23.5	20.4
Membership organization/service club/professional society	6.6	13.4
Informal social groups	3.8	13.4
Workplace/employer	2.0	20.3
Other	1.2	5.7

[a]Respondents could give multiple responses. The 1992 teenage survey was based on those between twelve and seventeen years of age. The 1990 teenage survey was based on those between fourteen and seventeen years of age.

[b]Teenage data from the 60.4 percent of respondents in 1992 and the 57.6 percent of respondents in 1990 who volunteered in the past year. Adult data from the 51.1 percent of respondents in 1992 and the 54.4 percent of respondents in 1990 who volunteered in the past year.

[c]Not available. This category was not included in the survey for that year.

[d]Teenage data from the 40.7 percent of volunteers in 1992 and the 44.0 percent of volunteers in 1990 who learned about their volunteer activities by being asked by someone. Adult data from the 35.9 percent of volunteers in 1992 and the 42.4 percent of volunteers in 1990 who learned about their volunteer activities by being asked by someone.

[e]Includes being contacted by an organization directly and through a teacher or a youth activities leader.

[f]Teenage data from the 31.3 percent of volunteers in 1992 and the 46.5 percent of volunteers in 1990 who learned about their volunteer activities through an organization. Adult data from the 36.1 percent of volunteers in 1992 and the 41.3 percent of volunteers in 1990 who learned about their volunteer activities through an organization.

Source: Data from Hodgkinson and Weitzman, with Noga and Gorski, 1992a, 1992b.

reported a friend, a teacher or school administrator, a family member or other relative, or someone at their church or synagogue. (Multiple responses were allowed on this question.) Adults most frequently cited a friend, someone at their church or synagogue, a member of their family or other relative, or someone at their workplace or their employer. These findings show that volunteers are most often asked to volunteer by friends or family, or by someone in an institution where they spend a lot of time, such as school and religious institutions for teens or religious institutions and the workplace for adults.

Teens and adults who reported that they found their volunteer activities through participation in an organization were asked: Which organization? (Multiple responses were permitted.) Teens most often mentioned their religious organization, their school, or a voluntary organization or service club. Adults most frequently reported their church or synagogue, a voluntary association or other organization or membership in service clubs, their workplace or employer, or their school or college. Again, the institutions that have the most influence in providing opportunities or information about volunteer activities are religious institutions, schools, voluntary organizations, and the workplace.

When adults and teens were questioned about whether they had been asked to volunteer in the past year, 44 percent of adults and 57 percent of teens said yes (Table 1.6). Among adults who were asked, 86 percent volunteered; among teens who were asked, 90 percent volunteered. Among the adults (55 percent) and teens (41 percent) who were not asked, less than one out of four volunteered. Survey results have consistently shown that people are more than three times as likely to volunteer when they are asked than when they are not.

When we examined the demographic characteristics of adults and teens who were asked, we noticed some disturbing patterns. While 46 percent of whites reported that they were asked to volunteer in the past year, only 32 percent of African Americans and

Table 1.6. Being Asked to Volunteer and Actual Volunteer Behavior (Percentage of Respondents).

	Adults				*Teens*			
	Were asked	*Volunteers*	*Were not asked*	*Volunteers*	*Were asked*	*Volunteers*	*Were not asked*	*Volunteers*
Total	44.1	85.6	55.0	23.5	56.6	89.7	41.4	22.7
Gender								
Male	42.0	85.5	57.4	22.5	54.9	90.4	42.4	22.4
Female	46.0	85.7	52.8	24.6	58.3	89.0	40.3	23.1
Race								
White	45.8	86.0	53.4	24.2	59.3	90.5	38.5	22.1
Nonwhite	32.8	81.9	65.4	19.7	44.7	84.7	54.0	24.6
Black	32.4	84.3	66.4	22.2	46.3	84.5	52.9	25.8
Hispanic[a]	33.1	80.4	66.7	16.4	NA	NA	NA	NA

	Adults			
	Were asked	*Volunteers*	*Were not asked*	*Volunteers*
Total	44.1	85.6	55.0	23.5
Age				
18–24	36.9	90.4	62.0	23.3
25–34	46.3	87.7	52.5	21.7
35–44	53.2	90.9	45.8	26.2
45–54	46.3	83.9	53.4	31.8
55–64	45.1	80.4	53.7	23.5
65+	32.4	73.0	66.9	18.1
Income				
Under $10,000	21.9	74.5	76.2	18.7
$10,000–$19,999	34.8	76.2	64.7	17.4
$20,000–$29,999	42.3	88.0	57.2	23.8
$30,000–$39,999	47.7	88.6	50.8	26.0
$40,000–$49,999	58.4	91.7	41.2	33.7
$50,000–$74,999	56.0	83.9	43.3	31.9
$75,000–$99,999	62.3	90.8	36.5	16.7
$100,000+	60.4	94.4	39.6	42.0
Marital status				
Married	48.4	87.2	50.7	26.5
Single	39.9	89.1	59.6	19.5
Divorced, separated, or widowed	33.2	70.9	65.4	18.7
Employment status				
Employed	49.8	89.6	49.7	28.5
Full-time	49.3	90.1	50.2	27.8
Part-time	52.2	87.2	47.3	31.9
Not employed	35.4	82.3	63.3	19.9
Retired	35.0	70.1	64.0	15.0

[a]Hispanics may be of any race.

Source: Data from Hodgkinson and Weitzman, with Noga and Gorski, 1992a, 1992b.

33 percent of Hispanics reported that they had been asked to do so. However, the rate of volunteer participation among these groups when they were asked was 80 percent or higher, demonstrating that regardless of race or ethnic background, if individuals are asked to volunteer they are more than three times as likely to volunteer than if they are not asked. The patterns were similar among the teen population. Six out of ten white teens reported that they were asked compared with less than one out of two blacks. Among whites who were asked to volunteer, 91 percent volunteered; among blacks, 86 percent volunteered. Among the 39 percent of whites and blacks who were not asked, about one out of four volunteered.

When we examined people who were asked to volunteer by age, we found similar patterns. A lower percentage of young adults eighteen to twenty-four years of age were asked to volunteer, as were a lower percentage of older adults sixty-five years of age and up. The same patterns of volunteer rates emerged among all those who were asked regardless of age compared with those who were not asked.

When we examined people by level of household income, similar patterns occurred. Only 22 percent of respondents with average household incomes of $10,000 or less were asked to volunteer compared with 58 percent of those with household incomes of $50,000 or more. Seventy-five percent of respondents with low household incomes volunteered if they were asked. This was nearly four times the volunteer rate of those who were not asked.

Finally, when we explored adults by marital status, we found that a higher percentage of married people were asked to volunteer than single people or those who were divorced, widowed, or separated. Again, similar rates of volunteering occurred among those who were asked compared with those who were not.

The findings in the 1992 survey were as graphic as those in the 1990 survey and demonstrate that certain conditions must occur for people to take action. Adults are three to four times more likely to volunteer if they are asked. When asked to volunteer, over eight out of ten adults and teens will volunteer; when not asked, less than one out of four will seek out the activity on their own. These findings hold true regardless of age, income, or racial and ethnic background.

Conclusion

The United States is a pluralistic nation made up of citizens that originally emigrated from most of the other nations in the world. Leaving countries where a single ethnic or racial group made up the majority of the culture also meant leaving many institutional forms of caring and participating, ranging from extended families, tribes, or guilds to nationally supported religious institutions or even government structures designed to serve homogeneous groups. In the United States, structural arrangements to bring disparate people into association with one another to conduct their public business have led to a predominance of institutions and cultural mores different both in number and in influence from those in other countries where the citizenry is not ethnically and racially diverse. The original intention of those who designed our research on giving and volunteering was not to explore membership in religious and other institutions. It became clear, however, that adults who were members of religious institutions reported household contributions and volunteering, not only to religious institutions, but to all other charitable causes at much higher rates than did nonmembers. In the 1992 survey, we explored the influence of membership in a whole range of institutions from service clubs to political organizations and found the same patterns, although total membership in other organizations (33 percent) is much lower than in religious institutions (70 percent) for the adult population.

What is surprising is that memberships in these institutions is totally voluntary. The United States was the first country to separate church and state in its constitution, and churches are voluntary institutions and are solely supported by voluntary service and contributions. Tocqueville ([1835] 1976) wrote about the importance of these moral and cultural associations in the early nineteenth century. He might be surprised to learn how well they have held up over time. One of the most powerful findings of our research is that membership in religious institutions and other voluntary and membership organizations leads to exceptionally high participation rates in household contributions and volunteering. Its correlation is also revealing. Nonmembership leads to low or exceptionally low participation.

Even more revealing and, perhaps, encouraging is that the experience and habit of membership start early in life—the earlier the better. Whether teens or adults, those who were members of religious institutions or youth groups as children were far more likely to exhibit high levels of giving and volunteering later as teens and adults. Those who were not members of these types of organizations when young continued to show a much lower level of participation throughout the age groups. In a nation without a uniform ethnic or cultural history, it seems that all children should have the opportunity to experience membership in a youth group, either in schools (and preschools), religious institutions, or voluntary associations.

These findings suggest that one of the important experiences of transmitting caring for others and citizen involvement is membership in a religious group or other voluntary organization—particularly a youth group in the case of children. These organizations provide regular opportunities for individuals to learn to participate with others, to work toward group goals, and to help others or work together with others to achieve those goals. What is discouraging is that only half of the adults surveyed reported membership in a youth group when they were young. What is encouraging is that 65 percent of the teens surveyed reported such membership. A goal we might set for the next generation is that over 90 percent of all young people have such an experience.

Another major finding is the importance of certain institutions in providing and encouraging values of caring and sharing with others, of serving others, and of participating in community activities. For young people, those are religious institutions, schools, and voluntary associations. For adults, they are religious institutions, the workplace, and voluntary and other membership organizations. Schools and particularly corporations and other institutions where people work need to realize that encouraging voluntary service and contributions to various causes is important to the continuation and strengthening of the tradition of giving and volunteering.

Studies show that schools that encourage voluntary service triple the participation rate of volunteering among young people. It is also striking that only 7 percent of adults report finding out about volunteer activities in the workplace. As institutions in the community, all businesses—for-profit or not-for-profit—and government agencies should be concerned about the level of citizen participation among their employees. Since a majority of adults spend a significant portion of their lifetime in the workplace, just as young people spend most of their time in school, these institutions need to support and encourage the kinds of voluntary behavior that sustain and strengthen the community.

Role models are important to young people. The highest incidence of volunteering among teens was among that small group who reported that both parents had volunteered. The next highest rate of volunteering came from young people who reported that their mother had volunteered. Having witnessed members of one's family or another respected adult help others has a lifelong impact that grows more important with age. Young children particularly need to see adults they admire helping others. Religious leaders, school administrators, employers, and voluntary organizations should offer more opportunities for family members—particularly parents with young children—to volunteer together.

There is no substitute for the direct experience of volunteering. Ervin Staub points out in Chapter Two that parents should give children opportunities to help even when they are very young. These experiences not only help to build a more caring person, but help to build self-esteem and confidence. Our surveys continue to show that volunteers are far more likely than nonvolunteers to be concerned about others and about social causes, and the surveys also demonstrate that volunteers believe they can help to solve some of society's problems and to improve the welfare of others. Children, including very young children, should be given an opportunity to volunteer at an early age. While religious institutions are more apt to engage young children in these activities, preschools and elementary schools should also be encouraged to provide them. Rather than having 33 percent of young people report that they had a volunteer activity before the age of eleven, we should set a goal that at least 90 percent of all children between the ages of three and eleven should have had the opportunity to experience a volunteer activity. Such intervention has positive outcomes in the short term as well as the long term for both the individual and society. It also is a cheap intervention with long-term value.

Finally, fewer than one out of five adults and teens reported finding their volunteer activity on their own. Over eight out of ten teens and adults reported that they volunteered when they were asked. More opportunities need to be made available to ask individuals to volunteer, and particularly from those groups that are not asked at the same time as white and higher-income persons. If we are truly to develop a pluralistic, multicultural, caring society, we need to ensure equal opportunity to serve and participate in society. Leaders of voluntary organizations, schools and colleges, and community organizations need to ask senior citizens, young people, single people, and people from a wide range of racial and ethnic groups to volunteer. Lack of participation among these groups results from the failure of those people and organizations who do not ask them to participate. The research reported here shows that if they are not asked, most people do not serve. Organizations might begin by building profiles of their volunteers and asking if these profiles reflect the demographic profiles of their communities; if they do not, they might set measurable goals to improve participation.

References

Hodgkinson, V. A. "The Future of Individual Giving and Volunteering: The Inseparable Link Between Religious Community and Individual Generosity." In R. Wuthnow, V. A. Hodgkinson, and Associates, *Faith and Philanthropy in America: Exploring the Role of Religion in America's Voluntary Sector* (pp. 284–312). San Francisco: Jossey-Bass, 1990.

Hodgkinson, V. A., and Weitzman, M. S. *Giving and Volunteering in the United States*. Washington, D.C.: INDEPENDENT SECTOR, 1988.

Hodgkinson, V. A., and Weitzman, M. S. *Giving and Volunteering in the United States*. Washington, D.C.: INDEPENDENT SECTOR, 1990.

Hodgkinson, V. A., and Weitzman, M. S., with Kirsch, A. D., Noga, S. M., and Gorski, H. A. *From Belief to Commitment: The Community Service Activities and Finances of Religious Congregations in the United States*. Washington, D.C.: INDEPENDENT SECTOR, 1993.

Hodgkinson, V. A., and Weitzman, M. S., with Noga, S. M., and Gorski, H. A. *Giving and Volunteering in the United States*. Washington, D.C.: INDEPENDENT SECTOR, 1992a.

Hodgkinson, V. A., and Weitzman, M. S., with Noga, S. M., and Gorski, H. A. *Volunteering and Giving Among American Teenagers 12 to 17 Years of Age*. Washington, D.C.: INDEPENDENT SECTOR, 1992b.

Hodgkinson, V. A., Weitzman, M. S., and Kirsch, A. D. *From Belief to Commitment: The Activities and Finances of Religious Congregations in the United States*. Washington, D.C.: INDEPENDENT SECTOR, 1988.

Hodgkinson, V. A., Weitzman, M. S., and Kirsch, A. D. "From Commitment to Action: How Religious Involvement Affects Giving and Volunteering." In R. Wuthnow, V. A. Hodgkinson, and Associates, *Faith and Philanthropy in America: Exploring the Role of Religion in America's Voluntary Sector* (pp. 93–114). San Francisco: Jossey-Bass, 1990.

Tocqueville, A. de. "Of the Use Which the Americans Make of Public Associations in Civil Life." *Democracy in America*. 2 vols. New York: Knopf, 1976. (Originally published 1835.)

Chapter Two

How People Learn to Care

Ervin Staub

How can we create a caring society, where individuals act on behalf of others, notice and respond to others' needs, and work to benefit their community as a whole? How can we also extend this caring to people beyond the borders of our own community? How can we create a world in which people are not passive bystanders?

What are the characteristics of people—their modes of thought, feelings, and values—that lead them to be concerned with others' welfare and to take action to benefit others? How do these characteristics evolve? What kind of socialization and experience do children require at home and in the schools to become caring persons? What kind of support do parents need to care for their children that way? Social conditions and culture provide an important background; they greatly affect individuals, their orientation to other people, even their patience and care for their children. In this chapter I will examine the origins of caring, of people turning toward (rather than against) each other, giving special attention to issues of our times that affect the transmission of caring to children and in society.

Societal Change and Caring

We live in a complex world at home and abroad, with tremendous changes in technology, social mores, and political systems under way. Economic problems, intense political conflict, and rapid social change represent "difficult life conditions" (Staub, 1989a). These conditions create social disorganization and have a profound impact on individuals. They give rise to intense needs for security and for a positive identity. Since it is difficult for human beings to exist without a worldview that enables them to anticipate the future and locate themselves in the present, social chaos or disorganization also gives rise to an intense need for meaningful comprehension of the world and one's place in it. Difficult life conditions intensify the need for connection, too. In the face of life problems, great changes, and social disorganization, people become self-focused, and connections diminish just when connection and support from others are most needed.

When difficult life conditions are especially intense, groups of people frequently deal with the resulting needs by turning against others. They elevate themselves by diminishing others, develop connections as they turn against other groups, and create visions of a better life while identifying presumed enemies who stand in the way of fulfilling these visions (Staub, 1989a). In the United States in recent decades we have had, I believe, moderately difficult life conditions, resulting primarily from the social change just mentioned. Even positive social movements like the civil rights movement, feminism, and the peace movement have created social disorganization and placed great demands on people to adjust to new social realities, including changed roles, new societal norms, and new forms of human relationships. The societal changes have been quite varied, including changes in social and sexual mores, family structure, drug use, and increased violence. Some of these changes preceded and in turn contributed to some of the other changes; all reflect difficult life conditions. Can we deal with them by turning toward each other and working together to fulfill the needs noted above, rather than turning against each other? How can we create this joining together?

Our concern cannot be only with ourselves in the United States. We live in a highly interconnected world. We must also be concerned with our relationship to the rest of the world and what we can do through our connections with other nations to facilitate people joining with rather than becoming antagonistic toward each other.

Personal Characteristics That Promote Caring and Helping

What are the characteristics of individuals that embody concern about others and are likely to lead people to reach out to and help others? Many characteristics can lead to helping, depending on specific conditions, but three core characteristics appear to be generally important. One is empathy—seeing and opening oneself to others' needs, understanding others' feelings, and feeling with others. Another is commitment to moral rules and the resulting feeling of obligation to help other people. Both of these characteristics are important motivators of helping. However, in my view the most important personal characteristic that leads to helping is a *prosocial value orientation*, which I have proposed on the basis of research my associates and I have conducted. It has three components.

The first is a positive evaluation of human beings or human nature—that is, seeing human beings in a positive light. This is a precondition for concern about human welfare. If you see people in a negative light, if you devalue people, why would you concern yourself with them? The second is a feeling of concern for others' welfare. The third is a feeling of personal responsibility for the welfare of other people (Staub, 1978). Responsibility adds a component to empathy, to feeling with others, that makes action on behalf of people in need more likely.

In one of our studies, we gave participants tests to measure their prosocial orientation and then assessed their willingness to help another person in physical distress. There was a complex scenario. Participants heard sounds of physical distress from another room. They could go into the other room when they heard the sounds of distress, or if they did not, the distressed person (a confederate) entered their room. In either case, an extended interaction followed in which people had varied opportunities to help. Some did very little, while others were almost impossible to stop. We conducted this study on the fourteenth floor of a building at Harvard University. A couple of the participants, before we could "debrief" them (explain the project to them) were already rushing down the stairs, running to Harvard Square to fill a prescription for the person in distress. The amount of helping participants engaged in was strongly associated with their prosocial orientation (Staub, 1974; Erkut, Jaquette, and Staub, 1991).

In other studies, we examined helping in response to psychological distress. It is not obvious what kind of reactions to another's psychological distress are helpful. Talking a lot to someone in distress may not help. A central measure of helping was the extent to which a person simply attended to the distressed person, rather than continuing to work on a task. This and other forms of helping were strongly associated with the helpers' prosocial value orientation (Feinberg, 1978; Grodman, 1979; Staub, 1978).

In a survey (Staub, 1991), a questionnaire I prepared was published in the magazine *Psychology Today* (Staub, 1989b). Readers were invited to fill out and send in the questionnaire, which included a new test of prosocial orientation, as well as questions assessing empathy and moral rule orientation. Over 7,000 people responded. People also reported the extent to which they helped others in a variety of ways. Prosocial orientation was more strongly related to varied forms of helping than was empathy or moral rule orientation.

On the basis of the information in the survey, I constructed four "worldviews": a caring worldview, a religious worldview, a liberal worldview, and a materialistic worldview. The caring worldview, which was essentially a person's prosocial orientation, was associated with the largest number of different kinds of helping, including helping in emergency situations. The religious worldview was strongly associated with charitable donations and helping in one's own community. The liberal worldview was strongly associated with working to create social change. People with the materialistic orientation, valuing power and wealth, tended to be unhelpful.

Information gathered from research in the laboratory and in surveys is corroborated by the study of a highly significant form of helping in the real world. "Rescuers"—people in Nazi Europe who endangered their lives to save the lives of Jews—were volunteers of the most special kind. Their characteristics include empathy, concern about moral rules, and for a substantial portion, a "caring" or prosocial orientation (Oliner and Oliner, 1988; Tec, 1986). Many were asked to help: about 50 percent of them initiated help in response to a request either by somebody in danger or an intermediary. In my view, the information gathered about rescuers indicates that many of them went through an *evolution* toward increased caring and helping (Staub, 1989a, 1993). Many at first decided to help for a limited time or in a limited way, like hiding people in their basement for a day or two, but as they helped, they changed and became more committed. If they succeeded in moving the people they were helping to safe places, they did not stop. They joined with others to help more, committing their lives to saving others. Perpetrators—people who harm others—also change over time and engage in more harmful, more violent actions. The inclinations to help and to harm others both develop and intensify as a result of our own actions (Staub, 1979, 1989a, 1993). We learn by doing, change through participation.

The *Psychology Today* study (Staub, 1989a, 1991) also showed a clear connection between a feeling of competence or power to help others and actual helping. The more people endorsed items like "It is in my power to do things that improve the welfare of others," the more helping they reported. In the same study the more help people provided, and the stronger their prosocial orientation, the greater the amount of life satisfaction they reported.

The Origins of Caring

What are the childhood origins of caring and helping? Feelings of connection and positive orientation to other human beings develop through experience. We cannot teach children caring values without experiences that predispose them to care. A child who experiences rejection and hostility and develops negative feelings about people is not going to learn through instruction to care about others. Caring about people is rooted in experiences of interaction with other human beings.

Parental Socialization and Childhood Experience

A large body of research suggests that nurturance and affection are required if children are to develop a positive connection to caretakers and a positive orientation to other human beings (Eisenberg, 1992; Staub, 1979). Affection and nurturance tell the child that other people are benevolent and trustworthy and make the child feel good about himself or herself. They contribute both to a positive orientation to other people and a positive sense of self. The opposite modes of relating to children—rejection, neglect, hostility, and violence—develop a negative orientation to others. Severe neglect or abuse break the affectional tie between adult and child or inhibit its development. Research on aggression shows this (Staub, 1994; Yoshikawa, 1994).

But nurturing is not enough. Children require guidance. Explaining the reasons for rules to children is a positive form of guidance, which contrasts with authoritarian rule setting. A form of reasoning that is important for the development of caring is "induction" (Hoffman, 1970; Staub, 1979), which refers to pointing out to children the impact of their behavior on others. This helps children to understand others' needs and concerns and to learn that they themselves have the power to affect others, both positively and negatively.

Occasionally, rules have to be enforced; the exercise of control or discipline by parents and other adult caretakers is important (Baumrind, 1975). Children need to learn that adults are serious about essential rules. But the forms of discipline are important. Highly punitive discipline counteracts affection and nurturance. Parents and teachers have to be ingenious, therefore, in developing positive discipline practices.

Another important source of caring and helping is learning by doing or learning by participation. In research, we involved children in helping others in a number of ways (Staub, 1975, 1979). They made toys for poor hospitalized children or taught younger children. Not everything works the same way with both boys and girls. For example, one of our measures of helping was asking children to write letters to hospitalized children. We found that fifth- and sixth-grade boys are poor letter writers, and few wrote letters regardless of their preceding experience. But on the whole, prior involvement in helping increased children's later helping behavior in comparison with children in control groups. The experience of benefiting others can connect others' welfare with one's actions and can provide a sense of one's own power and importance. In the course of helping, a child (or adult) may think about others' needs, develop increased commitment to others' welfare, and come to think of himself or herself as the kind of person who will help other people. Thus, both orientation to the other and the sense of self are affected.

Parents and other adult socializers can guide children to help others in varied domains: to share with and help peers, to contribute to the life of the family, or to volunteer in the community. Probably there will be some specificity in learning as a function of modes of participation, affecting the type of needs that activate children's concern about others and the forms of helping they are more or less inclined to. But learning by doing is also likely to promote a general tendency to be helpful.

Experiences early in the child's life affect caring and helping.

At about the age of six months, children begin to demonstrate "attachment" (Ainsworth, 1979), an affectional bond with primary caretakers. The quality of attachment varies. It has been categorized as secure, anxious, or avoidant, with a recently added category of "disorganized." Secure attachment indicates trust in caretakers and other people and contributes to later positive relations with peers (Sroufe, 1979; Waters, Wippmann, and Sroufe, 1979). Avoidant attachment has been found to be associated with aggressiveness in the preschool years (Shaffer, 1988; Troy and Sroufe, 1987; Yoshikawa, 1994). Loving parenting, involving responsiveness to the infant's needs, is associated with secure attachment (Shaffer, 1988).

Some psychologists who do therapy with young children have begun to identify "unattached" children. Not only do these children not show secure, positive attachment, but they do not show any kind of attachment. Usually these are children who were handed from family to family, foster home to foster home (Keogh, 1993). Since they lack affectionate ties to other human beings, they will not only be unconcerned about others' welfare, but will more easily become aggressive.

Creating and Overcoming "Us" and "Them"

Another issue is the relationship between "us" and "them." It is possible for children to have experiences that develop caring for people but that also teach sharp differentiation between "us," people in the in-group, and "them," people in other groups. We have a genetic *potential* for differentiating between us and them—not a given, but a potential. Young infants, as they begin to show attachment at the age of six months, also begin to show fear of strangers. This is a kind of metaphor for and rudimentary form of the differentiation between us and them. But early experiences of infants can diminish this differentiation. When young infants are securely attached and when they have secure and supportive experiences with a wide range of people, they show less stranger anxiety (Shaffer, 1988). The potential is there to experience positive connection to everyone.

However, most societies have developed strong devaluations of certain groups of people (Staub, 1989a). These devaluations are part of the culture and are taught to children. Piaget and Weil (1951) did a study of Swiss children's stereotypes in the late 1940s. Nine- to ten-year-olds had strong stereotypes of people in other nations, many of them negative. The French were thought of as dirty, the Russians as people who always want war. At that time, the children thought Americans were clever, since they were rich and had developed the atom bomb.

A woman who came from the South and became a committed civil rights worker in the 1960s gives an example of how the devaluation of others can be created (Colby and Damon, 1992). She grew up in a family with black servants. As a young child her favorite playmates were the children of these servants. When she was seven years old and was going to have a big birthday party, she was told that she could not invite these children. She threw a temper tantrum and was allowed to have a separate party for them. But by the time she got to Wellesley College at the age of eighteen and the first night was seated at the same table with a young black woman, she was outraged. How could the college do this to her? The influences on her had taken hold.

Hostility and antagonism also evolve when we discriminate against others. As we harm others, we change. In genocidal societies, there is an evolution of the whole society as it moves along a continuum of destruction. As the group harms members of another group, individuals change, institutions change, and new institutions get established that foster harm to others (Staub, 1989a). How can we move in the other direction, toward including other people in the realm of a shared humanity, toward greater connection to all people?

Here again the experiential element is essential. People cannot just learn through instruction and abstract concepts to accept others they had previously devalued. They need experiential connection. Deep connection to others across group lines, or "cross-cutting relations" (Deutsch, 1973), can bring about relearning. People can come together for community projects, problem-solving activities, and joint business projects (Staub, 1989a, 1992).

A good example of cross-cutting relations is cooperative learning in schools. One of the origins of the cooperative learning movement was the realization, following the desegregation of schools, that minority children continued to underperform academically, had low self-esteem, and had limited social interaction with white children. Cooperative teaching was designed in part to get children from different groups into meaningful contact with each other. For example, each child may learn a part of the material necessary for the completion of a task, then both teach his or her share of the material to others and learn their part from them (Aronson and others, 1978; Deutsch, 1973). Here deep contact takes place in the framework of relative equality. Unequal contact does not work because it recreates a preexisting relationship of superiority versus inferiority.

The Role of Schools

Schools have an important role in creating a caring and positive orientation to others, and overcoming a negative orientation and hostility. This is especially the case today, when there are many single-parent families and many families are disorganized, in need, or "dysfunctional," unable to provide children with love and guidance. Single parents, especially if they are young and poor, are much more likely to treat children harshly (Gelles, 1989), which in turn is an important cause of aggressiveness and ineffectiveness in children and youth (Gelles, 1989; Staub, 1994; Yoshikawa, 1994).

However, schools have an essential role not only by default. Schools inevitably socialize children. They not only teach content and cognitive skills; they shape children's personalities in the course of thousands of hours of interaction with teachers and other children. The question is not whether schools socialize children in terms of personality and character, but what kinds of personality, values, and social behavior they help to develop.

Many of the practices described earlier in relation to parents also apply to schools. Teachers can be affectionate and employ positive discipline practices as they guide children. But schools can also offer special possibilities and opportunities. They can create learning by doing by involving children in projects that help others in the school and in the community. Schools can provide children with significant roles, engaging them in meaningful, responsible activities. Children can participate in making rules for the classroom at an early age. One strategy is to create a bill of rights for students and teachers. This can be threatening to teachers, if they see it as a loss of authority, but it can actually have a positive effect on the life of the classroom. Children can feel empowered, develop a sense of responsibility for their community, and acquire cognitive skills as they assess which rules are beneficial or harmful.

Participation in creating rules and in decision making can help fulfill another important potential of schools, which is to develop critical consciousness and critical loyalty (Staub, 1988, 1989a, 1992). Critical loyalty means the ability and willingness to speak out against current policies and practices of one's group, when one judges them as contrary to important human values or the long-term interests and well-being of the group. This becomes crucial if the group embarks on policies that promote discrimination or antagonism, since an active response by the population can inhibit these negative behaviors, while passivity supports the evolution along a continuum of destruction.

Schools can also introduce instruction that humanizes members of different groups (Staub, 1988). Children can learn about both the differences and similarities between their own and other cultures. They can come to understand culture from a functional perspective by considering the roles or functions that cultural groups have evolved in dealing with particular conditions, like scarcity or enmity. This way, unfamiliar or unusual aspects of the other culture can become comprehensible.

Social Conditions and Culture

Societal conditions also affect the socialization of children. For positive socialization to take place in the home, parents need support. As I mentioned at the start, there have been great changes in U.S. society, creating intense needs on the part of many people. The government and the community can provide various kinds of support. For example, poor, young, single parents who are especially harsh with their children (Gelles, 1989) could greatly benefit from financial support and early education programs for children, especially those that involve parents as well (Yoshikawa, 1994). Social programs that reduce single teenage motherhood would also reduce the development of aggressive and ineffective children.

Since there are many struggling single parents and poorly functioning families, the creation of caring schools that provide the affection, support, and guidance that parents are not able to give becomes very important. Such schools can also provide a community for parents. They can involve parents, not the usual way, talking to them about their child's problems, but by identifying shared interests and common purposes, and by creating a cooperative community that serves both schools and parents. That is one way for parents to get significant psychological support.

We also need to work for cultural changes that contribute to positive socialization by parents. In much of the Western world, including the United States (Grevan, 1991), children used to be seen as willful by nature and obedience was greatly valued. To create well-socialized persons, it was believed that children's obedience had to be ensured, and their will broken, by any means necessary. The belief that physical punishment is desirable in raising children still persists (Straus, Gelles, and Steinmetz, 1980). However, the research findings indicate that nurturance, affection, and responsiveness, combined with guidance consisting of standards, guiding values, and positive discipline, raise well-socialized and caring children. Wide-ranging awareness of this, as well as the development of skills in positive socialization through the media, literature, and parent training, would contribute to the development of caring in society.

The Role of Bystanders

Everybody who witnesses but does not act in the face of others' needs is a passive bystander. We are bystanders to things happening both at home and abroad. It is difficult to create a caring world if we draw sharp lines between us and them.

What happens when individuals or nations are passive in the face of others' needs? It is nearly impossible to see others suffer, to do nothing, and to continue to feel empathy and caring. When people are discriminated against, homeless, abused, the objects of ethnic cleansing or mass killing and we do nothing, in order to protect ourselves from their pain and suffering and our empathic suffering with them, we tend to distance ourselves from them. We engage in just-world thinking—the belief that the world is a just place and people who suffer must somehow deserve it. In these and other ways, we devalue the sufferers (Staub, 1989a).

The United States has, like most other nations, an unfortunate history in this regard. In the 1930s, U.S. corporations—in the midst of the violent Nazi upsurge—continued with business as usual in Germany (Simpson, 1993). We supported Iraq while it was using chemical weapons to kill its own Kurdish minority. And while United Nations and other observers have reported that they had not seen, since the Second World War, the kind of suffering that existed in parts of Bosnia, the world has been wringing its hands, doing almost nothing. In cases like Nazi Germany or Bosnia, the earlier bystanders react the greater the eventual impact, and the less force is needed to have an impact. Very early, even speaking out can inhibit the evolution of destructive actions (Staub, 1989a, 1992).

While inaction creates passivity in us, action has the opposite consequence. Here again, there is learning by doing and a process of evolution. When we get involved in helping others, we begin to change. When as bystanders we become active, we also influence other people. When two people hear sounds of distress from another room and one of these people (a confederate) says "I don't think that concerns us, it is really nothing," the other person tends to do nothing. When the confederate says "that sounds really serious, we need to do something," the other person is likely to initiate helping action (Staub, 1974). Our potential to influence others by what we say and do is great.

Conclusion

We need to create a vision of a caring world and caring communities. People are hungry for connecting with others, and helping is a wonderful avenue for it. But they often feel hopeless and ineffective. Offering a vision of how to help can liberate their energy, open their hearts, and enable them to also serve their own needs by joining with and helping others.

People sometimes say to me: "What can I do? There are so many things in the world—it is so full of problems—we can't do everything." But most of us have special concerns dear to our hearts, whether the welfare of our children or children in general, or injustice against minorities, or hunger and homelessness. Being involved in the world does not mean that we act on all fronts all the time. We can choose a primary domain for our efforts. I believe we also have an obligation to speak out and act in response to emergencies, whether they involve a single person or groups, as in the case of starvation in Ethiopia or killings in Bosnia.

Sometimes when I talk about helping, people also say: "I would really like to do something. I have the time, I have the interest, I have the desire, but I don't know what to do." At times I have a vision of starting a universal volunteer organization that channels people into different activities depending on their interests, an organization that allows people to designate their particular concerns and has ways of directing people to activities that fit their concerns and needs.

Finally, when people act in courageous ways, when they try to bring about unpopular, difficult social change, they need a supportive community. For example, the abolitionists, as they went around the country making speeches, suffered abuse. But they had a community of the spirit with others who were doing the same things, and were greatly strengthened by that. Everywhere people who are devoting themselves to helping and volunteering can benefit from a spirit of community with like-minded others.

References

Ainsworth, M.D.S. "Infant-Mother Attachment." *American Psychologist*, 1979, *34*, 932–937.

Aronson, E., Stephan, C., Sikes, J., Blaney, N., and Snapp, M. *The Jigsaw Classroom*. Newbury Park, Calif.: Sage, 1978.

Baumrind, D. *Early Socialization and the Discipline Controversy*. Morristown, N.J.: General Learning Press, 1975.

Colby, A., and Damon, W. *Some Do Care*. New York: Free Press, 1992.

Deutsch, M. *The Resolution of Conflict: Constructive and Destructive Processes*. New Haven, Conn.: Yale University Press, 1973.

Deutsch, M. "Educating for a Peaceful World." *American Psychologist*, 1992, *48*, 510–518.

Eisenberg, N. *The Caring Child*. Cambridge, Mass.: Harvard University Press, 1992.

Erkut, S., Jaquette, D., and Staub, E. "Moral Judgment–Situation Interaction as a Basis for Predicting Social Behavior." *Journal of Personality*, 1991, *49*, 1–44.

Feinberg, J. K. "Anatomy of a Helping Situation: Some Personality and Situational Determinants of Helping in a Conflict Situation Involving

Another's Psychological Distress." Unpublished doctoral dissertation, Department of Psychology, University of Massachusetts, Amherst, 1978.

Gelles, R. J. "Child Abuse and Violence in Single-Parent Families: Parent Absence and Economic Deprivation." *American Journal of Orthopsychiatry*, 1989, 59, 492–501.

Grevan, P. *Spare the Child: The Religious Roots of Punishment and the Impact of Physical Abuse*. New York: Knopf, 1991.

Grodman, S. M. "The Role of Personality and Situational Variables in Responding to and Helping an Individual in Psychological Distress." Unpublished doctoral dissertation, Department of Psychology, University of Massachusetts, Amherst, 1979.

Hoffman, M. L. "Conscience, Personality, and Socialization Technique." *Human Development*, 1970, *13*, 90–126.

Keogh, T. "Children Without a Conscience." *New Age Journal*, Jan.-Feb. 1993, pp. 53–60.

Oliner, S. B., and Oliner, P. *The Altruistic Personality: Rescuers of Jews in Nazi Europe*. New York: Free Press, 1988.

Piaget, J., and Weil, A. "The Development in Children of the Idea of the Homeland and of Relations with Other Countries." *International Journal of Social Science Bulletin*, 1951, *3*, 570–580.

Shaffer, D. R. *Social and Personality Development*. Pacific Grove, Calif.: Brooks/Cole, 1988.

Simpson, C. *The Splendid Blond Beast: Money, Law, and Genocide in the Twentieth Century*. New York: Grove Press, 1993.

Sroufe, L. A. "The Coherence of Individual Development: Early Care, Attachment, and Subsequent Developmental Issues." *American Psychologist*, 1979, *34*, 834–842.

Staub, E. "Helping a Distressed Person: Social, Personality, and Stimulus Determinants." In L. Berkowitz (ed.), *Advances in Experimental Social Psychology*. Vol. 7. New York: Academic Press, 1974.

Staub, E. "To Rear a Prosocial Child: Reasoning, Learning by Doing, and Learning by Teaching Others." In D. DePalma and J. Folley (eds.), *Moral Development: Current Theory and Research*. Hillsdale, N.J.: Erlbaum, 1975.

Staub, E. *Positive Social Behavior and Morality: Social and Personal Influences*. Vol. 1. New York: Academic Press, 1978.

Staub, E. *Positive Social Behavior and Morality: Socialization and Development*. Vol. 2. New York: Academic Press, 1979.

Staub, E. "The Evolution of Caring and Nonaggressive Persons and Societies." In R. Wagner, J. DeRivera, and M. Watkins (eds.), *Positive Approaches to Peace*. Special issue of *Journal of Social Issues*, 1988, *44*, 81–100.

Staub, E. *The Roots of Evil: The Origins of Genocide and Other Group Violence*. New York: Cambridge University Press, 1989a.

Staub, E. "What Are Your Values and Goals?" *Psychology Today*, May 1989b, pp. 46–49.

Staub, E. "Values, Helping, and Well-Being." Unpublished manuscript, Department of Psychology, University of Massachusetts, Amherst, 1991.

Staub, E. "Transforming the Bystander: Altruism, Caring, and Social Responsibility." In H. Fein (ed.), *Genocide Watch*. New Haven, Conn.: Yale University Press, 1992.

Staub, E. "The Psychology of Bystanders, Perpetrators, and Heroic Helpers." *International Journal of Intercultural Relations*, 1993, *17*, 315–341.

Staub, E. "Altruism and Aggression in Children and Youth: Origins and Cures." Unpublished manuscript, Department of Psychology, University of Massachusetts, Amherst, 1994.

Straus, M. A., Gelles, R. J., and Steinmetz, S. K. *Behind Closed Doors: Violence in the American Family*. New York: Doubleday, 1980.

Tec, N. *When Light Pierced the Darkness: Christian Rescue of Jews in Nazi-Occupied Poland*. New York: Oxford University Press, 1986.

Troy, M., and Sroufe, L. A. "Victimization Among Preschoolers: Role of Attachment Relationships." *Child and Adolescent Psychiatry*, 1987, *26*, 166–172.

Waters, E., Wippmann, J., and Sroufe, L. A. "Attachment, Positive Affect, and Competence in the Peer Group: Two Studies in Construct Validation." *Child Development*, 1979, *50*, 821–829.

Yoshikawa, H. "Prevention as Cumulative Protection: Effects of Early Family Support and Education on Chronic Delinquency and Its Risks." *Psychological Bulletin*, 1994, *115*, 1–27.

Chapter Three

Children of the Left: Sharing Values Across Generations

Martin Halpern

How can we as a society raise our children so that they become adults who care thoughtfully and actively about the needs of others? We must first take note of the fact that our society is not organized to bring about such a goal. There is no central planning in the fields of child development or education, just as there is no central planning of the economy in the United States. Our society does not have a single "we" but rather many competing, conflicting, and cooperating "we's" and "I's." In the cacophony of conflicting subcultures, ideas, and values, it is not surprising that there is no shared goal of raising children to be thoughtful and actively caring about others in society. In practice, much of the responsibility for the transmission of caring values devolves on the family and the community. In some families and communities, the concept of caring is valued only for members of one's subculture. In some cases, caring is limited to members of one's family. In other cases, caring is viewed as a delusion: pursuing one's self-interest is the only meaningful goal.

Although families and communities may wish to transmit caring values to children, the diversity of power centers within our society means that the influences on our children are many and often conflicting. Our children are influenced by their parents, by their extended families, by their teachers and other adults in the

Note: The author wishes to thank Paul Schervish, Sally Lancaster, and Helen Webb for their thoughtful critiques of the manuscript and John Beck and Paul Mishler for helpful suggestions on sources.

school environment, by their peers, and by general societal institutions such as the media, the business community, trade unions, churches, civic organizations, and government. They also may be influenced by neighbors as well as by members of their family's subculture(s).

How important is membership in a caring subculture to the development of children into caring adults? How is the moral development of children brought up in caring subcultures affected by such other variables as the media, the schools, and peer groups? What happens when a caring subculture is "out of sync" with the larger society? Is it able to survive and pass on its traditions to the younger generation?

The Left as a Caring Subculture

To address these questions concretely, this chapter examines the attempts of members of one subculture—the left-wing movement in the twentieth-century United States—to pass on caring values to its children. A study of the left's experience is useful because activist caring is at the core of the left's value system rather than being a peripheral or subsidiary concern. Moreover, the left, while critical of the existing social system, has not sought to wall off its members into an unchanging sect. Accepting the reality of a rapidly changing society, left-wing families have sent their children into the public educational system to learn and eventually into the market economy to earn a living while attempting to transmit to them the value of caring for their people and all people, for the working class and all oppressed people. Children of the left have faced the problem of coming to grips with ideas and value systems coming from government, employers, the media, the schools, and peers that conflict with the ideas and values of their parents.

The left has shown a great deal of resilience but has also faced tremendous adversity. As a secular, modern, and egalitarian subculture, the left has supported scientific and technological progress and favored an end to the traditional subordination of minorities and women. The left's philosophical orientation thus has allowed it to adapt to rapid changes in twentieth-century American society while at the same time maintaining its core values. For example, left-wing understanding of women's oppression has evolved considerably during the course of this century, especially under the impact of the feminist movement that erupted in the 1960s (Buhle, 1983; Evans, 1979; Gatlin, 1987; Gosse, 1991). Because the left is a subculture that defines itself as oppositional to the existing social system, however, it has endured hostility from powerful groups determined to maintain the status quo. The left's experience, therefore, can highlight the workings of subcultural survival mechanisms.

The chapter will first explore the left's concept of care and its place in the overall left-wing outlook. It will then examine the role of leftists as parents and nonleft influences on children of left-wing families. The body of the chapter will survey the historical experience of left-wing families' attempts to raise caring children, focusing on how nonleft societal and peer influences interact with family and left subcultural influences in different periods. The chapter then turns to a comparison of the left's experience with that of other subcultures. The conclusion returns to an examination of the importance of growing up in the left and assesses both the left's survival mechanisms and the general significance of the left's experience.

The Concept of Care

What is the left's approach to care? The director of the Aliyah Senior Citizens Center in Venice, California, the subject of Barbara Myerhoff's anthropological work *Number Our Days* (1979, p. 117), noted that his mother was

> one of the important people in the Russian revolution. She was the first one in our town to carry the Red Flag. She was what you call a humanitarian, a most dedicated person. . . . In my life, she had the

> biggest influence. . . . I do all what I can for humanity, perpetuating the ideas of my mother, so that I want to carry that on for her. I'm not so big, like Abraham, Moses, Christ, and Buddha. But you should know, they too didn't want war. Those people left their footsteps on history, and in a smaller way, I may do that also.

At the most general level, the left's concept of care—helping humanity—is similar to that of the philanthropic community. As is implicit from the juxtaposition of the image of carrying the red flag and being a humanitarian, to the left being a caring person means being politically active for the working class. Also evident is the left's emphasis on history. Leftists feel connectedness to the past and the future of their movement. The dedication during difficult times to carry on for the sake of those who went before and for those who will come after provides important sustenance, similar to the spiritual faith of religious people. Although leftists generally favor scientific thinking and contrast it with religious beliefs, Elizabeth Gurley Flynn (1973, p. 44) acknowledged in her autobiography that "in a certain sense," socialism was her religion. "I found the Socialist movement at a very young and impressionable age. To me it was the creed of the brotherhood of man or 'to do on earth as it is in Heaven,' and I was an intense believer in socialism during my whole life."

In her study of the left-wing writer Tillie Olsen, Elaine Neil Orr focuses on the central role of caring in Olsen's vision of social and spiritual transformation. Olsen wrote: "'What's wrong with the world then, that it doesn't ask—and make it possible—for people to raise and contribute the best that is in them'" (quoted in Orr, 1987, p. 154). For Olsen, caring involves meeting the daily needs of children and others but also encouraging them to develop themselves and contribute to others. Orr explains Olsen's concept of caring and her critical view of the consequences of its practice being limited: "Olsen's 'truth' emerges as an advocacy that all learn the necessary human art of caring and encouraging. . . . If part of humanity offers all of the 'essential' care—whether that part be the half who are women or the more than half who are working class—those people are denied their human creativity in other areas. On the other hand, to live without offering to someone else 'essential' care and encouragement may be, in Olsen's view, a greater poverty" (p. 157). Orr summarizes Olsen's view: "Care and encouragement, given and received, liberate people toward their fullest being" (p. 159). When left-wingers write specifically about the concept of care, then, they include caring for others in one's family, caring for others through the medium of political and social activism, and the sociable caring provided to friends, neighbors, and strangers.

The Left-Wing Outlook

The left-wing movement's goal has been to transform society as a whole so that encouragement to caring becomes the society's organizing principle. A planned socialist economy would offer jobs, health care, and education to all who needed them, while support would be provided for those unable to work. Cooperative values would replace competitive ones. "In place of the old bourgeois society, with its classes and class antagonisms," Marx and Engels ([1848] 1948, p. 31) wrote, "we shall have an association, in which the free development of each is the condition for the free development of all." Having failed thus far to achieve its dream of a transformation of American society, how well has the left fared in the effort to transmit its values to succeeding generations?

America's left-wing subculture in the twentieth century is modest in size, but its activist orientation and the value it has placed on education have made it a significant and visible influence on twentieth-century American society. Leftists see themselves as members of a working class oppressed and exploited by the capitalist class. Although members of the working class may seek to advance themselves individually, the left-wing view is that real improvement in the lives of workers comes through collective action. Leftists are those members of the working class who actively organize against oppression and exploitation, promote united action of workers of both genders and of all races and ethnic groups, and seek the transformation of America's capitalist society into a socialist society run by the working class. Although they are anticapitalist and acknowledge that they seek to advance the interest of the working class at the expense of the capitalist class, leftists believe that socialism and communism would lead to a more just society in which all would gain the opportunity to develop to their full potential.

The left's concept of activism is based on a unity of the personal interest of the individual with the collective interest of all working people. The left thus recognizes and includes the concept of self-interest in its worldview, but the left is also a movement with significant psychological and spiritual dimensions. In practice, leftists laud those who make sacrifices to help the working class, the poor and oppressed, and other members of the left-wing movement. In certain periods, most notably during the period of cold-war repression of the late 1940s and the 1950s, the need to make sacrifices became overwhelming. The survival of a left-wing movement in the United States was in doubt.

For leftists as for other Americans, "personal interests" have generally included love, marriage, and children. Although child-rearing styles and practices are quite varied among leftists and have changed with the times, children do have a special place in left-wing philosophy. As people looking to the development of a future society organized on the basis of humanistic values, leftists view their current activities as a contribution to the welfare of their children and of future generations.

Leftists as Parents

Like most other parents, leftists want their children to adopt their values. Didactic instruction in right and wrong behavior and beliefs occurs in left-wing households as in other households. Those who think deeply about how to raise their children know that instruction in caring values entails many layers of involvement with their children. Two such parents were Ethel and Julius Rosenberg, who were arrested, tried on the charge of conspiracy to commit espionage in wartime, and executed in 1953 in what the left viewed as a cold-war frame-up. While separated from their two sons, Julius wrote that he and Ethel "'shared everything together and gave our all to help our boys develop as healthy, socially concerned human beings, holding dear the principles of democracy, liberty and brotherhood. In our behavior, in our play with them, in the stories we told them and by understanding and devotion to them we gave them more than just parental love. Through them and in them we mentioned a love for humanity for its basic goodness and its inherent creative genius'" (quoted in Meeropol and Meeropol, 1975, pp. 165–166).

As parents who love their children, leftists generally have wanted their children to acquire an education and to make a good living. Leftists advocate education both as an economic tool and as a necessary component of a full, humanistic life. While working for a socialist future, left-wing parents in most cases realize that their children must equip themselves to live in a capitalist society. As people of generally modest means, they want their children to become skillful and "successful" economically without advancing at the expense of others.

To meet the developmental needs of their children, left-wing parents sometimes find it necessary to employ activist techniques on their children's behalf. When her daughter Kim was in junior high school in the 1950s, for example, Rose Chernin went to the school to protest when the principal suggested secretarial school to Kim. "What do you mean giving such advice to this girl?" she asked the principal. "She has straight A's, doesn't she? She's the brightest girl in her class. This girl is going to college. How can you, a woman, advise her to sacrifice this? Don't you know how hard it is already for a girl to make the right choices? Shame on you" (Chernin, 1984, pp. 106–107).

According to left-wing thinking, children will successfully incorporate socialist ideas only if these ideas make sense in terms of their own experience. Each generation finds itself in new historical circumstances and tests out the ideas it learns in childhood in those new conditions. Given this emphasis on youth as a time of testing out ideas, left-wing theory posits the idea that youth should engage in their own autonomous political activity. As a result, the left-wing movement sponsors the development of youth organizations that share the philosophy of the adult movement but allow for independent decision making by young people.

Nonleft Influences on Children of the Left

Youth of left-wing families are influenced not only by their parents but by other individuals and organizations that tend to pull them in the same direction. Often, extended family members, neighbors, and friends are also left-wing activists or are influenced by left-wing thinking and thus reinforce parental ideas. There are meetings and picnics of left-wing organizations. Appropriate books, pamphlets, newspapers, and records are available for children to read and listen to. Depending on their resources, which vary with time and place, left groups sponsor outings, dances, Sunday schools, and summer camps for children and youth (Gornick, 1977; Liebman, 1979; Mishler, 1988; Teitelbaum, 1993).

Although the left-wing movement has multiple channels for influencing the children of its participants, there are substantial competing and sometimes antagonistic influences at work. From teachers, friends at school and in the neighborhood, the mass media, and nonleft community organizations and recreational centers, children and youth of left-wing families hear ideas different from and often hostile to those of their parents and the left-wing movement. Values formation among children of left-wing families results from the individual child's interaction with parents, peers, the subculture(s) of which they are a part, and the institutions of the larger society. Outcomes vary, according to the personality of the child, the characteristics of the parents, political attitudes of peers, the quality of subcultural support systems, and the degree of opposition to or support for "progressive" values by institutions of the larger society. An examination of parent-child interaction in different historical periods reveals some of the general problems involved in values formation and the specific importance of historical context.

Progressive Era Through the 1920s

Elizabeth Gurley Flynn was born in 1890 in Concord, New Hampshire. According to her autobiography (Flynn, 1973, p. 23), her ancestors were "'immigrants and revolutionists'—from the Emerald Isle." Her mother was a tailor and her father was a laborer in the quarries. The family experienced poverty even after her father became a civil engineer. Flynn's hatred of poverty developed when the family lived in the "drab bleak textile center of Manchester [New Hampshire]." She recalled watching a police officer put a "weeping old man" in jail. "He kept assuring us children he had done no wrong, he had no job and no money and no place to sleep. This episode caused me anxiety about all old people" (p. 36).

Both of Flynn's parents were critical thinkers and socialists who stimulated the intellectual growth of their children. "My mother was always interested in public affairs. She early became an advocate of equal rights for women. . . . Mama was no model housekeeper. But she was interesting and different and we loved her dearly. . . . All during our childhood she read aloud to us—from Irish history, poetry, fairy stories" (pp. 29–30). Her mother "was firm in teaching us respect for other people's nationality, language and religion" (p. 40). Flynn recalled her mother's special place in the South Bronx community where the family settled in 1900: "She was a good neighbor in time of need. She helped the sick, advised on domestic problems, and when she baked pies and cakes she shared them with the neighborhood children. It was a calamity to the area when she moved away to Brooklyn in the late twenties" (pp. 40–41).

Flynn became interested in socialist ideas at an early age: "In our household the children listened in on everything." At about age twelve, she enthusiastically argued the affirmative in a public school debate on the topic "Should the Government own the Coal Mines?" Her parents took her regularly to the neighborhood socialist Sunday night forum. Just after Flynn's fifteenth birthday, her mother suggested she read Edward Bellamy's *Looking Backward* (1898). She then began to read works by Karl Marx and Frederick Engels. She was not yet sixteen when she was invited to give her first speech to the Harlem Socialist Club. With her mother's encouragement, she accepted the offer. "I tried to select a subject upon which my father would not interfere too much," Flynn recalled, "something he did not consider too important. It was 'What Socialism Will Do for Women'" (p. 53). The speech was her own and its success led to many other invitations to speak. She quickly became a prominent soap box orator. Because of her many nighttime meetings, however, her grades in school declined dramatically. Flynn ignored the advice of her principal and her mother to concentrate on her studies and dropped out of school, an action she "deeply regretted" in later years (p. 64). Despite these regrets, she was launched on a career that included periods as a leading labor organizer, civil liberties partisan, and communist official (Flynn, 1973; Baxandall, 1987; Cole, 1991).

Armand Hammer was born in 1898 on the Lower East Side of New York into a family of Jewish immigrants. As a young person, his father, Julius, had become a steelworker, organized a trade union, and joined the Socialist Labor Party. "Throughout his life, my father was warmly emotional and sentimental, easily moved to anger and pity by the sufferings of the poor and the cruel labors of the underprivileged masses of that time," Hammer (1987, p. 45) recalled. Remaining a socialist, Julius became a small businessperson in pharmaceuticals and then a physician with a thriving practice. He achieved a modest prosperity. "He could have made himself many times richer," Armand commented, "if he had insisted on collecting all his bills; or if he could have restrained himself from giving money away" such as paying for his patients' prescriptions (p. 54).

Concern for the safety of their children led the Hammers to move from the crowded Lower East Side, which had both dangers and a vibrant radical subculture, to the then–sparsely populated Bronx. When the Bronx also became crowded and dangerous, twelve-year-old Armand was sent away to live with family friends in a small Connecticut town. During his four-year stay in Connecticut, he saw and interacted with well-to-do children from the other side of the tracks. He read Horatio Alger stories and biographies of financiers like Rockefeller, Carnegie, and Vanderbilt. "I began to see plainly that the American system made it possible for individuals to do great things," Hammer recalled, "to create lasting business enterprises which gave employment to millions and improved the living standards of everybody. I was particularly impressed with the charitable endowments of these vastly rich men—the colleges, libraries, art galleries, and medical facilities" (p. 59).

Although Hammer adopted a capitalist rather than a socialist vision, he shared some of his father's political views and was influenced by his ethical example. As a fifteen-year-old high school student back in the Bronx as World War I began, Hammer delivered an impassioned speech against the "horror and futility of war." Over seventy years later, he wrote, "I could make much the same speech today" (p. 60). Hammer believed the example of his father's "goodness" inspired him to compose what he calls his "personal creed" early in life. "In my bed at night, I would ask to be as good as I could be and give as much help as I could to others. I found that I liked myself best when I was helping other people—and I wanted to like myself" (p. 55). It was this personal creed that led him to regularly give away a large part of his fortune.

Like Hammer, Peggy Dennis (1977) was born into a family of Russian Jews in New York City. Her parents had been revolutionaries in Russia, and they immersed themselves in the socialist movement in the United States. When Peggy was three, the family moved from New York to Los Angeles for health reasons. Unlike the Hammers' relocation to the Bronx, the move by the Dennis family produced no separation from a radical subculture. Both of Dennis's parents were socialists, and in her memoirs, she recalled that the revolutionary Jewish subculture was the primary reality of her childhood: "We children grew and played in this self-contained, foreign-born, radical community. We were enrolled in the Socialist Party Sunday school at the Labor Temple at the time we started public school kindergarten, and the former was more important than the latter. Among my early memories are those of being lifted each week onto a table in stark meeting halls and lisping my way through recitations of revolutionary poems by Yiddish writers my parents and their comrades loved so passionately. Papa coached me at home, explaining the pathos and courage and hope of the words I was to recite" (p. 20).

In interactions with the larger world beyond their radical subculture, Dennis's family dramatically asserted its socialist distinctiveness. The children stayed out of school on May Day, proudly stating the reason for their absence. On the other hand, Dennis and her sister attended school on Jewish holidays. During World War I, Dennis refused to buy war savings stamps despite the criticism she received for keeping her class from a "100 percent patriotism record" (p. 21). As she recalled it: "We were belligerently atheist, internationalist, and anti-imperialist, and the narrow-mindedness of our block, our school, and our community only made us feel special and superior" (p. 21).

Despite the clear sense of a socialist identity, Dennis successfully competed in the academic, extracurricular, and peer-group activities in junior and senior high school in the early 1920s. She won schoolwide elective office, participated in statewide oratorical contests and Shakespearean festivals, won the lead in her senior play, and was editor of her junior and senior high newspapers. She "went steady with popular athletes and . . . belonged to the in-groups noted for being intellectual, service-minded, trend-setting" (p. 24). On evenings and weekends, on the other hand, she was involved in communist meetings and Marxist discussions and in organizing a communist children's group. Dennis kept her school and political lives separate, with the latter remaining "always the more important and real to us" (p. 24).

Their parents encouraged Dennis and her sister to enroll in Teachers College at the University of California so they could become "economically independent from whatever husbands we might someday acquire" (p. 25). Neither completed the course of study. Nevertheless, Dennis concluded: "We were happy, unconflicted, suffered no identity crises, saw no generation gaps. We lived in isolated security among our own kind. The goals and hopes of our parents were ours. We rejected those of society around us; ours was the dream of the Future" (p. 26). Her sister became a garment worker and trade union leader. Dennis became a revolutionary.

Dorothy Healey's childhood was similar to Dennis's. Healey's parents also moved the family to California for health reasons when she was a child. Her parents were Jewish immigrants from Hungary and became socialists in the United States. Born in 1914, Healey attended her first socialist meetings "when I was still in diapers" (Healey and Isserman, 1990, p. 22). "By the time I was twelve years old," she recalls, "there was no question in my mind what I was going to be when I grew up. . . . I knew . . . my life was going to be devoted to the revolution. Along with discussions with my mother, one of the greatest influences on me was reading Upton Sinclair's novels. . . . I just throbbed with indignation over the unhappiness of the miners and the oil workers and the injustice and cruelty of the bosses" (p. 25).

The views of her peers began to influence Healey when she was in junior high school in Berkeley. She "started feeling terribly self-conscious about all kinds of things about my appearance, especially my clothes. My mother, of course, thought people should ignore such nonsensical bourgeois details as how you looked and what you wore. The important thing was what was in your mind. Besides, we didn't have much money" (p. 24). Her mother made clothes but poorly. Healey did not rebel, however. "I was ashamed to say how much those dresses embarrassed me. I never learned the things that other girls were taught while growing up, how to fix your hair, or how to choose clothes" (p. 24).

Although she was not rebellious, Healey did branch out socially in junior high school. Most of her friends were top students who were well-to-do and lived in the Berkeley hills while her family lived in the lowlands. At fourteen, however, she joined the Young Communist League (YCL). "I quickly lost interest in the friends I had made in junior high school," Healey recounts. "The parties I had started being invited to up in the hills had never really been fun for me anyway" (p. 28).

Although she shared her mother's political outlook and values, Healey's adolescence was not problem-free. She had found a new social life in the YCL. Her new friends were in their late teens and early twenties. Healey lost interest in school, failed to do her homework, and stopped getting good grades. Two older siblings were both very good students and her indifference to school angered her mother, who placed a high value on education. In 1931 Healey dropped out of high school a month before graduating to accept a YCL assignment to go to work in a cannery. Both her brother and sister had gone on to the university and her mother was very disappointed. "In spite of her Communist loyalties, Mama considered the Young Communist League to have been a terrible influence on me. Here I was casually flinging away the chance for the education that she had been denied in her childhood" (p. 36).

Great Depression and New Deal

Less than a year after Healey became a YCL member, the stock market crashed. Left-wing organizing opportunities expanded greatly and she was involved in organizing unemployed councils and unions, speaking on street corners, and supervising a branch of the communist children's group, the Young Pioneers. With so many workers needing help, with the left-wing movement growing, Healey's vision as a twelve-year-old became a reality. She spent her youth organizing for a variety of left-wing organizations and unions and eventually became a full-time official for the Communist Party.

Another California communist was Rose Chernin, who remembers the thirties as the "golden time of our movement" (quoted in Chernin, 1984, p. 101). She recalls that "there was always an excitement," an excitement that was contagious for the children of communists. Rose's first daughter, Nina, was born in 1929 and, as Rose recalls it,

> Her entire life she lived in the movement. When I joined the party and began to organize full time, I always took her with me. I felt I had something to give to this little girl, an understanding to pass on to her. Children were very important in our movement; who else would carry on our struggle? . . . We knew, when she grows up, she will be joining the Young Communist League. She will be going down to write for the *Daily Worker*. She was very proud to be a Communist when she was in high school and this pride began when she was a little girl, holding my hand when we walked in the coop in the East Bronx. . . . She had a gentle nature, very thoughtful and our people loved her. You would look at her and you would think, Here is what a girl will be like under socialism [pp. 100–101, 167].

Nina's unstressed absorption of her parent's values and political ideology occurred in the context of a strong left-wing subculture that provided security and affirmation for parents and children. Thus the radical youth involved in the 1930s mass student movement saw their activism as an "auxiliary . . . to the labor movement and its struggle for a more egalitarian social order." Instead of rebelling against their parents, Robert Cohen (1993, pp. 248–249) found, 1930s student "activists seemed eager to link their own political activism to some legacy from their parents and siblings." Although the larger society was far from being pro-communist, opportunities for leftists to find affirmation there as well were numerous. Communists led protests of the unemployed in the early 1930s, became the left wing of the New Deal in the mid 1930s, and joined in the national effort to defeat Nazi Germany and militarist Japan in the 1940s. The larger societal framework turned decidedly hostile, however, with the onset of the cold war in the late 1940s. By the early 1950s, the country was in the grips of anticommunist hysteria. It was an especially difficult time for parents of young children and teenagers.

Postwar Red Scare

A memoir that focuses on that difficult time is Carl Bernstein's *Loyalties* (1989). Bernstein, who achieved fame with his colleague Bob Woodward for their exposure of Watergate in the 1970s, recalls his childhood in the 1950s and attempts to come to grips with the meaning of his parents' lives as left-wing activists. His father was a leader of the United Public Workers union and his mother was a leader of the Committee to Save the Rosenbergs. As a child growing up in the nation's capital during the 1950s anticommunist hysteria, Bernstein saw officials, neighbors, and friends turning against his parents. He rebelled. "I'm not sure exactly when the notion of my father being 'different' from other fathers began to tug so strongly, but the sense of shame, of being threatened, of being vulnerable to something over which I had no control, came early. Sometimes I hated him for it, and I articulated my rage through whatever misdemeanor was closest at hand" (p. 15).

Bernstein's rebellion against his parents took such forms as acts of shoplifting, reckless driving, and vandalism that got him in trouble with the law. These acts of what was then called juvenile delinquency greatly troubled his parents, as did his failure to apply himself to his studies and his poor grades. Bernstein also rebelled by joining in peer-group activities that involved associations antagonistic to the left-wing subculture in which his parents moved. When the family lived in a District of Columbia neighborhood, ten-year-old Carl's friends were Catholics, and he tried out for a Catholic Youth Organization football team. (The Bernsteins were nonreligious Jews.) His parents accepted positive peer-group activity. For his football tryout, Bernstein's father bought him a uniform costing more than a week's groceries. He made the team, and his father's support included attendance at a father-and-son prayer breakfast prior to the season's opening game.

Bernstein responded not only to peer pressure but to what he perceived as the dominant values of the larger culture. In 1952, at the age of eight, he donned "I Like Ike" and "Ike and Dick" buttons while his parents debated whether to support Adlai Stevenson or Vincent Hallinan of the Progressive Party. In 1954, after a report of his mother's appearance before the House Un-American Activities Committee, some of the Bernstein's friends, neighbors, and relatives cut off contact with them. Bernstein reacted to the family's difficulties by "becoming a patriotic nut" (p. 124). He was class air-raid warden, led the Pledge of Allegiance, read the Bible aloud on Wednesday mornings, and went to St. Columbia's Episcopal Church for optional prayer on Friday.

When the Bernsteins moved to a Maryland suburb, most of Carl's new friends were Jewish. He joined and became a leader in a religious Jewish fraternity and argued stridently and eventually successfully to have a bar mitzvah. Although they would have preferred he make different choices, his parents supported the positive forms of rebellion. The negative forms of rebellion caused them greater difficulty. After an incident in which Bernstein's driver's license was suspended and he was put on a year's probation for a second time, his father decided he had to do "something constructive." He helped his son get a summer job at the *Washington Star*, and thus began Carl Bernstein's career in journalism.

Despite his anger, hostility, and rebellion against his parents, young Carl assimilated many of his parents' values. His mother was a leader of the movement to integrate Washington's public accommodations in the early 1950s. In response to the sit-in movement that began in 1960, Bernstein wrote articles in the school newspaper arguing that "Jewish kids, Jews perhaps more than any other people, belonged in the civil rights movement" (p. 151). Advocating a social awareness platform, he then ran and was elected regional president of the Aleph Zadik Aleph (AZA) youth organization. The region stretched from the District of Columbia to North Carolina. When the train to a North Carolina AZA convention stopped for repairs, Bernstein and other AZA'ers and members of the BBG, a Jewish sorority, refused to leave the black waiting room at the Greensboro station despite threats of arrest. "I announced that anybody who didn't want to get arrested should get back on the train. Everybody stayed and waited." The police did not carry out the threat (pp. 151–153).

Although as an adult Bernstein has many political disagreements with his parents, he has an underlying respect for their values. He comments that he's always valued his father's judgment "more highly than anyone else's especially on questions that might be regarded as either moral or political. He has an innate sense of decency that leads him almost unerringly to the proper course. . . . He arrives at his judgments carefully, yet almost effortlessly, bringing pragmatism to a wellspring of what, in another age, might have been termed humanism" (p. 19).

When Communist Party leader Rose Chernin was arrested under the Smith Act in 1951, her daughter Kim was eleven years old. Like Bernstein's, Kim's attitude was a mixture of acceptance of her parents' values and rebellion against them. "Since I was a small girl I have been fighting with my mother. When the family was eating dinner some petty disagreement would arise and I'd jump from the table, pick up a plate and smash it against the wall. I'd go running from the room, slamming doors behind me. By the age of thirteen I insisted that Hegel was right and not Marx. 'The Idea came first,' I cried out from the bathroom, which had the only door in the house that locked. 'The Spirit came before material existence'" (Chernin, 1983, p. 7).

Kim was greatly affected by the death of her sister Nina in 1945. Her mother "fell apart" and thought about suicide. When the family moved to California, Kim was sent to a boarding school for a time. Then came the cold-war onslaught. Fear began to dominate Kim's thinking. "I figured things out. I figured out there was some new danger in the world. The fascists had gone. The concentration camps were gone. The Jews had gone to Israel. Now it was the turn of the Communists. We were Communists, it was our turn" (p. 215). Earlier she had been told to be proud of being communist, now "I wasn't supposed to tell the kids at school. I shouldn't repeat anything I heard my parents say at home" (p. 216). After her mother's arrest in 1951, the fear dominated her life. Kim's greatest fear was that she would be questioned herself and would inform on her family's friends. "Would they torture my mother in jail? Would they torture me? Would I tell the names I knew?" Nevertheless, Kim participated in the left-wing subculture and hoped to be a revolutionary like her mother (pp. 224, 303).

Peer relations became critical in Kim's development. After her mother's arrest, "old friends drifted away." When Kim spoke up to a teacher on behalf of a black student, she gained the friendship of the black, Mexican, and Asian students. For several years, the minority students were her social world. At one point, however, her rebelliousness won the admiration of even the well-to-do white students. She was invited to the parties of the school's social elite.

Despite guilty feelings, she left her black and Mexican friends who had provided her "a protective circle" during her time of difficulties. She even found herself laughing at and telling racist jokes, and making "fun of everything I loved and cherished. . . . I seemed to have felt that if I lied enough, and made enough racist comments, people would forget that I was a Jew and my parents were Communists" (pp. 225–227, 252–253, 255).

Kim tried at once to share her parents' values and to rebel against them and all authority. Her rebelliousness, the stresses on the family stemming from the arrest and trials of her mother, and peer pressure prepared the ground for a break with her parents' views. Rather than seeking an independent path to adulthood based on critical reflections on her own experiences, she saw her choices as becoming a professional revolutionary like her mother or rejecting her family's values. Kim chose to become an apolitical poet. For years, her political differences with her mother led to many hurtful arguments. But in the course of writing their story, they achieved a mutual respect for each other's different choices. In writing the story of her mother's courageous actions in defense of other radicals threatened with jail and deportation and in criticizing her own racist acts, it is clear that Kim writes not only out of love for her mother but also continues to share many of her parents' values.

Margaret Collingwood Nowak's memoir, *Two Who Were There: A Biography of Stanley Nowak* (1989), recounts the experiences of two of Michigan's leading left-wing activists. Stanley, an immigrant from Poland, was one of the first organizers of the United Automobile Workers and went on to serve for ten years in the Michigan state senate. Despite—or perhaps because of—his prominence in Michigan politics, the federal government twice tried to take away his citizenship, in 1942 and again in 1952. The second attempt, coming during the worst days of McCarthyism, was the most serious. The case came to trial in 1954 and resulted in conviction. Stanley won his case on appeal to the Supreme Court only in 1957.

Two Who Were There focuses on the Nowak's lifetime of political activities, but it includes a brief discussion of how the family successfully managed to survive the repressive onslaught and remain intact.

> Our relationship was a steadying factor. We were in complete agreement on the issues and values that had led to this period in our lives, and we would not have done anything differently even if we could have. The families of dear friends were destroyed in facing similar struggles. Men who had not fully shared their political beliefs and activities with their families saw them alienated by the price demanded in unfavorable publicity, ostracism, and condemnation. Divorces and separations resulted, and children were hurt and bitter. Because Stanley and I fully believed in what we did, were committed, and shared our goals, we were able to weather the difficulties and be supportive of each other. Because we had shared our beliefs and goals with Elissa, without preaching, she also reacted in this spirit and was proud of what her father had done and the principles for which he stood [pp. 237–238].

Being called before the House Un-American Activities Committee as the Bernsteins were, being fired or unable to obtain work due to blacklisting, and losing one's friends were common fates for left-wingers in the 1950s. The political trials to which Rose Chernin and Stanley Nowak were subjected were more harrowing than the repression suffered by most in that period. It was a decade of suffering and fear for both parents and children. Nevertheless, many children absorbed their parents' values by a kind of "osmosis." Linn Shapiro remembers the political discussions with her parents' adult left-wing friends as "absolutely intoxicating" (Kaplan and Shapiro, 1985, pp. 1–2). Another child of the fifties—David Goldring—recalls that "[my] political absorption came from the way my parents lived and dealt with problems more than from any explicit political direction. . . . Above all, there was a pretty strong, firmly established atmosphere of love in the home. People were dealt with as whole human beings" (Lukas, 1971, p. 23). Although weakened by repression, subcultural organizations such as *shules* and camps persisted and provided left-wing children of the 1950s with important sustenance. (*Shules* are after-school educational programs run by left-wing Jewish fraternal organizations to teach Jewish tradition and Yiddish literature.) The summer camp experience saved many left-wing children from isolation (Liebman, 1979). "My salvation was camp," Debra recalled. "There's no question that I spent ten months of the year counting down the days 'til I could get to the summer" (quoted in Kaplan and Shapiro, 1985, p. 25). Jeannie grew up in suburban New Jersey and found camp "a total revelation, that there were all these other people who were just like me. . . . I spent high school, every single weekend, running into New York to see my friends from camp, and discounting that anyone I went to school with could possibly be interesting" (quoted in Kaplan and Shapiro, p. 28).

The 1960s

As the repressive climate began to ebb in the late 1950s, new civil rights and peace movements developed and grew into a mass radical upsurge in the 1960s. In both the 1930s and 1960s, millions of people participated in demonstrations, picket lines, and strikes, wrote letters to Congress, campaigned for candidates, and joined organizations. A significant minority of these participants drew radical conclusions from their experiences in movements for social change. While 1930s radicalism centered around organizations and movements led by communists, there was no such focal point to 1960s radicalism. The institutions and the subcultural world of the left had been shattered by cold-war repression. Commentators, historians, and activists themselves labeled the 1960s radicals a "New Left." The label referred both to the youthfulness of the participants and a perceived discontinuity with the communist-oriented "Old Left."

The 1950s victory of anticommunist paranoia led participants and commentators alike to exaggerate the discontinuity between Old Left and New Left. Like Chernin and Bernstein, most children of communist, left-wing, and ex-communist families were affected by the shattering of the left in the 1950s and the anticommunist pressures dominating the larger society. In a great many families, both parents and children dropped some left-wing beliefs that had characterized the movement in earlier periods. Nevertheless, a core set of values survived among parents and children alike. With the much more hospitable climate of the 1960s, the children participated in the new radical upsurge and helped to shape it. Many developed a lasting commitment to social activism.

Among the young people participating in the radical upsurge were the children of Ethel and Julius Rosenberg. In their moving memoir, *We Are Your Sons* (1975), Robert and Michael Meeropol describe how they were "shielded from publicity by loving adults" and grew up in a secure and loving environment with Anne and Abel Meeropol, the couple who adopted them. At the age of ten, Robert Meeropol participated in his first peace march in April 1958 and then joined in the early picketing of Woolworth's to protest the store's segregation policy. "I shared the Meeropols' belief in civil rights and human dignity. . . . I harbored a strong sense of justice, was bothered when someone was picked on, and for the most part avoided the teasing that went on in school, thinking how badly I'd feel if I were teased. These feelings spilled over into politics, especially the issue of injustice to minority groups" (pp. 259, 269, 278).

It was, of course, the black-led civil rights struggle in the South that started a movement that expanded into the multi-issue radical upsurge of the 1960s. Angela Davis grew up in Birmingham, Alabama, in the 1950s when race-based repression was a daily reality for black Southerners. Although her family did not suffer from the anticommunist hysteria, Davis's mother had been a member of the radical Southern Negro Youth Congress in the 1930s and the Davises were friendly with families who were victims of the cold-war purges. As a teenager, Davis attended the alternative high school in New York City run by the American Friends Service Committee where the Meeropols also studied. She joined a communist youth organization and became one of the early participants in the new radical upsurge (Davis, 1974, pp. 75–113).

Citing a survey of participants in two 1980s gatherings of children of communists and his own interviews, Todd Gitlin (1987, p. 73) comments on these children of the left: "Many took in a powerful moralism. There are rights and wrongs, and it is important to live by the rights." In a study on the origins of the New Left, James P. O'Brien (1971, p. 23) found that children of left families brought to the campuses "a set of attitudes favorable to peace, civil liberties, and racial tolerance as well as a willingness to act in support of these goals." After interviewing a sample of fifty 1960s Chicago student activists and their parents, Richard Flacks (1967, p. 68) found that "the great majority . . . are attempting to fulfill and renew the political traditions of their families."

For her influential study on the origins of the women's liberation movement of the 1960s, Sara Evans (1979) sought out New Left activists to interview. "Again and again," she writes, "I was surprised to discover a radical family background" (p. 120n.) Evans notes that "the experience of girls growing up in activist families tended to encourage independence and self-confidence and to place a premium on egalitarian ideals" (p. 121). Commenting on one such woman she interviewed, Evans notes that

> her family was infused with a great sense of morality and social concern. . . . As a very small child she expected herself to defend anyone who was being mistreated. In the first grade she stepped into a circle of children throwing stones at a black child; in the second grade she intervened to stop an Italian child from being beaten; and in the third grade she defended a student against a teacher who was administering corporal punishment. Such an intense sense of identification with the downtrodden coupled with a strong sense of self

> led her to become active in civil rights, SDS, the antiwar movement, and to provide key leadership in the initial phases of the women's liberation movement [p. 121].

Although Evans found that activists with radical family backgrounds were a minority among New Leftists, "women with such backgrounds provided much of the key leadership in developing a new feminism. . . . They . . . had learned a willingness to question and a deep sense of social justice. . . . Again and again, when a voice was raised within the new left pointing out male domination . . . it came from one of these women—these 'red diaper feminists'" (p. 124).

Since the 1960s

Although many children of Old Left parents became activists in the 1960s, the institutional structure of the left began to crumble during the repressive 1950s and was not rebuilt in subsequent decades. The post-1960s left-wing movement has no single organizational center comparable to the Socialist Party in the period prior to 1920 and the Communist Party in the period between the early 1930s and the mid 1950s. Left-wingers participate in a multitude of causes—for peace, solidarity with Latin America, the feminist, civil rights, and environmental movements—but the post-1960s left is fragmented organizationally. It has fewer, smaller, and different geographical centers of concentration than in the past. In the 1930s and 1940s, there were lively centers of left influence in a number of working-class neighborhoods in many major cities. Now, left strongholds are university towns like Cambridge, Massachusetts and Berkeley, California. Children of left-wing working-class parents have usually become professionals, entered a national job market, and become geographically dispersed. Leftists wishing to transmit their values to their children in the past twenty years often have to travel to visit relatives, find few people in their neighborhoods and workplaces who come from similar backgrounds, and lack the institutional support system of camps, cultural groups, fraternal organizations, and left-led trade unions available in earlier periods.

In 1982 and 1983, when a group of red diaper babies (most of whom grew up in the 1950s) gathered together, a focal point of their concern was how to transmit left-wing values to their children in the absence of the vibrant left subculture they had experienced when they were growing up. For example, Bill regrets that there's no "Sunday school or a camp" for his eight-year-old son to "get any political help" when he's older and is contemplating organizing a "sort of Sunday school for the kids in my neighborhood" (Kaplan and Shapiro, 1985, p. 63). Steve, father of ten- and five-year-olds, also is "interested in finding support networks for Left culture for my children. How do you give them the support you know they can't get in the general community?" (pp. 63–64). Molly, the mother of a fourteen-year-old son, commented: "I feel a real vacuum. We [1960s activists] left no institutions or groups or anything for our kids to move into. Now he's out there trying to figure out what to do. . . . He's not gonna fight. He's not gonna register [for the draft]. I want to make sure that that's his belief and not [just] my belief. How do you teach children to develop their own beliefs so that they're solid?" (p. 64). Elizabeth finds that her five-year-old daughter

> needs more support than just my husband and I can provide. She needs to know that there are other people in the culture who have our beliefs. We're vegetarians. We don't eat the same kind of foods. We're not religious. She just can't seem to find any place where she fits in. Who is she like? She's not like her friends. . . . The problem is that we're so few and far between that I feel like we need some type of institution . . . an extended family or an extended culture to take care of the problem of being different, to make her feel she is less different [p. 65].

One avenue of influence that some parents use is taking children to demonstrations. One parent explained that she takes her daughter to events such as the June 12, 1982 nuclear freeze march "where there are a lot of people and they're singing. . . . There are things going on; there's excitement. She's really enjoyed herself. She listens to those speeches" (p. 69). Another parent recounted how he took his daughter to the labor movement's 1981 Solidarity Day demonstration: "We set it up so that she did a report for her class. She wanted to make sure there would be leaflets, took pictures with her camera. She went back and convinced her whole class to hate Reagan" (p. 69). Aside from demonstrations, the channels for reinforcement of left ideas are limited. Some parents take their children to one of the small number of progressive camps that remain. One group in Brooklyn has organized a *shule* (pp. 71, 73).

Some of the older children attending the red diaper weekends along with their parents expressed their views on left-wing values and culture. As in earlier generations, these youth of the 1980s were picking up their parents' ideas. A Boston University college student commented on his acceptance of his parents' views: "I myself have always been aware of their philosophies and agreed mostly, because that's where I got most of my beliefs from" (p. 87). Niki, a seventeen-year-old, reported that she "relied on them [her parents] for telling me everything that's right and wrong. For a while, if somebody would ask me a question, I would say, 'I can't answer this until I ask my folks.'" She and other children with similar experiences decided they needed to read, study, and think more for themselves. "It's been a real hard thing for me to learn they're not always right, or maybe they are, but I have to develop my own opinions," Niki concluded (p. 89). Another youth agreed: "Although I still believe in most of what they believe in, I've done a lot more reading and come to conclusions on my own" (p. 89).

Some of the 1980s children of the left are already activists. Maggie Levenstein was born in 1962. Her parents were first-generation radicals active in the Cambridge area. Levenstein and her younger siblings attended a Black Panther Party Liberation School when she was eight or nine. At twelve she became active in the Cambridge Tenants Organizing Committee. "I remember that I stopped watching Saturday morning cartoons when I started going to meetings every Saturday morning" (p. 8). Nevertheless, she felt relatively isolated. Even in Cambridge, Levenstein knew only one other leftist kid. She reported feeling different, ashamed, and "wished my mother looked like other mothers . . . act[ed] like other mothers" (p. 8). Living in an integrated working-class neighborhood, her parents wanted them to participate and be like the other kids. Levenstein's mother was active in the new feminist movement and she herself reports the "Women's Movement was probably the major influence, in terms of defining myself and who I was." She finds it difficult, however, "to balance the feminist expectations from your family with not so feminist expectations from outside. . . . Maybe I want to do all these things so boys care about what I look like and that's the worst thing in my mother's mind, something I'm never supposed to do. I think those are hard things to work out when you have your parents' values and you exist in the world and those other values are there" (p. 93). Adding to her difficulties is that she feels "a lack of connectedness between us and past generations" and the absence of "a culture to participate in . . . so that you feel like you're part of something that has come from someplace" (p. 93).

Children of 1980s socialists experience many of the same difficulties as the children whose parents were raised as communists. Commenting on her teenage children's situation, Barbara Ehrenreich, chair of the Democratic Socialists of America (DSA), reported: "One of the worst things now is that they don't know other kids who are political" (p. 4). Although DSA'ers Beth and Steve Cagan's oldest daughter was active in an antiapartheid group, Beth noted that their children "tend to feel like oddballs, charting new territory" (Phillips, 1986, p. 4).

To summarize, despite the development of broad new mass

movements during and after the 1960s, the left subculture has not recovered from the trauma of the 1950s. As in the past, however, children of left-wing parents are absorbing their parents' values and entering into social and political activity. The children are also experiencing the pain of being different but, unlike their parents, they do not have the extended family networks, social support systems, and subcultural institutions such as camps to sustain them. Left-wing parents are succeeding in raising caring children, though they miss the help and the sense of wholeness of the communist subculture in which they grew up. The Communist Party persists, but it is not central to the vast array of new movements as it was to the progressive movements of the 1930s, 1940s, and 1950s.

Comparisons of the Left with Other Subcultures

The left-wing approach to care can be usefully compared with that of other subcultures to clarify the distinctiveness of the left's view. The value of caring is present to one degree or another in many subcultures, and academic researchers have developed recommendations to help parents, schools, and universities promote caring values among children and youth (Staub, 1992). The discussion here focuses on a comparison of the left's concept of care with those in the upper class and in nonleft working-class families, both white and African American.

In *Women of the Upper Class* (1984), Susan Ostrander provides a portrait of upper-class families in a large Midwestern city, paying particular attention to child-rearing practices, values transmission, and volunteer activities. Like left-wing parents, upper-class parents want their children to be happy and to do well in life. The upper-class women interviewed by Ostrander also want their children to become caring adults. What Ostrander's subjects mean by these ideas, however, is distinct from what left-wing families believe. There are also formal similarities between the parenting practices of Ostrander's subjects and the left-wing families described in this chapter, but once again the content of the children's upbringing is quite different.

Ostrander found that upper-class parents had "stringent expectations" and expressly "channeled" their children into a specific world (p. 142). The children are sent to class-segregated schools, participate in debuts, are expected to succeed in careers such as business, medicine, and law, and are expected to make compatible marriages within the upper class. The upper-class women were active volunteers, Ostrander found, and "want their children to be seen as people who 'contribute to the community.'" Although they themselves complain about "the pressures of living up to a family name . . . [and] the burdensome obligations of being expected to contribute to the community . . . they want their children to carry on as they have" (p. 77). There are family and class traditions to uphold, a sense of "noblesse oblige," that in Ostrander's view function "to justify and legitimate their class privilege" (pp. 77, 128–129). Thus the concept of caring in this subculture involved an emphasis on the difference and superiority of the carer. This approach is markedly different from the egalitarian and collectivistic approach to care characteristic of the left subculture.

Although upper-class children are relatively isolated from the larger society, Ostrander found that their parents nevertheless are concerned about such negative phenomena as use of drugs, poor performance in school, or inappropriate marriages or career choices. Given their family's economic resources and their mother's expenditure of time devoted to child rearing, upper-class children are assisted in overcoming problems at school and negative peer and societal influences. "Upper class children," Ostrander maintains, "including those who are admittedly poor students, are simply not allowed to fail academically or personally" (p. 84). If poor behavior persists, the negative sanction of reducing or eliminating the child's access to family money may be used. As in the left, parental and subcultural influences work in the same direction, to acculturate children to parental and class values.

The children of the upper class, while sheltered for many years, are influenced by peers and do come in contact with the larger society. They may pull away from the narrowly circumscribed path set for them by getting involved in drug use, picking an inappropriate interest such as rock music, or falling in love with the wrong person. In that larger society, moreover, upper-class children may have to contend with ideas, attitudes, and people hostile to the upper class. In contrast to the left's usual experience, however, the larger society also provides a great deal of positive reinforcement and respect for members of the upper class as the leading citizens of their community (pp. 78–79).

Much is expected of children both of the left and of the upper class. The material advantages enjoyed by the children of the upper class are many and assist them in successful transitions to adulthood along the lines of their parents' expectations. On the other hand, the rigid expectations do lead to difficulties for some of these youth. The independence central to adulthood is carefully circumscribed in the upper-class world, especially for women. Caring is seen as a necessary but subsidiary complement to assuming one's elite status in the world. In many ways, children of the left face a bumpier road to adulthood. Their path is far less clearly drawn for them and they tend to be independent in their thinking and actions. Nevertheless, children of the left often assimilate the left's concept of caring in a deep and lasting way. One cares for others who are suffering not because one is different or superior to them but because one is like them. Leftists see themselves as members of a class or group that is oppressed and exploited and therefore feel a oneness with all people suffering from injustice in the world. Upper-class women who choose to challenge their oppression as women may also feel a oneness with others suffering from injustice. In pursuing such a course, however, such women are seeking to develop a new set of caring values rather than the elite "noblesse oblige" approach described by Ostrander.

How similar are leftists to nonleft members of the working class?

Like left-wing working-class families, the working-class families that are the subject of Lillian Breslow Rubin's 1976 study, *Worlds of Pain: Life in the Working Class Family*, have often faced severe economic hardship. Rubin's interview subjects recalled "parents who worked hard, yet never quite made it; homes that were overcrowded; siblings or selves who got into 'trouble'" (p. 48). Rubin reports few happy memories of childhood among the people she interviewed. They accepted their parents' lack of attention to their emotional needs as an inevitable consequence of their parents' lives of pain and deprivation and do not criticize them for it. These attitudes contrast with those of children of left-wing families, who recall many happy times and have positive things to say about the parental attention they received as well as a number of criticisms.

Since her interviewees were preoccupied with "the daily struggle for survival," Rubin finds that "in the context of their lives and daily struggles, looking either backward or forward makes little sense; planning for the future seems incongruous" (pp. 39, 48). While Rubin's subjects looked neither forward nor backward, having a sense of history is central to the left-wing outlook. "History sat down with them" is the way Vivian Gornick (1977, p. 7) put it in her study of the communist milieu. "I believe this was the feeling most Communist Party members had," Annette Rubinstein (1993, p. 242) maintains; "history sat down with us. We were a functioning part of history, a small part or a large part depending on our specific contributions, but all part of a tremendous and ultimately victorious movement."

Rubin discusses two major subgroups in her study: "settled-livers" and "hard-livers." The settled-livers had "stable work histories . . . were cautious, conservative, church going, and if they drank, they did so with moderation" (p. 31). Settled-livers believed in conforming, were strict with their children, and valued the ethic of hard work and "the American myth that everyone can pull themselves up by their bootstraps." The hard-livers, in contrast, were "the nonconformists—those who cannot or will not accept their allotted social status" (pp. 34, 36). The rebellions of the hard-livers take the form of "explosive episodes of drinking and violence, the gambling away of a week's wages . . . unexplained work absences . . . and . . . sudden, angry quittings" (p. 34). The hard-liver's protest is a "personal rebellion," Rubin argues, "rooted in the individualistic ethic of American life." Neither hard-liver nor settled-liver engages in "constructive action directed at changing the social system" (p. 34).

In contrast to the individualism of both the settled-livers and the hard-livers, leftists have a collectivist approach. The left, indeed, orients itself on "constructive action directed at changing the social system." Those of Rubin's subjects who are union members acknowledge some of the benefits of belonging but "more commonly . . . gripe about it" (pp. 201–202). Left-wingers, by contrast, tend to be active members of their trade unions and have played important roles in strengthening these working-class institutions. Both they and their co-workers have thereby benefited (Keeran, 1993, pp. 163–197).

Given their present-mindedness, it is not surprising that interest in school and, indeed, in reading is limited among both Rubin's settled-livers and hard-livers. Left-wing parents typically expect their children to do well in school, and many students meet their parents' high expectations. Literacy is emphasized in left-wing families and in the left subculture generally. Somewhat paradoxically, then, members of this collectivist subculture have an important advantage as individuals participating in the market economy. They more readily acquire new skills and are more knowledgeable and sophisticated participants than similarly situated nonleft people in the struggle to survive in an increasingly complex and crisis-ridden economy.

Ostrander's and Rubin's studies indicate that the values of children of upper-class and nonleft white working-class families are quite different from those of the working-class left. Some African American memoirs describe upbringings in nonleft families that resemble those of left families in their emphasis on education and on identification with and service to the oppressed group of which one is a member. Angelo Herndon was born in 1913 in Wyoming, Ohio. His father was a miner and his mother was a servant. The family was extremely poor; they often had too little to eat. The Herndon family was highly religious rather than politically radical. Nevertheless, the message that Herndon received from his parents was similar to that of children in left families. Education, his father advised him, "was a powerful weapon with which to fight poverty and the handicaps of racial discrimination. Once he said to me in his soft quiet voice that he and Mother wanted me to become an educated man so that I could be of service to my people" (Herndon, 1969, pp. 5–14).

In her foreword to Comer's *Maggie's American Dream: The Life and Times of a Black Family* (1988, p. xiv), television newscaster Charlayne Hunter-Gault recalled her father's expectations that she would get good grades and her mother's "hands-on involvement in my schoolwork, as well as in my school." Mothers, grandmothers, and teachers supplied children with "a sense of pride in who we were and where we came from and where we were going. As routinely as they continued to raise the pennies, the notion of education as an essential ingredient of my life became a part of my thinking. It never occurred to me that I wouldn't go on to college after high school. Or achieve my goals. . . . Every day was black-history day" (p. xv).

"Church was the center of our family's life," James Comer (1988, p. 137) recalls. Comer's father was active as a deacon in the church. His mother, however, "often privately challenged the message in the church," which led the children to develop a critical mode of thinking: "'We ought to be talking about getting together to do something about life on these cement streets we live on now rather than golden streets in heaven we don't know nothing about'" (p. 137). Comer's commitment to formal religion was also shaken by examples of unchristian practices of Christians that he observed: "I became increasingly wary of people who talked a Christian game and played an unchristian game. Gradually we [he and his siblings] moved from our usual seat on the second row to the middle and then to the back of the church" (p. 139).

There was a vibrant intellectual life in the Comer family as the children engaged in after-dinner debates. Maggie Comer listened to her children's clever game and only intervened occasionally. James Comer recalled his mother's troubled reaction to his proposal to scrap the welfare system. "'But Jim, how would the poor people take care of themselves?'" She was relieved when her son replied that "there should be a job for everybody and that the government should provide jobs when there weren't enough to go around" (p. 125). Like children in families affiliated with the left-wing movement, the Comer children were learning both about caring for others and the necessity of social change.

Maggie Comer focused her attention on the development and proper upbringing of her children. "'I believe in talking with children, taking time with them, taking them to places of interest, doing things together,'" she declares. "'You explain to the child and they want to learn more'" (pp. 93–94). Her son recalled: "Mom and Dad had this notion that there were fine things in life that kids should experience—educational places and activities, successful people going places and achieving great things. They felt that would cause us to strive to do the same" (p. 131). The Comers expected their children to get good grades and to go to college. All did so. James Comer became a Yale University child psychiatrist, and his siblings also received graduate degrees. As is the case in left families, the Comers instilled a social vision in their children as well as a striving for success. Comer has been active with the New Haven public schools in developing projects to help low-income children achieve. "Life in a world changing ever faster because of science and technology is like a relay race with each generation almost desperately passing the baton on to the next. Past and present policies and practices which made it extremely difficult for black Americans to achieve at the level of their ability is like dropping the baton" (p. 226).

The transmission of caring values to children in the Comer, Hunter, and Herndon families resembles the process that takes place in many left-wing families. Parents show concern for the development of the child, emphasize the value of education and literacy, and expect their children to achieve in school. At the same time, parents also provide firm moral guidance to their children, emphasizing the importance of acting for justice by their own example. Finally, parents also set an example and teach their children to demonstrate concern for other oppressed blacks or working-class people and for all of humanity. Left-wing parents have a particular philosophical, political, and historical approach that assists them in transmitting caring values to their children. A broadly similar approach to caring for others is sometimes conveyed by families with a somewhat different political outlook.

Conclusion

Transmitting the values of caring to children is as challenging and difficult as it is necessary. The left's experience indicates that there are four levels at which the values of each generation are formed. The influence of the immediate family, of the parents, is the most obvious and usually the strongest factor. Three other principal factors can be identified, but their significance varies with time, place, and circumstance. The particular subcultural niche in which a family is located is influential. It may, in fact, be a meeting ground of more than one subculture. Members of the extended family, neighbors, and members of one's church, social organization, political group, or trade union all contribute to the shaping of the child's values.

Often most troubling to parents is the impact of peers. Although parents—left, right, and center—are often negative about the influence of peers on their children, this is an inevitable part of youth's development. To become mature adults, children must break free and establish their own independent identities. They look to their peers because it is among members of their own generation that they make the attachments that mark their independent adulthood.

Finally, the larger society influences children and youth through the state of the economy and such institutions and media as government, schools, newspapers, television, and film. Such a fundamental reality as the degree to which decent, well-paying jobs are available reverberates through family, subcultural life, and peer interactions. For the left, government repression and hostile presentations of the communists and communist ideas in the media also have been enormously important.

For much of this century, left-wing parents had the support of a rich subcultural world to assist them in guiding their children into adopting a radical vision and a caring approach to others. Although societal influences hostile to the left as well as peer-group pressures pulled their children in different directions, particularly during the 1950s, left-wing parents often succeeded in transmitting their values to their children. However, the strength of the left subcultural world appears to have declined in the past few decades. The left continues to be "out of sync" with the dominant political philosophies of our society and has been unable to fully recover from the setbacks suffered during the height of the cold war, when it was most "out of sync."

Nevertheless, on an individual and scattered basis, left-wing parents are managing to transmit caring values to their children. As they go about their separate tasks of overcoming gender and race inequality, preserving the environment, supporting world peace and solidarity with so-called Third World countries, and fighting for jobs and health care for all, they feel a need to rebuild that subcultural world and to achieve the kind of unifying oneness available to their parents' and grandparents' generations. Despite its difficulties, the left persists and continues to seek the development of a society and a world that care for all people.

References

Baxandall, R. F. (ed.). *Words on Fire: The Life and Writings of Elizabeth Gurley Flynn*. New Brunswick, N.J.: Rutgers University Press, 1987.
Bellamy, E. *Looking Backward, 2000–1887*. Boston: Houghton Mifflin, 1898.
Bernstein, C. *Loyalties: A Son's Memoir*. New York: Simon & Schuster, 1989.
Buhle, M. J. *Women and American Socialism, 1870–1920*. Urbana: University of Illinois Press, 1983.
Chernin, K. *In My Mother's House*. New York: HarperCollins, 1984.
Cohen, R. *When the Old Left Was Young: Student Radicals and America's First Mass Student Movement, 1929–1941*. New York: Oxford University Press, 1993.
Cole, S. C. "Elizabeth Gurley Flynn: A Portrait." Unpublished doctoral dissertation, Department of History, Indiana University, 1991.
Comer, J. P. *Maggie's American Dream: The Life and Times of a Black Family*. New York: New American Library, 1988.
Davis, A. *An Autobiography*. New York: Random House, 1974.
Dennis, P. *The Autobiography of an American Communist*. Westport, Conn.: Hill, 1977.
Evans, S. *Personal Politics*. New York: Knopf, 1979.
Flacks, R. "The Liberated Generation: An Exploration of the Roots of Student Protest." *Journal of Social Issues*, 1967, *23*, 52–75.
Flynn, E. G. *The Rebel Girl: An Autobiography; My First Life (1906–1926)*. New York: International Publishers, 1973.
Gatlin, R. *American Women Since 1945*. Jackson: University Press of Mississippi, 1987.
Gitlin, T. *The Sixties: Years of Hope, Days of Rage*. New York: Bantam Books, 1987.
Gornick, V. *The Romance of American Communism*. New York: Basic Books, 1977.
Gosse, V. "'To Organize in Every Neighborhood, in Every Home': The Gender Politics of American Communists Between the Wars." *Radical History Review*, 1991, *50*, 109–141.
Hammer, A., with Lyndon, N. *Hammer*. New York: Putnam, 1987.
Healey, D., and Isserman, M. *Dorothy Healey Remembers: A Life in the American Communist Party*. New York: Oxford University Press, 1990.
Herndon, A. *Let Me Live*. New York: Arno Press and the New York Times, 1969.
Kaplan, J., and Shapiro, L. (eds.). *Red Diaper Babies: Children of the Left*. Privately printed, 1985.
Keeran, R. "The Communist Influence on American Labor." In M. E. Brown, R. Martin, F. Rosengarten, and G. Snedeker (eds.), *New Studies in the Politics and Culture of U.S. Communism*. New York: Monthly Review Press, 1993.

Liebman, A. *Jews and the Left*. New York: Wiley, 1979.
Lukas, J. A. *Don't Shoot: We Are Your Children!* New York: Random House, 1971.
Marx, K., and Engels, F. *Manifesto of the Communist Party*. New York: International Publishers, 1948. (Originally published 1848.)
Meeropol, R., and Meeropol, M. *We Are Your Sons: The Legacy of Ethel and Julius Rosenberg*. Boston: Houghton Mifflin, 1975.
Mishler, P. "The Littlest Proletariat: American Communists and Their Children, 1923–1950." Unpublished doctoral dissertation, Department of History, Boston University, 1988.
Myerhoff, B. *Number Our Days*. New York: Simon & Schuster, 1979.
Nowak, M. C. *Two Who Were There: A Biography of Stanley Nowak*. Detroit, Mich.: Wayne State University Press, 1989.
O'Brien, J. P. "The Development of a New Left in the United States, 1960–1965." Unpublished doctoral dissertation, Department of History, University of Wisconsin, 1971.
Orr, E. N. *Tillie Olsen and a Feminist Spiritual Vision*. Jackson: University Press of Mississippi, 1987.
Ostrander, S. A. *Women of the Upper Class*. Philadelphia: Temple University Press, 1984.
Phillips, M. "Family Ties of Parents, Politics, and Progeny." *DemocraticLeft*, 1986, *3*, 3–5, 11.
Rubin, L. B. *Worlds of Pain: Life in the Working Class Family*. New York: Basic Books, 1976.
Rubinstein, A. T. "The Cultural World of the Communist Party: An Historical Overview." In M. E. Brown, R. Martin, F. Rosengarten, and G. Snedeker (eds.), *New Studies in the Politics and Culture of U.S. Communism*. New York: Monthly Review Press, 1993.
Staub, E. "The Origins of Caring, Helping, and Nonaggression: Parental Socialization, the Family System, Schools, and Cultural Influence." In P. M. Oliner and others (eds.), *Embracing the Other: Philosophical, Psychological, and Historical Perspectives on Altruism*. New York: New York University Press, 1992.
Teitelbaum, K. *Schooling for "Good Rebels": Socialist Education for Children in the United States*. Philadelphia: Temple University Press, 1993.

Chapter Four

Passing It On: The Transmission of Wealth and Financial Care

Paul G. Schervish

Over the next two decades, between $6.5 and $8 trillion of wealth will be transferred from the current generation of parents to their immediate descendants. Some of the inheritances will be modest sums transferred from middle-class parents to their children. But the bulk of the money will pass to children of the wealthy, virtually doubling or tripling the number of millionaires from approximately 1.5 million today to perhaps 4.5 or 5 million in twenty years. Even without this vast transference of wealth, an important question is whether the growth in the number of wealthy will be accompanied by a parallel growth in the number dedicated to philanthropic giving. That is, will there be an intergenerational transfer of charitable commitment along with the transfer of wealth? The most obvious answer is that the passing on of a philanthropic commitment will occur in some instances and not in others. But to encourage a broader transfer of philanthropic identity to the next generation, it is important to discern the factors that have encouraged the successful transmission of philanthropic identity where it has occurred in the current generation of the wealthy.

During the course of our interviews with 130 millionaires in the Study on Wealth and Philanthropy, respondents frequently

Note: I am grateful to the T. B. Murphy Foundation Charitable Trust for supporting the research reported here and to Ethan Lewis and Platon E. Coutsoukis, who graciously and competently assisted in the preparation of this chapter.

signaled their intention to pass on to their children a sense of financial care along with a financial inheritance. (For a discussion of the research methodology and other technical details of our study, see Schervish and Herman, 1988.) A frequent theme in these narratives of the wealthy was the relationship between parents and children surrounding the inheritance of wealth and the imparting of the parents' financial morality—a morality that frequently includes a philanthropic orientation. It is the question, as one wealthy parent terms it, of "How do we pass the torch?"—or, as we identify it, of "passing on and passing it on." Early on we learned that from the point of view of parents (and children), "passing on" means more than dying; it means the transferring of family leadership from one generation to another. Similarly, "passing it on" connotes more than disbursing one's wealth to others in the family. It also entails the disbursement of identity and responsibility regarding that wealth.

In this chapter, I draw on those interviews to explore the various factors that wealthy parents report either encourage or obstruct their efforts to establish a legacy of a financial morality of care. By "financial morality of care," I refer to a sense of duty and even self-interest around the meaning and practice of money, an anxiousness to connect the empowerment and beneficence of wealth in a way that is personally appealing. Taking money seriously means taking children seriously in the sense of educating the next generation to appreciate the responsibilities and not just the privileges of wealth. I do not wish to imply that every wealthy parent is equally concerned about teaching such financial care. We found several instances in which the wealthy appeared remarkably nonchalant about this parental chore. But in most cases, the wealthy were more likely to agree with the father who insists that in this important realm of cultural generativity, "the way to err is on the side of more involvement rather than on the side of less."

Five Elements in the Intergenerational Transfer of Financial Care

Wealthy parents and their children mention five categories of factors when describing the social and cultural factors affecting the generational transfer of wealth and financial morality. Such influences range from simply setting an example, to intentional guidance, to explicit stipulation of how an inheritance must be used. In addition to noting positive influences, parents often indicate an assortment of social and psychological impediments in communicating financial morality. Such impediments, we learn, sometimes lead parents to relay contradictory signals to their children and cause the children to resist their guidance.

The following five elements appear most influential in the intergenerational transfer of financial care:

1. The *specific historical forces* facing the current cohort of wealthy children, with a particular emphasis on circumstances that differ markedly from those the parents faced
2. The effect of the family's *economic life-style*, such as the level of luxury allowed, type of housing, amount of allowance, extent of household duties, and extent to which parents seek to convey their achievement ethic to the children
3. The extent of de facto or intentional *parental modeling* around life-style issues of money and philanthropy
4. Offered or required *institutional training*, such as participation in a family investment portfolio, business, philanthropy, or foundation
5. Explicit parental teaching of *frameworks of consciousness* aimed at conveying a morality of money and a specific morality of philanthropy

Specific Historical Forces

The transmission of a morality of wealth is intrinsically problematic, for it requires parents to transform an economic ethic appropriate to the circumstances of an earlier era into an ethic relevant to the circumstances of their children. This problem of translation has two related dimensions. The first concerns the historical trends of consumerism and affluence affecting most of today's youth. The second involves the generational differences that parents born poor or with modest means encounter in relation to children who became accustomed early on to the privileges of wealth. Parents address these issues by speaking about the dangers of decadence associated with their children's enjoying but not having to earn wealth, being wrapped up in the culture of consumption, not understanding how to handle money, and not being able to relate to common people. For their part, however, the children born into wealth emphasize a different problem. Without denying the importance of the issues highlighted by their parents, the kids emphasize the problems associated with establishing an identity in regard to wealth that is independent of their parents' own roles and expectations for them. It is not that they eschew the responsibilities of wealth. Rather it is a matter of determining their own responsibilities and being free to decide which responsibilities to attend to in a particular phase of their lives.

The most frequently cited generational difference that parents fear will make it hard for their children to assume a financial morality is that the children have never experienced material want. Put simply, their kids have not experienced the trauma of the Depression and the virtues it instilled. The fact that his family "lost everything" during the Depression has made a lasting impression on Chicago contractor and former National Football League great Raymond Wendt:

> I look at that [period in my life] many a time and I try to talk to my

> children about that, about all of the things that we have now and should be thankful for. I look at material things and treat money in a different way than they do. They might call me frugal. I'm not a wealthy man but I am not a poor man, but I just don't throw money around. I have respect for it, let's put it that way, and I try to teach my children that. Of course, money is not the most important thing in our lives but being young, I guess, and struggling all the time made an impression on me.

Many children of the rich also recognize the importance of the Depression as a formative experience. "A lot of the kids that I went to school with never have seen [poverty]," reports Camile Russo, twenty-seven, who now works as a middle-level manager in her family's brewery. "They were very, very sheltered. They were very much into status, they were very into how wealthy they were. I find for a large percentage of wealthy people born into wealth, inherited wealth, there's definitely a difference. There's for sure a difference between second and third generation wealth. No question. Through my father, I have direct contact with his being born very poor, and now being very rich. I can feel that." As second-generation wealthy, Russo recognizes how different she is from one of her third-generation friends who is "so far removed" from any contact with a life of modest means. "I think it's just a matter of how you gear yourself, that and how you are raised, as far as how humble you are. My father and mother are very, very humble. You'll never hear them talk about themselves. They're just real low key. They never forget where they've come from. They always remind us. They always tell us, 'don't ever brag, we could go bankrupt.' I think they raised us with really important values." Even so, Russo recognizes important differences between her and her father in regard to the value of a dollar. "I might go out and spend 40 bucks and think no big deal, where he's more sensitive to what that 40 dollars represents, so what's a lot of money to me, and what's a lot of money to him, that's two different things."

What is different about the orientation of what Robert Coles calls "the children of privilege"? For Russo, it is an attitude of humility. For Eileen Case Wilson of Chicago, it is the recognition of vulnerability. "When we were being raised [economic insecurity] was always a threat. I think that anybody that came from my parents' generation and survived the Depression realized how vulnerable in effect you are—that things beyond your control could wipe you out. Now that I have reached forty-five, I don't feel that vulnerable anymore," Wilson explains, recalling how feelings of vulnerability inched their way into her thinking as well. But now, she says, "I feel almost too secure, and I'm afraid that my children are going to feel that way." This results in two problems, according to Wilson. First, today's youth "have no recollection of war, the Depression, or anything. As a result, the children we're raising today in wealthy families live in a fairy world because they have no basis of knowing what this life was like." This is different from Wilson's experience, where her riches "increased in increments of wealth at such levels that I never really ever had all I wanted. There's always something else that you're striving for, so you never have the feeling of having too much, so therefore you're [always] sort of insecure." The second problem Wilson worries about derives directly from "raising the children in an unrealistic world based on material goods." Wilson claims that "particularly in the 70s and 80s kids are so acquisition oriented. They don't have established lives yet. So they don't have a sense of responsibility of sharing wealth by sharing of themselves. I don't think it's even entered my daughter's head yet that she could give it away. In other words, they take it for granted."

When wealth is taken for granted the wealthy child becomes morally at risk, insists Gerald Simpson, who himself grew up wealthy in and around the prep school culture. "You know about children who inherit money," he says; "they get a check from a lawyer or from the bank once or twice a month. They live on that, they get into drugs, they go to a place to dry out, they get into trouble with the law. But the lawyer provides for them, whatever they do, everything is taken care of, right? And they become spoiled and horrible, and antisocial, and everybody looks askance at them. And this is the product, of the rich." Not all parents are as cynical as Simpson. But as we will see, those who share his concerns strive to counteract the negative tendencies they perceive.

Russell Spencer is one parent who worries about his kids growing up without the virtues wrought by economic accountability. "I worry more about the kids and the atmosphere that they live under, the Westchester and Forest Hills tennis crowds that they'll be moving in," says the New York real estate entrepreneur. "Kids don't have paper routes there. I did as a kid. I mowed lawns. Kids don't mow lawns, you hire somebody to mow your lawn," observes Spencer, who is proud to have grown up in what he calls "Smalltown U.S.A." "These are the things that I worry more about than about myself. I worry about the material things that the kids see and are getting, though I would hope that my own values and my wife's values, which are terrific, will be able to show some principle and balance to the kids." For Boston software entrepreneur Brian Riley, the major temptation facing his children is to be financially "reckless." He regrets that his oldest daughter has assumed "somewhat of a jet-setter mentality, in terms of spending." Although he tried to educate her differently, she "lives very luxuriously," making him wonder how he lost his sway over her and turned into "the heavy" in her life.

All of this presents a profound dilemma to wealthy parents. Especially for the entrepreneurial wealthy—but for those with family wealth as well—the quandary is how to teach their children the responsibilities of wealth while also providing for their needs. Having gone through hard times, they do not want their children to face the same insecurities. As a result, they furnish a life of affluence for their children while at the same time attempting to instill frugality, humility, and responsibility. For Wendt, the problem is that once he chose an affluent neighborhood in which to live, his children automatically became exposed to an environment that threatens to make them materialistic. That his kids "are exposed to so much luxury" bothers Wendt. Despite his best efforts,

> It was hard for 9, 11, 12, or 13 year-old children to understand [deeper dimensions of life] when they weren't exposed to anything else. They were exposed to the good life, country clubs, trips to Florida, you know. They were in a position where they saw all of these things and they thought that everybody had those things. They weren't exposed to not having clothes, not having televisions, not going to a country club where you can sign your name. So as a result, it's difficult on the one hand to have all of these luxuries, and on the other hand say "no, you can't have these certain things."

A similar dilemma haunts Detroit importer Rebecca Jacobs. "The thing that's been my success, is I was hungry," she says. But her kids are "never going to be hungry, and I don't mean hungry for food." But at the same time, she wonders whether it is necessary to surrender all her advantages just to motivate her kids. "I'd say to myself, 'for God's sakes, Rebecca, you've worked this hard to have this housekeeper in the house, and to be able to have a swimming pool outside, and to be able to have all those things, the Cadillac if I wanted to drive it.' Am I willing to give up all those things so my kids can be hungry?" Like virtually all other wealthy parents, Jacobs answers her question in the negative. She concludes that her best strategy is give her kids "a lot of extra love so that they can know who they are and who their mother is."

The commonsense observation of Seattle real estate developer Lisa Rayburn summarizes the problem of transmitting an ethic of financial care to the next generation. "The impression that I have taken away from my experience with wealth is that it's a double-edged sword." Nowhere is this truer than in the complex parent-child relations surrounding issues of money—how it is to be earned, invested, conserved, given to philanthropy, and used for the necessities and pleasures of life. Parents are more or less devoted to instilling financial ethics in their children and, of course, more or less proficient in doing so. But across the board, parents are keenly aware of the effect money has on their children and of the importance of providing at least a basic sense of financial responsibility. For this reason, we hear much about the formal and informal strategies parents use to inculcate financial virtue even as they bestow a life of affluence.

Economic Life-Style

Later sections describe the factors that appear to instill an ethic of financial care in the children of the wealthy. One such factor that respondents frequently cite is the economic life-style they design for their children. We have already heard how parents view life-style issues as a major concern in raising their children to embrace economic virtues. The question here is what parents do to realize this goal.

One strategy is to insist that children earn their allowances or work to obtain money to pay for what they want. This does not always guarantee that the children learn the meaning of money, as Jacobs points out. Even though her son had to work for much of his money, he still ended up being "very impressed with what money can buy and is very interested in buying a lot. He's a very kind, decent, wonderful guy. But I suppose he's used to a lot of things," she laments. "They feel they deserve it, that it's their birthright." Wendt also recognizes how hard it is to stave off his children's consumption. He and his family live in the affluent Chicago suburb of Wilmette, where "a lot of people just arbitrarily give their kids whatever they want."

A second strategy to constrain consumerism in children is to provide a limited allowance to keep the children from knowing how rich they really are. Jacques Katkov, for instance, tries to ensure that his family's "private life-style" is changed only in a "small" way by its wealth. "We have purposefully resisted wealth being a drastic change. In fact one of our concerns has been not to have it corrupt our children," says the electronics entrepreneur. "For that reason, I don't think my oldest daughter, who's now twenty-two, knew about our substantial wealth until she was fifteen or sixteen, and even then she's had a budget and an allowance so that she's had to learn to manage her affairs. Our younger children, who are eight and eleven, still don't know it, although my eleven-year-old's been asking some questions which are very suggestive."

A third approach for instilling the proper economic values is to restrict the luxury of daily life. Detroiter David Stephanov is proud to own "four nice homes." But he still insists on setting limits. "I was going to put a Rolls Royce down there at my home in Palm Beach, and I said to myself, 'What am I doing with those children? That would be terrible to do.' That's the reason I didn't put a Rolls Royce down there. I know most people would flip if they even had the privilege to do something like that. I had it. And I called up my dealer who sells me all my cars. But then I called him back and said, 'I can't let my kids drive that car around Palm Beach. I'll distort them, screw them up more than maybe they're already screwed up.'" What really counts is his kids' educational success. "[My son] came out with a 3.6. That's all I asked. As long as they get a 3.5, they get anything they want: airplanes, boats, travel, anything they want. But they got to get those grades first." Restricting luxury is also important in the style of home and the absence of servants. Jacques Katkov emphasizes that his family expenditures are "moderate ones," including what he and his wife spent on their home. "We were able to build in '74 an attractive house without having to finance it any way. And we're talking well under a hundred thousand dollars, so when I say attractive, I'm not talking about a Ming palace, nor would we wish it."

Holding the line on luxury is also important to East Coast media magnate Michael Hollander:

> I think probably most anyone would agree that we live very conser-

> vatively for what we are able to do and have not overly spoiled our children in the process and have used whatever funds are required to pay the bills. We do have two homes, one down on the Eastern Shore and one here. We have one or two cars, and no yachts or anything extensive; and airplanes we've never had. I didn't want to spoil the children with too many material things although what we always wanted to do was to make our home very comfortable and make that the central part of their activities and the attractive place that it could be, hoping that they would continue to come back to it which they have done. So that's been central to us.

Stressing the relatively ordinary quality of their life-style, Hollander adds, "I don't think we've spent any more in doing that than anybody, than any wealthy dentist around here, but we do it well." He elaborates that "our kids did not grow up with maids and butlers and valets and chauffeurs. They could have, obviously, but we never did that, wouldn't permit it. And they were always expected to do their share of chores and help with everything as I do. I still do. And that's the way we run our personal lives." Moreover, "They've been productive kids who have worked at their education and their lives and we're very very fortunate about that. Maybe it's by example, maybe it's we're just lucky."

There are other aspects of their life-styles by which the wealthy teach their children the lessons of moderation and responsibility: an insistence on a good education, living within the family's means, and so forth. But if the foregoing demonstrates anything, it is that avoiding the decadence of wealth is a major concern. Indeed, despite such concern, Jacobs, Stephanov, and others report that their children may still become spoiled and consumption-oriented. For according to what we hear, the wealthy inundate their children with conflicting messages. There is surely a discourse of limits, but there is just as surely a reality of opulence. Immediately on recounting how his household has no maids and how his kids must do their chores, Hollander reveals that "nobody stints on travel. If they want to take a nice trip, it's always been given to them." Katkov also concludes his statement about limiting materialism by noting that "whenever we've had the time or the inclination, we've been able to take up vacations without being worried about what are often substantial travel costs. We've been able to provide a first-class education among our children without having to make sacrifices so there are a variety of ways in which it's been personally enjoyable." Listen, finally, to Dean Devlin, the New England regional manager of a major investment firm. He and his wife actually tried to dissuade their kids from getting jobs while in college, "but for some reason they all insist on working. Every single one of them has insisted on going out and getting a part-time job during the school year. And we've not been entirely successful in keeping them from working. Our oldest child worked every summer when he was in college and during the year he had a part-time job. Our oldest daughter, we finally were able to convince her to take a summer in Italy and to go to school in Italy. But still they insist on earning their own money."

Given such an imposing environment of wealth and the mixed messages from their parents, it is not surprising that additional factors offset the tendencies toward materialism and contribute to financial responsibility.

Parental Modeling

If setting limits on the opulence of the family life-style and requiring that children share in household chores is a first step toward instilling economic morality, parental example is an important second step. Parents' actions can impart an ethic of financial responsibility in a number of ways. These involve the development of moral character, especially learning to care for others.

Russo feels the influence of her parents in teaching her to always do her best. "My parents never say it," she notes, but simply watching how they work in the family business has led her to internalize an "inner pressure that makes you want to get your own business" and feel "you're going to disappoint them if you're the director of the department and don't make it the best. You're going to disappoint them if you don't get your own business." She also quietly learns the value of gratitude:

> Although it was never said, it was something I always felt obligated to do. Because of all these things I had watched. I felt like it was time for me to pay back what I'd been given. And only did I start to feel that when I started to realize really how fortunate, and what a head start I had on life because I was born wealthy. It was such a head start. So I think of the opportunities that I was given, I look back and I say, "Geez, I was so fortunate to have all these opportunities. If I don't succeed, I'm a fool. How can I fail? I have to succeed. I've been given all these wonderful things." Really there is pressure that I feel. Luckily I have an ambition that goes hand in hand with that. There is something inside me that I want to do.

For Russo, the key to her growth is her father's example: "My father's the type of person that never demanded anything," she reports. But in his quiet way he still "pretty much just taught us to be honest, be nice, work hard, and things will go your way." Her father "never expected us to work for him, although we all do." Most of her personal and business education transpired informally:

> I think as a young person growing up—just dinner talk and being around the family business, being around people who are very high achievers—something is instilled in you that [makes] thinking skills become very practical. I never had any public relations training, I never took one writing class, I've never taken any communications, but I do well in my job because I'm very knowledgeable in the company and I have practical sense. Some decisions I make, I don't know where I've even heard it sometimes before. But just subconsciously, growing up, just from the nature of being around, there's

just certain things I know about our business that would take years to learn.

More directly relevant for learning an ethic of financial care is the example parents set around issues of philanthropy. Katkov, for instance, makes sure even his younger children know that "nine-tenths of the money had been spent on what I still call philanthropic activities, in the form of contributions to social change and social progress" and that he and his wife "derive great pleasure from that." The same is true for St. Louis real estate developer Sheldon Lewis, who devotes an extraordinary amount of time to fundraising on behalf of the Jewish Federation. In addition to yearly contributions, which he hopes to make "for the rest of my life," Lewis has "bought some zero coupon bonds with the gift money [going to] the Jewish community twenty-five years or so from now." It is equally vital to Lewis that his children someday do the same. "I hope that my children will emulate my example if they can. I've tried to let them observe what my wife and I do, but they don't have the financial means right now to emulate what I'm giving." At present, his kids have learned enough "to do a modest amount of charitable giving," but philanthropy is still "secondary to their other needs for money within their growing families."

Our youngest daughter was just moving to Philadelphia and her husband has finished his training at a Cleveland clinic and they will be starting a new life there, but they need money for a home, furniture, cars and all the things that you and I have already been through, so they are very limited financially as to what they can give to charity, but I hope as they become more successful they will increase their giving and have some of the same feeling. I think it's a worthwhile feeling to have. To me it's the opposite of being totally selfish. Part of the frustration with fundraising is to meet the challenge of people who have no feeling at all.

Hollander also hopes his children will imitate his philanthropic regimen. "I have been very happy to have Media East designations on things and sometimes my family name because I think it is very meaningful to children coming along in the family to see and understand that their family . . . is a responsible family." Hollander recognizes how important that is as "part of the teaching process." He now wants to set the same example for his children that his father set for him:

> They see it as a visible example, it's under their nose, they can't help but see it and they have to live up to something when they see that. There's an obligation that's implicit in the teaching process so I believe in that. It starts with a sense of responsibility to the community which is very strong. It's strong in me, it was strong in my father, I started at home growing up and I've done my best to carry it on in an effective, aggressive way I might say. And hopefully, by example, I've been trying to teach it to my children.

Does such parental modeling in philanthropy affect the children? Many of the younger respondents born into wealthy families testify that it does. Children of the wealthy often criticize the causes and style of their parents' philanthropy. Yet they almost always recognize their debt to their parents' example. "Mom was very active in the community, very active in the Junior League—was president of that—was head of the United Way of Oakland County and did a lot of volunteer work," recalls Ruth Robbins, the founder of Detroit's Victoria Women's Fund. "So I had from her definitely a sense that you put something back into the community and you didn't just go to the country club every day." It is a matter of learning a vocation of care, even though Robbins directs her attention to more political and activist concerns than her mother did:

> I think that there are people who have their basic needs met and

> they have a generosity of spirit and personality that wants them to do something else. I know that I learned from my parents that you give back to the community. So I did have that kind of example, which was not like my aunts and uncles. They didn't participate, volunteer and do all those kind of things like Mom did, but I think they gave money too and my grandmother's sister and husband started a foundation and she gave stuff to the hospital and whatever. There was always this sense, you know, in church you always gave your money. There was always a sense that you put, you were supposed to contribute to society as well as enjoy the benefits.

Institutional Training

Just as important as parental example for the generational transmission of economic responsibility is the involvement in various economic institutions parents offer to and sometimes impose on their children. To properly train their children in the duties of wealth, parents deliberately enmesh their children in business, money management, and philanthropy.

Jacobs recognizes that in many ways she "could have done a better job" in raising her children. She wishes she had spent more time "reading to them, rough-housing with them, and driving them to piano lessons, and football games, and doing those kinds of things." What she did do, however, was to lug them with her to the offices of her fledgling import business. "I didn't get to spend a lot of time with them, so I had them all work. I made them all take typing as soon as they could, so all of them worked here as typists. And of course, when they got to college they all thanked me for that. That's the best thing I could have ever done for them. At the beginning they hated me for it." Now, her children are grateful for their early exposure to her company. "It's either, I sell the business or involve the kids. But since they've been working here for years, I'm kind of grooming them to take over the business. That's the whole joy of it, that's the fun. And that's I think one thing that prevents me from selling, that my kids like the business."

Proclaiming "I do believe in nepotism," Ralph Pellegrino has also brought his kids and other relatives into his metro Los Angeles hardware business, insisting they learn his concern for quality and courtesy. "My son Robert, who is very, very bright, has a Pellegrino Hardware Center. My son Andrew is also in Pellegrino Hardware. And my son Anthony, who went to Yale, he's up in the office, manning all phases of it. He's into lumber, remodeling departments, and electrical, and he's a very bright young man who's president of his class at Choate and graduated with honors from Yale." But as important as his son's academic success may be, Pellegrino appears prouder of the way Anthony has picked up the torch: "He's just a great, delightful kid. They love him in all the departments where he works, and when he leaves, they're angry at me for pulling him out. He's got to learn all phases of it."

In addition to involving them in the family business, wealthy parents formally establish procedures to ensure that their children learn to handle their inheritances properly. We hear accounts from a number of wealthy heirs about the turmoil that arose in their lives from being too young or too inexperienced to deal with their inheritances. To help their children avoid these problems, many parents take steps to pace the generational disbursement of wealth and to educate their children about handling their windfalls.

Eileen Case Wilson and her husband David have staggered disbursements to their children at the ages of eighteen, twenty-one, and twenty-six. "We've portioned it out so they wouldn't get it all at once, cause that's gonna be a scary situation," she explains. "If my children were to inherit today, from me, directly, their incomes would exceed $30,000 and they're not even of age yet. And that would be very terrifying to them, so we set up that they would get part in 5 years and part in 5 more years, so they would have a little time to get used to it." This is something to which she has given much thought. "I don't know what the truly wealthy do, but you think in terms of putting all that money on kids, who aren't even out of school, that part is frightening. I don't want them to inherit until I have a chance to lead them into this as I was led in by my parents. So that's a concern. Money management is teaching them how to use what they're getting at the age of 18 and I'm working on [my daughter] Elizabeth right now."

Riley also delimits a period of time in which an organized framework can facilitate responsibility. "My kids are all set, they all have trust funds that they can't get at until they're 30." Again the strategy is well conceived to create fiscal competence. Riley designates two categories of inheritance. The first is what he calls "funding that is in place" while he is still alive. "I don't want them to be living like fat cats, in their 20's. I want them to see what it's like to have a job or earn money that you need to subsist on and realize that it doesn't always reach both ends of the week. I figure by 30 they should all have had enough experience, have some level of wisdom, so that they won't be crazy and go out and just blow it." The second category of inheritance is what he will pass to his children on his death. "If I should die my will stipulates that they don't get any [money immediately]. That all goes into another trust that they can't get till age 35. My thinking is that if they boot things [mess things up] at age 30, they might have learned by age 35 how to handle the next one."

Devlin began the formal training of his children when they were in their middle teens. "We've transferred bank accounts to them as soon as we legally could," he reports. "We tried to give them at an early age the ability to manage their own money without us looking over their shoulder saying you must do this, you must do that." This turned out to be a fortuitous tack, for even with this independence his kids have "insisted" on his and his wife's counsel. Hollander, too, started his children's financial training at an early age, giving "a great deal of thought and effort to that." Like Devlin, he and his wife "have provided wealth in the children's own names at young ages." But unlike Devlin, Hollander admits to keeping "a reasonably strong advisory position on how their assets are invested." Following his recommendations "is not mandated," however, so the kids are free to "make some decisions that go contrary to the advice." Regarding how well he has ignored his kids, Hollander's appraisal is that "they have a long way to go in terms of some financial maturity, but I think we've done well on sophistication."

> We have seen to it that our children have some investment funds at their disposal, and this started really, oh, at about the time each of them reached 19, 20 years old. They are now into their, well they are 25, 26, and 31. So they've had some years of involvement with investment funds in their own name. They all have been brought up in an atmosphere where they were surrounded by professionals and money managers who serve them. Their lawyers, accountants, and money managers who serve each of them have all been introduced by me, but they have an independent relationship with each one of them and have learned how to conduct those relationships and have been through a little bit of change in some of them as well. So all three of them have gained some degree of comfort in dealing with those kinds of issues. Today, they each have as a result of that program substantial wealth in their own names, mostly in the form of company stock but that generates dividends and the dividends are cashed, not needed for current living, and they do get invested, so that's the pattern each of them are involved in and I think they are well started.

In addition to providing training in the family business and money management, wealthy parents teach financial care by formally involving their children in their philanthropic endeavors. Harold Bacon, an executive in charge of corporate charity at a Big-Three auto company, links money management to philanthropic training. "A number of years ago I gave each of my four children some tax-free bonds. I said, 'There's a string on them. Half the income has to be given away to charity.'" Apparently his strategy worked because "each of the four children has become charitable in their own way and one of them still sends me a list of the charities he gives to every year."

Norman Guano always understood the importance of early philanthropic involvement. As a youth he was brought into active involvement with his family's major foundation. He regrets, however, that his kids were not as receptive to such training as he was. "I would like in principle to involve my kids in my giving by—I have five of them and they are very, very different people. And I have tried to encourage them. I wanted to get them involved with the Guano Fund very, very, very badly and that's the trouble with it. In those days I was even more unwise than I am now and I pushed, pushed, pushed, pushed. And the kids' reaction was to pull back and say 'my God, what's Dad trying to do to us.'" Still Guano recommends involving the children "to anybody or to any foundation."

Numerous wealthy parents understand this. One of the most common stories we heard concerned the steps parents take to induct their kids into a charitable ethic by involving them in their family foundations. But, as we hear from San Francisco heir Christopher Burke, such involvement should extend to direct contact with the projects and people benefiting from his foundation's largesse. His children "are all members of the board at the foundation. And that's automatic. Whether they are really interested or not." In fact, he has built into the job description of his foundation director that "she really work on getting family trustees—we call family directors, trustees—into the field."

Frameworks of Consciousness

Theories of socialization emphasize the importance of communities of participation for inculcating ways of thinking and behaving. Socialization theories also stress the importance of frameworks of consciousness for shaping orientations and dispositions. The previous sections have discussed aspects of the community of participation through which the children of the wealthy become educated to a morality of money. In this section, I explore the various parental teachings that help fashion their children's financial care. There are five categories of instruction by which parents convey the lessons of money: finances, entrepreneurship, family, religion, and philanthropy.

We have already seen how schooling in the management of money is an important goal of many experiences parents provide their children. But just as important is what the parents articulate. "My kids know not only everything about what they have now," explains Burke, "but they know right down to the last nickel where future money is going to come from, how it's going to be managed, what the likelihood of its distribution will be, how they need to think about it, how that affects their lives today, as compared to how it's going to affect them in twenty years." In fact, says Burke, "we talk about it constantly."

Teaching the work ethic and its application to entrepreneurship is also a topic of frequent exhortative conversation. "I'm going to share with my kids what my sport is. It's being an entrepreneur," remarks Stephanov. "This is a game. It's a big game, like squash, like racquetball, like skiing. That's all it is; that's all it is." His philosophy is deceptively simple: "You find a piece of land, you think about it, you look at seven pieces of land. You say 'I'll take that piece and put up 120,000 square feet. Then we'll resell it in six months and we'll make nothing but money on it.' It's a game," he teaches his children. "You're looking at an opponent." It's a matter of learning to "play for big money."

So much of what the parents have to say about the responsibility of money concerns teaching priorities. The major problem he confronts, Wendt explains, is convincing his kids that the meaning of life revolves around family rather than consumerism. "My kids would come home and say, 'well so and so has a boat,' maybe they have a snowmobile, they have all these things." Wendt's reaction is typical of many respondents. "And I said, 'you don't need those things, it's not important for you to have those things.'" Still, it is hard for Wendt to buck the trend: "When you have kids growing up in that environment it's difficult to explain to them why they don't need that. Of course at their age they still couldn't understand, at least they didn't want to understand it. All they look at is the enjoyment they are receiving from it," he laments. "And so I tried to explain that we're not here to have all these things. Maybe later in your life you can get those things if you work for them and you strive and become successful. We're here mainly to be a family and try to teach you other things which are more important than material things."

Another central tenet in the manual of parental teaching is a set of religious principles. These principles emphasize the appreciation of wealth as an undeserved gift and the subordination of one's desires to a divine path. "I just think that we all should attempt to do what we can. This is what Christ said to do, you know. He's only got our hands, so to speak. It sounds corny, but it's the way I feel," says Boston homebuilder Charles Dore. He is unashamed of his religious values and makes sure his family knows just where he stands. "My kids know that, my wife knows that. They don't laugh at it, they think it's good, you know. My kids never argue with me about how much I give away, even though eventually it's coming out of their pocket. Plus the fact they have more stock in the company now than I do so they can say, 'Hey Pop, you're out.' But I don't worry about things like that." Hollander addresses the same issue from his Jewish faith. "There is a tradition amongst Jewish people to be charitable to their own. Not just to their own, to be charitable in general," he points out. This is "part of the training that is given to Jewish children," including his own: "To not be selfish and not to only be concerned about yourself but to be aware of what is going around you in a community. Be aware that there are people that have problems, social problems, and they need help and that not all social problems are solved by federal budgets."

The foregoing elements of moral education contribute to learning the proper handling of money, the rules of entrepreneurship, the priority of family over material goods, and a commitment to follow a spiritual path. But to the extent that they come together as a general framework of consciousness and basis of conscience, they provide a foundation for explicit teaching about financial care in the form of philanthropy. "I try to get my kids to think of something valuable [even though] they say it's all easy for you because you've made it and you can now give the time and the effort and the money too," recounts Bacon. I told them that has nothing to do with it. If you don't have it then you don't have it. But I'm getting the message through I think. I don't know whether it'll stick, but a part of their life should be to help people less fortunate than they."

Conclusion

This chapter has discussed five family influences that contribute to the intergenerational transmission of financial care. Let me conclude by citing one additional factor and by indicating the next step in this research. The additional factor involves the various extrafamilial influences that encourage or discourage the transmission of financial care. Respondents speak about several such influences from the vantage point of being parents or children: the broad range of experiences encountered at school and work, contact with the needy in connection with travel or volunteer work, friends and marriage partners, politics and religion, and influential occurrences of fortune and misfortune.

Janet Arnold is a third-generation Detroit philanthropist whose lifelong dedication to issues of poverty began with her childhood travels to developing countries. "We just learned from those experiences," explains Arnold. Her father's business took him frequently and for extended periods to Latin America, and as the children got older he would take them along. "Because of that, we were exposed to people who were not wealthy. We didn't move in a very narrow circle the way many people of wealth do." In addition to being exposed to "the little people," as her father used to put it, Arnold tells how "several of my brothers and sisters and I worked in Latin America in summer jobs when [my father] had business there." At sixteen, she worked for a year in Venezuela in a community center linked to an experimental farm program. The following summer, Arnold lived in a Brazilian village where "we fed the little children in the morning, taught them about brushing their teeth and all that kind of thing. And we worked with the mothers, teaching them how to cook these new vegetables, and planting them on raised beds to deal with the flash rain and flood type things. It was marvelous. I absolutely loved it."

While Arnold's formative experiences occurred abroad, those of Devlin's kids occurred here at home. Each of his kids has become more caring as a result of engagements outside the family. His oldest daughter goes to Georgetown University, where she participates in a tutoring program for high school kids in the Washington, D.C. school system. "She ran that program for a year at Georgetown," says Devlin proudly. "She's also done volunteer work at the Peace Corps and last summer she received a commission from the Public Health Service and worked on an Indian reservation in Wisconsin, and that's the field that she wants to go into now—public health," says Devlin, connecting his daughter's philanthropic involvements to her choice of career. One of his sons volunteers at a Boston halfway house connected to a drug and alcohol counseling program for high school youth and has done "some unpaid manual labor for the Appalachian Mountain Club cleaning trails and things like that." Finally, Devlin's youngest daughter at the age of fifteen has just "started into a tutoring program in Roxbury [an inner-city district of Boston], where she goes one afternoon a week to help tutor elementary school kids."

At this point in my research, I feel confident that I have located at least some of the key variables that propagate the intergenerational transmission of financial care. The next research task in regard to the interview data is to describe the various ways these variables come together to form a set of distinct story lines about the successful and unsuccessful transmission of financial care. For example, there are important differences in the communication of economic morality between entrepreneurial, first-generation families, and established second- and third-generation families. Also important are the dynamics that distinguish cases where the children become independently dedicated to philanthropy and where they do not. A second direction for research would be to operationalize the variables mentioned above with data collected in INDEPENDENT SECTOR's biennial Survey on Giving and Volunteering. Although there is no direct measure of the intergenerational transmission of a philanthropic identity, respondents provide considerable retrospective information about the orientations and activities that led to their commitment to charity.

While awaiting more thorough analysis of the transmission of financial morality, one can still learn much from this preliminary listing of the challenges parents face in conveying their charitable instincts to their children. In the end, the intergenerational transmission of financial care is a matter as homely and honorable as that of teaching the children well.

Reference

Schervish, P. G., and Herman, A. *Empowerment and Beneficence: Strategies of Living and Giving Among the Wealthy*. Final report on the Study on Wealth and Philanthropy. Chestnut Hill, Mass.: Social Welfare Research Institute, Boston College, 1988.

Part Two

Children as Givers and Receivers of Care

As we have already heard, an important factor in shaping the philanthropic orientation of adults is their participation as youth in charitable activities. Such involvement is not always completely voluntary in that it is often urged if not required by parents, schools, or youth groups to which a young person belongs. Still, this is as it should be. If later in life adults are to choose to be truly voluntary caregivers, some early exposure to the responsibilities and satisfactions of service provides invaluable background for that decision. Moreover, as the three chapters in Part Two point out, the philanthropic activity of youth provides not just a training ground for future involvement but a catalyst for personality development and a substantive contribution to social welfare. All three chapters imply that helping children become caregivers is a profound and effective way to care for children.

We hear much about the monumental pressures imposed on today's children and youth by the cultural perversities of television, violence, drugs, sex, excessive work for pay, and materialistic consumerism. In Chapter Five, Silvia Blitzer Golombek reviews recent changes in scholarly and popular thinking about the role of the young as caregivers, and without being naively optimistic suggests that involving children in charitable activity may be one of the most salutary countertendencies to improve our children's lot. Traditional conceptualizations of child development emphasize the maturational stages by which children move from being merely *potential* to *complete* human beings who only later in life have something to contribute to society. Fortunately, a new theoretical paradigm is emerging that views children more as productive members of society. Youth advocates too are beginning to link responsibility and education by calling for children to be involved in serving others. Such involvement reinforces academic performance and reduces problems of self-esteem and discipline. In a word, youth become empowered agents and realize they are valued members of their community. Golombek's study of children in three Baltimore public schools confirms that these children are treated too narrowly as objects of protection, care, and constant supervision. Needed instead, insists Golombek, is for society to hike its expectations about and to facilitate the contribution of children to their communities. KIDS IN ACTION, a volunteer service program founded by Golombek in Baltimore, is one effective model by which children learn by doing. It brings children into the web of society as responsible agents while, at the same time, enriching the life of the children, their families, and the community.

Virginia A. Walter's research on how child volunteers, even under the age of twelve, learn by doing supports the paradigm shift Golombek promotes. Although various trends in child psychology have begun to highlight the importance of social and political engagement for early childhood development, surprisingly little systematic research has been done on how children take their place in a caring society. In Chapter Six, Walter begins to fill this research gap with her study of children who volunteer in their local library, a Camp Fire group engaged in community service, and the adults who work with these children. She finds that children respond to both affective and instrumental motivations, that children as young as nine are capable of making useful contributions, that volunteer work by children provides positive links to adults, and that esteem and affection are more important than supervisory style for inspiring children's enthusiastic collaboration. Walter concludes that volunteering provides a natural opportunity for children to try on adult roles in a process of what sociologists call anticipatory socialization. The children develop leadership and participation skills and learn to value themselves as responsible members of the community. What children need is not coddling from adults but a respectful invitation to work alongside them.

In Chapter Seven, Steven Schinke and Roxanne Spillett complement Walter's research by describing the effect of Boys and Girls Clubs on promoting care in a public housing development. They argue that the presence of these clubs creates a more caring community for all the residents and helps develop more caring children and adolescents. Based on a three-year study of fifteen public housing developments, the authors found that children in developments with a Boys and Girls Club took part in less deviant and dangerous activities, were exposed to programs that advanced their well-being, had parents who were more involved in youth activities and school programs, and enjoyed living conditions with less juvenile crime and drug activity. In addition to engendering a healthier community environment, the clubs make the kids themselves more caring. The major implication is that the presence of more Boys and Girls Clubs and other kinds of indigenous youth groups would go a long way toward revitalizing hard-pressed communities from within.

Chapter Five

Children as Philanthropists: The Younger, the Better

Silvia Blitzer Golombek

"Children should be seen and not heard"; "Children are the future"; "Youth leadership and empowerment." Such phrases summarize a society's perception of its younger generation. Moreover, these phrases have research and programmatic implications for those working with children and youth.

This chapter provides an overview of recent developments in the sociology of childhood and establishes some links with changes in the field of philanthropy. First, the review of the literature presents the traditional conceptualization of children inspired by Jean Piaget's model of developmental stages. This is followed by a discussion of what James and Prout (1990) call the "new paradigm" in children's sociology, which emphasizes their role as social agents. In both cases, the underlying questions are the following: How are children encouraged to or prevented from participating in philanthropic efforts? How do the prevalent theoretical frameworks assign children a role as passive recipients or active providers of care?

Next, the chapter reviews ongoing initiatives that operationalize the current paradigm of "youth leadership and empowerment." The remaining sections of the chapter analyze the implications of the new sociological paradigm when applied to young children as philanthropists. The question here is how old a person has to be to be allowed to serve on behalf of his or her community. To answer this question, I draw on data collected in a research study conducted in three public elementary schools in Baltimore—data that support the early involvement of children in philanthropic endeavors.

They Are Not Persons Yet

The "children should be seen and not heard" era is, fortunately, a thing of the past. Kids are very much a part of today's society—something toy and clothing manufacturers know all too well. But how do scholars and policy makers perceive the young?

Research on children's issues in our society has been dominated by psychology and has been especially strongly influenced by Piaget's studies of maturational development. According to Piaget's theory, children go through distinct development stages marked by age, during which they acquire increasingly complex and abstract forms of knowing and relating to their social and natural environment. The "end product" of this process is the adult individual, the person who is complete, having learned to behave in accordance with society's expectations. For this model, age is considered a key variable in determining behavior. Little or no attention is paid to the social environment and circumstances a child faces, which also influence conduct. From this traditional perspective, children are seen more as "human becomings" than as complete human beings with talents, skills, and experiences to contribute to society (Qvortrup, 1987).

This teleological perception of the young—"children are the future"—is present in other areas of scholarly discourse as well. Political science, anthropology, sociology, and education have all been influenced by the notion that children are not full-fledged individuals. These fields often reflect the belief that children are empty vessels into which society pours its cultural values and norms of conduct—a process that turns children into adults, the "proper" status to actively participate in today's world. This perspective is evident in the way some sociology textbooks have defined the concept of socialization as "the learning process by which infants are made into normal human beings, possessed of culture and able to participate in social relations" (Stark, 1989, p. 146).

The "children are the future" notion clearly pervades the popular discourse. When government officials, policy makers, and activists discuss children's issues, it is in the context of ensuring society's survival. We need to help our children, because they will be the workers of tomorrow; they will care for us in old age; they are an investment in the country's future. Seldom is a plea made for children's role and potential today, for a recognition of children's condition as individuals in the present. The focus is rarely placed on children's own participation in social life, which may explain the scarcity of sociological studies taking children's point of view into account. Social scientists have traditionally looked "at" children but seldom "through" them (Blitzer, 1991).

According to this perspective, children need not concern themselves with playing the role of caregivers in practical ways. Their philanthropic role is limited to "learning to share in class" or studying the social values of consideration and good neighborliness in theory. This perspective tends to emphasize children's role as "recipients of care" while they develop and grow up to be responsible adults.

A New Paradigm

In the past few years, a new perspective on the status of children and youth in today's society has begun to emerge. One of the best examples of research within this new framework is a volume edited by Allison James and Alan Prout (1990) in which the contributors question the ideology that sees children as "persons in the making" and replaces it with one in which the young are "active, constructive members of society" (Qvortrup, 1990).

Two contributors to that volume illustrate the emergence of the new conceptualization of childhood. The first contributor, Martin Woodhead (1990, p. 60), urges that the concept of children's needs be outlawed from "professional discourse, policy recommendations and popular psychology." He argues that cultural values, not biological realities, cause us to see children as weak, helpless, passive recipients of care, while conferring all the power on adults, who are charged with fulfilling such needs. He cites the case of rural societies where children work alongside their parents for the family's subsistence. In those cases, "children's needs" are surely defined differently—in connection with household requirements—than in a society where the children's role is limited to receiving care, studying, and playing.

Woodhead's observations reflect on a new theoretical model. Whereas the traditional perspective on childhood stressed biological determinism, and most explanations of children's behavior were connected to development stages and little else, more recent analyses recover the cultural and historical factors that affect the status of children in society. Consider, for example, the October 1990 issue of *Environment and Urbanization*, which was entirely devoted to different aspects of the relationship between children and the environment in developing countries. The special social and economic circumstances in which many of these children live lead to roles that are far from passive. Diana Lee-Smith and Taranum Chaudry (1990, p. 27), writing on a children's environmental knowledge project in Kenya, call attention to the fact that "children are important agents of change. They have time to think in school and are usually the most literate people in rural communities." Under these circumstances, children can disseminate what they learn in terms of environmental resource management within their communities, a strategy also used in rural villages where the Van Leer Foundation of the Netherlands conducts public health education projects.

Jens Qvortrup (1990, p. 85)—the second contributor to the James and Prout volume—focuses on the absence of children from European official statistics and accounting methods: "Family statistics provide us with one of the best examples of the general rule that children are not the unit of observation in the production of statistics. It is the rule that families, parents, women, marriages, households, etc. are counted, but not children. This means that a number of distortions and omissions are introduced as far as children are concerned." Qvortrup offers a possible solution to the current exclusion of children as a population category from the national statistics; his proposal recognizes that their role is to accumulate essential knowledge for a society's long-term development.

The absence of children and their role as a population category is also a problem in U.S. statistics. An example is the difficulty in assessing the true number of working children, especially in agricultural activities. Similarly, it is difficult to find statistics for child volunteers or even solid documentation and reports on the philanthropic activities of young people (see Chapter Six).

Woodhead from a theoretical viewpoint, and Qvortrup from a methodological standpoint, agree on the need to replace society's present attitude toward children with one that sees them as able, productive individuals who are part of society and whose voice needs to be heard. Until recently, sociology textbooks contained separate chapters for women, the elderly, and ethnic minorities but no consideration of children as a separate category. However, that may change; in 1992, the American Sociological Association recognized the uniqueness of the child population as a distinct social agent and created a section exclusively devoted to the Sociology of Children. The newly created group includes Scandinavian scholars, who are among the forerunners in the emergence of the new paradigm. A new journal published in Norway—*Childhood*—prints analyses of the concept and realities of childhood from a social and cultural perspective, stressing "an international, interdisciplinary, view of the culture, language, health, social networks and peer relationships of childhood, with a new emphasis on the rights of the child and the child's position in society" (Frones, ed., 1993).

Authors like Jonathan Kozol (1992) and Robert Coles (1971–1977, 1986a, 1986b, 1992) have subscribed to this new perspective for many years. They have portrayed children in America and, in Coles's case also in other countries, as individuals who have been forced to live the life of adults even at a young age. Kozol's and Coles's children have much to say about the world around them, and both authors know how to listen. From a journalistic perspective, Richard Louv (1990) argues for the need to educate the media to pay attention to children as front-page news. Louv argues that family and children's issues are frequently dealt with as "soft journalism" and therefore fit only for the "home and garden" section of the newspaper. Louv interviewed parents and children in ten American cities to gather their views regarding the current situation of the American family. He stresses that unless children's issues are truly placed at the top of the political agenda and the media deal with them at a different level, children's future will continue to be threatened.

It is easy to see how scholars and practitioners adopting this paradigm would encourage the participation of youth in philanthropic projects in leadership roles: recognizing children and youth as persons, as citizens in their own right, encourages their participation as active members of society and capable individuals who can make a contribution on behalf of others. This theoretical model supports the recognition of children's skills and talents, which can be applied in community service projects.

"Youth Leadership and Empowerment"

The emerging scholarly paradigm seems to be mirrored by similar shifts in other levels of discourse and action. A growing awareness of environmental depletion, public health problems, and poverty seem to be spurring renewed attention to youth as an untapped resource. In other words, there are increased opportunities for young people to become the "doers" and to exercise an active role in their communities.

Youth advocates are now stressing the need to link service and education, citing advantages both for the community and for the young volunteers themselves. Proponents of youth service often support their argument with references to John Dewey's educational philosophy, where academic and social development are stimulated through actions, especially those performed on behalf of others. "The most remarkable benefit," writes Barbara Lewis (1991b)—a middle school teacher in Salt Lake City—"is that as students reach outward to solve problems to benefit others, the process internalizes, and they learn to better control their personal lives."

There are numerous programs throughout the country, school-sponsored or organized as youth corps, aimed at involving young people in community service projects. In a majority of cases, volunteers are middle and high school students, and the areas in which most students volunteer are environment-related projects, tutoring elementary school and special education children, helping the homeless, and visiting nursing home residents. Evaluations of the service experience by educators, community agencies, and students are consistently positive.

Advocates of youth service also agree that, while involvement in community projects is beneficial to all, students with poor academic performance, discipline problems, and low self-esteem gain the most. By taking responsibility for a social cause or caring for someone else, these students internalize a different self-image: they learn they can produce change and can be problem solvers (Lewis, 1991b).

Among the most frequently cited advantages of early involvement in volunteer service are that academic skills are reinforced (some teachers suggest that tutors make as much or even more progress as their tutees), that youngsters learn to care and be responsible for others, that they are connected to a community that needs them and so become better citizens, and that overall self-esteem, motivation, and autonomy increase. Even from a developmental psychology perspective, the search for adult role models outside the immediate family and intense concern for social and political issues during adolescence can find a niche in volunteer service activities.

The general principle shared by all initiatives is that youth are empowered through service; they learn to make decisions and to lead and realize that they can make a difference in the life of their community. Concerned about the future of philanthropy, some foundations and nonprofits are incorporating youth into the decision-making levels of their organizations. The Youth as Resources Program sponsored by the National Crime Prevention Council, for example, funds youth-designed and executed projects; the board itself consists of adults and youth with equal voting power. In 1987, the Kellogg Foundation granted $2 million to be distributed to community foundations in Michigan, requiring that youth be involved both in the grantmaking process and in raising the matching funds. In the words of Mary Leonard, coordinator for Grantmakers for Children and Youth, the way to ensure the continuity of philanthropy is for foundations to "grow their own philanthropists" (Goss, 1991).

In November 1990 the youth service movement received a strong thrust when the National and Community Service Act was signed into law and a special commission was created to distribute the funds appropriated. A total of $287 million was authorized for the support of youth corps, school-based service projects, and state demonstration models that incorporated service-learning into their programs. Different from traditional community service or volunteerism, the service-learning approach seeks to infuse the traditional academic curriculum with hands-on service experience, changing educational roles by allowing student volunteers a much more active participation in project delivery, from design to final evaluation.

In the volunteerism model the teacher organizes and makes decisions, while students follow directions in atomized projects usually taking place only out of class. Under the service-learning model the teacher, community, and students become partners in projects integrated into the curriculum; students are self-directed and reflect on their actions before and after the service is completed. Critical elements in service-learning projects are preparation, action, and reflection, without which a service project is considered to have less educational value.

Many states have instituted some type of community service

program in their schools. In Minnesota, for example, the majority of the K-12 student population is involved in some type of service-learning project. In July 1992, Maryland became the first state to require students to engage in community service for high school graduation. The decision sparked a great deal of debate between those who see the initiative as "involuntary servitude" and supporters of the service-learning requirement as a vehicle to teach students citizenship through reading, researching, and especially by *doing*.

A wave of new publications on the infusion of service-learning into the curriculum, software to keep track of student volunteers and projects, books, and catalogues especially geared to recruiting, organizing, and rewarding youth for their service, and even a new civics textbook by Ralph Nader on the "how-to's" of citizen involvement point to the emergence of this new perspective on youth.

The emphasis is on youth as an untapped resource; more and more people believe that they need to be respected as full-fledged individuals and that everyone benefits from their empowerment. A wealth of titles like *The Kid's Guide to Social Action* (Lewis, 1991a), *Volunteers in Public Schools* (National Research Council, 1990), *The Helping Hands Handbook* (Adams and Marzollo, 1992), *Kids Can Save the Animals* (Newkirk, 1991), and *What Would We Do Without You?* (Henderson, 1990) make it clear that youth are increasingly considered a rich community resource that should be encouraged to participate actively on behalf of many social causes.

However, this discussion leads to another question: How long do students need to wait to be recognized as valued members of their community? What age does an individual need to be to put into practice the values he or she learns at school and at home? The following discussion and examples will attempt to show that, from a very young age (before they reach the middle school years), children are aware of their social and natural environment and are willing to become involved in its improvement.

Children as Social Agents

A study I completed in 1990 explored how elementary school children experience urban life, how they use the city in a role other than in their role as students, and how they evaluate that experience. Further, if encouraged to search for solutions to urban problems, what would their priorities be?

The study was conducted in three Baltimore City public schools located in very different neighborhoods in terms of socioeconomic levels. The sample—eighty fifth-graders—also varied in terms of gender and ethnicity. One-on-one interviews were conducted with each child. These interviews included both a structured questionnaire on the students' evaluations of urban scenes and open-ended questions on their use of public areas, concerns regarding urban problems, and their priorities and suggestions for solving problems.

The interviews confirmed that elementary school children are aware, through the media or through their own experience, of the dangers and pleasures of urban life (Golombek, 1993). They have strong opinions about what is right or wrong with our cities. What is more important in terms of the present volume is that they are also eager to offer and be part of the solutions. Ten-year-olds often made it clear that they did not feel free or safe in the city; in a sense, it did not "belong" to them. This was particularly true for inner-city children and especially girls. Common responses to questions regarding their assessment of urban life were:

> Mine is a noisy street. You hear gunshots, accidents and it just doesn't feel safe around my block. It's violent. I'd like to move to a place where it's quiet and nice.

> I don't like living in the city because of people hanging out in corners and stuff, cursing; I don't like to see people lying down on the street with no homes, real poor.

The potential dangers of urban life naturally restrict children's freedom of movement. For some, it is "the crowds and confusion" that really disturb them, as is the case with middle-class children who are used to looking at the city through a car window. Inner-city children, on the other hand, are faced with other types of challenges:

> Sometimes I like to go off when I'm with my mother, but then I stop doing it 'cause I get lost and I start crying, even though I'm growing up.

> I'm not allowed to catch the bus by myself but I would like to go someplace by myself, but when I see strange people or dogs I wouldn't like to go by myself.

> I don't like that much about the city, 'cause of the shootings and killings and they take drugs and also they have people that try to rape you.

These quotes indicate how cities reinforce children's role as passive members of society who need protection, care, and constant supervision. Urban life, according to these children, increases their vulnerability. However, if following the new paradigm, children are offered opportunities to participate, they will not remain passive observers of reality but active contributors to collective efforts.

When given the opportunity to discuss what they saw as problems in today's larger urban areas, particularly in Baltimore, these ten-year-old citizens were quick to offer their views and propose solutions. Two types of responses emerged: while middle-class children were concerned with infrastructure, landscaping, and the general aesthetics of the urban environment, inner-city children had more pressing matters that needed attention: freeing their neighborhoods from drugs and alcohol, violence and homelessness. Compare, for example, the urgency of the problems referred to in these two quotes:

> Well, a problem is pollution and dirty buildings. And sometimes it's a tiny bit too crowded, a tiny bit. That's just about all.

> They should change the way they treat the homeless, especially kids! Because they should give them jobs and enough money to buy a small apartment. And clean up the trash. Clean city and people in their houses!

What needs to be emphasized is that, as these few examples confirm, children are not passive observers of reality; already at the elementary school level they internalize the urban social environment with its advantages and limitations, and most important, have ideas, opinions and concerns about it. Giving them opportunities to participate in community projects is a way of allowing them to appropriate the city, to "own" it as much as its older residents. Facilitating and encouraging their participation is a way of reducing their sense of vulnerability, of marginality, of powerlessness, the feeling that the city belongs to grown-ups. But they need scholars, activists, and policy makers to offer them a chance to voice their concerns and work on the solutions.

Citizenship 101

Citizenship is a broad concept, encompassing not only the ability to vote and serve on a jury, but also the responsible and active participation of an individual in and for the community. It is an acquired quality; *citizenship must be learned*. However, because of the traditional perception of children as "future persons," society does not expect or facilitate the younger generation's contribution to the life of a community.

In science classes, elementary school children learn about germination and marvel as a plant grows out of the seed they placed in a cotton-filled cup. They count pennies, nickels, and dimes to learn the value of money and work on creative projects on favorite books in language arts. In social studies and the vaguely defined "character education" curriculum, children dutifully study the meaning of such concepts as responsibility, caring, and considera-

tion. But they are not regularly offered the ch
concepts in concrete projects outside the class
could only occur within the limits of the schoo
they learn to be good citizens, good neighbors,
nity is more than the grocery store, the cleane
the post office? How do children learn that they themselves are a part of their community, that they build it every day in their relationships, and that they can have an active role and apply what they learn at school for the good of others?

It is common for young children to play "doctor" or "teacher." This can be interpreted as a reflection of their profound desire to prevent pain and to bring joy to others. The following first-graders' quotes confirm such an interpretation:

> When I grow up I want to be a doctor and make people healthy and strong, so they can work and play.

> When I grow up I want to be a teacher because I want to help people. I want kids to learn.

> When I grow up I want to be an author because I like cats and want to write about cats. I want to tell people about cats.

Others are deeply concerned with the fate of animals and the rest of nature:

> Whales are big. Whales are being extinct. So please help the whales. Let's bring the whales back. Please help the world.

The traditional question "What do you want to be when you grow up?" implies that teleological perspective that children are expected to wait to become caregivers and community participants, when they are in fact ready to help in the present, and derive great satisfaction and pride from the opportunity to do so.

KIDS IN ACTION

Encouraged by my research findings, I founded KIDS IN ACTION, a volunteer service program currently established in Baltimore City (Maryland) public elementary schools and adding more schools to its network. Its main elements are offering young children (five- to ten-year-olds) opportunities to change their traditional role of passive recipients of care to one of givers, to reinforce in them the sense that they can act on behalf of their community, and to raise their self-esteem and motivation by enabling them to help others. Giving children opportunities to lead, to design and implement their own service projects, and above all to help others is a potent way of reducing a future sense of powerlessness—the belief that our social problems are too overwhelming to even attempt a solution.

What skills can elementary school children put at the service of their community? A dichotomy seems to exist between what children are taught in school and adults' expectations of how children can apply that knowledge. Rarely are children encouraged to utilize what they learn at school in practical experiences throughout the community: a teacher taking her young students to practice their reading skills at a senior citizens' center is still quite exceptional. However, once children have learned how to read, they can entertain preschoolers and the elderly; they can work on their fine motor skills by making crafts for nursing home residents; they can do gardening projects to improve the appearance of their school and neighborhood; they can practice the uses and applications of graphs to record the number and type of canned goods collected to donate to a local shelter; they can write short stories and poems for hospitalized children. These are only a few examples of the skills the younger children already have but that are seldom thought of as resources for the community.

In KIDS IN ACTION's brief but rich experience, a successful transmission of philanthropic values to future generations can and should start as early as possible, especially taking into account that children are being taught such values although in a purely theoretical fashion. At the same time, responsibility and the ability to make decisions are acquired with practice. For that reason, KIDS IN ACTION projects are designed on the basis of the children's own interests, concerns, and ideas. When they know their input is respected and encouraged, they feel more responsible for the projects' success. Offering children opportunities to assume a more active role in their communities not only teaches them that their contribution is valuable but also makes them aware of their own skills, as indicated in the following quotes by KIDS IN ACTION participants:

> It helped me learn that helping other people makes you feel good about yourself.
>
> I learned that I can do things. And that I am good at them.
>
> [I learned] about places in my community and I've been to places I had never been before.
>
> A small group of kids can do a lot!

What programs such as KIDS IN ACTION achieve is to show children in a different light. Community organizations start to turn to children's groups for help with specific activities. KIDS IN ACTION, for example, has received requests to participate in "penny collection" projects for community agencies; Parent-Teacher Associations consider their young volunteers as allies in their fundraising and community outreach efforts. Children's programs are also seen as "setting a good example" for adults. When children participate in environmentally safe practices such as recycling, they take those behaviors home: parents tend to feel embarrassed if their children see them throwing away recyclable products. Or, as expressed by the director of a homeless shelter that benefited from a KIDS IN ACTION project: "The less fortunate need the support of everyone, and if a child can help so can the community." This recognition of children's role as young citizens is also being recognized at other levels. In some cases—such as Children for a Clean Environment (KIDS F.A.C.E.), which received funds from Wal-Mart to strengthen their operations—children's volunteer efforts gain corporate support. KIDS IN ACTION members, for example, were invited to participate in a meeting of citizens concerned with issues of homelessness hosted by the mayor of Baltimore in recognition of the group's advocacy campaign to save a shelter from closing down. More important, the children who participate in volunteer service activities are encouraged to make decisions as to what projects are carried out and how, which gives them a sense of their own ability to produce change.

The Road Ahead

As the children and youth service movement grows, longitudinal and case studies of different programs will contribute to a better understanding of the links between education, service, and students' social and academic development. To date, scattered but significant evidence suggests that involvement in community service projects is a positive experience for all children, but especially so for the less assertive or those with disciplinary and academic problems.

Research could also establish if leadership training through community service can prove especially beneficial for children who, in my study, felt "on the margins" of urban life, always the followers, seldom the leaders: girls, black children, and those from lower income groups. For example, Steven Schinke and Roxanne Spillett's study on the effect of Boys and Girls Clubs in public housing (see Chapter Seven) supports the hypothesis that involvement in philanthropic activities has positive effects in especially difficult social environments. Similarly, and recognizing the potential of volunteer service involvement for some students, teachers in the three schools where KIDS IN ACTION is operating have recommended students for participation in the program (a child in foster care, students with a poor self-image, and children with discipline problems).

The implications of incorporating philanthropic activities into the elementary school curriculum are many. The shift would produce a renewal in terms of teacher training, since educators would be socialized into less conventional forms of teaching that establish direct and practical connections between the concepts and skills they teach and their application in community projects. Another potential effect of such a shift would be the strengthening of ties between schools and communities. When children volunteer in neighboring institutions, these organizations are encouraged to support the schools. For example, it is common for adult day-care centers to offer to serve as trial audiences for school plays, to support schools' fundraising efforts, or even to send their healthier clients to the school as tutors or older volunteers.

The most important implication of engaging children as caregivers, however, is that when an individual is encouraged to help others, he or she is being recognized as a valuable community member. When a teacher assigns students leadership roles and public responsibilities, students become aware not only that they have something to contribute but that their skills and ability to give are respected and legitimized by those in authority.

Specifically, experiences such as KIDS IN ACTION's confirm that children learn by doing. Experiential learning that combines service and work with fun activities offer children new angles in the study and acquisition of moral standards (the purpose of "character education" units in the elementary grades). For example, children begin to question myths about homelessness and gain a better understanding of the issue when visiting and playing with the young clients of a day-care center for homeless children than when discussing the topic in theory.

Conclusion

The growing number of school programs and youth organizations devoted to community service would indicate that the trend toward youth involvement in service activities will continue, especially with the legislative and funding support of the National and Community Service Act and the creation of a Corporation for National and Community Service. It is also likely that funding for programs geared to the involvement of young children as volunteers will increase as well, instilling and reinforcing philanthropic attitudes early on.

Active, responsible, and concerned youth who have internalized the value of philanthropy since elementary school are likely to wish to continue such behavior as adults, and especially as parents—not an easy task for working families. The will to volunteer will be there, but not the time; it is possible that the links between individual and community will once again be broken.

Under such circumstances, how is the development of a caring society possible? In *Childhood's Future* (1990, p. 7), Louv discusses what he calls the need to reweave "the web." This term encompasses the personal contacts between parents and children, between families and community, what is sometimes called a social safety net, the need "to connect to something bigger than ourselves, bigger even than our individual families." One mother Louv interviewed expressed this clearly:

> I just feel we blew it somehow. All that sixties idealism has been lost. . . . After all these years, we're no more gratified or satisfied than when we started. And all the good we wanted to get from our parents and for our parents, our kids are waiting to get from us. The solution to where we're at is to focus on our children [p. 7].

Louv's proposal to reweave that web, essentially the reconstruction of a caring society, is what he calls "A Family Ties Bill." The main components of this proposal are that employers give every employee two to four hours a month to volunteer at their child's school or day-care center or a parent's nursing home or to do volunteer work in one such setting. Employees would have to submit proof of their service. Included in Louv's proposal are company-sponsored continuing education programs and parent support groups for employees that would ensure that employers value good parents and community volunteers.

Utopian as it may seem, it can happen. Louv cites the example of the Southland Corporation—owner or franchiser of most 7-Eleven stores in the country and abroad—which has already established a program similar to the "Family Ties Bill." A national advocacy organization—PARENT ACTION—is working so that government, workplaces, and communities institute policies ensuring that children will grow into caring, competent adults. PARENT ACTION promotes the "Family Ties Bill" and as an employer has adopted the policy for its own staff. If, through legislation or tax incentives, the concept were adopted by the public and private sectors and expanded to encourage volunteering in schools and nursing homes as well as in other areas of need (environment, homelessness, literacy), the notion of a caring society would be restored.

The "reweaving the web" argument goes hand in hand with what so many schools claim is absent: parent involvement. With the employers' cooperation, parents could join their children in their service-learning activities at school. This would bring parents and schools closer together, parents' involvement in their children's education would be facilitated, and family members would be offered the opportunity to work together on behalf of the community. Providing regular opportunities for parents to volunteer with their children in school or youth corps service projects would establish a continuum of service from elementary school to adulthood, strengthening the connections "to something bigger than ourselves, bigger even than our individual families."

References

Adams, P., and Marzollo, J. *The Helping Hands Handbook*. New York: Random House, 1992.

Blitzer, S. "They Are Only Children, What Do They Know? A Look at Current Ideologies of Childhood." *Sociological Studies of Child Development*, 1991, *4*, 11–25.

Coles, R. *Children of Crisis*. 5 vols. Boston: Little, Brown, 1971–1977.

Coles, R. *The Moral Life of Children*. New York: Atlantic Monthly Press, 1986a.

Coles, R. *The Political Life of Children*. New York: Atlantic Monthly Press, 1986b.

Coles, R. *Their Eyes Meeting the World: The Drawings and Paintings of Children*. New York: Houghton Mifflin, 1992.

The Earthworks Group. *50 Simple Things Kids Can Do to Save the Earth*. Kansas City, Mo.: Andrews and McMeel, 1990.

Frones, I. (ed.). *Childhood*, 1993, *1*(1), inside front cover, quoted in G. Lenzer, *Childnews*, 1992, *1*(1), 11.

Golombek, S. *A Sociological Image of the City: Through Children's Eyes*. New York: Lang, 1993.

Goss, K. "Turning Kids on to Good Works." *Chronicle of Philanthropy*, 1991, *3*(22), 10–14.

Henderson, K. *What Would We Do Without You? A Guide to Volunteer Activities for Kids*. White Hall, Va.: Betterway Publications, 1990.

James, A., and Prout, J. (eds.). *Constructing and Reconstructing Childhood*. Bristol, Pa.: Falmer Press, 1990.

Kozol, J. *Savage Inequalities*. New York: Crown Publishers, 1992.

Lee-Smith, D., and Chaudry, T. "Environmental Information for and from Children." *Environment and Urbanization*, 1990, *2*(2), 27–32.

Lewis, B. *The Kid's Guide to Social Action*. Minneapolis, Minn.: Free Spirit Publishing, 1991a.

Lewis, B. "Today's Kids Care About Social Action." *Educational Leadership*, Sept. 1991b, pp. 47–49.

Louv, R. *Childhood's Future*. Boston: Houghton Mifflin, 1990.

National Research Council. *Volunteers in Public Schools*. Washington, D.C.: National Academic Press, 1990.

Newkirk, I. *Kids Can Save the Animals: 101 Easy Things to Do*. New York: Warner Books, 1991.

Qvortrup, J. "Introduction." In J. Qvortrup (ed.), *International Journal of Sociology*, 1987, *17*, 3–38.

Qvortrup, J. "A Voice for Children in Statistical and Social Accounting: A Plea for Children's Rights to be Heard." In A. James and A. Prout (eds.), *Constructing and Reconstructing Childhood* (pp. 78–98). Bristol, Pa.: Falmer Press, 1990.

Stark, R. *Sociology*. Belmont, Calif.: Wadsworth, 1989.

Woodhead, M. "Psychology and the Cultural Construction of Children's Needs." In A. James and A. Prout (eds.), *Constructing and Reconstructing Childhood* (pp. 60–77). Bristol, Pa.: Falmer Press, 1990.

Chapter Six

Children as Volunteers: Learning by Doing

Virginia A. Walter

What kind of society are we talking about when we talk about a "caring society"? President George Bush tried to conjure up a vision of a "kinder, gentler" society illuminated by "a thousand points of light," each one a spark of voluntary individual or collective action, privately initiated and implemented. Ultimately, the model was not convincing. Alternatively, we can invoke a number of academic constructs: Benjamin Barber's (1984) strong democracy, the communitarian society of Amitai Etzioni (1988), Jon Van Til's (1988) active society, or the good society of Robert Bellah and others (1992). While these models differ in emphasis, they share at least two characteristics. They offer mechanisms for institutionalizing altruism, for facilitating voluntary donations of time and money for the good of others; and they are utopian or normative visions. They reflect only bits and pieces of current reality, offering instead the possibility of a better future.

We adults may or may not succeed in implementing a caring society, a communitarian, active, good society in our lifetimes. It is, however, a vision that represents a desirable, perhaps even necessary, future for our children and grandchildren. Educating children to take their places in that caring society then becomes a matter of some importance. This chapter deals with that question directly, focusing specifically on the nature of children's volunteer experiences. How do these experiences prepare children to create and maintain a caring society? What do child volunteers do? What do they learn? What do these experiences teach children about participating in civic life? Where do children volunteer, and how do their adult supervisors structure their experiences? What elements in children's voluntary action are most likely to contribute to positive learning? What research is still needed to help us understand children and voluntarism? What policies might encourage more voluntary action by children?

Relevant Research

Surprisingly little systematic research has been done on voluntary action undertaken by children under the age of twelve. One exploratory study suggested that membership in a youth organization, which provides an opportunity to actually practice the skills of democracy through voluntary social action, may be a more salient factor than the more frequently cited socialization agents—television and the school curriculum—in developing a sense of political efficacy in children (Walter, 1990). Not all youth organizations provide volunteer opportunities, however, and there is little reliable evidence on the number of children who belong to youth organizations or on the number of children age twelve and under who volunteer in any context. There have been studies focusing on voluntary action by adolescents (Hamilton and Fenzel, 1988; Hanks, 1981; Hedin and Conrad, 1987; Lewis, 1988), but these have not considered the activities of children. INDEPENDENT SECTOR released the findings from an important national survey, *Volunteering and Giving Among American Teenagers 12 to 17 Years of Age*, in 1992 (Hodgkinson and Weitzman, with Noga and Gorski, 1992). This report establishes that volunteering and giving are pervasive activities among American adolescents, with 61 percent of all teenagers volunteering an average of 3.2 hours a week (p. 7). No comparable study has yet been done on volunteers under the age of twelve, even though one-third of the teen respondents in the INDEPENDENT SECTOR study reported that they started volunteering before they were eleven years old (p. 23).

There has been considerable interest in voluntary community service as a component of young people's school experiences, but this practice has also been largely limited to junior and senior high schools (Carnegie Task Force on Education of Young Adolescents, 1989; Conrad and Hedin, 1991; Schine, 1990). There are scattered accounts, however, of school-based community service programs being implemented in lower grades. Mary S. Harbaugh (1990), for example, reports an ongoing program in an Albuquerque fifth-grade class to help clients of a day shelter for homeless adults and a volunteer immigrant assistance program that was developed and implemented by Pennsylvania fourth-graders. Joe Nathan and Jim Kielsmeier (1991) describe volunteer environmental cleanup efforts undertaken by fourth- through sixth-graders and a new playground designed, funded, and built by a group of inner-city children age five to nine.

Most of what we know is based on such journalistic and anecdotal reports, but an interesting picture of childhood voluntarism can be drawn by accumulating the evidence from a growing body of these accounts. There are remarkable young individuals, such as eight-year-old Teddy Andrews, who is chair of the Berkeley, California, Committee on Homeless and Needy Youth (Clurman, 1989). Children help other children as peer tutors ("Kids Helping Kids: An Old Idea That's Working in Today's Schools," 1985) and as assistants in their school libraries (McHenry, 1988). Children under the age of twelve have volunteered in geriatric convalescent homes, collected food for homeless people, held fundraising events for local government services, conducted Easter egg hunts for disabled children, and repaired used toys for distribution to needier children (Ellis, 1983).

Children have been particularly effective volunteers in the environmental movement. A survey sponsored by the World Wildlife Fund indicated that children are more motivated to work actively on behalf of the environment than their parents are and indeed are active in setting the environmental agenda (Koenenn,

1992). Another study, recently released by Environmental Research Associates, showed that many children have been effective in persuading their parents to make consumer choices that protect the environment, urging them to recycle, buy reusable products, and save energy by turning off lights (Bond, 1993). The efforts of children to protect the environment have gone beyond influencing family decisions, however. One resource list includes eight children's activist groups dedicated to environmental causes throughout the United States ("Resources: Children and the Environment," 1991). There are certainly many more groups whose existence has not been documented. As members of these youth-oriented groups or as participants in adult environmental action projects, children have planted trees, cleaned up polluted streams and waterways, and produced environmental programs for cable television (Lewis, 1991).

There is a body of research from the discipline of child development that, while not dealing directly with childhood volunteer experiences, is helpful in understanding their significance in the lives of children. The stage theories of childhood development, pioneered by Jean Piaget (1965), suggest that constructs about society as well as critical beliefs and attitudes related to a child's sense of political efficacy and self-esteem are formed between the ages of ten and twelve. As Conrad and Hedin (1991, pp. 747–748) point out, it has been difficult to quantitatively establish the causal relationship between community service and political efficacy, but there is considerable qualitative evidence that participating in meaningful voluntary action is empowering to children. We also know that experiential learning is particularly salient at this age; children under the age of twelve benefit from learning by doing. It seems reasonable to assume that children who *do* volunteer work such as cleaning up a polluted stream or feeding homeless adults will learn more than children who merely read or hear about such issues.

One of the more convincing trends in child psychology has been the integration of the child's place in the social world with the stage theories of such influential researchers as Jean Piaget. James Garbarino (1989, p. 8) has added what he calls an ecological perspective to the developmental model. This accounts for both the child's changing capacities and the interplay of social systems in the child's social environment. Garbarino and other researchers in social development help us understand the significance of children's social experiences such as participating in community tree planting or volunteering at a local library in their development as evolving civic beings.

Research on childhood political socialization is also helpful in illuminating the significance of early voluntary experiences in social action. Most of this research was conducted in the late 1960s (Easton and Dennis, 1969; Greenstein, 1969; Hess and Torney, 1967). It attempted to discover the processes by which children acquire political learning. Among the relevant findings from the political socialization research is the fact that children have little interest in politics when it is narrowly defined as electoral politics and political institutions. They also have few direct interactions with the political system, so their learning tends to be indirect, acquired through informal learning provided by parents, teachers, and peers. This suggests that the few opportunities children have for direct political learning may be particularly salient, above all in the years from nine to eleven, which Piaget characterized as "concrete operational."

Research Methodology

Like so much of the work on children's voluntary action, this study, too, turned out to be less systematic than intended. Because of the lack of documentation about children's volunteer opportunities, the quest for child volunteers and child activists turned up fewer local programs than expected. Many initial leads turned out to involve adolescents rather than the children age twelve and younger that I had targeted. The sample of actual subjects who were finally interviewed is therefore opportunistic; these are the child volunteers and activists and their adult supervisors or directors that I was able to locate in the Southern California area over a limited time period.

Extended focus-group type interviews were conducted with two groups of children who volunteer in their local library and with one Camp Fire group that is actively involved in community service. A total of fifteen children between the ages of nine and twelve were interviewed. These young people reflect the ethnic diversity of Southern California; there were eight European Americans, four Hispanics, two Asian Americans, and one African American. One group of library volunteers is from a working-class community; the second group of library volunteers are more traditionally middle class. The Camp Fire group was upper middle class. Boys are underrepresented in the subject population; only two boys are included, both library volunteers.

In addition to the children, six adults were interviewed—the two children's librarians who work with the library volunteers, the Camp Fire leader, two youth ministers, and one director of an active nonprofit environmental organization run by young people. It is a limitation of the study presented here that logistical problems prevented my interviewing the children associated with the two churches and the environmental action program. Follow-up studies will include them as well.

The interviews were in all cases open-ended and designed to elicit qualitative information about the perceived nature of children's volunteer experiences. All participants were candid and articulate in their responses.

Research Findings

The following four findings emerged as the most pervasive and salient themes in the interviews with the children who volunteer and the adults who work with them.

1. *Children's motivations for volunteering vary and include both affective and instrumental reasons*. For children in the subject popu-

lation, the original reasons for volunteering varied. Some children were bored and looking for something to do. Others responded to a request for help or a suggestion from an adult they respected. In all cases, however, children who continued to be active volunteers reported strong social bonds with the adults who guided their activities and in some cases with the other children who were involved. The library volunteers, in particular, talked about their positive relationships with the library staff. A typical comment was, "I like the people here; they're fun." The Camp Fire members reported strong support from their peers as an enabling factor in their volunteer work. One girl said, "I'd feel silly just showing up at the convalescent home and just saying, like, here I am. When we go together as Camp Fire girls, it feels more comfortable."

The children also were able to articulate how their activities helped the library or the community or the individuals who were the recipients of their efforts. They could see that their volunteer efforts resulted in strong, positive social relationships and positive good in the outside world. They felt that their efforts were needed and recognized. A library volunteer said, "I guess they need us to get the work done. Like Carole said, 'I couldn't get this done without you.' If books weren't on the shelves, people couldn't find them. It gets really busy in the summer, and they need a lot of help then." A Camp Fire girl explained, "It was really neat when we'd been visiting the old people's home awhile and they got to know us and they really liked to see us come in. You could see that they got happier after they got to know us." Another said, "It's nice to have someone who needs you. As a kid, the only thing you get to take care of is a pet."

More instrumental reasons were also given for volunteering. One girl said that she started volunteering at the library because she wanted to improve her library skills. "I wanted to find out how things were organized so I could find things myself easier," she said. Another girl confessed that she hoped her volunteer work would be remembered in a few years when she applied for paid employment at the library. One of the Camp Fire girls said that she liked to volunteer because it was an easy way to accumulate honor beads and patches.

2. *Children as young as nine and ten are capable of performing many useful tasks in organizations and communities*. The children and adults interviewed for this study reported a wide array of tasks that the children performed, ranging from library clerical work to feeding the homeless to producing an environmental quiz show for cable television and organizing a national environmental summit for young people. None of the work described was trivial. It had real value in the adult world. One of the children's librarians said that the child volunteers were as responsible and competent as the adults who had volunteered at the library. The other librarian said that during the summer she was so busy coordinating activities that the young volunteers essentially took over her routine work. "I couldn't run this kind of intensive summer reading program without their help," she added.

The adult coordinator of the youth environmental action group pointed out that the children were not constrained by adult concepts of "what is possible" and therefore took on projects that adult organizations would have rejected as being unrealistic. She cited the cable television program as a significant example. "I never would have tried that with an adult group unless I knew in advance that we had the resources to do it," she said. "But we told these kids when they were younger that they could be anything, do anything. They believed us, and now they have set out to save the world."

The youth minister in the inner-city church reported that children were expected to share with adult parishioners many of the tasks involved with maintaining the church and its activities. They babysat for younger children, sang in the choir, helped with outreach efforts, contributed to charitable activities such as bagging groceries for needy families, and assisted with clerical duties. They operated copy machines, licked stamps, and answered telephones. These activities were considered to be as important for the child's own spiritual and social development as they were for the operation of the church. "These children need to be empowered and cherished. We give them a place to develop roots and grow," the youth minister explained. Children at the more affluent church appeared to be much less involved with activities that supported the work of the church and more involved in volunteer activities sponsored by the church for the benefit of less fortunate people in the community. "Some children choose to be involved in our social ministry," the minister said. "This helps them prepare for roles they will have as responsible adults."

3. *Children's volunteer work links them in positive ways with adults*. One librarian explained that the children who volunteer get to know her as a colleague. This is a different relationship than she has with most of the children she meets professionally. "They get to know me in a different way, as a friend and colleague. A few years ago one of my girls came in. She had had her bike stolen at the market, and she came to me because she was afraid to tell her Mom. I know she wouldn't have done that if she hadn't gotten to know me better while she was a volunteer here." The other librarian expressed another aspect of this. He explained that the children who volunteer get to see the off-stage side of library work; they get to see how it operates and what kind of work people do there. "They get to see what grown-ups really do at work," he said. The children also talked about this, saying how they enjoyed being able to interact with other workers in the nonpublic parts of the library. They liked having access to the staff workroom and the staff lounge. One child said that he was surprised at how much the librarians ate!

The Camp Fire girls found that volunteering at a geriatric convalescent hospital gave them experiences with older people that were special. One girl said that her grandparents lived far away and visiting the people at the hospital helped make up for missing them. Another girl said that she was afraid of the senior citizens at first. "After I got to know them better, I could see that they really liked me and wanted me to come and then I liked them better too."

The young people who volunteer with the environmental action group take on many adult roles and participate actively in the adult world. They speak at city council meetings and solicit funds from corporations. Their volunteer activities give them access to many arenas of social life that would ordinarily be barred to children.

4. *Children respond enthusiastically to a variety of supervisory styles as long as the adults who are directing and/or guiding them demonstrate respect and affection for the children.* The six adults interviewed for this study work with children in different institutional settings—public libraries, churches, a youth group, and a nonprofit environmental action group. Their personal styles are also different. The head of the nonprofit group is a self-acknowledged child advocate as well as an environmental activist. She sees herself as empowering children, giving them tools for success. One of her techniques is to open doors to the adult world for the children. She said, "I'll call ahead to the newspaper office and tell them to expect an article from Susie Jones. Then Susie is less likely to experience age bias from the newspaper staff and to have a successful experience."

The male children's librarian is very casual and informal with the children, and they clearly think he's wonderful. He said that he tries to give them jobs requiring minimal supervision. He keeps rules to a minimum as well. "It's about hanging out," he said. "The kids are here; they want to work. It helps us, and it helps them. It's no big deal." The Westside youth minister is also very casual, with a collection of vintage surfboards in his office. He sees himself primarily as a counselor and only secondarily as a supervisor of youth volunteers. He uses the volunteer activities as opportunities to get to know the children in a different context and for them to see him in a different role.

Both the inner-city minister and the other children's librarian are more structured and formal. "I want them to learn to be responsible," the minister said. "We respect them, and they must respect us; our whole philosophy is based on mutual respect and caring." In the second librarian's program, the children sign a contract, committing to a specific amount of volunteer time. "I want the children to know that I am depending on them," she explained. In return, she arranges for formal city council recognition of the child volunteers. The children are impressed by the adult validation of their efforts. One child showed me the picture of the mayor presenting him with a certificate of appreciation that had been in the paper three years before; he had preserved it carefully as a precious souvenir.

What the adults have in common is respect and affection for the young people they work with. They seem to genuinely enjoy working with children and to have no reservations about what the children can accomplish. One of the librarians acknowledged that it took time to supervise the children but that it was well worth it. "Some of my colleagues think I'm crazy to do this," she said, "but on a personal level, I benefit too. And so does the library. It is a privilege to be able to have this kind of relationship with children."

Conclusion

While this study only documents isolated examples of children who volunteer, it does suggest that there is value for both the child and the community. For the child, volunteering is an opportunity to try on some positive adult roles. Peter Berger and Thomas Luckmann (1966) describe socialization as the process by which we come to understand and be a part of the reality of everyday life, an intersubjective world that is characterized by a web of human relationships. We do not learn about that world by independent reasoning or by rote learning but rather by trying on roles and seeing how other people react to them. We acquire the social knowledge we need by developing understandings and meanings that are shared by others who occupy the same time and place. Children who volunteer have the opportunity to try on new roles—library clerk, choir member, environmental activist, tutor—and to acquire skills and information from new domains of knowledge. They are able to develop leadership and participation skills. They are able to see and experience firsthand the importance of what social philosopher Laura Purdy (1992) has called *enabling virtues*, the desire to work hard and achieve excellence, reliability, and rationality. Psychologist Ervin Staub (1992) urges that children be provided with experience participating in many roles and activities. "As a consequence," he explains, "the child comes to perceive himself or herself as an actor rather than an audience, as an agent rather than helpless in shaping events, as responsible for others' welfare as well as his or her own, and as a responsible member of the community" (p. 405).

That early volunteer experiences indeed influence later behavior can be seen in one set of findings from the INDEPENDENT SECTOR study, *Volunteering and Giving Among American Teenagers 12 to 17 Years of Age* (Hodgkinson and Weitzman, with Noga and Gorski, 1992). Fifty-eight percent of the respondents in this survey reported doing some kind of volunteer work when they were children; of these, 84 percent still volunteer. Membership in youth groups, institutions that typically encourage leadership development and democratic processes, was another factor that seemed to lead to adolescent volunteering. Of the 65 percent of total respondents who reported belonging to a youth group as a child, 72 percent were currently volunteering (p. 27). Stephen F. Hamilton and L. Mickey Fenzel (1988, p. 65) remind us that research in human development shows that while we continue to learn and grow throughout our lives, "there is an undeniable efficiency to teaching young people the kind of behavior we value in adults: they are likely to learn it more quickly and they will demonstrate it longer."

Children's voluntary efforts also contribute to the betterment of their communities. Children have energy and vision; they still think they can save the world. After all, it is their future that they are trying to save. The director of the environmental action group read from the statement of purpose of one of the youth members of her board: "I want to save the world while there is still a world to save."

While I have focused in this discussion on the benefits of childhood volunteer experiences, it is important to mention some possible negative consequences that deserve further exploration. Some of the children devote a great deal of time to their volunteer efforts, time that might arguably be better spent on schoolwork or a more varied set of activities. The leader of the environmental action group confessed to worrying about this sometimes but added, "They learn to juggle and manage their time, just like we busy adults do." There were hints of condescension in some of the remarks from the affluent Camp Fire girls: "We took presents to poor kids' houses at Christmas." "We sang songs for old people." Are they learning to contribute to the construction of a caring society or to be patronizing "Lady Bountifuls"? There is also the danger that child volunteers may be manipulated by adults for personal or political purposes. Phyllis LaFarge (1987, pp. 155–156) has written about how the peace movement of the 1960s and early 1970s used children as potent symbols, inspiring a sense of connectedness of future generations. While mostly sincere, the use of children in marches and media coverage was sometimes exploited and sentimentalized, she adds. More recently, the militant Pro-Life movement has also involved children as participants in their demonstrations against abortion clinics. The crucial theoretical issue to be resolved here is to what extent a dependent child can *ever* be said to truly volunteer.

This small study suggests the much larger research agenda that remains to be addressed. It would be enormously helpful to have national statistics on the extent of children's voluntarism. We need to have a better understanding of the settings in which children volunteer. Churches, schools, youth organizations, and social action groups need to be surveyed to see to what extent they offer a platform for children's voluntary action. There may be more children volunteering in government agencies such as libraries and recreation centers than people had suspected. Longitudinal studies are needed to begin to establish the causal relationships between childhood volunteer experiences and adult civic participation. More qualitative studies such as this one could begin to tease out the experiential aspects of children's voluntarism and help us to develop models for effective youth volunteer programs. We need to know more about children's volunteer activities in particular ethnic and religious communities.

There are policy implications as well. Policy initiatives could be developed that would facilitate children's volunteer efforts. Some municipalities have insurance requirements that prohibit children from volunteering. Susan Ellis (1983) recommends ways that these can be eased. City governments and nonprofit boards could explore ways to include youth representatives. Kathlyn Thorp (1983) has written a manual for the Wisconsin Department of Health and Social Services, showing how young people could be meaningfully included on adult committees. Nonprofit and government agencies such as libraries, museums, and hospitals could be provided with incentives for creating volunteer opportunities for children.

This study indicates that children want to participate in meaningful social roles. They will even seek out volunteer opportunities in adult environments. They are capable of making meaningful contributions to the work of an organization. They are capable of taking on leadership roles in their communities. To do so, they need to be supported by adults who respect them and like spending time with them, who will not manipulate them or exploit them. The children ask little in the way of reward or recognition; the opportunity to participate seems to be reward enough. Children do learn by doing. We can provide them with opportunities to learn to do good.

References

Barber, B. *Strong Democracy: Participatory Politics for a New Age*. Berkeley: University of California Press, 1984.

Bellah, R., and others. *The Good Society*. New York: Knopf, 1992.

Berger, P. L., and Luckmann, T. *The Social Construction of Reality: A Treatise on the Sociology of Knowledge*. New York: Doubleday, 1966.

Bond, R. M. "In the Ozone, A Child Shall Lead Them." *New York Times*, Jan. 1, 1993, sec. 4A, p. 7.

Carnegie Task Force on Education of Young Adolescents. *Turning Points: Preparing American Youth for the 21st Century*. New York: Carnegie Council on Adolescent Development of the Carnegie Corporation, 1989.

Clurman, C. "A Young Voice for Needy Children." *Governing*, 1989, *2*(4), 67.

Conrad, D., and Hedin, D. "School-Based Community Service: What We Know from Research and Theory." *Phi Delta Kappan*, 1991, *72*(10), 743–749.

Easton, D., and Dennis, J. *Children in the Political System: Origins of Political Legitimacy*. New York: McGraw-Hill, 1969.

Ellis, S. J. (ed.). *Children as Volunteers*. Philadelphia: Energize, 1983.

Etzioni, A. *The Moral Dimension: Toward a New Economics*. New York: Free Press, 1988.

Garbarino, J., Stott, F. M., and the Faculty of the Erikson Institute. *What Children Can Tell Us: Eliciting, Interpreting, and Evaluating Information from Children*. San Francisco: Jossey-Bass, 1989.

Greenstein, F. I. *Children and Politics*. New Haven, Conn.: Yale University Press, 1969.

Hamilton, S. F., and Fenzel, L. M. "The Impact of Volunteer Experience on Adolescent Social Development: Evidence of Program Effects." *Journal of Adolescent Research*, 1988, *3*(1), 65–80.

Hanks, M. "Youth, Voluntary Associations, and Political Socialization." *Social Forces*, 1981, 60(1), 211–223.

Harbaugh, M. S. "Kids Can Make a Difference!" *Instructor*, 1990, 99(2), 45–50.

Hedin, D., and Conrad, D. *Youth Services: A Guide Book for Developing and Operating Effective Programs*. Washington, D.C.: INDEPENDENT SECTOR, 1987.

Hess, J., and Torney, D. *The Development of Political Attitudes in Children*. Chicago: Aldine, 1967.

Hodgkinson, V. A., and Weitzman, M. S., with Noga, S. M., and Gorski, H. A. *Volunteering and Giving Among American Teenagers 12 to 17 Years of Age*. Washington, D.C.: INDEPENDENT SECTOR, 1992.

"Kids Helping Kids: An Old Idea That's Working in Today's Schools." *Better Homes and Gardens*, Sept. 1985, pp. 25–28.

Koenenn, C. "Now the Kids Are Writing Green Agenda for Parents." *Los Angeles Times*, Feb. 18, 1992, pp. E1, E10.

LaFarge, P. *The Strangelove Legacy: Children, Parents, and Teachers in the Nuclear Age*. New York: HarperCollins, 1987.

Lewis, A. C. *Facts and Faith: A Status Report on Youth Service*. New York: William T. Grant Foundation Commission on Work, Family, and Citizenship, 1988.

Lewis, B. A. *The Kid's Guide to Social Action: How to Solve the Social Problems You*

Choose—and Turn Creative Thinking into Positive Action. Minneapolis, Minn.: Free Spirit Publishing, 1991.

McHenry, C. A. "Library Volunteers: Recruiting, Motivating, Keeping Them." *School Library Journal*, 1988, *35*(5), 44–47.

Nathan, J., and Kielsmeier, J. "The Sleeping Giant of School Reform." *Phi Delta Kappan*, 1991, *72*(10), 739–742.

Piaget, J. *The Child's Conception of the World*. Totowa, N.J.: Littlefield, Adams, 1965.

Purdy, L. M. *In Their Best Interest? The Case Against Equal Rights for Children*. Ithaca, N.Y.: Cornell University Press, 1992.

"Resources: Children and the Environment." *Environmental Action*, 1991, *23*(2), 26.

Schine, J. "A Rationale for Youth Community Service." *Social Policy*, 1990, *20*(4), 5–11.

Staub, E. "The Origins of Caring, Helping, and Nonaggression: Parental Socialization, the Family System, Schools, and Cultural Influence." In P. M. Oliner and others (eds.), *Embracing the Other: Philosophical, Psychological, and Historical Perspectives on Altruism*. New York: New York University Press, 1992.

Thorp, K. *Youth Participation in Adult Committees*. Madison: Wisconsin Department of Health and Social Services, 1983.

Van Til, J. *Mapping the Third Sector: Voluntarism in a Changing Social Economy*. New York: The Foundation Center, 1988.

Walter, V. A. "Children as Citizens in Training: Political Socialization for a Strong Democracy." *Nonprofit and Voluntary Sector Quarterly*, 1990, *19*(1), 7–20.

Chapter Seven

The Effect of Boys and Girls Clubs on Promoting Caring in Public Housing

Steven Schinke, Roxanne Spillett

In the United States today, there are more than 6,500 multiple-unit public housing developments. Many provide marginal living conditions for their residents. Indeed, an estimated 86,000 individual units have been classified as severely distressed (National Commission on Severely Distressed Public Housing, 1992). Public housing in general, and severely distressed units in particular, are often described as some of the bleakest and most dangerous environments in America. Trapped in poverty, the young people who live in distressed housing units often grow up without positive role models or adequate social supports. Many of these youth exist in substandard living conditions with inferior neighborhood schools and are surrounded by drugs and violence. Compounding these social pathologies is the reality that many public housing communities fail to provide caring environments for their children.

Accepted theory and empirical evidence strongly support the idea that caring communities contribute to the development of healthy, caring children and adolescents (National Commission on Children, 1991). This chapter reports the results of an evaluation of newly established Boys and Girls Clubs with substance abuse prevention components. A corollary of this research supports the hypothesis that Boys and Girls Clubs in public housing developments create a more caring community for residents,

Note: The research described here has been supported by grants from the U.S. Office of Substance Abuse Prevention and the Henry J. Kaiser Family Foundation.

thus contributing to the development of more caring children and adolescents.

Culling from the larger study that focused on Boys and Girls Clubs with substance abuse prevention programs (SMART Moves), this chapter discusses the relationship between substance abuse prevention and the fostering of caring. Specifically, the chapter seeks to answer four important questions related to caring: What effect does a Boys and Girls Club have on promoting caring in public housing communities? What activities and strategies help to develop the caring capacity of young people? What strategies are effective in galvanizing support for the creation of more caring communities in public housing? Who are the key individuals and organizations that can provide the leadership needed to transform public housing developments into more caring communities?

About Boys and Girls Clubs: The Intervention

The mission of the Boys and Girls Club Movement is to help youth of all backgrounds (with special concern for those from disadvantaged circumstances) develop the skills and qualities needed to become responsible citizens and leaders. Currently, 1,450 Boys and Girls Clubs in the United States serve approximately 1.85 million boys and girls, age six to eighteen. Each Boys and Girls Club facility is professionally staffed and fully equipped with daily programs that promote youth development. Based on the physical, emotional, and cultural needs and interests of boys and girls, and recognizing key developmental principles, Boys and Girls Clubs programs focus on six core areas: citizenship and leadership development, personal and educational development, cultural enrichment, health and physical education, social recreation, and outdoor and environmental education. Typical programs include homework help and tutoring, sports, cooking classes, community service projects, educational games and projects, field trips, drug prevention activities, career exploration, and arts and crafts.

Boys and Girls Club programs are designed to promote in youths a *sense of competence*—the feeling that there is something they can do and do well, a *sense of usefulness*—the opportunity to do something of value for other people, a *sense of belonging*—the feeling that they "fit in" and are accepted, and a *sense of power or influence*—a chance to be heard and to influence decisions.

In 1987, the Boys and Girls Club movement launched a major nationwide offensive to reach and serve the neediest children in America. Public housing was targeted as one of several likely areas to fulfill this commitment. With funding from the Office of Substance Abuse Prevention and the Henry J. Kaiser Family Foundation, Boys and Girls Clubs of America initiated a demonstration project in which five Boys and Girls Clubs with substance abuse prevention programs were established in public housing. An independent evaluation conducted by Columbia University and the American Health Foundation measured the impact of these newly established clubs on the public housing developments where the clubs were established.

Research Design

This three-year comparative study assessed the overall effects of Boys and Girls Clubs on children and adolescents who live in public housing developments. Toward that end, the study assessed parental involvement in youths' lives, volunteerism, the availability of recreational, educational, social, and community supports for children, and the levels of criminal activity, delinquency, drug use, and drug dealing in the indexed public housing developments.

The study took place in fifteen public housing developments in a representative sample of American cities. Over a three-year period, the external evaluation team compared public housing developments under three different conditions: five public housing developments with no Boys and Girls Clubs, five public housing developments with newly established Boys and Girls Clubs, and five public housing developments with well-established Boys and Girls Clubs. To evaluate the five newly established clubs in public housing, each was assigned two control sites: a public housing site with a well-established Boys and Girls Club and a public housing site without a Boys and Girls Club. These control sites were geographically and demographically matched. Matching criteria included the size of the public housing site, its geographical locale, and demographics of the population.

By including three types of housing developments, the design concurrently compares the effects of a public housing development with a newly established Boys and Girls Club to a public housing development with a well-established club and to a public housing development with no club. Thus, the evaluation research design provides a measure of confidence about the effects of two types of Boys and Girls Club programs. In addition, the design permits an empirical examination of the processes and outcomes of an applied program. As such, the design and the evaluation generated important findings for policy, programming, and future research.

Measures

To assess the influence of the Boys and Girls Clubs on public housing developments, data were collected on informal support networks, observed external supports, and perceptions and attitudes of parents, teachers, and local authorities toward the housing developments. Members of the outside evaluation team visited every public housing site. During these visits, the team carried out several measurement procedures and collected data from multiple sources. Among the variables of interest were the presence of crack and estimated rates of drug-related activity in the housing developments, parental involvement in the Boys and Girls Club programs, and the incidence of juvenile criminal activity.

Informal support network data came from semistructured questionnaires distributed to a randomly selected 33 percent of all housing units in each development. These surveys gathered data on perceptions of the Boys and Girls Club, the perceived level of delinquency problems in the area, and the needs that should be addressed through the club.

Observed external supports were gathered by research assistants blind to condition assignments. External support data came from public housing sites and surrounding neighborhoods. In these settings, research assistants recorded evidence of tangible, structural, and institutional supports to encourage healthy program and recreational activities among young people. Tangible supports for purposes of data collection included posters, signs, and literature on youth activities, alcohol and other drug use prevention, and so on.

Unobtrusive measures provided additional data. These means of data collection are assumed to have fewer biases than self-report. By having access to and collecting confirmatory findings on alcohol and other drug use and related behavior and prosocial activities among youth in public housing sites, the evaluators scientifically examined the validity of outcome measurement results. Members of the evaluation team gathered juvenile and adult crime statistics from local police and housing authorities at each site for the study. The evaluation team also reported their observations of graffiti, garbage, and vandalism within each public housing site. Finally, any presence of drug paraphernalia and drug dealing was documented.

Findings

For youth who live in public housing developments and who have access to a Boys and Girls Club, the influence of the club was manifest in their involvement in healthy and constructive educational, social, community service, and recreational activities. Relative to their counterparts who did not have access to a club, these youth were less involved in unhealthy, deviant, and dangerous activities. Moreover, youths involved in Boys and Girls Club programs (both newly established and well-established clubs) were regularly exposed to positive role models who consistently demonstrated a caring attitude.

Organized sports, a key element of Boys and Girls Clubs, prevailed in study sites that contained clubs. Such activity for youth in public housing without Boys and Girls Clubs was rare. When a recreational or sports facility did exist for youth in public housing without Boys and Girls Clubs, it was usually not staffed by professionals or other trained personnel. These unregulated facilities were susceptible to drug dealing and other illicit activities. In contrast, the Boys and Girls Clubs were, without exception, professionally staffed. Boys and Girls Club programs staffed by adults who know youth members send a message that the Boys and Girls Club and the public housing community care about its children.

Data from the evaluation indicated that adult residents of public housing were also positively affected by Boys and Girls Clubs. Compared with parents in public housing sites that did not have club programs and facilities, adult family members in communities with clubs were more involved in youth-oriented activities and school programs. This appeared to be due to Boys and Girls Club staff encouraging parents to volunteer for and participate in club activities. Also, Boys and Girls Club staff encouraged parents to respond to student evaluations and conferences at school. The greatest parental involvement was recorded for well-established clubs, suggesting that parental involvement increases with the length of time the club is in existence. Once the clubs are embedded in the community, their caring atmosphere seems to have a ripple effect on the larger community.

Based on archival records obtained from public housing authority administrators at each of the fifteen study sites, comparisons were also possible on selected parameters of quality of life. Quality of life, for purposes of the study, was operationalized as the rates of unoccupied and damaged units within each development. Most housing authority administrators agree that unoccupied and damaged units are sensitive indicators of the overall economic well-being and morale of a public housing development. The percentage of damaged units and unoccupied units was higher in housing developments without Boys and Girls Clubs than in housing developments with the clubs.

Factors That Promote Children as Caregivers

Although the scientific evaluation of the Boys and Girls Clubs did not specifically assess caring, it did assess factors inextricably linked with caring. From observations and interviews with Boys and Girls Club staff and public housing residents, it was clear that club staff routinely modeled behaviors consistent with caregiving. Residents and Boys and Girls Club staff spoke of members emulating such club staff behaviors as respect for others, attentive listening, helping, teaching, and coaching fellow members. Of special note was the particularly strong influence of Boys and Girls Club staff who were themselves club alumni. This suggests that caring skills were internalized during youths' formative period of development and then employed when these alumni were in a position of authority and leadership.

Also through observations and interviews, the evaluation team noted that older members appeared to serve in a mentoring role to younger members. These older members helped orient newer or younger members to club activities and rules. Older members, like the alumni Boys and Girls Club staff, served as a reminder to newer or younger members that a level of competency, usefulness, and influence was well within their reach. In addition, each Boys and Girls Club encouraged adult residents to participate as volunteers. Adult residents assisted in program activities, provided homework help, chaperoned trips, and organized and implemented fundraisers. Such visible volunteerism served as further example of caregiving to youth Boys and Girls Club members.

Finally, every year Boys and Girls Clubs record a set of "best practices" in a self-assessment document known as *Commitment to*

Quality. These best practices are also the focus of training for Boys and Girls Club professionals. Many of these best practices are specifically directed at developing and nurturing a caring capacity in young people. The following statements appear in the *Commitment to Quality* assessment tool:

- Members actively participate in keeping the Club neat and clean, putting away equipment and supplies after programs and activities.
- There is genuine caring and respect demonstrated between and among staff and members. There is no name calling, labeling or stigmatizing.
- Walls and bulletin boards in all program areas are covered with names, photos and notes giving recognition to members.
- Staff, volunteers and junior leaders demonstrate, consistently reinforce, and encourage honesty, responsibility, fairness and respect for people and property.
- Staff, volunteers, and junior leaders continually praise members for good deeds and appropriate behavior and encourage participation in all program areas.
- Older members with appropriate training serve as volunteers or junior staff leaders.
- Members participate in a wide range of activities which enable them to get along with others and make new friends.
- Members participate in Club and/or community service projects conducted quarterly (e.g., hospital visits, tutoring, big brother/big sister, working with disabled, etc.).
- Members receive training and opportunities for helping other members with decision making, school work, personal issues.

Without question, the above principles contribute to the development of caring among the Boys and Girls Club members and staff. Nationwide, Boys and Girls Clubs strive to adhere to principles that clearly encourage caring, both between members and staff and among members themselves.

Strategies for Success

The apparent success of Boys and Girls Clubs in creating more caring communities in public housing developments can be partially attributed to the community organizing that accompanies the establishment of a Boys and Girls Club, as well as to the club's staff and programs. These fundamental strategies include involving residents and resident councils in the establishment of each club. Thus, parents and other adult residents are given the opportunity to guide club operations by serving as members of an advisory committee and supporting the club through volunteer activities and fundraising. Further opportunities are available as parents and other residents meet with and mobilize community leaders from business, industry, law enforcement, education, and government to improve the environment and create a safer community for children, adolescents, and adults. As a result, the establishment of a Boys and Girls Club is a collaborative effort among housing authorities, residents, and Boys and Girls Clubs of America.

At the time of the study reported in this paper, forty Boys and Girls Clubs existed in public housing. Today, there are 200 clubs in 200 public housing developments across America. Clearly, the results of the evaluation reinforced the impact of Boys and Girls Clubs on the community and, by extension, contributed to the increase of Boys and Girls Clubs in public housing.

Conclusion

Based on analyses of data collected from public housing sites that have newly established Boys and Girls Clubs, existing clubs, or no clubs, several conclusions from the longitudinal study are empirically warranted. Foremost among these conclusions is that the establishment of a Boys and Girls Club in public housing positively impacts that housing development. Boys and Girls Clubs exert a positive and palpable influence on the human and physical environment of public housing sites.

Through interviews, members of the evaluation team discovered that the presence of Boys and Girls Clubs in public housing encourages residents to organize and improve their community. Residents serve on the club advisory committee, participate in club activities, raise funds for the club, and serve as club volunteers. Moreover, Boys and Girls Clubs stimulate communication between public housing residents, the police, housing authority managing personnel, and other community groups. That increase in communication enriches the safety and the social life of the public housing environment. For example, the evaluation team noted such safety measures as more police presence and installation of outdoor lighting after the establishment of a Boys and Girls Club. Similar communication led to increased services for families, such as counseling for drug users, parenting classes, and social events for families, in other club environments. Such interaction and communication is perhaps one of the most important effects of the Boys and Girls Clubs.

Although social support services are critical for youth in housing projects, comprehensive and sensitive services for young people in housing projects are practically nonexistent. These housing project communities are the ones that most urgently need the kind of attention, community organization, and carefully designed intervention programs that the Boys and Girls Clubs have generated. Yet research funding is rarely available for the type of evaluation necessary to document the impact of such a youth development program.

Although the long-term impact of Boys and Girls Clubs in housing projects is yet to be seen and is difficult to measure, our evaluation reveals the clubs' positive influence on caring in the communities surveyed. Our society urgently needs the kind of cost-effective strategy of intervention the Boys and Girls Clubs provide, so that we can learn to prevent substance abuse and other kinds of maladaptive behavior before they become too costly and too entrenched to treat.

References

National Commission on Children. *Beyond Rhetoric*. Washington, D.C.: National Commission on Children, 1991.

National Commission on Severely Distressed Public Housing. *Final Report*. Washington, D.C.: National Commission on Severely Distressed Public Housing, 1992.

Part Three

Civic and Religious Traditions of Care

While Part One explores the range of variables that create a disposition of care and Part Two examines specific programs in which children are the givers and receivers of care, Part Three focuses on the civic and religious frameworks of consciousness that shape our understanding of the philosophical nature and practical duties of care. There are of course numerous cultural traditions actively shaping the philanthropic values of contemporary Americans. The following chapters address four such traditions. The first is the American humanitarian ethos, according to which individuals are taught the responsibilities and trained in the skills of public service. The remaining three chapters examine the impact, respectively, of the Jewish, Islamic, and Christian religious faiths on the conduct of charitable activity. But in each instance, the crucial point is that cultural beliefs actively shape the intensity and direction of people's voluntary commitments. The chapters in this section are on solid research footing when they imply that sentiments, emotions, values, and conscience are as important as institutional factors in mobilizing the performance of care.

In Chapter Eight, Peter Dobkin Hall traces the historical ebb and flow of the ethos of *leadership education*, which he defines as the range of activities that include "values and citizenship training, character building, and forms of experiential education that feature voluntary community and national service." This effort to identify and train citizen leaders to make democracy work is rooted in the Jeffersonian concern to encourage an "aristocracy of talent." Religious bodies, evangelicalism, informal education societies, mutual improvement groups, and value-laden formal education all actively tried to form individuals as moral agents capable of shaping their institutional environment. By the 1930s, however, there was growing concern that the transmission of the public moral ethos had disappeared from the public agenda. There was little sympathy for the mission of character formation until President Kennedy's Peace Corps and President Johnson's Great Society revived the idea of transmitting the virtues of social concern and national service to youth. Although floundering during the Bush-Reagan era of self-actualization, leadership education appears to have undergone a renewed impetus as President Clinton's national service program and groups like the Christian Coalition once again enlist the traditions of civic and religious values for character formation aimed at public service.

Chapter Nine—featuring Eliezer David Jaffe's discussion of free loan associations in Israel—is the first of three chapters on religious faith as a mobilizing framework of consciousness for transmitting care across generations. In the Jewish tradition, *gemiluth chasidim* (mutual aid) refers to an act of benevolence that expects no recompense, and in particular to the granting of interest-free loans designed to avoid embarrassing the recipient and to observe the prohibition against accruing interest from fellow Jews. Jaffe's research focuses on neighborhood-based interest-free loan associations in the Jerusalem area that grant interest-free loans of money and goods ranging from baby bottles to medicines. Jaffe finds that these associations tend to be founded by religious Jews, serve the religious sector, are funded by local and international private sources rather than government, tend not to be officially registered as nonprofit associations, and are run by volunteers. They also receive many more appeals than they are able to fill, require that their applicants be Jews, and seldom grant loans worth more than $500. Although these loan associations are often insular, their moral intention, concrete service, and familial style make them worthy of international emulation wherever there is a need for innovative local initiatives with an ethos of self-help.

The second chapter on the effect of religious faith on philanthropy—Chapter Ten—is Amani Kandil's study of Islamic nonprofit organizations in Egypt. Kandil points out that *Zakat* or obligatory charitable tithing of 2.5 percent of income to benefit the poor is one of the five pillars of Islam. *Zakat* funds are often distributed directly to those in need but are also a major source of funding for Islamic nonprofit organizations. In addition to *Zakat*, Islam also embraces the less obligatory tradition of *Sadakat*. This is a form of personal voluntary giving used to help the poor, to fund voluntary activity among members of a mosque, and to support Sufi orders dedicated to an ethos of service. Due to their form of governance and dedication to *Zakat* and *Sadakat*, Islamic nonprofit organizations are particularly effective in mobilizing volunteers and addressing social needs. Comprising 34 percent of Egypt's nonprofits, Islamic organizations make a substantial contribution to health, education, and assistance to the poor. In view of such effectiveness, the government of Egypt has partly adopted Islamic discourse to promote individual care even though the secular state tends to distrust Islamic civil institutions because of their potential to create political dissent.

In Chapter Eleven, John E. Tropman continues the examination of the relationship between religious frameworks and philanthropy by focusing on the distinctive charitable orientation of the Catholic ethic. As opposed to the Protestant ethic, the Catholic ethic is communally based, cooperative rather than competitive, and encourages a culture of sharing. Tropman summarizes research findings documenting a distinctive Catholic perspective and suggesting how a Catholic approach to charity might differ from a Protestant approach. He concludes that more research is needed to confirm the indications that the two ethics produce different charitable behavior.

Chapter Eight

A History of Leadership Education in the United States

Peter Dobkin Hall

The term *leadership education* has historically embraced a broad range of activities, including values and citizenship training, character building, and forms of experiential education that feature voluntary community and national service. Although sometimes differing in their motives and methods, these seemingly diverse activities have in common the conviction that individuals do not stand alone but are part of larger communities. Accordingly, a central part of the educational task is to teach individuals the values that define their obligations to these larger communities as well as ways that they can carry out these obligations.

Leadership education, as an effort to transmit to future generations the values of a caring society, has a long history. Americans today, who are making major investments of time, money, and expertise nurturing leadership, have much to learn from these efforts. This is true regardless of whether leadership is defined narrowly, as a matter of educating executives and board members with particular skills, or broadly, as a matter of training people willing to assume broad responsibilities for the well-being of their communities.

Note: The research on which this chapter is based was generously supported by the Lilly Endowment, the Rockefeller Archives Center, the American Association of Fund Raising Counsel Trust for Philanthropy, and the Program on Non-Profit Organizations, Yale University.

Leaders for a New Nation

There is nothing new in Americans' anxieties about leadership. The domination of economic life by market relationships—a transformation largely complete by the beginning of the nineteenth century—eliminated any easy means of discerning "natural" leadership. Distinguished forebears and inherited wealth, which had counted for so much in the colonial period, became less and less important.

As soon as Americans realized that their "republican experiment" precluded any possibility of "natural" leadership defined by lineage or wealth, they began to worry about how to create and identify leaders. Some worried more than others. Thomas Jefferson believed that the people needed no special preparation for self-government and that the major threat to freedom came from oppressive Old World institutions: primogeniture, entail (limiting the inheritance of property to certain heirs), the Common Law, and established religion. With the vestiges of feudal privilege abolished, Jefferson believed that an "aristocracy of talent" would emerge—leaders who would prove their worthiness by their superior knowledge and their powers of persuasion capable of reinventing and reshaping institutions to suit the nation's needs.

Leaders like Timothy Dwight were far less optimistic. A Calvinist who deeply distrusted human nature, Dwight believed that republican institutions were insufficient, in and of themselves, to preserve freedom. Without the proper values to guide them, the darkest and most anarchic impulses would be let loose in individuals and in society. While Dwight strongly supported the Revolution, he wondered how the new nation could survive once its founding generation passed from the scene. Unlike Jefferson, who was relatively indifferent to educational issues, Dwight believed that people could be schooled in virtue and that the workings of the electoral and economic marketplace could, with the proper influence, bring superior leaders to the fore (Jefferson, [1778] 1990a, 39–47, 131–155; Cunningham, 1942).

Popular assumptions notwithstanding, Americans at the end of the eighteenth century were unsupportive—if not openly hostile—to education and religion. Outside of New England, few states required citizens to support schools, and even where common schools existed, their quality was miserably poor. Churches too were in decline. Plunged into turmoil by a half-century of intense religious controversy following the Great Awakening, threatened by efforts to abolish their tax-supported status, and openly challenged by atheists and freethinkers, by the 1790s, according to some estimates, fewer than a third of the population even bothered to attend church (Dwight, 1817, vol. 4, pp. 410–411). Even in New England, churches and schools languished, especially in the poorer rural areas.

Thus, while conservatives like Dwight worried about leadership and about the problems of passing intact to the future the new nation's hard-won liberties, they found that they lacked even the most fundamental means of acting on their concerns. While believing that formal institutions—schools and churches—were the vehicles of choice for inculcating knowledge and values in the mass of the people and for bringing forward future leaders, the lack of reliable public support for these institutions posed a seemingly insurmountable problem. Added to this was the fact that, even with public support, educational institutions would hardly have a universal impact, since a large proportion of the young entered apprenticeships at early ages.

The response of Dwight and his fellow conservatives was to spearhead a new wave of religious revivals—the Second Great Awakening—which explicitly played on the fears and anxieties of post-Revolutionary Americans. The bloody excesses of the French Revolution were made to resonate with local disturbances like Shays' and Fries' rebellions in fiery sermons, poems, and pamphlets. These stirring messages circulated through New England towns and in the South and West, where New Englanders were settling in great numbers (Dwight, [1788] 1954; Parrington, 1954; Phillips, 1983). Framed by an explicit political agenda, the Awakening went far beyond strengthening churches, which were used as the foundations for the establishment of new kinds of civic institutions. In addition to setting up religiously oriented Bible, tract, temperance, moral reform, and other kinds of benevolent associations, the evangelicals established schools, libraries, colleges, and charitable institutions (Foster, 1960; Hall and Hall, 1982; Marsden, 1990).

Informal Institutions and Leadership Education

By the 1820s, foreign observers like Alexis de Tocqueville believed that the most important mechanism of citizen education was the political life of the towns and villages: "Town meetings are to liberty what primary schools are to science; they bring it within the people's reach, they teach men how to use and how to enjoy it. A nation may establish a free government, but without municipal institutions it cannot have the spirit of liberty" (Tocqueville, [1835] 1945, vol. 1, p. 63).

Unlike other political arenas, where property qualifications and other impediments largely restricted participation to men of property and standing, town government was open to virtually any white male. Still, formidable obstacles remained in the way of popular leadership. Effective participation in public forums required access to information, knowledge of law and procedure, and a capacity to formulate and express ideas about public issues—none of which were freely available before the early decades of the nineteenth century.

In this setting, the notions of self-education and mutual education by voluntary groups described by Benjamin Franklin in his *Autobiography* (1961) take on particular relevance. A printer's apprentice of humble origins, Franklin joined with others like himself in the 1730s to form "a club for mutual improvement which we called the Junto." Meeting once a week, every member was required to "produce one or two queries on any point of morals, politics, or natural philosophy, to be discussed by the company, and once in three months produce and read an essay of his own writing on any subject he pleased" (pp. 72–74).

The group, which read, studied, and conducted debates was, in Franklin's view, "the best school of philosophy, and politics that then existed in the province" (p. 74). The apprentices learned the basic techniques of reasoning and persuasion, learned to address public issues, and, most importantly, learned to frame and act on common purposes. Not surprisingly, the club became the basis for other more ambitious public projects such as Philadelphia's subscription library, volunteer fire company, hospital, and university.

Franklin's experiments in self and mutual education were widely emulated. By the 1780s, even in small towns and villages, such associations, in which young men pooled their resources to buy books and which featured debates and discussion of public issues, were becoming the nuclei for broader kinds of political and economic mobilization—often to the dismay of the wealthy, learned, and respectable.

Citizens in one small Connecticut town recalled "a Society formed in Durham about thirty years since, by the youngerly and middle aged men, which excited considerable anxiety among the people." "We used frequently to discuss religious questions and sometimes political ones," recalled farmer and shoemaker Manoah Camp. Its purpose was "to accustom us to express our ideas and induce us to read. . . . The object of the Society was to make us bold, and learn to read—to be friends to each other, and friends to the world—to watch the sick, &c. In our discussions I don't know as we calculated to side according to principle, but to strengthen the mind" (Converse, 1822, p. 51).

While Durham's Esothian Society eventually broke up, its influence endured. Much as Franklin and his self-schooled friends moved to positions of ever-greater influence in Philadelphia and ultimately in the life of the colonies, so Durham's ambitious young men became the leaders of political and religious dissent in the town. The Society also became the model for other more sharply honed instruments of political and economic empowerment. They organized dissenting religious congregations, political associations, and business firms, which transformed the economy of their isolated village and helped to move it into the center of the state's intense debate over political freedom and religious tolerance (Van Beynum, 1959).

Evangelical Religion and Secular Leadership

Groups like Durham's Esothian Society redoubled the concerns of conservatives and caused them to redouble their commitment to building church-related institutions. Curiously, the formal institutions of education, while framed by explicit concerns about preparing citizens to meet the challenges of democracy, did little in their curricula to address these needs. For example, the Yale Report of 1828, which boldly outlined the college's educational mission and in many ways set the agenda of American higher education for the next half century, stressed the importance of the values underlying the curriculum. But little in the curriculum came close to providing the knowledge and skills that bore directly on public life. Offering studies of Scripture and ancient languages and literature, Yale and other colleges would not feature courses on American history, government, or other relevant subjects until after the Civil War.

Ironically, students probably were better prepared for public life by the religious values that permeated the curriculum than by the subjects themselves. The transformation of Calvinism wrought by Timothy Dwight and his protégé, Nathaniel W. Taylor, in stressing the importance of the individual as a moral agent capable of influencing and changing social and political institutions unquestionably provided young minds with "*discipline* and *furniture*." These attributes rendered Yale men and other graduates of evangelical colleges extraordinarily prolific as founders and directors of voluntary associations. At the same time, the continuing use of disputations as part of the educational process helped to hone the debating and public speaking skills of students. Nevertheless, the major arenas for leadership training remained informal. Reacting to curricula that were largely indifferent to public issues, students at American colleges emulated their nonacademic peers in forming societies for study, debate, and good fellowship.

Recognizing their power, younger evangelical leaders like Lyman Beecher turned their attention to organizing these Junto-like clubs. Although one of Dwight's protégés and nominally a supporter of church establishment, Beecher came to believe that voluntary support actually made churches stronger because it ensured that they would be gatherings of genuinely committed believers. Further, as he watched with dismay the increasing political and economic disorderliness of the Jacksonian era, Beecher became convinced that the churches could play a particularly powerful role—not as direct political actors, but as forces for the political empowerment of their members.

After taking up a pastorate in Boston in the early 1820s, Beecher began experimenting with methods of politically educating the young men of his congregation. "When I came to Boston," he would recall, "evangelical people had no political influence there, and in civil affairs those who joined them had but little chance. All offices were in the hands of Unitarians—perhaps a Baptist occasionally; hence, as young men came in from the town, there was a constant stream of proselytes to them. But as the revival went on, I had a large number of young men that joined the church . . . the finest set you ever laid eyes on" ([1864] 1961, vol. 2, p. 107). He invited one of his young parishioners to come to his parsonage, where he proceeded to explain to him "the operation of political patronage." "The whole influence of Unitarianism a poisonous bribery," he continued,

> "My opinion is, we can stop it. There must be ten men in our Church—you one—that can assemble in a confidential meeting, and make such arrangements as will do it." I named twelve to bring

to me. He did. I explained to them, and said, "You may exert a power that shall be felt throughout the United States. . . . Now organize a society. Go to primary meetings; go to this and that man, and persuade them to go and do up the business. . . .

These young men met monthly (the "Hanover Association of Young Men" they called it), and had committees on various important matters relating to state of city and things needing to be done. . . .

One of their reports was on lotteries, and it was so well drawn that afterward, when it came into the Legislature, it was embodied in the law that was passed. Nobody ever knew where that movement came from. They never knew what hurt 'em.

They got up a petition to sweep off the booths for ardent spirits on the Common on public days. They got Channing's name, and the deputy-governor, and supreme judges, and lower judges, merchants, and carried into the city council the largest number of signatures ever before known before that time to any such document. It failed the first year, but carried the following. The next public day there was not one of the booths, and they have never been put back since. But they never knew where *that* came from either.

The Association was organized in January, 1827, and before the year was out there were four other Associations of the same kind formed in the city [vol. 2, pp. 107–108].

Beecher's efforts to teach young people the power of voluntary action were astoundingly successful. But they were not confined to denominational, political, or public morality issues alone. As Franklin had discovered three-quarters of a century earlier, the empowering character of voluntary action made it difficult to confine to any one sphere of action. In 1850, Amasa Walker, one of the founders of the Hanover Street Association, described its role in establishing lyceums—public educational lectures, often featuring well-known writers, orators, and ministers (Beecher, [1864] 1961, vol. 2, pp. 109–110). "It is impossible," Walker declared, "to realize the great importance of this Lyceum effort in changing the public state, and in giving a higher and better tone to the public mind. Individual voluntary associations pass away, but ideas become impressed upon society never to be obliterated. Lyceums, however transient as organizations, have produced a social revolution in a most essential particular, and the several lecturers who now traverse the broad territory of the United States, entertaining thousands with their eloquence, have been created by the new tastes generated by the Lyceum movement" (vol. 2, pp. 109–110).

Walker went on to summarize what he regarded as Beecher's "vast influence" in Boston "through the various agencies he set in motion." The young men's associations he created—and that were emulated by other congregations—gave "such an impetus to the public mind that societies of young men were formed for a great variety of kindred objects" (vol. 2, p. 110).

Leadership and Stewardship

While Beecher concerned himself with the practical dimensions of the "voluntary system"—throwing his energies into advocating voluntarism and establishing and mobilizing new organizations—he left the task of working out the conceptual implications of voluntarism to others. The conceptual side of voluntarism was crucially important because, at the beginning of the nineteenth century, neither democratic political theory nor Protestant theology regarded voluntary associations as legitimate instruments of public purpose. Assailed by liberals and conservatives alike as "instruments of faction" dangerous to republican institutions, proponents of voluntary associations were hard put to create a rationale that would define their public character. Efforts to impart public character to associations through incorporation by legislatures were objectionable because they expanded the power of government into constitutionally protected domains, such as religion and private morality. They also created "little commonwealths" of privileged individuals who, while acting under the cover of public purpose, reaped personal gain.

Leonard Bacon (1832), a protégé of Beecher's, overcame these problems, first by refining his mentor's conceptions of individual moral agency in ways that deemphasized the role of the church as direct political actor and stressed its role as an institution that empowered individual believers to be moral agents whose primary arena of action was the secular world. Bacon's subsequent work directly engaged the issues of organizational legitimacy and authority in a democracy by suggesting that these, rather than proceeding from electoral or political accountability, proceeded from the fiduciary responsibilities imposed on trustees as managers of the property of others. These involved both religious elements of stewardship and formal legal elements that proceeded from the equitable relationship of trustees to donors and beneficiaries, living and dead (Bacon, 1847b, pp. 28–40).

The notion that there were legitimate alternatives to democratic government that were, at the same time, grounded in the popular will and that nurtured and sustained it, spurred the growth of voluntary organizations and encouraged their expansion into new domains of activity. More important, by firmly linking the idea of values and character to private institutions, this idea legitimated the evangelicals' claim that they were responsible for training those who would take the lead in public life.

From Evangelicalism to Character Education

The influence of clergymen like Beecher and Bacon went far beyond New England. Their eloquence, tireless lecture tours, and strategic location within the extensive organizational networks of the evangelical movement guaranteed the rapid spread of their ideas. Domestic missionary and tract societies ensured that the evangelical message was carried not only to the new settlements on the frontier, but into the cities. The impact of these efforts was reinforced by privately funded "education societies," which made scholarship funds available to pious and indigent young men who, after completing their degrees, went on either to become ministers or laymen active in the evangelical movement. These institutions were further sustained by an outpouring of New Englanders—including Beecher himself, who eventually settled in Ohio—to the cities and new settlements of the West and South.

Wherever they went, the New England evangelicals used their organizational abilities both to promote their own fortunes and to work for what they defined as the public good. And, while sometimes physically isolated from one another, they remained closely linked, not only through the comings and goings of touring lecturers and evangelical preachers like Beecher, but also through the newspapers, periodicals, and, eventually, the national lyceum lecture circuits. Thus Tocqueville ([1835] 1945, vol. 1, p. 32) would observe that "the principles of New England spread at first to the neighboring states; they then passed successively to more distant ones; and at late, if I may so speak, they *interpenetrated* the whole confederation. . . . The civilization of New England has been like a beacon lit upon a hill, which, after it has suffused its warmth immediately around it, also tinges the distant horizon with its glow."

Though certainly exaggerating the extent of New England's influence at the time he wrote, by the 1860s his prophetic observation had been largely fulfilled. Moreover, the evangelical influence was both *extensive* and *intensive*. The basic focus of evangelicalism was neither building church membership nor making public life more virtuous: its objective was, in Weber's terms, the "thoroughgoing Christianization of the whole life" (p. 124) and its transformation into a "methodically rationalized system of ethical conduct" (Weber, [1904–1905] 1958, p. 125). Thus, the reorganization of domestic life, and along with it the reconfiguration of the roles of parents and children, were part and parcel of the broader reorganization of society (Cross, 1965; Sklar, 1973; Douglas, 1977). Parenting was important because it prepared the young for the institutional ministrations of church and school—which, in turn, empowered them as moral agents in the worlds of commerce, politics, and the professions.

It became evident by mid-century that the evangelicals had largely succeeded in bringing Americans back to the fold of organized religion—with some 75 percent of Americans church affiliated (Finke and Stark, 1992). Heralded by the writings of Catherine Beecher and ministers like Horace Bushnell, whose controversial essay "Christian Nurture" (1847) focused on the relation of parental influence and training to the formation of Christian character in children, the evangelicals' emphasis shifted from saving the unconverted to overseeing the shaping the lives of children and teenagers.[1]

The evangelicals had always been interested in the young: Timothy Dwight was writing about the importance of education and character formation as early as the 1780s, and the Sunday school movement dated back to the 1820s. But because Calvinist theology required believers to undergo a conversion experience, institutional energies were primarily directed to adults who had attained some measure of intellectual and emotional maturity. As Bushnell (1847, p. 178) put it, because "the Church of New England recognized no gradual growth into Christianity . . . , children had no participation in the religious life of their parents, and no rights in the church as a home." Christian nurture downplayed the importance of individual conversion and suggested that children could be gently and steadily led toward belief through "Christian nurture" in the family setting.

In response to this focus on the family as a vehicle for transmitting values, the churches began shifting their institutional energies toward the young. Sunday schools, originally intended to serve the poor, were redesigned for the children of believers, and their programs became increasingly elaborate. To provide for children too old for Sunday school, congregations began forming young people's societies.

The Christian nurture movement coincided—and eventually

meshed with—the transformation of mutual improvement groups that served young men. Because such young men's societies had originally been tinged with political radicalism and were often openly antireligious, they became particular targets for evangelicals who, like Beecher, understood their power. Although Christian societies serving young men were established in various places from the 1820s on, these efforts began to coalesce in the 1850s, with the formation of the Young Men's Christian Association (YMCA) in Boston in 1852 at a ceremony presided over by Lyman Beecher (Hopkins, 1951, p. 18). Featuring libraries, prayer meetings, Bible classes, employment bureaus, boarding house registers, and aggressive social programs, YMCAs spread rapidly: by 1856, such organizations had been established in some fifty-six cities.

The founders of the Y understood early on that, to muster broad support, the organization would have to be nondenominational and would have to offer programs and services that would make them attractive to the footloose and fancy-free young men of the cities. They early on began providing recreational facilities, including gymnasiums, baths, and programs designed to foster physical development. Disciplined and supervised recreational activity, with its emphasis on teamwork and sportsmanship, was more than a come-on: it was seen as an important means of character and values training.

Interpenetrated and sustained by the values- and character-training efforts of families and churches, the Y's became the seedbed of more far-reaching efforts to transform American community life. Although they were nonpolitical institutions, the civic values that infused every aspect of the Y's activities necessarily encouraged various kinds of—usually nonpartisan—reformist activism in their members. Most often these took the form of efforts to extend values-training endeavors to the public schools, through public parks and recreation programs, and through the establishment of such character-building voluntary groups as the Boys Club (1906), Boy Scouts (1910), and Girl Scouts (1912).[2]

To a significant extent, values-training efforts in the early twentieth century replicated their predecessors in that they were not merely directed to the rote learning of values, but stressed learning by doing. Both voluntary efforts like the scouts and public ones based in the schools encouraged the young to practice and master democratic forms of conduct. By the 1920s, schools increasingly featured "student governments" and fostered the growth of athletic teams and special interest clubs as a means of helping students learn how to govern themselves.

The study of Muncie, Indiana, by Robert Lynd and Helen Lynd (1929) noted that by 1925, the "informal kind of training" offered by school "athletics, clubs, sororities and fraternities, dances and parties, and other 'extracurricular activities'" had become "a fairly complete cosmos in itself. . . . Here the social sifting devices of their elders—money, clothes, personal attractiveness, male physical prowess, exclusive clubs, election to positions of leadership—are for the first time set going with a population as yet largely undifferentiated." This widening of the school function had taken place since the 1890s, when the only organized extracurricular activity was a single literary society (Lynd and Lynd, 1929, pp. 211–222). At the same time, these endeavors served as sorting mechanisms for identifying and giving encouragement to students with leadership abilities.[3]

The contributors to *Recent Social Trends* (President's Research Committee on Social Trends, 1933) suggested that the expansion of the extracurriculum was hardly spontaneous. Lawrence Frank (1933, pp. 751–752) of the General Education Board, writing on childhood and youth, noted the "outstanding development" in the field was "the growing belief in directing and controlling social life through the care and nurture of children" (also see Steiner, 1933, pp. 912–957). This was taking place not only through the increasing interest of educators and child welfare professionals in "the provision of better opportunities for wholesome child life" through organized youth programs like the scouts and better playgrounds and recreational facilities, but also through the schools, where one of the major objectives had become "preparation for social life."

Noting the expansion of character, moral, and citizenship education programs in the schools, Frank declared that such "efforts to prepare the individual for social life" illustrated "the assumption by the schools of responsibilities formerly considered the duty of the home and church." Especially important, he believed, was the *ethos* of activities that, in pledging "their members to a definite code of conduct," both fostered "specific ideals of conduct and citizenship" and emphasized teamwork rather than competition. Part and parcel of these efforts was a shift in pedagogical emphasis from "teaching to learning." This shift involved "the use of project methods, activities, units, and similar procedures, especially those of group work, to evoke the child's interests and activities within a socialized environment" (p. 752).

Two especially noteworthy facets of the growing investment in character, moral, and citizenship training during this period were the central importance of academically trained professionals—including not only teachers, but social workers and guidance counselors—and the growing attention to the psychological dimensions of education and child development. Through the 1920s, 1930s, and 1940s, these two factors fundamentally transformed both the rhetoric and practice of this aspect of education. The professionals, with their batteries of tests and increasingly arcane jargon, gradually redefined character education from being a set of moral concerns, closely tied to the mission of the churches and core civic institutions, to a set of measurable criteria of psychological and social adjustment.

At the same time, communities themselves were changing, as commuter railroads, rapid transit, trolley and interurban lines, and the automobile permitted increasing numbers of middle-class Americans to move away from the center city (Jackson, 1985). The settlers on the "crabgrass frontier" brought with them many of the institutions that had defined public life in the city—the church, parks and playgrounds, schools, and youth groups. But these institutions came to serve quite a different function in the relatively exclusive and privatized enclaves of the suburbs. Rather than directing the attention of the young to their place as citizens and moral agents in a broad, heterogeneous society, both the extracurriculum and community organizations like the scouts, the Y's, and the churches tended to focus their interests on themselves and to affirm their sense of themselves as members of a privileged class.

Combined with the professionalization and psychologizing of the domains of character and citizenship training, this disagreement of older communities drained such programs of moral content or overarching mission. Thus, by the 1950s, while organized in-school and community activities continued to serve a sorting function, identifying and rewarding those with leadership qualities, they had become merely mechanisms for the replication of adult cliques and the reproduction in miniature of class distinctions. In other words, they had forsaken any claims to a broader leadership training function (Hollingshead, 1949, pp. 163–242).

Reinventing Leadership Education

As early as the 1930s, a handful of Americans were expressing concerns about the decreasing ability of schools and communities to engage and transmit the kinds of encompassing moral and ethical values that they viewed as essential to sustaining a caring society. In the mid 1930s, two books by social psychologists, Ernest M. Ligon's *The Psychology of Christian Personality* (1935) and Henry C. Link's *The Return to Religion* (1936), criticized the increasingly secular, materialistic, and selfishly uncaring tendencies in American society. They also called for the reintroduction of explicitly Christian character education components in family, school, and community. These concerns were echoed from a far more prestigious source, with the publication of *The Crisis of Our Age: The Social and Cultural Outlook* (1941), by Harvard's senior professor of sociology,

Petirim Sorokin. Identifying the crisis in Western civilization as a product of pervasive materialism and "ever expanding appetites for sensory values" (p. 195), Sorokin called for "a change of the whole mentality and attitudes in the direction of the norms prescribed in the Sermon on the Mount" (p. 319) through nurturing "more familialistic and altruistic relationships" (p. 324).

These books came to the attention of Eli Lilly, a wealthy Indiana pharmaceutical manufacturer and philanthropist, who fully shared their authors' views—and who had the resources to act on his convictions (Madison, 1989, pp. 188–223). In the hope of restoring the traditional social values in which he so strongly believed, Lilly provided Ligon and Sorokin with generous funding for academic centers—the Character Research Project at Union College and the Harvard Research Center in Creative Altruism—to underwrite further research and dissemination of their views.

Sorokin's center engaged the participation of such prominent scholars as Paul Tillich, Gordon Allport, F.S.C. Northrop, and Erich Fromm, and Ligon's project, as the primary center of character education in the United States, influenced the activities of churches, Y's, and youth groups. But their activities had little impact on the mainstreams of academic research and education. On the academic side, social and behavioral scientists, funded by government and secularly oriented private foundations to focus on issues of domestic and foreign policy, were uninterested in the kind of broad questions of social philosophy that preoccupied Sorokin and Ligon.[4]

On the community side, despite opinion researchers finding that more Americans than ever believed in a supreme being and that America was a "nation of joiners," neither churches and character-forming youth groups nor the public schools were able or willing to hold such controversial and essentially sectarian positions on ethics and morality.

In spite of broad resistance to the idea of revitalizing character-training and leadership education efforts, a number of influential figures in the business world continued to encourage interest in these issues. A group of top executives at AT&T, which included Chester I. Barnard, Arthur W. Page, and Robert Greenleaf, produced an influential body of literature. This literature both called attention to the moral and ethical dimensions of management and encouraged expansion of the scope and scale of corporate social commitment.

The uniquely reflective corporate culture at AT&T was created by company president Walter S. Gifford, who had begun his career working at Western Electric and living at Jane Addams's Hull House (Gifford, 1924–1949). Arthur W. Page, his classmate at Harvard, had been a progressive journalist and publisher before being recruited by Gifford to run AT&T's public relations office. Page was one of the leaders of a group of executives who, after the Second World War, worked to call corporate America's attention to the nation's values and the role in preserving them (Curti, 1965). These efforts not only stimulated new forms of corporate philanthropy but also helped to focus them on aspects of college curricula specifically concerned with values issues. Barnard, who was president of New York Telephone (an AT&T subsidiary), devoted significant attention to these issues in a pathbreaking volume on the theory of management, *The Functions of the Executive* (1938). Robert Greenleaf, who served as AT&T's director of management research, developed conceptions of "servant leadership" that explored ways of applying Christian ethics to organizational leadership. He summarized this approach in *Servant Leadership* (1977). All of these executives served on the boards of foundations: Gifford and Barnard at the Rockefeller Foundation and the General Education Board, Page at the General Education Board and the Carnegie Corporation, and Greenleaf at Russell Sage. As a consultant to the Lilly Endowment in the late 1970s, Greenleaf played a key role in shaping the foundation's continuing commitment to leadership education.

"Ask Not What Your Country Can Do for You . . ."

Despite the prominence of individuals like Lilly and the AT&T group, concerns about American leadership and how to systematically nurture it remained on the margins of public discourse. Ignored by the academic and religious mainstream, Ligon's work on values education had its greatest impact on fundamentalist denominations, especially the Southern Baptists, who, by the early 1950s, had launched ambitious church-based leadership education programs. These programs had a profound influence on the generation of American political leaders that began to emerge in the 1970s and 1980s: Jimmy Carter, Bill Clinton, and Al Gore were among those whose leadership skills were molded by these efforts.

The religious locus of leadership education efforts began to broaden in the 1960s, as international and domestic political turmoil began to shake American national confidence. With a clarion call for national self-sacrifice, President Kennedy's Peace Corps was the first federal program since the Civilian Conservation Corps to promote youth involvement in national service. Under Lyndon Johnson's War on Poverty, this emphasis was vastly expanded through Volunteers in Service to America (VISTA) and other efforts to develop leadership, citizenship, and community organizing skills among the disadvantaged young. Later, the Youth Development Program (YDP), a component of the Community Action Agency program of the Office of Economic Opportunity, sought to create "a trained cadre" of community advocates who could give the poor a voice in efforts to fight the War on Poverty.[5] These programs garnered more than their share of adverse publicity—and were among the first to disappear as the Nixon administration dismantled Lyndon Johnson's Great Society.

As the Great Society disintegrated in a welter of intensifying protest, much of it initiated by young radicals, John D. Rockefeller 3rd, convened a task force to explore the dimensions of the "so-called youth revolt."[6] Unlike most of the American establishment, Rockefeller believed that the rising tide of political dissent among the young betokened "a profound shift in cultural values" in which young people, "deeply concerned about basic values, [were] rejecting what they regard as an overly materialistic society resisting necessary change."

In a widely publicized speech made in the fall of 1968, Rockefeller challenged the Establishment to "bring together our age and experience and money and organization with the energy and idealism and social consciousness of the young." Instead of seeking to suppress the youth revolution, "we of the older generation should be worrying about how to sustain it." The student activists, he declared, "perform a service in shaking us out of our complacency. We badly need their ability and fervor in these troubled and difficult times." "We of the older generation," he continued, "must reexamine our attitudes, our assumptions, and our goals. . . . We must have a sense of responsibility, individually and collectively, for solving the massive problems of our society." He urged that Americans work to "revitalize our existing institutions, whether they be in education, government, religion, or politics. They must be made more relevant to today's problems, have a greater sense of mission . . ." (Rockefeller, 1973, pp. 5–6).

Rockefeller organized a Task Force on Youth, which commissioned extensive surveys on the values and attitudes of young people and which promoted dialogue between young people and business and community leaders.[7] Insights from these efforts were incorporated into Rockefeller's book *The Second American Revolution: Some Personal Observations* (1973). As he made clear, he was not only interested in examining and engaging the values of the young—he wanted to empower them through training programs that would enable "the disenfranchised (youth, minorities, etc.) to acquire the skills necessary for a participatory role in their communities."[8]

Identifying with the youthful dissenters' frustration with institutional unresponsiveness and self-serving public and private bureaucracies, Rockefeller believed that revitalizing America's philanthropic and voluntary organizations was central to his efforts to engage the changing values of American young people. To this end, in 1974 he convened a Commission on Private Philanthropy and Public Needs (the Filer Commission) to explore and redefine the scale and scope of voluntary and philanthropic activities in the United States. Had Rockefeller not died in 1978, the institutionalization of the Filer Commission's efforts would probably have included a greater emphasis on training young people to participate in Third Sector organizations.

"A Thousand Points of Light"

The neoconservative revolution heralded by the 1980s election of Ronald Reagan was accompanied by a rising chorus of concern over the nation's future and, in particular, the strength of its values. While attempting to dismantle government social commitments, the new administration aggressively promoted "traditional" values of family, church, community—and voluntary action. Early in 1981, the president convened a Task Force on Private Sector Initiatives, which brought together business, philanthropic, and community leaders to discuss the ways private initiatives could take on responsibilities for the poor and dependent.

As with so much else in the Reagan-Bush era, the promotion of private initiative was long on rhetoric and short on substance. The administration failed to understand that, by the 1980s, the federal government had become the largest single source of revenue for nonprofits—and that cutbacks in federal programs would inevitably cripple the very sector it hoped to sustain (Salamon and Abramson, 1982). While it dramatically cut taxes for the wealthy, it made no effort to strengthen incentives for philanthropic giving. And its stress on "traditional values" was meaningless in a nation increasingly diverse religiously, ethnically, and racially, in which ever-larger numbers of families were headed by single parents, and in which public and private community institutions were being devastated by cuts in government spending.

While national philanthropic and voluntary organizations flourished during the 1980s, they showed surprisingly little interest in youth-oriented citizenship and leadership education efforts. Although they made significant efforts to promote teaching and research on philanthropic and voluntary activity and in building degree programs for nonprofit managers, these programs focused more on philanthropy and voluntarism as an academic subject than as a means of community empowerment (Hodgkinson, 1988; Hall, 1992). Moreover, along with efforts to recruit and train trustees, they were aimed more at adults than at the young, who had traditionally been the target for leadership and citizenship training.

By the end of the 1980s, there were a few encouraging signs of real concern for "transmitting the values of a caring society to future generations" (INDEPENDENT SECTOR, 1993). A handful of foundations, notably the Lilly Endowment, maintained and expanded their commitment to leadership education in programs operating in universities, churches, and schools.[9] Many universities, encouraged by such groups as Campus Compact and Campus Outreach Opportunity League (COOL), have encouraged student voluntarism and community service and a few have made such service a requirement for graduation.[10] Some communities have created programs of this sort aimed at younger children in public and private schools. And a welter of programs intended to encourage national and community service have been debated in Congress, which in 1990 passed the National and Community Service Act to provide funds, training, and technical assistance to states and communities to develop and expand service opportunities.

These efforts were strangely disconnected from the motives that had traditionally underlain efforts to serve communities. The continuing social commitment of American religion was reflected in its growing investment in community-based social programs ranging from day care and soup kitchens through such ambitious programs as Habitat for Humanity. Yet neither religious rhetoric nor involvement by churches and denominations was anywhere evident. This was not, it appears, accidental. As Harry Boyte (1991, p. 626)—a critic of the movement—has written, the new community service movement has adopted "the therapeutic language of personal development that now pervades society." The learning objectives for its activities include goals like "self-esteem," "a sense of personal worth," "self-understanding," "independence," "personal belief in the ability to make a difference," "consciousness about one's personal values," "openness to new experiences," "capacity to persevere in difficult tasks," "exploration of new identities and unfamiliar roles," and "skills in caring for others."

At the same time, Boyte noted, the movement is singularly devoid of political content and, because of this, lacks a capacity to grasp either the policy dimensions of poverty, homelessness, drug use, and illiteracy, or "the complex dynamics of power, race, and class" that underlie them (p. 627). Because it does not give student volunteers a conceptual framework, the movement differs significantly from the traditions of citizen and leadership education.

The single encouraging sign that the programs promoting student voluntarism might begin in the 1990s to reanchor themselves in the greater traditions of civic and religious values came in September 1992, when President Clinton spoke to student volunteers at Notre Dame University. After reiterating his own involvement in such citizenship education efforts as the American Legion's Boys' Nation program and his wife's involvement with the Grant Foundation–sponsored Commission on the American Family, Work, and Citizenship, he discoursed at length on the religious roots of community service. "We all have the right to wear our religion on our sleeves," Clinton declared, "but we should also hold it in our hearts and live it in our lives."

> And if we are to truly practice what we preach, then Americans of every faith and viewpoint should look for ways to come together to

> promote the common good. . . . Echoing down the ages is the simple but powerful truth that no grace of God was ever given for me alone. To the terrible question of Cain—am I my brother's keeper?—the only possible answer for us is God's thunderous yes.
>
> As I've traveled across this country, I've spoken with people whose daily experience testifies that a new sense of community is not just a moral imperative, but a practical necessity. . . .
>
> I want an America where service is a way of life. . . . I want Americans to learn in their own way the lesson that you've learned from Catholic social teaching, that our individual rights flow from our essential dignity as creatures of God, but that each one of us reaches our fullness as human beings by being of service to our fellow men and women. . . .
>
> I want an America where every young person and every not so young person understands . . . [that] service is the rent we pay for living [Clinton, 1992].

Conclusion

Clinton's comments suggest that leadership education may be moving into a new phase. While the therapeutic motifs of self-actualization that characterized such efforts during the 1980s seem likely to persist, there appears to be an increasing willingness to justify educating the young for community and national service in explicitly religious and political terms. Part of this stems, no doubt, from the increasing activism of fundamentalist groups like the Christian Coalition, whose efforts to shape political life remarkably resemble those of nineteenth-century evangelicals like Beecher and Bacon. Events in the former communist countries and in the Third World may also be helping leadership education rediscover its religious and political roots. During the cold war, American philanthropy responded to Congressional critics by portraying itself as apolitical and values neutral. However, after 1990, as it became engaged in the task of reconstructing democratic societies abroad, it began to appreciate the extent to which philanthropy and voluntarism were integral to the creation and maintenance of the public and private values that make such societies possible (Etzioni, 1993). Inspired by an awareness of the moral and historical roots of voluntarism, this effort to include civic values as a part of the educational process may yet become a powerful force for transmitting to future generations the traditions of a caring society.

Notes

1. Beecher's writings in this vein include *The Moral Instructor for Schools and Families: Containing Lessons on the Duties of Life, Arranged for Study and Recitation, Also Designed as a Reading Book for Schools* (1838), *Treatise on Domestic Economy for the Use of Young Ladies at Home and at School* (1843), and *The Evils Suffered by American Women and American Children: The Causes and the Remedy* (1846). On the controversy engendered by Horace Bushnell's *Views of Christian Nurture and of Subjects Adjacent Thereto* (1847), see Leonard Bacon, "Bushnell on Christian Nurture" (1847a) and Mary Bushnell Cheney, *Life and Letters of Horace Bushnell* (1880, pp. 178–183). For an excellent appraisal of the importance of Bushnell's work, see Howard A. Barnes, *Horace Bushnell and the Virtuous Republic* (1991).
2. While there has been no systematic study of the civic activism of Y.M.C.A. members, my work on Allentown, Pennsylvania, suggests that, like Franklin's Junto, the Y played an important role in socializing and networking among community leaders. This was not, moreover, merely a matter of confirming those who were already destined for leadership by wealth and family. Allentown's top leaders in the early twentieth century were largely men like Harry and Frank Trexler, who had been born in the countryside and come to the city as young men. Once there, the Y gave them opportunities to

build friendships with others like themselves who worked together to further their economic and political ambitions. The Trexlers and their friends became the key figures in the expansion of the public schools, the abolition of child labor, and the creation of public parks and recreational facilities. On this, see Karyl Lee Hall and Peter Dobkin Hall, *The Lehigh Valley—An Illustrated History* (1982, pp. 75–134), and Hall and Hall, "Allentown, 1870–1900" and "Allentown, 1930–1941" (1987, vol. 1, pp. 289–340; vol. 2, pp. 81–146).

3. Despite the attention devoted to the growth of the extracurriculum by contemporary observers like the Lynds and the contributors to *Recent Social Trends* (President's Research Committee on Social Trends, 1933), there has been no systematic effort to study this phenomenon, which so profoundly shaped the character of American schools. Lawrence Cremin's *American Education: The Metropolitan Experience, 1876–1980* (1988) only mentions in passing efforts to transform the school into a "total educational environment" and the growth of "ancillary institutions intended to strengthen the school's effort to shape adolescents in desirable social directions" (pp. 309–311). And the important bibliographical essay that concludes the volume mentions only a handful of studies on the subject, none of which are primarily devoted to the schools. These include Macleod's *Building Character in the American Boy: The Boy Scouts, YMCA, and Their Forerunners* (1983), Dominick Cavallo's *Muscles and Morals: Organized Playgrounds and Urban Reform, 1880–1920* (1981), Helen Bucker's *Wo-He-Lo: The Camp Fire History* (1980), and Lawrence A. Finfer, "Leisure as Social Work in the Urban Community: The Progressive Recreation Movement, 1890–1920" (1974). Primary sources on the extracurriculum include Thomas M. Deam, *Socializing the Pupil Through Extra-Curriculum Activities* (1928), and A. O. Bowden, *Tomorrow's Americans: A Practical Study in Student Self-Government* (1930).

4. Sorokin and several other prominent older sociologists who shared his views criticized the "empiricist" and overly quantitative research favored by the major foundations in testimony to Congress's Special Committee to Investigate Tax-Exempt Foundations (Reece Committee) in 1954. Sorokin's appearance as a "friendly witness" before a red-baiting committee at the height of the McCarthy era could have hardly made the views he sought to advance attractive to his colleagues. See *Report of the Special Committee to Investigate Tax-Exempt Foundations and Comparable Organizations*, 83rd Congress, 2nd Session, House Report No. 2681 (Washington, D.C.: U.S. Government Printing Office, 1954), pp. 60–95.

   On the increasing importance of government in shaping the focus of the social and behavioral sciences during this period, see Alvin W. Gouldner, *The Coming Crisis of Western Sociology* (1970), Ellen W. Schrecker, *No Ivory Tower: McCarthyism and the Universities* (1986), Robin W. Winks, *Cloak and Gown: Scholars in the Secret War, 1939–1961* (1987), and Sigmund Diamond, *Compromised Campus: The Collaboration of Universities with the Intelligence Community, 1945–55* (1992).

   I am especially grateful to Jay Demerath, who knew Sorokin, whose father was his colleague at Harvard, and who himself was a student in sociology there during the 1950s and 1960s, for sharing with me his recollections and insights into the outlook of his generation of young scholars and their attitudes toward Sorokin's work. He suggests that Sorokin's diminished influence was due less to the politics of the period than to a more general effort to retrieve sociology from the social welfare/reformist orientation into which it had fallen during the 1920s and 1930s.
5. For a good overview of YDP, see *Community Action Agency Youth Development Program Manual* (1972). See also *Leadership Development—A Technical Assistance Pamphlet* (1972).
6. "John D. Rockefeller 3rd," biographical memorandum dated

November 1971 (Rockefeller Archives Center, Family Collection, RG-17, Associates, Box 1, Folder: General).

7. The work of the Task Force is summarized in a memorandum entitled "JDR3rd Fund Form 4653—Amended: Statement re: status as a private operating foundation," dated 4/24/1973 (Rockefeller Archives Center, Family Collection, RG-17, Associates, Datus Smith, Box 1, Folder: JDR3rd Fund/Corporate). The surveys, conducted by Daniel Yankelovich, which were published and widely circulated, included *Youth and the Establishment* (1971), *Youth's Agenda for the Seventies* (1971), *Changing Values on Campus: Personal and Political Attitudes of Today's College Students* (1972), and *Changing Youth Values in the 1970s: A Study of American Youth* (1974).
8. "The Institute," undated memorandum outlining activities to follow from the Youth Task Force's efforts (Rockefeller Archives Center, Family Collection, RG-17, Associates, Datus Smith, Box 2, Folder: JDR3 Fund/Youth/General).
9. For an overview of the scale and scope of the Endowment's commitment to this field, see Lilly Endowment (1990). This workbook contains summaries of some thirty-four research, teaching, and training projects being conducted by universities, consulting firms, community groups, and individual researchers and community activists.
10. I am grateful to Jon Van Til, who generously provided me with an overview of the development of experiential learning and community service programs in American colleges and universities. Published sources on this movement include Benjamin Barber, *An Aristocracy of Everyone: The Politics of Education and the Future of America* (1992), Eric B. Gorham, *National Service, Citizenship, and Political Education* (1992), Jane C. Kendall, *Combining Service and Learning: A Resource Book for Community and Public Service* (1990), William F. Buckley, Jr., *Gratitude: Reflections on What We Owe to Our Country* (1990), Charles C. Moskos, *A Call to Civic Service:*

National Service for Country and Community (1988), and Donald J. Eberly, *National Service: A Promise to Keep* (1988) and *National Service: Social, Economic, and Military Impacts* (1982). Certainly the key document in the current wave of interest in this area is the study *Youth and America's Future* (1988), produced by William T. Grant Foundation–sponsored Commission on Family, Work, and Citizenship. There is an extensive literature of articles about this movement. Especially worthy of note are Harry C. Boyte, "Turning on Youth to Politics: Beyond Community Service" (1991); James Bennet, "1,000 Points of Lite: Bush's Youth Service Scheme" (1988); Thomas Moore and Marianna I. Knight, "Idealism's Rebirth" (1988); William Raspberry, "Not All Students Are Greedy" (1988); and John E. Gallagher and Melissa Ludtke, "Silver Bullets for the Needy: Campuses Are Seeing a Revival of Student Voluntarism" (1987).

References

Bacon, L. *The Christian Doctrine of Stewardship in Relation to Property: A Sermon Preached at the Request of the Young Men's Benevolent Society of New Haven, Connecticut*. New Haven, Conn.: Whiting, 1832.

Bacon, L. "Bushnell on Christian Nurture." *New Englander*, 1847a, 8, 1–47.

Bacon, L. "Responsibility in the Management of Societies." *New Englander*, 1847b, 5, 28–40.

Barber, B. *An Aristocracy of Everyone: The Politics of Education and the Future of America*. New York: Ballantine Books, 1992.

Barnard, C. I. *The Functions of the Executive*. Cambridge, Mass.: Harvard University Press, 1938.

Barnes, H. A. *Horace Bushnell and the Virtuous Republic*. Metuchen, N.J.: Theological Library of America, 1991.

Beecher, C. *The Moral Instructor for Schools and Families: Containing Lessons on the Duties of Life, Arranged for Study and Recitation, Also Designed as a Reading Book for Schools*. Cincinnati, Ohio: Truman & Smith, 1838.

Beecher, C. *Treatise on Domestic Economy for the Use of Young Ladies at Home and at School*. Boston: Webb, 1843.

Beecher, C. *The Evils Suffered by American Women and American Children: The Causes and the Remedy*. 2 vols. New York: HarperCollins, 1846.

Beecher, L. *Autobiography*. Cambridge, Mass.: Harvard University Press, 1961. (Originally published 1864.)

Bennet, J. "1,000 Points of Lite: Bush's Youth Service Scheme." *New Republic*, 1988, *199*(19), 22.

Bowden, A. O. *Tomorrow's Americans: A Practical Study in Student Self-Government*. New York: Putnam, 1930.

Boyte, H. V. "Turning on Youth to Politics: Beyond Community Service." *Nation*, 1991, *252*(18), 626–628.

Bucker, H. *Wo-He-Lo: The Camp Fire History*. Kansas City, Mo.: Camp Fire, Inc., 1980.

Buckley, W. F., Jr. *Gratitude: Reflections on What We Owe to Our Country*. New York: Random House, 1990.

Bushnell, H. *Views of Christian Nurture and of Subjects Adjacent Thereto*. Hartford, Conn.: Hunt, 1847.

Cavallo, D. *Muscles and Morals: Organized Playgrounds and Urban Reform, 1880–1920*. Philadelphia: University of Pennsylvania Press, 1981.

Cheney, M. B. *Life and Letters of Horace Bushnell*. New York: HarperCollins, 1880.

Clinton, W. "Remarks of Governor Clinton at the University of Notre Dame, Sept. 11, 1992." *U.S. Newswire*, Sept. 14, 1992.

Commission on Family, Work, and Citizenship. *Youth and America's Future*. New York: William T. Grant Foundation, 1988.

Community Action Agency Youth Development Program Manual. Prepared by Project MAP, Inc., for the Office of Economic Opportunity. Washington, D.C.: Office of Economic Opportunity, 1972.

Converse, S. *Report of the Case of Joshua Stowe vs. Sherman Converse for a Libel*. New Haven, Conn.: Converse, 1822.

Cremin, L. *American Education: The Metropolitan Experience, 1876–1980*. New York: HarperCollins, 1988.

Cross, B. M. (ed.). *The Educated Woman in America: Selected Writings of Catherine Beecher, Margaret Fuller, and M. Carey Thomas*. New York: Teachers College Press, 1965.

Cunningham, C. E. *Timothy Dwight, 1752–1817*. New York: Macmillan, 1942.

Curti, M. *Philanthropy in the Shaping of American Higher Education*. New Brunswick, N.J.: Rutgers University Press, 1965.

Deam, T. M. *Socializing the Pupil Through Extra-Curriculum Activities*. Chicago: Sanborn, 1928.

Diamond, S. *Compromised Campus: The Collaboration of Universities with the Intelligence Community, 1945–55*. New York: Oxford University Press, 1992.

Douglas, A. *The Feminization of American Culture*. New York: Knopf, 1977.

Dwight, T. *Travels in New England and New York*. 4 vols. New Haven, Conn.: Published by Timothy Dwight, 1817.

Dwight, T. "The Triumph of Infidelity." In Vernon L. Parrington (ed.), *The Connecticut Wits*. New York: Crowell, 1954. (Originally published 1788.)

Eberly, D. J. *National Service: Social, Economic, and Military Impacts*. New York: Pergamon Press, 1982.

Eberly, D. J. *National Service: A Promise to Keep*. Rochester, N.Y.: John Alden Books, 1988.

Etzioni, A. *The Spirit of Community: Rights, Responsibilities, and the Communitarian Agenda*. New York: Crown, 1993.

Finfer, L. A. "Leisure as Social Work in the Urban Community: The Progressive Recreation Movement, 1890–1920." Unpublished doctoral dissertation, Department of History, Michigan State University, 1974.

Finke, R., and Stark, R. *The Churching of America: Winners and Losers in Our Religious Economy*. New Brunswick, N.J.: Rutgers University Press, 1992.

Foster, C. I. *An Errand of Mercy: The Evangelical United Front, 1790–1837*. Chapel Hill: University of North Carolina Press, 1960.

Frank, L. K. "Childhood and Youth." In Research Committee on Social Trends (eds.), *Recent Social Trends*. New York: McGraw-Hill, 1933.

Franklin, B. "Autobiography." In J. Lemisch (ed.), *Benjamin Franklin: The Autobiography and Other Writings*. New York: Signet Books, 1961.

Gallagher, J. E., and Ludtke, M. "Silver Bullets for the Needy: Campuses Are Seeing a Revival of Student Voluntarism." *Time*, Mar. 16, 1987, p. 72.

Gifford, W. S. *Walter S. Gifford: Addresses, Papers, and Interviews*. New York: American Telephone and Telegraph Company, 1924–1949.

Gorham, E. B. *National Service, Citizenship, and Political Education*. Albany: State University of New York Press, 1992.

Gouldner, A. W. *The Coming Crisis of Western Sociology*. New York: Basic Books, 1970.

Greenleaf, R. *Servant Leadership*. New York: Paulist Press, 1977.

Hall, K. L., and Hall, P. D. *The Lehigh Valley—An Illustrated History*. Woodland Hills, Calif.: Windsor, 1982.

Hall, K. L., and Hall, P. D. "Allentown, 1870–1900" and "Allentown, 1930–1941." In Mahlon Hellerich (ed.), *Allentown, 1762–1987*. 2 vols. Allentown, Pa.: Lehigh County Historical Society, 1987.

Hall, P. D. "Teaching and Research on Philanthropy, Voluntarism, and Nonprofit Organizations." *Teachers College Record*, 1992, 93, 403–435.

Hodgkinson, V. A. *Academic Centers and Research Institutes Focusing on the Study of Philanthropy, Voluntarism, and Not-for-Profit Activity: A Progress Report*. Washington, D.C.: INDEPENDENT SECTOR, 1988.

Hollingshead, A. *Elmtown's Youth: The Impact of Social Classes on Adolescents*. New York: Wiley, 1949.

Hopkins, C. H. *History of the Y.M.C.A. in North America*. New York: Association Press, 1951.

INDEPENDENT SECTOR. *Transmitting the Values of a Caring Society to Future Generations*. Washington, D.C.: INDEPENDENT SECTOR, 1993.

Jackson, K. T. *Crabgrass Frontier: The Suburbanization of the United States*. New York: Oxford University Press, 1985.

Jefferson, T. "A Bill for the More General Diffusion of Knowledge." In *Jefferson: Public and Private Papers*. New York: Vintage Books/Library of America, 1990a. (Originally published 1778.)

Jefferson, T. "Report of the Commissioners for the University of Virginia." In *Jefferson: Public and Private Papers*. New York: Vintage Books/Library of America, 1990b. (Originally published 1819.)

Kendall, J. C. *Combining Service and Learning: A Resource Book for Community and Public Service*. Raleigh, N.C.: National Society for Internships and Experiential Education, 1990.

Leadership Development—A Technical Assistance Pamphlet. Prepared by Project MAP, Inc. for the Office of Economic Opportunity. Washington, D.C.: Office of Economic Opportunity, 1972.

Ligon, E. M. *The Psychology of Christian Personality*. New York: Macmillan, 1935.

Lilly Endowment. *Lilly Endowment Leadership Education Conference, December 3–5, 1990*. Indianapolis, Ind.: Lilly Endowment, 1990.

Link, H. C. *The Return to Religion*. New York: Macmillan, 1936.

Lynd, R. S., and Lynd, H. M. *Middletown: A Study in Modern American Culture*. Orlando, Fla.: Harcourt Brace Jovanovich, 1929.

MacLeod, D. I. *Building Character in the American Boy: The Boy Scouts, YMCA, and Their Forerunners*. Madison: University of Wisconsin Press, 1983.

Madison, J. *Eli Lilly: A Life, 1885–1977*. Indianapolis: Indiana Historical Society, 1989.

Marsden, G. M. *The Evangelical Mind and the New School Presbyterian Experience: A Case Study of Thought and Theology in Nineteenth-Century America*. New Haven, Conn.: Yale University Press, 1990.

Moskos, C. C. *A Call to Civic Service: National Service for Country and Community*. New York: Free Press, 1988.

Parrington, V. L. (ed.). *The Connecticut Wits*. New York: Crowell, 1954.

Phillips, J. W. *Jedidiah Morse and New England Congregationalism*. New Brunswick, N.J.: Rutgers University Press, 1983.

President's Research Committee on Social Trends. *Recent Social Trends in the United States*. 2 vols. New York: McGraw-Hill, 1933.

Raspberry, W. "Not All Students Are Greedy." *Washington Post*, Feb. 3, 1988, p. A19.

Rockefeller, J. D. 3rd. *The Second American Revolution: Some Personal Observations*. New York: HarperCollins, 1973.

Salamon, L. M., and Abramson, A. J. *The Federal Budget and the Nonprofit Sector*. Washington, D.C.: Urban Institute Press, 1982.

Schrecker, E. W. *No Ivory Tower: McCarthyism and the Universities*. New York: Oxford University Press, 1986.

Sklar, K. S. *Catherine Beecher: A Study in American Domesticity*. New Haven, Conn.: Yale University Press, 1973.
Sorokin, P. *The Crisis of Our Age: The Social and Cultural Outlook*. New York: Dutton, 1941.
Steiner, J. F. "Recreation and Leisure Time Activities." In President's Research Committee on Social Trends, *Recent Social Trends in the United States*. New York: McGraw-Hill, 1933.
Tocqueville, A. de. *Democracy in America*. 2 vols. New York: Vintage Books, 1945. (Originally published 1835.)
Van Beynum, W. "The Esothian Library." Unpublished term paper, Graduate Liberal Studies Program, Wesleyan University, 1959.
Weber, M. *The Protestant Ethic and the Spirit of Capitalism*. New York: Charles Scribner's Sons, 1958. (Originally published 1904–1905.)
Winks, R. W. *Cloak and Gown: Scholars in the Secret War, 1939–1961*. New York: Morrow, 1987.

Chapter Nine

The Role of Free Loan Associations in Jewish Communities

Eliezer David Jaffe

The interest-free loan concept is an excellent example of the embodiment of Jewish civic and religious traditions in a social service geared to the care of disadvantaged populations. Free loan associations stem from religious motivation to copy spiritual traits and fulfill religious commandments, expressed in the form of this unique socioeconomic nonprofit service (Jaffe, 1992a).

In Jewish tradition the general meaning of *gemiluth chasadim* refers to an act of benevolence toward one's fellow human beings, for which neither remuneration nor recompense is expected (Eisenstein, 1917). Most often, *gemiluth chasadim* refers specifically to interest-free loans. In this chapter, I explore the religious traditions that motivated the establishment of free loan associations throughout the Jewish world. I also describe the nature and variety of these organizations in a specific geographical setting: Jerusalem, the capital of Israel. The empirical research from the Jerusalem survey also includes nonprofit associations that lend various goods free of charge, in addition to the classic free loan associations that loan money without interest.

The goal of this research was to examine an important area of volunteer activity available to the population at large in Israel and in most Jewish communities around the world. This study of Hebrew free loan associations—which appear to provide a unique socioeconomic service—should result in a better understanding of their nature and role. The study should also highlight the usefulness of these associations and may inspire others to create similar organizations in other cultural contexts.

Anchored in Jewish religious law and societal tradition, the Hebrew free loan association represents a distinct transgenerational institution in Jewish communities that care about the welfare of their co-religionists. Through repayment of (interest-free) loans and reissuance of new loans, the result is a permanently revolving, locally supported and administered self-help institution that has lasted for many generations in most large Jewish communities in North America, Europe, Israel, and elsewhere. In many localities, "membership" (involving annual dues and donations) in the local Hebrew free loan association is a family tradition, religiously motivated, and often reflected in transgenerational family representation on the board. Another important feature of many free loan associations is that borrowers eventually tend to become donors and board members after they establish themselves in business and professional pursuits.

Although the free loan concept is unique to the Jewish community, the model has great relevance for non-Jewish communities, particularly in depressed neighborhoods where interest-free loans could revitalize private enterprise and disadvantaged individuals.

Gemiluth Chasadim in the Jewish Sources

The institution of *tzedakah* ("charity"), including mutual aid (*gemiluth chasadim*), has always existed among the Jewish people. Many different charity associations operated both in the Land of Israel and in the Diaspora. Some concentrated on a particular area of aid, while others served as sources for general, undifferentiated assistance. Among those with specific, limited objectives were: *hachnasath kallah* societies (providing dowries for poor brides), *hachnasath orchim* societies (providing shelter for poor or homeless travelers), and funds and associations that provided free meals to the indigent. General financial assistance was offered by charity funds and loan societies (Neipris, 1975; Jaffe, 1982).

The roots and ethos of these institutions are deeply embedded in Jewish religious tradition and sources, which deal more comprehensively with the issue of charity in general and *gemiluth chasadim* specifically. The subject is first dealt with in the Torah. Interpretations of these concepts later appear in the *Mishna* and the *Gemara*, in Maimonides and many other commentaries, all of which expand on the discussion regarding the essence of *gemiluth chasadim*, its objectives, and ways of implementing it. In the following paragraphs, I will cite some of the Jewish sources that deal with *gemiluth chasadim* in its general meaning (that is, charity, deeds of kindness, and assistance to one's fellow human beings), as well as with *gemiluth chasadim* in the sense of an interest-free loan, which developed to operationalize the principles of not embarrassing the recipient and of observing the prohibition against taking interest from fellow Jews.

Gemiluth Chasadim in Its General Sense

According to the sources, *gemiluth chasadim* includes a number of precepts whose ultimate purpose is to assist one's fellow men and women to the greatest extent possible in any circumstance where help might be required. The sources attest to the fact that *gemiluth chasadim* is one of the fundamental precepts of Judaism. Thus, for example, in the words of Simon the Righteous: "The world is based on three things: the Torah, divine service, and *gemiluth chasadim*" (*Ethics of the Fathers*, chap. 1). Simon the Righteous considered *gemiluth chasadim* to be on a par with the supreme values of Torah study and service in the Temple, and made it one of the foundations of the universe that constitute the very reason for human existence. The importance of *gemiluth chasadim* is also mentioned in other sources: "The sages attributed three characteristics to the people of Israel: mercy, modesty, and *gemiluth chasadim*" (*Talmud*, *Yebamot*,

p. 79). Also, "The Torah begins with *gemiluth chasadim* and ends with *gemiluth chasadim*" (*Talmud, Sota*, p. 14).

Jewish sources emphasize doing kindness and *gemiluth chasadim* in contrast to other commonly accepted values such as the study of Torah and bringing sacrifices during the Temple period. For example: "Rabbi Hanina the son of Teradyon said to the son of Parta [when they were both arrested by the Roman authorities]: "How fortunate you are, for you will be saved from death because you occupied yourself with the study of Torah and with *gemiluth chasadim* while I will not be saved because I occupied myself exclusively with the study of Torah" (*Yalkut Am loez*, 77:17); Rabbi Yohanan was wont to say: "*Gemiluth chasadim* is more precious than charity and the study of Torah" (*Jerusalem Talmud, Pe'ah*, p. 81). Likewise, "*Gemiluth chasadim* is greater than the Temple sacrifices, as it is written: 'For I have desired benevolence and not sacrifices'" (*Yalkut Shimoni* on *Hosea* [1762], 60).

Gemiluth Chasadim as Interest-Free Loans

The sources distinguish between *gemiluth chasadim* as an interest-free loan (of money or goods) and charity. They place *gemiluth chasadim* on a higher plane for many different reasons. These include educational-rehabilitative reasons, egalitarian reasons, and humanitarian reasons (not to embarrass the recipient).

The rehabilitative value of a loan versus charity is expressed in Maimonides: "There are eight progressive levels of charity. The highest, of which there is none greater, is supporting a person instead of giving him a gift or providing a *loan* or making him a partner or finding him a job so as to hold his hand so that he will not have to turn to other people [for charity]" (Maimonides, *Mishneh Torah: Zeraim*, Laws of Gifts to the Poor, 10:7). Thus, a loan is more worthwhile to the giver than charity: "Rabbi Eliezer said: '*Gemiluth chasadim* is greater than charity,' as it says: 'Sow according to a measure of charity; reap according to a measure of benevolence.' When a man sows, it is questionable whether he will be able to eat the produce. When a person reaps, he will certainly eat the produce." (*Babylonian Talmud: Sukkiah*, 49:2). And "[the merit of] *gemiluth chasadim* is eternal, while [the merit of] charity lasts for only three generations, as it says: 'The benevolence of the L-rd is eternal and His justice is unto the sons of sons.' From here we learn that *gemiluth chasadim* is greater than charity" (*Yalkut Tehilim*, 56:859) and also intergenerational.

Other sages also noted the educational element of loans and stated that the precept of lending must be practiced toward everyone. This did not apply, however, when the would-be borrower was known to be frivolous and careless with someone else's money, or if the loan would abet immoral practices.

The Principle of Not Embarrassing the Recipient

Gemiluth chasadim as a loan is distinguished by the fact that the recipient is spared embarrassment. In his book on *tzedakah* among the Jewish people, Bergman (1944, p. 94) cites the *Sefer Hachinuch* regarding the importance of preserving the poor person's sense of self-respect:

> The religious duty of giving loans is a stronger and greater obligation than the *mitzvah* of giving charity. For if someone's penury has become revealed and known among people, and he has to publicly ask for charity of them, his distress and suffering is not as great as that of a person who has not yet been reduced to this ignominy and who fears to enter this state. If he will have the small help of a loan so that he can find a little relief, perhaps he will never need to come asking (for charity). Then, when G-d will mercifully grant him financial ease, he will pay his creditors and live from the rest [*Sefer Hachinuch*, Precept 66].

Bergman (1944, p. 95) also cites quotations from the *Sefer Chasidim* that indicate the importance of preserving the poor person's sense of self-respect. Here is an example: "The Holy One Blessed be He commanded giving gifts and loans to the poor, and by right one should not give the poor a loan, but should give him a gift, but the Torah knew that sometimes the poor man is ashamed to receive a gift but would rather have a loan, as is granted by one rich man to another, who is not ashamed to take it. So the poor person will not be ashamed to take a loan, and will say: I will work and labor until I pay back my debt" (*Sefer Chasidim*, 9).

Here is another example: "Sometimes a loan is better than a gift: Reuben the Righteous asked Simon to lend him some money. Immediately Simon came and said to him: 'I am giving this to you as a gift.' From then on, Reuben was embarrassed and ashamed to request a loan of Simon. We find that it would have been better if he had not given it to him" (*Sefer Chasidim*, 10). And to quote Maimonides: "We were commanded to lend to the poor person in order to lighten his burden and make it easier for him. This is the strongest commandment and the most obligatory of all the precepts dealing with charity, because for someone who must expose himself and be shamed to ask of other people, there is no distress like that of a person who is trying to hide his penury and who needs help but who fears being exposed and shamed" (*Hilchot Harambam*, Maimonides, Precept 197).

The Prohibition Against the Taking of Interest

The precept of lending without interest as a form of *gemiluth chasadim* is related to the prohibition against taking interest, which serves to protect the poor person. The Hebrew word *neshech* ("usury") itself—which derives from *neshicha* ("biting")—indicates wounding and suffering, and reflects the extent to which the Jews considered usury to be the ultimate immorality. During their exile in Babylon and later Assyria and Europe, some Jews became moneylenders for profit among non-Jews—their assigned role in society by decree of the ruling powers who used this as a method of discrimination.

In contrast to the Code of Hammurabi—which fixes interest rates for every type of loan, whether monetary or food—the Torah (Exodus 22:24, Leviticus 25:35–37, Deuteronomy 23:20–21) absolutely prohibits the taking of any interest whatsoever from fellow Jews, either from poor people or for commercial purposes. The severity of this prohibition is first stressed by the prophet Ezekiel (18), who lists it as no less grave a transgression than adultery or murder. He who lends money for interest is one of the evildoers listed in Proverbs (28:8), and he who refrains from doing so is listed among the righteous (Psalms 15:5). Someone who calls in a debt is mentioned with disapprobation several times in the Scriptures (Samuel I 22:2, Kings II 4:1, Isaiah 50:1). Taking usury from anyone is in direct contradiction to the dictates of the Torah.

The literature of the sages during post-Talmud (*Tanaitic* and *Amoraitic*) periods deals extensively with the laws of interest, expands their definition, emphasizes their conceptual aspects and their severity, and cites many examples in every generation where the sages fought against the taking of interest. According to the *Mishna*, interest mentioned in the Torah refers to simple, direct interest. The *Tanaim* expanded this prohibition to include any form of benefit: "He who lends his fellow-man money should not live rent-free in his home and may not rent from him at a lower rate, for this is interest." Likewise, it was prohibited to exploit the labor of the borrower, since this might resemble interest.

The sages emphasized the severity of taking interest and equated it with murder and apostasy. They also stressed the economic dangers of paying interest and the resultant, inevitable deterioration of the borrower. They compared the "bite" of interest to the bite of a snake, for in both cases the victim is oblivious to it until it is too late. Thus they said that it is better for a person to sell his daughter into servitude than to become involved with interest payments (*Hebrew Encyclopedia*, 1978, "Interest"; also see *Hebrew Encyclopedia*, 1976, "Charity and Philanthropy").

German Jews also considered lending money with interest to be sinful, predicting that whoever lent his money or cheated with weights or measures or merchandise would eventually lose his property, and his children would rebel and become dependent on charity. The reason given for this prohibition against the taking of interest is that when someone lends to a fellow human being, the latter is rehabilitated at no loss to the lender. Moreover, people have a responsibility to deal benevolently and without remuneration with someone in trouble. Therefore, whoever is able to earn a living should not take interest.

From all of this we learn that the fundamentals of *tzedakah* in general, and of *gemiluth chasadim* as an interest-free loan, are deeply rooted in the Jewish sources, in the Torah and commentaries. As the citations from the sources attest, the lending of money is considered of much greater merit than charity as a gift. We see that charity is also considered inferior because it is in the category of a "hit-and-run" operation. In other words, giving—minus any responsibility or obligation—is sometimes more harmful than beneficial. Lending is far superior in that it necessitates greater personal and often professional involvement, reflects a true desire to help, has greater educational and rehabilitative significance for the recipient, and does not shame the person.

This commandment to provide interest-free loans—which is so central to our moral system—has been a guiding light to the establishment and operation of free loan associations in both the past and present in all countries where Jews live and especially in Israel.

While free loan associations originally lent money, Ungar (1988) says that the idea of interest-free loan associations for goods became increasingly popular in the Orthodox neighborhoods of Jerusalem and other towns. The free loan associations for goods are often highly specialized, and many of the goods they lend out are related to items needed for Jewish holidays, ritual occasions, and family celebrations.

Aside from "Yad Sarah," an Israeli nonprofit, national association for lending medical equipment, most of the free loan associations are unknown outside their immediate neighborhoods and are publicized by word of mouth. Most of these societies do not seek publicity, for fear of oversubscription.

The free loan associations for goods are generally funded and operated privately, and their monetary worth varies from several hundred to several thousand *shekalim*. The goods they lend out vary widely, ranging from baby bottles, cutlery, and linens to bridal gowns, furniture, and medicines.

Because this phenomenon is so widespread, free loan associations for goods were included in my research, in addition to the monetary free loan associations, in the Jerusalem area.

Methodology

This is the first exploratory research study in Israel that deals with the characteristics and operation of free loan associations.

The Population

The research included two types of free loan associations in Jerusalem: those that lend money and those that lend goods, specializing in a particular item. The latter were included because of their popularity and because of the great interest they arouse (some of them being quite unique). The research deals with Jerusalem alone, since an initial exploration of the subject showed that the large number of such associations in the entire country—several thousand, according to our estimates—was beyond the scope of our resources to investigate.

Since little is known empirically about the free loan associations and their characteristics—something that made it difficult to obtain a representative sample—the research group decided to examine the entire population of free loans in Jerusalem.

Methodology of Locating Free Loan Associations

Several methods were utilized to locate both types of free loan associations. We placed two different ads in the classified column of the local weekend newspaper *Kol Ha'ir.* The first announced that university researchers conducting research on free loan associations were looking for information on free loan associations. The second ad, which appeared the following week, was a fabricated personal request for help from free loan associations by a distressed family. There was no response to either ad. In retrospect, this was an indication of the special populations and geographical areas served by most free loans.

We asked the Ministry of Religion for information on free loan associations in Jerusalem, but none was available. We also wrote to synagogues, the office of the Chief Rabbinate, and various religious and other organizations for names of free loan associations, and engaged in "detective" work based on networking, rumors, and bits and pieces of information. In this way, we located a list of associations, including many not publicized anywhere or known to religious institutions. In all, we located 412 free loan "associations" in Jerusalem. This is a considerable number, but we believe that most were extremely small groups rather than established loan associations. Many free loan associations among the religious population are known only to relatives of those who operate them and a small clientele—since, for a variety of reasons such as the inability to serve an expanded population, many are not interested in being exposed to the public at large. For example, in one particular block-long housing unit in a religious neighborhood, the majority of the families ran small free loan "associations," lending $50 to $150 on the average. On three adjacent streets in the same neighborhood, twenty-five families had free loan associations. The multiplicity of free loan associations and their concentration in religious neighborhoods, on the one hand, and their concealment from the general public, on the other, led us to conclude that more small free loan associations exist than we were able to locate.

Research Instrument

Initially, we investigated seven free loan associations for the purpose of developing a questionnaire relevant to different types of free loan associations. This was because of the wide variety of associations lending goods versus those lending funds of larger and smaller amounts. Obviously, we needed to create a research tool suitable for examining the entire gamut of free loans. During this stage, we personally interviewed people connected with the free loan associations to clarify any ambiguities due to unclear formulation of questions or redundancy, and to identify content areas that had not been included.

The amended final questionnaire was sent to the Jerusalem free loan associations we had located. Materials were sent by mail, since our budget did not allow for personal interviews. The packets sent included a questionnaire and a self-addressed, stamped envelope. After a month, we sent a second mailing that included the original material plus a reminder to free loan associations that had not responded. We also tried to locate the correct addresses for free loan associations whose envelopes had been returned due to an inaccurate address.

Out of the 412 free loan associations to which we sent questionnaires, 68 associations (or 17 percent) responded. Evidently, most of these involved religious people operating very small loan funds who did not wish to publicize their services.

They included forty-one money-lending associations (60 percent) and twenty-seven free loan associations for goods (40 percent).

Limitations of the Research

Our research was limited by the fact that we were perceived as a secular group investigating many small loan funds, primarily within the ultra-Orthodox religious sector, known only within the circles of those who operated them. It is possible but improbable that the sixty-eight funds whose responses we studied represented the entire population of the free loan associations, in that they agreed to cooperate with a secular (university) research group, and thus were different from the nonrespondents. We think it highly probable that the nonparticipating free loans also fit our main findings about the ultra-Orthodox nature of most Jerusalem free loan associations, which are clearly described in the research.

Results

The results of the research were divided into categories that dealt with the background of the free loan associations, sources of funding, registration and tax status, operating characteristics, accessibility, and guidelines for eligibility and other rules.

Background of the Free Loan Associations. The findings show that almost one-half of the free loans (48 percent were established in the 1980s. An additional third (32 percent) were established in the 1970s. Only one free loan fund established in the nineteenth century—in 1870—is still operating.

The majority of the free loan associations (77 percent) were established by several members or an individual; 9 percent were created by an organization, such as a synagogue. Not a single free loan association was established by the government; 74 percent were established through private initiative, 18 percent were founded as public not-for-profit associations, and none was created as a government agency. Missing data are 14 percent and 8 percent for these items respectively, but it is safe to believe that in each case the free loans were established by private individuals.

One of our central hypotheses was that the founders of the free loan funds are mostly Orthodox Jews—those whose daily lives are guided by religious observances—rather than secular Jews. The data show that more than half (55 percent) of the founders of free loan funds consider themselves *haredi* (ultra-Orthodox), while another 21 percent consider themselves "national religious" Jews. In other words, 76 percent of the founders of free loan associations identify themselves as religious. In contrast, only 3 percent identified themselves as "secular." Another 21 percent did not answer this question.

In line with this finding, the data point to two primary reasons for the establishment of a free loan association: a personal need of the founders, such as a desire to memorialize loved ones or contribute to their own immortality (38 percent), or to "do good deeds" and "help needy people" (62 percent) as part of religious obligation.

Sources of Funding. The survey showed that 31 percent of the free loans were funded by the founders of the free loan themselves; another 31 percent were funded by private donors and 26 percent by both. An interesting finding was that the government—national or local—contributed nothing to the funds. Of the total number of free loan associations, 51 percent are funded by sources in Israel, an additional 20 percent obtain between 50 percent and 90 percent of their funding in Israel, and about 30 percent of the associations receive only about 50 percent of their funding in Israel. Of those receiving assistance from out of the country, 47 percent were helped by contributors primarily in the United States.

Overhead expenses of the free loan associations such as salaries and office costs are absorbed primarily by the owners of the associations (about 40 percent), while an additional 15 percent were covered by private contributions. The balance was funded by other sources, such as donations from users. Only 19 percent of the associations engaged in fundraising by advertising (15 percent) or public appeals (4 percent), but the major source of funding is independent private giving (81 percent) by the operators of the free loan funds.

We found that the total current financial capital (or value of goods) of 21 percent of the free loan associations was only $100 to $1,000; 23 percent of them had $1,000 to $5,000, 7 percent had between $5,000 and $9,000, and 39 percent had $10,000 or more. In contrast, only 11 percent of the total number of free loan associations indicated that the amount available at the time of the establishment of the association was $10,000. In other words, the scope of these funds is relatively small, but for many of them the sum at their disposal increased over the years. About half of the free loans (48 percent) indicated that their financial resources had increased over time, 33 percent indicated no change, and only 8 percent experienced a reduction of capital.

Sixty-five percent of the free loan associations try to maintain the value of their capital, 36 percent by linkage to the dollar, 12 percent by linkage to the cost-of-living index, and the balance in other ways. The majority (57 percent) indicated that maintaining the value of their assets was the major difficulty in running the association.

Registration and Tax Status. The registration of free loan associations as nonprofit organizations means adhering to particular rules of the Ministry of the Interior and accepting supervision by the Registrar of Non-Profit Associations of the Ministry. Findings show that the majority of the free loan associations (57 percent) are not officially registered as nonprofit associations. Of these, 68 percent are registered in the Ministry of the Interior and 18 percent received tax-deductible status from the Ministry of Finance, which requires more stringent accounting and broader membership than does the Ministry of the Interior.

Registration as a nonprofit association with the Ministry of the Interior must precede registration as a recognized tax-exempt fundraising institution by the Ministry of Finance. Findings show that approximately 82 percent of the free loan associations lack such a tax exemption.

This finding is consistent with the fact that most of the free loans are not even registered as nonprofit associations, the most basic type of formal registration, which may explain why they were so difficult to locate. Contrary to government regulations for registered nonprofit organizations, only 9 percent of the loan funds used an accountant, and only 5 percent reported to any government agency. In most cases, supervision and administration were a completely private affair.

Operating Characteristics. The majority of the free loan associations (64 percent) are run by volunteers. Of these, 55 percent are run by one or two volunteers, another 34 percent are run by three to six volunteers, and one was even run by ninety-nine volunteers. Thirty-six percent of the total number of free loan associations are operated by a paid staff, with the largest staff (in one case) consisting of thirty-one paid employees. Likewise, the majority of the free loan associations (57 percent) use nonprofessional help, with only 14 percent using only professional employees and 29 percent using both.

An examination of the role of contributors in administering and operating the free loan associations shows that in most cases (79 percent), there is no involvement of donors. Of the 21 percent that responded that donors were involved, 43 percent indicated that this involvement took the form of fundraising; 36 percent said that it took the form of ongoing administration and 21 percent that it was a combination of the two.

Similar to the findings on the religious affiliation of the founders, we found that 61 percent of those that operated the free loan associations were ultra-Orthodox (*haredi*); 26 percent were national religious. Not a single free loan association indicated that it was operated by secular Jews.

The majority of the free loan associations (77 percent) are run independently by a person or family and 11 percent belong to a religious organization. Only 2 percent belong to a political party, and an additional 2 percent to an ethnic organization. Similarly, 83 percent are independent and not part of any network.

Accessibility. More than half of the free loan associations (52 percent) turned away hundreds of applications each year for lack of funds, and 10 percent noted that they turned away "thousands." The rest reported tens of applicants rejected each year. These findings show that not all requests are granted. Table 9.1 compares the percentage of free loan associations that report applications of thousands, hundreds, and tens of people, respectively, as opposed to grants actually made. While 10 percent of the free loan associations reported applications by the thousands, only 7 percent reported granting thousands of loans. Likewise, 52 percent of the free loan associations reported hundreds of applications, but only 38 percent reported granting hundreds of loans. In contrast, while 35 percent reported tens of applications, almost half (48 percent) reported granting these loans. In other words, small loans were given to large numbers of people.

Fully 62 percent of the free loan associations publicize themselves. For 45 percent, the publicity is by word of mouth, and in only 6 percent of the cases is it done commercially, by means of ads in the telephone book or the media. None of the free loan associations turn to those in need (loan recipients) for fundraising purposes.

Most of the free loan associations we studied (71 percent) are located in private houses. Another 8 percent are located in offices, 3 percent in synagogues, and 2 percent in various other settings and institutions. Ninety-two percent can easily be reached by bus lines. In contrast to their relative accessibility by public transportation, most (77 percent) report that they have no street signs indicating their location; a person either has the home address or does not.

Confidentiality is an important factor in free loan work and in religious strictures related to helping people. Nevertheless, only 71 percent of the associations reported that they maintain the confi-

Table 9.1. Distribution of Free Loan Associations According to Yearly Number of Applicants and Loans.

Number of applications for loans	*Percentage of free loan associations that reported this no. of applications*	*Percentage of free loan associations that reported granting this no. of loans*
Thousands	10	7
Hundreds	52	38
Tens	35	48
Not known	3	7

dentiality of their applicants. Those that did not stated as a reason that "there was no need."

Guidelines for Eligibility and Other Rules. We wanted to study whether the religious, national, or ethnic affiliation of the borrower and the borrower's financial situation or geographical location constituted criteria for receiving help. The data indicate that about half (52 percent) of the free loan associations give help to everyone who appeals for assistance. Of those who limit their help to people meeting particular criteria, the main criterion is national-religious affiliation; 100 percent of the free loan associations only help Jews. We also found that 27 percent grant assistance according to religious affiliation: 61 percent help only national religious and *haredim*, and the rest help various Jewish religious groups. Additionally, 30.8 percent grant assistance according to geographical location. Of these, 30 percent are limited to residents of certain (mostly religious) neighborhoods, 45 percent are limited to residents of the city of Jerusalem, and 25 percent give loans out of the city as well. Almost all the free loan associations responded that they did not grant assistance according to any means test, and only 11 percent limit their help in accordance with the financial situation of the applicant and help the needy exclusively. Of those that indicated taking into consideration particular criteria, 80 percent reported strict compliance with those criteria.

Findings show that 44 percent of the free loan associations have an application form, 17 percent are satisfied with an oral promise to pay back the loan, only 3 percent require some form of documentation, and the rest use various other procedures or a combination of the above. Those who make the decision about whether to grant the loan or not are, in 52 percent of the cases, the association's director; in 28 percent, the loan committee; and in 20 percent, someone other than the above—for example, the founder-owner. If the request is turned down, most free loan associations (86 percent) do not permit an appeal.

The guiding criterion in the majority of the free loan associations (55 percent) in determining the priority of granting a loan is the principle of "first come, first served."

The amount of the loan or value of the goods loaned is relatively limited; 34 percent of the free loan associations loan the equivalent of up to $250 (in shekels), 37 percent loan up to $500, 8 percent loan up to $750, 13 percent loan up to $800, and only 4 percent loan up to $1,500. Forty-four percent of the free loan associations determine the amount of the loan according to their preestablished bylaws and 32 percent according to assessment of need. Another 24 percent decide according to a combination of the above. In the majority of the free loan associations (54 percent), the loan is not limited to specific purposes; no reason is required and no questions are asked.

We found that most loans were small. Table 9.2 shows the distribution of loan associations according to the range of the loans. For 93 percent of the free loan associations, the amounts loaned are from $100 to $500, and larger loans—from $500 to $900—are given by only 7 percent of the free loan associations.

Almost none of the free loan associations (91 percent) limit the number of times requests for a loan may be submitted, and 59 percent estimated that the percentage of applicants to whom more

Table 9.2. Range of Loans Granted by Free Loan Associations (in U.S. Dollars).

Average amount of loan	*Percentage of free loan associations granting the loan*
\$100–\$199	34
\$200–\$249	38
\$250–\$499	21
\$500–\$900	7

than one loan was granted is more than 30 percent. One quarter of the associations had no restrictions on repeated loans, and 75 percent answered that their limit was up to five loans per person.

Almost half of the free loan associations (49 percent) respond immediately to the applicant's request for a loan; another 30 percent reply within a month of the request and the remainder give their answer within three months. Once they decide to give a loan, most of the free loan associations (77 percent) request a security from the recipient before the loan is granted. In 24 percent of the cases this means postdated checks, 20 percent require collateral, 8 percent request guarantors, 2 percent request a promissory note, and the rest (18 percent) require various combinations of the above or other forms of security.

The average repayment period for the majority of the free loan associations (62 percent) is six months or more. The majority (67 percent) of free loan associations allow six to ten payments; 8 percent permit more, and the remainder less. About half of the free loan associations (49 percent) state that they are highly flexible about repayment, 47 percent allow little flexibility, and only 4 percent allow no flexibility at all.

When the free loan associations were asked to estimate the percentage of people who failed to adhere to the repayment schedule, the majority (65 percent) reported a default rate of up to 10 percent. The rest gave a figure of up to 32 percent. When the loans are not repaid on time, 85 percent of the free loan associations use sanctions. Of those, 34 percent try to locate the borrowers and pressure them; another 34 percent use a combination of a few methods such as keeping the collateral or refusing to grant another loan, as well as trying to locate the borrowers and putting moral pressure on them. Only 2 percent resort to legal prosecution. This may relate to our finding that in 59 percent of the associations, the loan agreements lack legal validity. Nevertheless, we found that only a very small percentage of the loans are actually not paid back. Twenty-five percent reported complete repayment, an additional 25 percent reported that only a percent or two failed to repay, and another 31 percent indicated that 3 to 5 percent of the borrowers did not repay their loans.

Only about half (51 percent) of the free loan associations have constitutions. Rules are determined by the administrators (64 percent) or by the founder-owners (31 percent). The majority (69 percent) have not altered their procedures and criteria over the years. Of those who have, 50 percent have made them more inflexible and 50 percent more flexible.

Conclusion

This exploratory research has examined the characteristics of interest-free loan associations and associations for lending out goods in Jerusalem. Our interest stemmed from an awareness of the importance of this particular social institution, which is an integral part of Jewish welfare and religious tradition but which has rarely been studied by scholars.

To casual observers, free loan activity is often thought of as a universal service for all segments of the population. In contrast to our expectations, however, research findings showed that most free loan associations in Israel are generally operated by religious people and primarily serve the religious sectors. The research showed that 7 percent of the founders and volunteer staff of free loan associations are religious, the majority *haredim* (ultra-Orthodox). Eighty-seven percent of those benefiting from the loans are also religious, most of them *haredim* (Jaffe, 1992a, 1992b). In contrast to general social programs, the services provided by the free loan associations are more concealed than publicized. Despite the finding that 52 percent of the associations claim that they provide assistance to all applicants, the overwhelming majority publicized their services by word of mouth. This practice indicates that the community most of them serve is almost exclusively religious, since the information would not be likely to reach the ears of those not in the network. This fact limits the extent to which the free loan associations can contribute to meeting the needs of the broad population, especially since secular groups have not developed this service to any significant degree.

Moreover, we found that, typically, the free loan association has a familial-personal rather than an organizational-bureaucratic character. The findings show that the majority of those who established and operate the associations are families or individuals, and the majority of the societies are located in private homes. The bulk of their funding is private, with 57 percent provided entirely or partly by the owner or owners. We learned that the government is not involved in the funding, operation, or supervision of most of the associations. The majority are not even registered as "nonprofit" organizations, though this would certify them as fundraising organizations and would give both them and their contributors tax exemptions.

The finding that the majority of the free loan associations are run by families or individuals seems to explain why most associations that participated in the survey were established within the last two decades. Any organization with limited funds operated exclusively by and dependent on one person or family is likely to be relatively short-lived. The fact that most of the associations are independent and not part of any network also meshes with the familial-personal character of the associations. The "Shaarei Hesed

Association," which was founded in 1870, claims to be the oldest free loan association established in Jerusalem that is still functioning—and it is exceptional in this regard. A more intensive study of the nature of this association and a few similar to it would shed light on our hypothesis that there exists a connection between the familial-personal nature of a free loan association and its longevity.

The research also demonstrated that the guidelines for granting loans were typically informal and lacked institutionalization and bureaucracy. This is reflected in the fact that the loan agreements generally lack legal validity. The findings show that only about half the free loan associations have a constitution and about 86 percent have no apparatus for appeal. Likewise, it appears that there are generally no clear criteria regarding eligibility for receiving a loan, and loans are granted on a first-come, first-served basis in 55 percent of the associations. These facts all further testify to the absence of institutionalization.

The absence of bureaucracy can be seen from the fact that in half of the associations, all that is required of the applicants is to fill out an application form, for 17 percent an oral promise is sufficient, and only 3 percent require documentation. The basic guidelines are convenient and flexible, and the forms are easily filled out by the applicants and do not require documents and other information, thus making the service easily available. In half the free loan associations a reply is given to the applicants immediately, and in 91 percent there is hardly any limit to the number of repeated applications. As further evidence of informality, the most common sanction in the case of default is an attempt to locate the borrower and to put moral pressure on the person; only 2 percent of the loan associations resort to legal procedures. Additionally, 67 percent assert that they are flexible about the predetermined repayment schedule and 49 percent note that they are very flexible.

The flexibility and absence of formality and bureaucracy are presumably related to the religious motif and the relatively low amount of the loans. Comparative studies by Bergman (1944) show that in

Europe, loans from Jewish free loan associations were given primarily for needs that centered on work, establishing oneself commercially or professionally, and study. In the United States and Canada loans are also given for such purposes as setting up a business, the purchase of a home, and immigrant absorption (Tennenbaum, 1993). These purposes necessitate significant sums. In Israel, however, our survey showed the size of the average loan for 72 percent of the free loan associations to be between $100 and $300. This is a small amount, of negligible rehabilitative value—precisely the point that Maimonides emphasized in his writings.

The picture that emerges from the survey is that in Jerusalem today there are hundreds of small free loan associations of limited financial scope. In the United States and Canada, on the other hand, there are seventy-six free loan associations; their scope, however, is estimated to be in the millions of dollars and the loans they grant are relatively high and help to rehabilitate the borrower. For example, the San Francisco Hebrew Free Loan Association has $5 million in circulating interest-free loans. There is also an umbrella organization of Hebrew free loan associations in the United States that meets annually to exchange information and ideas (*Association of Hebrew Free Loans*, 1988; Krasnel, 1988; Norman, 1986; Siegel, 1990).

A similar umbrella organization also existed in Israel called the Center for Free Loan Associations in Israel, but it closed down for reasons that are unclear. Such an organization in Israel might perhaps have served as a way of networking among the various interested free loan associations and could perhaps have stimulated several of them to merge, to create associations having greater reserves of money that could lend out significant sums.

However, this possibility seems unrealistic in view of the separatist nature of most free loan associations and the primary motivation of the founder families. Nevertheless, the involvement of national and local economic institutions in the establishment, operation, and funding of free loan associations could, in our opinion, help transform them into universal institutions that would serve a larger cross section of the population and would constitute an element of the welfare system in Israel. The establishment of a national free loan association with the power to recruit many resources would make possible loans of much greater amounts than are now granted and would serve a rehabilitative purpose. Likewise, Israel would do well to adopt the model of the umbrella organization that exists in the United States, as a central body that would share the activities of the associations and would also maintain contact with similar institutions abroad. Only one Israeli free loan, the Israel Free Loan Association (IFLA), has membership in the American umbrella association (*Association of Hebrew Free Loans*, 1990).

The IFLA, founded by a small group of volunteers in 1990, is an example of a universal, national, nonpolitical free loan association. It provides loans, primarily to new immigrants from the Soviet Union and from Ethiopia who need money for mortgage and rent payments and for a variety of other items, such as dentists' bills, food, medical supplies, and college tuition. In late 1993, nearly $3.5 million was in circulation as revolving loans. Additional funds enabled provision of loans for mortgages and small businesses, ranging from $3,000 to $10,000. All instructions regarding eligibility and loan procedures are provided in Hebrew, Amharic, and Russian, in writing and verbally by staff at the IFLA office in Jerusalem. Applicants are required to be employed, to have two employed guarantors, and to supply postdated checks to cover the number of monthly paybacks requested by the applicant (between ten and thirty-five payments). Loans are tied to the U.S. dollar but are interest-free. No overhead is deducted from donations due to special overhead grants received for this purpose.

Grants come from foundations, private donors, legacies, and fundraising events in Israel and abroad. The scope of the loan fund is constant due to the fact that loans are "rolled over" for reuse each time they are paid back. For example, a $10,000 grant, divided into average loans of $1,000, rolled over for a ten-year period, provides 100 loans, with a total value of $100,000, or ten times the original grant. This is a unique feature of free loan funds ("Israel Free Loan Association," 1993). New grants have dramatically enlarged the loan fund.

"Yad Sarah," an association that lends out goods (medical equipment for home use) serves as another example of free loan activity worthy of international emulation. It has a broad national scope, is universal in its target population, and maintains branches in other areas in Israel. Yad Sarah publicizes its activities, its existence is known to the welfare agencies, and its services are widely utilized.

Interest-free loan funds are important institutions with great social value, but their operation and use are limited to a relatively small segment of the population—as found in Jerusalem—while there are many Israelis that could benefit greatly from these services. Economic conditions in Israel, the many government cutbacks in social services, and the growing number of people experiencing economic difficulties suggest to us that interest-free loan associations could serve as a means of social assistance and development.

We believe that this free loan system could be a model for depressed neighborhoods in both Western and developing countries. A consortium of local economic interests, such as businesses, banks, and community funds, could provide the capital for establishing a large revolving loan fund in these communities—without interest and with reasonable payback arrangements. Federal funds might also be attracted to this type of nonprofit service, which might be used to promote the creation of local employment and businesses, as well as to serve individuals in temporary need (Salamon, 1987; Oleck, 1980; Kramer, 1984).

We hope that this study will make some contribution in underscoring the economic and social potential of free loan associations and bringing them to the attention of the general public and especially to social workers and social planners.

Since many social workers deal with financial problems as a central part of their work (Jaffe, 1975), they must be aware of the gamut of institutions and services that can help their clients. Free loan associations constitute a welcome area of volunteer and community activity characterized by individual initiative on behalf of one's fellow human beings. In addition to being an important economic resource, free loan associations provide supplementary income to many middle-class families struggling to make ends meet. This population is also handled by social workers in various service delivery frameworks, and referrals to free loan associations can be helpful in times of economic crisis.

Social workers must not only make do with information and referrals to municipal and national services; they should also be well acquainted with the network of local nonprofit services and be able to direct clients to any source that can help them in time of distress. There is no doubt that the network of free loan associations in Israel constitutes a key part of these resources.

For many people at risk, loans can play an important role in self-help and rehabilitation, without stigma and without creating dependency. Professionals must be able, however, to clearly differentiate between a client's need for public welfare and the potential for self-help through the free loan system.

The free loan model described in this chapter has great potential for advancing a special kind of care based on a coalition of the self-help and philanthropic sectors in society. Philanthropic foundations and individuals may find the free loan concept compatible with their need for innovative, catalytic uses of funding that can perpetuate services after the initial investment. They may also find this model attractive because it relates to economic need by helping people help themselves rather than by providing charity, and it involves working in partnership with nonprofit and volunteer free loan associations.

Ideally, I would like to see the establishment of a free loan movement in the United States and many other countries, including sharing of knowledge, skills, concepts, and technology developed for this special new area of economic assistance. I think that there is a need and a fertile ground for creating such a network because of my basic belief that many people would, given the opportunity, rather help themselves and pay back loans than depend on long-term charity as a way of life. This applies, however, primarily to people with adequate income prospects or the likelihood of acquiring the needed skills to pay back loans—not to people impoverished by structural and chronic economic disability. In these cases, government and social policy must be held responsible.

References

Association of Hebrew Free Loans (AHFL) News. San Francisco: Association of Hebrew Free Loans, May 1988.

Association of Hebrew Free Loans (AHFL) News. San Francisco: Association of Hebrew Free Loans, 1990.

Bergman, Y. *Charity in Israel: Its History and Institutions*. Jerusalem: Tarshish, 1944.

"Charity and Philanthropy." *Hebrew Encyclopedia*. Vol. 28. Jerusalem, 1976.

Eisenstein, J. D. *A Treasury of Laws and Customs*. New York: Hebrew Publishing Co., 1917.

"Gemilut Hasadim." *Encyclopaedia Judaica*. Jerusalem: Keter, 1971.

"Interest." *Hebrew Encyclopedia*. Vol. 30. Jerusalem, 1978.

"Israel Free Loan Association." *IFLA Update* (Jerusalem), winter 1993.

Jaffe, E. D. "Activating Manpower Before and After the Separation of Roles in Welfare Offices." *Megamot*, 1975, 3(11), 346–353.

Jaffe, E. D. *Child Welfare in Israel*. New York: Praeger, 1982.

Jaffe, E. D. "The Role of Nonprofit Organizations Within the Ultra-Orthodox Community in Israel." In K. D. McCarthy, V. A. Hodgkinson, and R. Sumariwalla, and Associates, *The Nonprofit Sector in the Global Community: Voices from Many Nations* (pp. 280–303). San Francisco: Jossey-Bass, 1992a.

Jaffe, E. D. "Sociological and Religious Origins of the Nonprofit Sector in Israel." *International Sociology*, 1992b, 8(2), 159–176.

Kramer, R. M. *Voluntary Agencies in the Welfare State*. Berkeley: University of California Press, 1984.

Krasnel, H. "Hebrew Free Loan Associations Still Handing Out the Cash." *Jewish Telegraphic Agency Special Feature*, June 24, 1988, p. 2.

Neipris, J. "Social Services in Israel." *Kidma*, 1975, 4(2), 16–23.

Norman, J. *Hebrew Free Loan Association: A Tradition That Lives*. San Francisco: Hebrew Free Loan Association, 1986.

Oleck, H. L. *Nonprofit Corporations, Organizations, and Associations*. (3rd ed.) Englewood Cliffs, N.J.: Prentice Hall, 1980.

Salamon, L. M. "Partners in Public Service: The Scope and Theory of Government-Nonprofit Relations." In W. W. Powell (ed.), *The Nonprofit Sector: A Research Handbook* (pp. 99–117). New Haven, Conn.: Yale University Press, 1987.

Siegel, Dranny. *Annual Report of the ZIV Tzedaka Foundation*. Rockville, Md.: ZIV Foundation, 1990.

Tennenbaum, S. *A Credit to Their Community*. Detroit, Mich.: Wayne State University Press, 1993.

Ungar, C. "Stopping the Gap." *Jerusalem Post*, Oct. 7, 1988, p. 4.

Chapter Ten

Islamic Nonprofit Organizations: In the Process of Promoting a Caring Society

Amani Kandil

Substantial work on the role of religion in developing nonprofit organizations has been done in Western countries, in relation to Christianity and Judaism. But less research is available on the situation in Islamic countries in general and Arab countries in particular. Unlike the situation in the West, where research on philanthropy is well established and theoretical models to explain variations are emerging, the philanthropic experience of the contemporary Muslim world is undocumented. In Egypt—our main concern—this subject is particularly important.

Islam was, and still is, a major factor in the development of nonprofit organizations (NPOs) in Egypt. The early history of Egypt reveals a deep relationship between Islam—as a religion and a set of traditions—and the development of a caring society, through a social movement that has depended on voluntary organizations, individuals, and mosques.

In recent history, Islam has played a major role in the development of NPOs. This is especially obvious when we recognize the size of Islamic organizations, since 34 percent of the NPOs in Egypt are Islamic ones involved in the teaching of religion and in philanthropic, health, education, and development activities. In recent history the role of Islam in promoting a caring society has become more and more important, in light of the increasing political and social role of the Islamic movement. The *political* role of Islam has to do with the increasing power of fundamentalism in political life, since fundamentalist groups are a major source of opposition to the government and to all other secular political powers in Egypt. The *social* role refers to all nonprofit Islamic services, which are mostly free of charge—an indirect role that helps in attracting supporters to what we call "Islamist" groups. In a country like Egypt, where Muslims are 93.5 percent of the total population (which reached 59 million in 1993), and where Islam is an integral component of the culture, the major research efforts have been concerned with the political aspects of Islam and the fundamentalist movement. Only a few works have focused on the social dimensions of Islam, in particular the relation between Islam and the development of NPOs. One of these works (Berger, 1970) explores the important role of mosques, *wakf*, and Islamic organizations in promoting a caring society in Egypt up to 1968. The other work (Kandil, 1993) surveys the historical background of the phenomenon and the recent role of Islam in NPOs in Egypt.

A few other case studies have concentrated on Islamic NPOs, but without relating them to their political and socioeconomic context. This explains the inability of these studies to explain the success of Islamic NPOs in responding to societal demands on the one hand, and their efficiency in resource mobilizations (volunteers and funds) on the other hand. This chapter approaches the Islamic NPOs, in a multidisciplinary way, to test the efficiency and capabilities of these organizations compared with other NPOs. The chapter also aims at clarifying the Islamic traditions in promoting a caring society, and their implications for motivating giving and care.

The results presented here are based on a survey I conducted in 1991 (Kandil, 1992), since national data on NPOs in general are not comprehensive. Documented information on Islamic NPOs are not available, because national data do not classify this type in an independent category; instead they are incorporated in the cultural category. The chapter also draws on interviews with some leaders of NPOs. The following topics are addressed:

1. Islamic traditions in promoting a caring society
2. How Islamic NPOs operate in Egypt
3. Profile of Islamic NPOs

In addition, the conclusion touches on the implications of Islamic NPOs for public policies.

Islamic Traditions in Promoting a Caring Society

Islam has been crucial in providing and stimulating private giving and philanthropic work. Encouraging caring on the part of individuals and the development of a caring society are major emphases in the Koran. In the following paragraphs, I will point to some specific principles and traditions related to Islam that have profoundly affected the history of NPOs in Egypt, and philanthropic work in Islamic and Arab countries in general.

Zakat or charitable tithing is an Islamic philanthropic tradition—indeed one of its five pillars. The others include prayer, fasting, pilgrimage, and the belief in one God. Zakat is obligatory; it requires allocating a fixed percentage of one's income to benefit the poor (2.5 percent). Thus, one of the five pillars of the faith is a regular tithe of personal and corporate income. In the past, wealthier households would distribute Zakat in the form of clothing and food during religious feasts, following the traditional formula of giving first to less advantaged relatives, then extending it to community members and finally to the broader society. Zakat support orphans, widows, the disabled, the homeless, and the poor.

Mosques, since the early years of Islam, have played a crucial role in distributing Zakat, in particular in urban communities. Now there are more than 4,000 Zakat committees established in mosques to play the role of mediator between donors and poor people. Zakat is also one of the main sources of funds to support NPOs, especially Islamic ones—a fact that helps to explain the efficiency of Islamic organizations. The trend in recent years has been toward increasing contributions to these Zakat funds, both in terms of the number of people contributing and in the proportion of income devoted to Zakat. This is hard to document, however, because philanthropic work in Islam is supposed to be kept quiet and should not be accompanied by publicity or fanfare. One of the principles in Islam is that "the left hand must not know what the right hand is giving," a saying of the profit Mohammed to motivate Muslims to give in secret.

A recent institution established in the 1970s called the Nasser Bank has accepted responsibility for allocating Zakat and distributing it to poor people and to some philanthropic organizations. In 1992 it was documented that Zakat funds had reached $10 million (Nasser Bank, 1992). But we should keep in mind that the majority of Muslims tend to give Zakat to poor people directly, so it is difficult to document the proportion of income devoted to Zakat. In conclusion, Zakat is a basic tradition or practice in Islam, one that has played a major role in developing the idea of a caring society.

Sadakat—another tradition in Islam—is a personal, voluntary form of giving mentioned more than thirty times in the Koran. Although (unlike Zakat) it is not obligatory from a religious standpoint, it aims at helping the poor "as a way to be near God." One of the most important practices developed from the idea of Sadakat is wakf. *Wakf* is a system of property bequests representing a continuous giving of Sadakat even after the death of the donor. This system emerged in the second century of Islam and still exists. Wakf property was traditionally real estate, agricultural land, or money. Literally translated as "stopping" or "holding," this form of bequest takes property out of circulation in perpetuity, so that its income can be devoted to specified beneficiaries like schools, hospitals, orphanages, mosques, NPOs, and similar institutions.

The other important tradition in Islam, related to the idea of the caring society, is the *role played by mosques*. These Islamic institutions are more than places to pray, since they encompass social, cultural, and sometimes political activities. The word for "mosque" in Arabic is *Al Gameh*, which means a place to gather and to meet other Muslims. So the mosques (or Al Gameh) have afforded scope for voluntary activity and community initiations responding to the needs of the community and to societal problems.

In recent periods, mosques have evolved and acquired new forms. Thousands of mosques have been joined by nonprofit organizations registered under Law 32 for associations and private institutions for public benefit, where there are clinics, literacy classes, libraries, educational services, and philanthropic centers. These activities are run mainly by Islamic NPOs and address the needs of the community, in particular in the health sector. All these activities pertain to the social component of Islam.

This recent role, combining secular and religious objectives, has generated serious debate in Egypt, since some people believe that this social Islam is an introduction to the political Islam. In fact, most of these Islamic NPOs have succeeded in mobilizing resources and in addressing basic needs, while the government is involved in handling the economic crisis, with limited ability to reach poor people.

The early organized popular type of today's NPOs were Sufi orders, which arose in the first and second centuries of Islam (the seventh and eighth centuries A.D.). Sufi orders are popular voluntary organizations based on the main principles of Islam. They have usually been founded by a religious teacher or scholar, who attracted followers through intelligence, charisma, and asceticism. The followers—members of these informal organizations—have built a common life involving social solidarity, support for the poor, and the observance of certain religious practices. These Sufi orders are very attractive to Muslims. Their membership was estimated at three million in 1989—a figure that tells a lot about the success of Islamic NPOs (Abdel Rachid, 1988).

To sum up, many principles and practices have grown out of Islam that advocate and inspire the values and practices of a caring society.

How Islamic NPOs Operate in Egypt

Law 32, enacted in 1964, organizes the establishment and activities of NPOs, in particular the private voluntary organizations (PVOs). According to this law, PVOs must consist of at least ten people and must not operate for profit (Kandil, 1993, p. 10). They can operate in the social welfare field (providing general social assistance and help with disability, aging, and childhood problems), the health sector, education, the cultural and scientific arenas, religion, and other areas benefiting the public.

These organizations—according to Law 32—enjoy tax deductions and are eligible for public subsidies. They also receive benefits in the form of personnel paid by the state, which is important in light of scarce resources and a limited number of volunteers.

Law 32 imposes numerous constraints on both the establishment and the activities of NPOs. Restrictions on the creation of new groups are imposed for four broad reasons: national security, preservation of the nation's general political system, support for social morals, and opposition to the revival of previously dissolved organizations.

Concerning the PVOs' activities, the government exercises control through several key provisions. The Ministry of Social Affairs has the right to check the documents and records of organizations to make sure they conform to various laws and to the PVOs' own regulations. The Ministry also has the right to appoint a temporary board of directors, when it seems necessary. The most important restriction is the government's right to terminate the "material and legal entity" of PVOs.

These restrictions have an obvious impact on Islamic NPOs and on organizations in general. The capacity for self-government, without which these organizations cannot survive, is tested by their ability to mobilize volunteers, funds, and other resources. Islamic organizations seem the most capable of doing the job, since they depend on Islamic principles and traditions. Islamic NPOs express these values by adopting procedures that conform with Islam. The most important are adopting Islamic discourse, allocating Zakat and Sadakat to poor people in the community, mobilizing volunteers, and addressing the basic needs of society.

It is important to compare these capabilities of Islamic NPOs with those of other organizations operating under Law 32, because the more independent organizations become, the more efficient they become. For this purpose, we will focus on the problem of obtaining resources (volunteers and funds).

In Egypt, NPOs in general face two main obstacles: limited participation and volunteers, and limited funds. The first problem could be clarified by pointing out that half the total membership of PVOs (estimated at three million in 1992) are not paying their annual dues. Also, 65 percent of the PVOs depend mainly on paid labor, while in some other cases, the Ministry of Social Affairs appoints its employees to work for the PVOs.

Islamic NPOs—dedicated to a religious mission—have succeeded in mobilizing volunteers to support their activities. Some doctors explained their volunteer work in mosque clinics as a "kind of Zakat and Sadakat, so as to have the feeling that [they are] near God." The same point was repeated by others in interviews with the writer. Islamic NPOs have large budgets, which come mainly from Zakat, Sadakat, and other donations. Most of these organizations are autonomous, which means limited or no government subsidies or foreign funds. But these general characteristics should not obscure variations between organizations. There are differences between the Islamic NPOs in size, membership, funds, grassroots involvement, capabilities, and efficiency.

To summarize, Islamic NPOs have been more successful than other organizations in mobilizing volunteers and raising funds. This success is due mainly to the Islamic principles adopted by these organizations, and more generally to the status of religion in Egyptian culture. By using Islamic discourse, it becomes easy for these organizations to encourage people to give and to foster the spirit of a caring society—but from an Islamic angle.

Profile of Islamic NPOs

Islamic NPOs are registered like other organizations under Law 32, for "Associations and Private Institutions for Public Benefit." Asking the state for legal status, both Islamic NPOs and Christian organizations tend to adopt a range of activities not confined to religious functions. Apart from their religious role, they engage in social welfare activities—in particular, in philanthropy, education, and health care. The following paragraphs elaborate on the profile of Islamic NPOs, in terms of their size and geographical distribution as well as types of activities and beneficiaries.

Size and Geographical Distribution

The total size of NPOs (operating as PVOs) was estimated to be 12,800 in 1990 (Kandil, 1992). Nearly 34 percent of this total number are Islamic organizations. In 1980, the percentage was less than 25 percent. The trend reveals the greater impact of the Islamic movement on social life, coinciding with its growing political role (Kandil, 1992). Even more important is the distribution of Islamic NPOs in Egyptian localities outside the capital.

Table 10.1 shows part of the phenomenon in some Egyptian regions, accompanied by the percentage of Christian PVOs. The table reveals the high concentration of religious organizations outside the big urban regions—Cairo and Alexandria. The survey indicates the increasing weight of these organizations in Upper Egypt, where a rural, conservative life-style prevails, where public services are poor in number and quality, and also where radical religious movements flourish. So, the important role played by Islamic NPOs in certain Egyptian localities can be explained in light of these socioeconomic and political factors. The survey's results reveal in particular that 51 percent of the total NPOs in some areas are Islamic.

Table 10.1. Distribution of Private Voluntary Organizations in Egypt.

	Percentage of total VCOs	
Location	*Islamic PVOs*	*Christian PVOs*
Upper Egypt		
Menia	56.8	12.8
Assiut	44.3	8.3
Urban regions		
Cairo	21.8	7.0
Alexandria	33.3	5.6

Moreover, the "local development PVOs," which have an important role in the process of development in rural areas, also operate as Islamic organizations. A field study of a sample of 400 local development PVOs indicated that 53.5 percent of these organizations operate in the religious as well as the secular sphere (Ministry of Social Welfare, 1992). This was explained—in interviews—in terms of the role the Islamic groups can play in attracting and mobilizing the community.

In Cairo and other large cities, the proportion of Islamic NPOs (which represent 23 percent of the local NPOs) is relatively smaller than in Upper Egypt and rural areas. This result also can be explained by the greater influence of secular culture in Cairo and other cities, and by the better performance of public agencies.

To sum up, Islamic NPOs make up nearly a third of all NPOs in Egypt and more than half in some localities. These organizations operate in rural areas as well as urban ones, and may be the only grassroots NPOs in Egypt.

Types of Activities and Beneficiaries

In general, PVOs in Egypt are formally classified into two main types (Ministry of Social Welfare, 1991, p. 170):

1. Local development (3,276 organizations, making up 25.5 percent of the total)
2. Social welfare (9,556 organizations, representing 74.5 percent of the total)

By law, these PVOs should serve in one or more of the following fields: child and maternal care, family care, social assistance, aging, disability; cultural, scientific, and religious services; local development; family planning; international friendships; and social advocacy.

What are the main activities of Islamic NPOs? Spiritual activities include religious services such as Islamic lectures, lessons in the Koran for children and youth, organizing pilgrimages, and establishing mosques. But this chapter is more concerned with the social welfare functions of the Islamic NPOs. In this arena, health care, educational services, and social assistance for the poor are major responsibilities.

Health Care. A large number of the NPOs operate in the health sector. This has especially been the case since the 1980s, when health services were gradually privatized (before that, these services were free). Poor people, and some segments of the middle class, could not afford the high cost of private doctors. At the same time, the social security system in Egypt provides insufficient coverage and can be inefficient—important factors that encourage Islamic NPOs to try to fill the gap in delivering health services. Islamic organizations have extended their activities to mosques, where they have established clinics and hospitals, depending mainly on volunteer doctors and donations to provide equipment and the necessary services. Thus, the phenomenon of delivering health services through mosques was and still is central in Egypt.

In 1980, the beneficiaries of these services were estimated by experts in the field to be 4.5 million people, but in 1992, they were estimated at 15 million, an obvious indication that Islamic NPOs play a key role in delivering health services and in addressing basic needs.

This means of providing care has important implications for philanthropy in general, because philanthropic work used to rely on more traditional methods of meeting the needs of poor people (distributing money and clothes). But offering health services to limited-income families means better accessibility to the service, which directly affects the quality of life. Also, health services through Islamic NPOs have succeeded in producing new types of volunteers—in particular, physicians and pharmacists, who can provide free medicines.

Philanthropic work in Egypt now encompasses more than social assistance in the traditional sense. Addressing basic needs is an approach particularly suitable to society with its current problems. Zakat is now funding and supporting the establishment of clinics and hospitals in conjunction with Islamic NPOs, indicating the response of these organizations to the Islamic emphasis on a caring society. "Social solidarity" is the Islamic concept that expresses the meaning of a caring society, though this has to be accompanied by Islamic philanthropy.

Social Assistance. The second broad area where Islamic NPOs have succeeded in promoting a caring society is in terms of philanthropic activity. Philanthropic organizations—depending on principles of giving and social solidarity—receive sufficient resources from Zakat and Sadakat to distribute them among the poor. The number of these organizations and their level of activity tend to increase in poor urban areas and in rural villages, where the poverty rates are higher. The credibility of Islamic NPOs in the community helps these organizations in allocating funds and in motivating volunteers, a privilege characterizing Islamic organizations.

Beneficiaries were estimated in 1992 to be two million families, which represent more than half the total beneficiaries from all PVOs. There were 5,671 NPOs operating in the social support field all over Egypt. Generally these were Islamic organizations dedicated to reminding people about Islamic teachings while distributing funds among the poor.

Educational Services. The other important field where Islamic NPOs are active is educational services. These NPOs have established schools with a special emphasis on religion, aimed at delivering a reasonable quality of educational services at a reasonable cost. Literacy classes have also been established in some mosques, since the literacy rate in Egypt is only 44 percent. The ability of the volunteers—especially among educated youth—is another indicator of the success of Islamic discourse in promoting caring individuals.

Conclusion

The political economy in Egypt has weathered serious crises in the last two decades. The population has increased from 40.5 million in 1976 to 56 million in 1993. The rate of urbanization reached 43.9 percent in 1986. Unemployment has become a major problem, since 14 percent of the total population and 38 percent of university graduates are unemployed. Housing is another severe problem. International indicators on poverty reveal that 23 percent of the total population is under the poverty line.

Facing such severe problems, the government's socioeconomic policies, having limited capabilities, have not been able to provide comprehensive solutions., As a result, the Islamic NPOs have gradually increased their role by presenting nongovernment options (in particular, health services) to poor communities. The state, which distrusts the Islamic movement in general, and political Islam in particular, has been unable to oppose or stop social Islam in the nonprofit sector, since the Islamic groups have been responding to society's basic needs. Thus, although the Islamic movement constitutes the primary opposition to the Egyptian government, no procedures have been formally adopted by the government to abolish the Islamic NPOs. These organizations are operating within a legal framework, and they are cautious in staying away from politics. They have supporters all over Egypt and have gained the trust of the people—especially the lower and middle classes.

The Islamic NPOs have succeeded in addressing large sectors of society, and in motivating these individuals and groups to participate in solving some societal problems. The notion of a caring society is now built on Islamic institutions, which have succeeded in transmitting the notion of a caring society from one generation to the next. NPOs have represented the most convenient channels in this process, within a social and cultural context that gives religion a prominent role.

The government has recognized that Islamic NPOs succeed in promoting a caring society, so the state political discourse has partly adopted the Islamic discourse to motivate and encourage caring individuals.

Thus a serious problem with three angles has arisen. The first is a secular state distrusting Islamic civil institutions, the second is a political economy in crisis, and the third is a strong Islamic movement depending on NPOs to fill the gaps in the provision of public services. The future of this dilemma will be determined by the capacity of the government to provide essential services and the success of its socioeconomic policies aimed at addressing basic needs. A solution could be achieved through a long-term development process and the strengthening of democratic institutions.

References

Abdel Rachid, M. *Egypt: Sufi Orders and Development*. Menia University, Menia, Egypt, 1988.

Berger, M. *Islam in Egypt Today: Social and Political Aspects of Popular Religion*. Cambridge, England: Cambridge University Press, 1970.

Kandil, A. "Survey on Private Voluntary Organizations in Egypt." Unpublished manuscript, Comparative Nonprofit Sector Project, Johns Hopkins University, 1992.

Kandil, A. "Defining the Nonprofit Sector: Egypt." In L. M. Salamon and H. K. Anheier (eds.), *Working Papers of the Johns Hopkins Comparative Nonprofit Sector Project*, no. 10. Baltimore, Md.: Johns Hopkins Institute for Policy Studies, 1993.

Ministry of Social Welfare. *National Social Indicators*. Cairo: Ministry of Social Welfare, 1991.

Ministry of Social Welfare. *Survey of 400 Local Development PVOs*. Cairo: Ministry of Social Welfare, 1992.

Nasser Bank. *Annual Report*. Cairo: Nasser Bank, 1992.

World Bank. *World Bank Reports on Development Indicators*. New York: World Bank, 1992.

Chapter Eleven

The Catholic Ethic and the Protestant Ethic

John E. Tropman

There is a need for a fresh examination of the relationship between religious orientation and philanthropy. Attention to religiously based cultural systems has been scant (with the exception of the Protestant ethic), and consequently little attention has been paid to the impact that religious cultures may have on the subculture of care and concern. The Protestant ethic has received considerable attention (Weber, 1956; Marshall, 1982). The Catholic ethic is a parallel concept—it is a set of beliefs and dispositions organized around and through a set of religious commitments. Recently, discussion has begun concerning the presence of a Catholic ethic (Tropman, 1986; Greeley, 1990; Novak, 1993; Mueller's 1978 piece focused on more theological concerns). And work is being developed on the concept of a Jewish ethic (Jacobs, 1994; Weiner, 1994; for a historical consideration, see Sombart, 1913).

These "cultures" or "ethics" contain, as an important component, views about others, their needs, and how these needs might be addressed. Such views include perspectives on poverty, encouragement to care for fellow humans in need, and injunctions to think about the needs of others as well as one's own. Sometimes these views are a part of the very core of the tradition and have a historical dimension; in other cases, they are more peripheral.

Note: Work on this project was supported in part by a grant from the Lilly Endowment. Its support is gratefully acknowledged. Ralph Pyle of Purdue University performed the data analysis for the original work in Table 11.3. His work is deeply appreciated.

Like all cultures, religious cultures are made up of conflicting values. It is not a question of either-or but rather of "dominant-subdominant." For this reason, most ethical systems—religious ones included—are best seen as a kaleidoscope: similar stones but different arrangements, making up a different picture (Tropman, 1989, especially Table P-1, pp. xvii–xviii).

While religious cultures have dominant and subdominant elements, religious cultures are unlike other cultures in that they have more difficulty with this situation. Religious cultures tend to appear one-sided and unidimensional. Thus one could not think of being a "little" Protestant and a "little" Catholic. But that is only because these value systems have the word *religion* in them. Otherwise it would be easier to think of blending.

Two of the themes here involve blending. The first looks at individual and collective orientation, or a solo versus an ensemble perspective. For some religions the role of the individual is dominant, while others take community orientation as more dominant. A second area is concern for others. While all religions support such caring, for some, this focus is more dominant; for others, more subdominant. It seems likely that ethics that emphasize the individual, the solo self, might also not be as oriented toward a caring culture; those oriented toward communal perspectives might see helping, prosocial behavior as crucial.

The Catholic and Protestant ethics are of particular interest here. Let's begin by looking at them in an overall way, and then explore in more detail the way they configure their concern for others.

Central Features of the Catholic Ethic

The Catholic ethic has existed as long as Catholicism itself. It draws from the founding ethos of Christianity/Catholicism and retained many of its central features even against the onslaught of the Reformation.

The central features of the Catholic ethic include orientations toward the community, toward family, toward the self-in-context. There is also a heavy emphasis on concern for others. These twin themes drive more specific views having to do with work, money, and forgiveness. There is a tradition of "share-ity" and a bias in favor of the poor.

The Catholic ethic is family and community oriented or "centered." Ethno-Catholicism is one way this focus has been expressed. The Catholic ethic sees self as fundamentally embedded in family and community. Born as an outcast religion, largely among the have-nots of the time, it is not surprising that early Catholicism was formed with an orientation toward the community and toward caring for those in need. Everyone in the community was in need.

The Catholic ethic sees work and money in instrumental rather than transcendental terms. *One is not a better person* because of one's job. Work is good—it keeps you busy, is a vehicle for the performance of necessary tasks, and is a place to meet people—but it is not sacred. The same arms-length approach applies to money. Money is good; money gets things you need. However, it should never be confused with the important things in life, and the richer person is in no way the better person; often the reverse is thought to be true.

The Catholic ethic is forgiving, merciful. It has a fault-forgiveness structure built into it. There is a recognition that there is sin in the world, and that there is forgiveness, too. The Catholic ethic accepts the cycle of sin and redemption, and provides mechanisms through which one can work one's way out of a state of sin. While it recognizes the responsibility for commission of sin, it also is aware of occasions for sin—something that tempers, or contextualizes, a sense of individual responsibility.

And finally, the Catholic ethic encourages a "share-itable" orientation (being altruistic, benevolent, bountiful, charitable, compassionate, generous, humane, philanthropic). Within the Catholic ethic there is a sense that, from a community perspective, you share and assist in providing for those who have less, and they will provide for you when you have less and they enjoy more. This point is stressed by Michael Novak (1993, p. xiv), who sees the Catholic ethic as providing a "counterbalance to the Protestant ethic." Novak stresses the contemporary "social Catholicism," dating essentially from the turn of the twentieth century and the encyclical *De Rerum Novarum*. What needs to be stressed is that the social Catholicism and social encyclicals derive from a 1,900-year tradition of "share-ity." This tradition sees the poor as close to Christ ("Christ's Poor") and supports those aspects of the church structure that allow parishioners to gain grace through good works. Of the many changes the Reformation wrought, a change in thinking about the poor and their status, and hence the role of aid to the poor, was one important element.

The Catholic ethic, then, leads to (or accompanies and expresses) a worldview that emphasizes self-in-community (the ensemble self). It is cooperative, is oriented toward sharing, and is perhaps captured by the phrase "a rising tide lifts all boats."

The Protestant Ethic Thesis

The concept of the Protestant ethic contains a paradox. Relatively speaking, the Protestant ethic is new—it began with the Reformation. On the other hand, the description of it is old, having been developed about a century ago by sociologist Max Weber. Perhaps because the Catholic ethic was so implicitly accepted and understood, no one until recently thought to explore it in any detail. Thus, for many years the Protestant ethic has stood alone as a religiously oriented ethical concept. Its aloneness seemed to exemplify its individualistic focus.

When Weber wrote *The Protestant Ethic and the Spirit of Capitalism* ([1904–1905] 1956) he unleashed a powerful idea, one that has been vital for almost 100 years—that the development of capitalism, the so-called "Western miracle"—was the result of an interrelated set of values developed through and unleashed by the Protestantism of Luther and Calvin. ("The Western miracle" is a phrase used to refer to the transformation of the West from a sleepy, medieval village into a world power, as noted by Rosenberg and Birdzill, 1990.) Though a popular idea, the concept of the Protestant ethic has not yet received complete verification in social science research. Disagreement still exists about several issues, such as the exact definition of the concept, the forms it takes, and whether it preceded capitalism or developed simultaneously.

The Protestant ethic is thought to have three main components: a transcendental orientation toward work, an either-or disposition toward salvation (predestination), and a "sacredized" view of worldly success.

First, Protestantism made work sacred, through the concept of the "calling." The calling meant that God had blessed all work, and all work was, therefore, God's work. No matter how menial, any task was now of supreme importance.

Second, Protestant beliefs about salvation differ from Catholic beliefs. Rather than achieving and losing a state of grace, a person's salvation is predestined. The concept of predestination implies that all decisions about salvation have already been made. A dualistic system was thus set up consisting of the elect and the nonelect. The problem, of course, is that people do not know if they are among the elect or not. There is little people can *do* about their salvation status. Prayer and "indulgences" cannot alter fate. This situation created a need for reassurance.

Novak quotes a passage from Benjamin Nelson that shows the similarities and differences between the two religions: "In many ways the Catholic man of the middle classes was like his Protestant opposite number. He too believed in being frugal, respectful, clean, time-saving, prudent. Yet the self-made man of Catholic France was in fact relatively free of the fearful anxieties which Weber has ascribed to the Protestant Saint of the sixteenth and seventeenth centuries. He had little taste for agonizing self-reexamination, living on the boundaries in an unending quest for the assurance of election" (Novak, 1993, p. vii).

This need for assurance brings us to the third element. People might be able to *infer* whether they were saved. Worldly success—money and other forms of wealth, and the high social position they conferred—became an *indicator of sacred status*. The social ladder was now Jacob's ladder. Of course the inference was still just that. People lost their money. Having no money was bad enough; damnation was worse. Newman's discussion of the "sacred" implication of losing one's job and resources is captured in the title of her book: *Falling from Grace: The Experience of Downward Mobility in the American Middle Class* (1988).

This set of views changed people's thinking about the nature of charity. Now the elect and nonelect became synonymous with the worthy and unworthy poor. Poverty was seen as something resulting from "personal failings" rather than social conditions. Of course, the so-called "casualty poor" were never unworthy since they were poor through fire, flood, and so on. The problem was always finding out whether a person was worthy or not. Segalman (1968) argues that it was surprising that support for the poor developed in such a culture. He seems to overstate the case. However, the Protestant ethic, focusing on the self and its election, does create a focus on the individual. And the change in orientation toward others in need that was one of the by-products of the Reformation has been with us to this day.

The Protestant ethic leads to a worldview that stresses individualism, fair play, and competition and could be captured by the metaphor that "each tub floats on its own bottom." It was not surprising that it developed as it did. Indeed, to stand Novak on his head a bit, one can see the Protestant ethic responding to its developmental conditions and "correcting" Catholic emphases of the times. For one thing, the newly acquired wealth of the emerging middle class needed some legitimacy. Second, some emphasis on the individual might provide a strength and reassurance that Catholicism lacked. Predestination can be seen as God's "tough love" posture, avoiding the "give 'em another chance" posture of Catholicism.

A Look at International Data

Was Weber right? Did the Protestant ethic "cause" capitalism? That question obviously cannot be answered here. How could these contentions be assessed, anyway? Most scholars agree there is an association between the Protestant ethic and capitalism, but the details and causality remain unclear. It also seems that the association is becoming weaker, as cultures spread and diversity within different cultures increases. Two points seem to emerge from the data in Table 11.1. First, Protestant countries had a substantially greater economic growth rate than many other countries in the past; second, that "edge" is now receding.

What may have been true in the past for economic growth is no longer true of the present.

If the Protestant ethic is associated with capitalism, could the Catholic ethic be associated with "welfarism"? Some data suggest that this relationship exists. There is, of course, the historical association of the Catholic church with prosocial work, including hospitals, leprosariums, and so on. And the social encyclicals that Novak (1993) stresses reinforce this point as well. (See also the work of Gremillion, 1976.) Moreover, Harold Wilensky (1981) did a multiyear study of Catholic political parties in power and their support of welfare state legislation. He was able to show that in European countries where Catholic parties were present, welfare state legislation advanced when these parties were in power. Misner made the same point in his book *Social Catholicism in Europe* (1991).

A Look at Data for the United States

The Catholic ethic is something of an "ideal-type" construct. Thus individuals would be mixed in their individual expression of it; the

Table 11.1. Economic Growth Rates in Protestant Countries, as Compared with Catholic Countries and Japan, 1870–1984.

Rank	*1870–1913*	*1913–1938*	*1949–1965*	*1965–1984*
1.	U.S. (P)	Japan (B)	Japan (B)	Japan (B)
2.	Canada (P)	Norway (P)	W. Germany (P)	Norway (P)
3.	Denmark (P)	Netherlands (P)	Italy (C)	France (C)
4.	Sweden (P)	U.S. (P)	France (C)	Belgium (C)
5.	Germany (P)	Switzerland (P)	Switzerland (P)	Italy (C)
6.	Belgium (C)	Denmark (P)	Netherlands (P)	W. Germany (P)
7.	Switzerland (P)	Sweden (P)	Canada (P)	Canada (P)
8.	Japan (B)	Italy (C)	Denmark (P)	Netherlands (P)
9.	Norway (P)	Canada (P)	Norway (P)	Denmark (P)
10.	Great Britain (P)	Germany (P)	Sweden (P)	Sweden (P)
11.	Netherlands (P)	Great Britain (P)	U.S. (P)	U.S. (P)
12.	France (C)	France (C)	Belgium (C)	Great Britain (P)
13.	Italy (C)	Belgium (C)	Great Britain (P)	Switzerland (P)
Mean economic growth rate in Protestant countries, as a percentage of mean economic growth rate in Catholic countries				
	152%	120%	98%	72%

Note: P indicates countries in which a majority of the population was Protestant in 1900; C indicates countries having a Roman Catholic majority in 1900; B indicates countries having a Buddhist majority in 1900.

Source: Inglehart, 1990, p. 60. The 1870–1965 rankings were calculated from data in Maddison, 1969, pp. 148–149; the 1965–1984 rankings were calculated from data in World Bank, 1986.

same is true of the Protestant ethic for that matter. How much of it actual Catholics have is a matter of current interest. Survey research data from the National Opinion Research Center are presented in this chapter to explore the extent to which contemporary American Protestants and Catholics do differ in general along charitable lines. These data support the general hypothesis that Catholics have a greater charitable orientation than Protestants, at least in the contemporary United States.

Work Values

Since "work" is often thought of as the central element of the Protestant ethic (sometimes called the Protestant work ethic), an examination of differences in work values is of interest. One of the earlier sociological works on this topic—*The Religious Factor* by Gerhard Lenski (1963, p. 357)—comes to the following conclusion based on data collected in 1958: "Our study has provided striking support for Weber's basic assumption—at least as it applies to major religious groups in contemporary American society. As the findings . . . make clear, the four major socioreligious groups differ from one another with respect to a wide range of phenomena affecting economic, political, kinship, and scientific institutions. Furthermore, these differences cannot be accounted for in terms of the economic position of either the individuals involved or the groups."

Other scholars have reexamined and challenged Lenski's findings. Andrew Greeley (1964), in particular, raised questions and objections. Howard Schuman reported a replication in 1971. This replication was important because it used the same survey approach that Lenski used, based on data compiled in the Detroit Area Study, and because Schuman was able to adopt many of the methodological and technical advances that had been made since the earlier research was carried out. He said: "Most of our conclusions about an intrinsically religious factor, therefore, must be negative. But not quite all, for a single question on work values, repeated in 1966 . . . did replicate Lenski's results; moreover, stronger results were produced in favor of the hypothesis than were apparent in 1958. Also the question seems theoretically closer to the conceptual meaning of the "Protestant ethic" than most of the other variables. . . . In particular, under a variety of controls, Protestants significantly more than Catholics rank as most important their attitude 'that work is important and gives a feeling of accomplishment'" (pp. 45–46).

Lenski, and later Schuman, asked respondents to rank five

values involved in choosing a job in order of importance: (1) high income; (2) no danger of being fired; (3) working short hours; lots of free time; (4) chances for advancement; (5) the work is important and gives a feeling of accomplishment. The results are given in Table 11.2.

In sum, it seems that there are significant differences between Protestants and Catholics in work orientation, but these differences are lodged largely in the upper middle classes. (These differences also emerge in my own analyses using a national data base. See Tropman, 1992, p. 197, Table 11.10.)

Family, Association, and Community

Another follow-up to Lenski examined the connections of individuals to family, friends, and voluntary associations. McIntosh and Alston (1982) used a different data set—the combined National

Table 11.2. Detroit Area Study: Survey Responses of White Males, 1958 and 1966, Giving First Rank to the Value "The Work Is Important and Gives a Feeling of Accomplishment" Versus Other Values When Choosing a Job.

Year	*Percent choosing "Protestant ethic response" ("Work is important")*		
	Catholics	*Protestants*	*Jews*
1958	44	52	48
1966	44	49	52
Social Class 1966			
Upper middle	58	68	[a]
Lower middle	44	47	[a]
Upper working	38	40	[a]
Lower working	37	37	[a]

Note: For details on class categories, see Schuman, 1971, p. 35.

[a]No data available.

Source: Data from Schuman, 1971, pp. 34–35. Reprinted with permission.

Opinion Research Center General Social Survey for 1974, 1975, and 1977 ($N = 3{,}278$). While the zero-order relationships between religion (a dummy variable: Catholics = 0; Protestants = 1) were not large, they were statistically significant. "Not large" means, for the dependent variables of spending time with relatives, friends, or neighbors, or being a member of a voluntary association, *r*'s of .042, .052, .021, and –.027 (McIntosh and Alston, 1982, p. 863, Table 1). McIntosh and Alston say this about social class: "What we have shown . . . is that what social class divides, religion unites. Religious commitment leads to greater secondary and primary ties, in particular tying family, neighborhood, and voluntary organizations together" (p. 876).

In a way, one could conclude that the Catholic ethic is spreading. Since these data are more recent than Lenski's, they seem to indicate that Protestants, in this dimension—religious commitment being linked to ties to family, and so on—are moving closer to Catholics. It is a hypothesis worth considering. In any case, we can expect a substantial mixing of attitudes in a pluralistic country like the United States. After all, Catholics have been converging with Protestants in terms of economic achievement (Lachman and Kosmin, 1993), if not in work values, so some movement the other way is not out of the question.

A Comparison of Worldviews

Lenski's structural predictions were generalized and codified, though not directly, by the work of Greeley (1990). Greeley clearly believes that Catholics and Protestants have different values. Members of each group "imagine" things differently, he says, drawing on David Tracy's (1989) concept of *analogical imagination*, which contrasts with *dialectical imagination*. Greeley (1990, pp. 47–48) extends this notion to outline a specific set of expected behavioral consequences rather than the "population tendencies" described by Lenski:

> Catholics will be more likely than Protestants to value social relationships. . . . Catholics will be more likely than Protestants to value equality over freedom. . . . Catholics will be more likely than Protestants to advocate decentralization. . . . Protestants will value in their children the virtues of initiative, integrity, industry, and thrift more than Catholics, while Catholics will value loyalty, obedience, and patience. . . . Protestants are more likely to emphasize personal responsibility (Weber's "worldly asceticism") than Catholics; they will also be more likely to emphasize the "work ethic" than Catholics, who will be more likely to work because they have to than because they want to.

Greeley's thinking in his 1990 work both reflects and extends Lenski's research, and he does so with a much wider base of empirical data (using several countries) and more sophisticated analytical techniques. The distinctions between Catholic and Protestant values were clear but were not really strong in Greeley's data. There seems, then, to be evidence for a Catholic ethic, but it competes with other belief systems people have as well.

Another way of looking at the matter might be to develop a religious "scale" to measure attitudes. There is a Protestant ethic scale but as yet no Catholic ethic scale. Studies of the Protestant ethic include Albee, 1977; Feather, 1984; Fine, 1983; Ganster, 1981; Gonsalves and Goodwin, 1984; Greenberg, 1977, 1978, 1979; Heaven, 1980; Merrens and Garret, 1975; Mirels and Darland, 1990; Mirels and Garret, 1971; Philbrick, 1976; Ray, 1982; Segalman, 1968; Stephens, Metz, and Craig, 1975; Waters, Batlis, and Waters, 1975. Greeley (1991, p. 41), though, has developed something similar called the "GRACE" scale (a seven-point scale between forced choices of pictures of God: mother/father, master/spouse, judge/lover, king/friend). About the GRACE Scale, Greeley says, "Religion, I saw, could be profitably approached as a predictor variable that is of some considerable importance in understanding social attitudes and behaviors" (1991, p. 43). Almost echoing Lenski's comments of decades earlier, Greeley comments, "The religious imagination, then, does contribute to people's social and political attitudes and behaviors, and its contribution cannot be reduced to either demographic or political orientation" (p. 42). Could these effects be manifest within a concept called the Catholic ethic? The answer must be affirmative.

In his scholarly work, Greeley has shown that a distinctive Catholic "imagination" exists; it could be called a Catholic ethic. The Catholic ethic is global, like the Catholic Church itself. Greeley's multinational data, and McIntosh and Alston's (1982) data from many ethnic groups within the United States, pointed to differences between religious groups that, while significant, were modest in strength. So our thinking about the power of the Catholic ethic needs to be tempered; perhaps by extension, the same is true of our thinking about the Protestant ethic.

What other differences in worldview might be seen between Catholics and Protestants in America? Data from the Times Mirror Center, taken from a survey conducted by Gallup between May 13 and 22, 1988, provide one of the most complete pictures of these differences (see Table 11.3). The data presented in the table suggest the presence of a Catholic ethic. Some differences are greater than others, of course, but the consistency of the differences suggests that Catholics, on the whole, think differently about things than Protestants do. However, race is a factor. African American Protestants (called black Protestants in the survey) had significantly different views from white Protestants in many areas. Racial differences within Protestantism are a fascinating topic, one that goes beyond the scope of this chapter.

Notice too that the confirmations (in italics) come in the areas considered parts of the Catholic ethic—work, otherworldliness, fault-forgiveness. However, the data do show some surprises. In regard to family ties, Catholics were less family oriented than I would have predicted, though the results were consistent with the McIntosh and Alston (1982) findings. Obviously this area needs

Table 11.3. Similarities and Differences Between Protestants and Catholics; White Protestants Only (Percent Agree with Statement), Times Mirror/Gallup Survey, 2,294 U.S. Adults.

Question	*Protestant*	*Catholic*	*Protestant-Catholic differences (P – C)*
Other Worldly			
Success in Life is pretty much determined by forces outside our control.	38.3	43.9	–5.6
Work			
Hard work offers little guarantee of success.	29.2	32.8	–3.6
The strength of the country today is mostly based on the success of American business.	81.8	78.9	2.9
Fault/Forgiveness Cycle			
We have gone too far in pushing equal rights in this country.	51.3	45.3	6.0
I think it's all right for blacks and whites to date each other.	35.7	53.1	–17.4
School boards ought to have the right to fire teachers who are known homosexuals.	59.8	44.5	15.3
Books that contain dangerous ideas should be banned from public school libraries.	55.4	50.3	5.1
There are clear guidelines about good/evil that apply to everyone regardless of the situation.	84.3	75.2	10.1
Family			
Too many children are being raised in day-care centers these days.	72.4	71.8	0.6
I have old-fashioned values about family and marriage.	91.5	85.8	5.7

Note: Italics indicates support for the Catholic ethic thesis.

Source: Data from *The People, the Press, & Politics, Survey III*, May 13–22, 1988, Times Mirror Center. Reprinted with permission. Italicized question headings added by John E. Tropman.

further attention. Alwin (1985) found a similar lack of difference in parental values.

Another relevant data set has been collected by the National Opinion Research Center at the University of Chicago in the General Social Survey (GSS). Some of their data examine general attitudes held by Catholics and Protestants, providing yet another way to approach the Catholic ethic question. In these surveys, Catholic-Protestant differences were assessed in terms of questions about the presence of good versus evil in human beings and the world and the need to act versus the need for caution. Some results are presented in Table 11.4.

The questions about evil in the world, evil in human beings, and the need to be wary, turned up consistent, definite differences between Catholics and Protestants. Catholics are more likely to think the world is good (by 8 percent), more likely to think that human beings are good (by 10.9 percent), and more likely to think that the good must act (by 9.4 percent).

Based on this review of data from global sources as well as the United States, there seems little question that religious culture is an important force in the lives of individual citizens and countries. *Catholic ethic* is an appropriate term, just as *Protestant ethic* is, to describe possible variants. But that leaves a second question: To what extent do these spiritually based cultures differ in their views of the disadvantaged and their willingness to provide assistance to those in need?

The Catholic Ethic as a Charitable Ethic

Some elements of a charitable approach and support for welfare state initiatives have already been hinted at in the earlier data. The question on whether "the good must act" suggests that the impulse to translate "Christian" principles into action is present in both Protestants and Catholics, but is stronger among Catholics.

Other data from the Gallup poll illustrate differences between

Table 11.4. Contrasting Worldviews of Protestants and Catholics.

The World Is Evil (*N* = 5105)			
Religion	*Evil (1–3)*[a]	*Uncertain (4)*[a]	*Good (5–7)*[a]
Catholics	13.5	26.6	59.9
Protestants	21.2	27.0	51.8

Man Is Corrupt Versus Good (*N* = 5097)			
Religion	*Evil (7–5)*[a]	*Uncertain (4)*[a]	*Good (3–1)*[a]
Catholics	9.7	21.5	68.8
Protestants	19.2	22.7	57.9[b]

The Good Must Beware Versus Good Must Act (*N* = 1341)			
Religion	*Beware (7–5)*[a]	*Uncertain (4)*[a]	*Act (3–1)*[a]
Catholics	14.6	28.3	57.1
Protestants	24.0	27.4	48.5[b]

[a]Based on answers from a 7-point scale.

[b]Rows that do not add up to 100 percent are due to rounding errors.

Source: Data from National Opinion Research Center General Social Survey, 1983–1989 combined.

Catholics and white Protestants on charity-related questions. Relevant data are presented in Table 11.5. Items that support a pro-charity/pro–welfare state orientation are in bold type.

In six out of nine cases, the responses indicated a more charitable orientation among Catholics, an orientation that supports government action to care for the needy. But while the differences between Catholics and Protestants are obvious, they are not striking. The largest distinction is found in responses to the last item on the list: "The Government should guarantee every citizen enough to eat and a place to sleep." On that item, there was a substantial difference (–11.5 percent), with 59.4 percent of the Protestant respondents and 70.9 percent of the Catholic respondents in agreement. Differences are present, and in the direction that I have hypothesized. They are modest differences rather than huge ones, however, suggesting that other key variables play a role.

Table 11.5. Similarities and Differences Between Protestants and Catholics, Welfare State/Charity-Related Questions; White Protestants Only (Percent Agree with Statement), Times Mirror/Gallup Survey, 2,294 U.S. Adults.

Question	P	C	(P – C)[a]
The federal government should run only those things that cannot be run at the local level.	82.0	74.3	7.7
The federal government controls too much of daily lives.	64.3	54.6	9.7
The government is really run for the benefit of all the people.	51.6	58.1	–6.7
Business corporations strike a fair balance between making profits and serving the public interest.	43.6	41.1	2.5
There is too much power concentrated in the hands of a few companies.	77.2	77.8	–0.6
Our society should make sure everyone has an equal opportunity to succeed.	91.1	90.7	–0.6
It is the responsibility of government to take care of people who can't take care of themselves.	72.4	72.8	0.6
The government should help more needy people even if it means going deeper into debt.	48.4	54.4	–6.0
The government should guarantee every citizen enough to eat and a place to sleep.	59.4	70.9	–11.5

[a]Protestant minus Catholic.

Source: Data from *The People, the Press, & Politics, Survey III*, May 13–22, 1988, Times Mirror Center. Reprinted with permission.

The GSS included other variables that allow us to look specifically at "share-itable" orientation and religion, but now we add the factor of social class. A striking finding is that the differences in orientation toward helping appear most prominent among upper-class Catholics, something true in all but one of the rows (Table 11.6). This point is mentioned by McIntosh and Alston (1982).

A second piece of evidence for Catholic charity lies in the extent to which Catholics want to see increases in public spending

Table 11.6. Percentage Results of "Share-ity" Variables by Catholic/Protestant (White) Religious Identification and Level of Socioeconomic Class.

Charity variable	*Catholic*			*White Protestant*		
	LoSES	*AveSES*	*HiSES*	*LoSES*	*AveSES*	*HiSES*
Assistance to the poor						
% too little	72	72	69	73	62	49
Should government improve standard of living						
% favor government	38	33	30	35	24	15
Should government spend less on poor						
% disagree	70	64	57	75	54	41
Should government reduce income differences						
% agree	57	51	45	57	46	31
Responsibility of government to meet needs						
% agree	67	65	54	63	45	39
Social welfare benefits are a disincentive						
% agree	45	47	32	60	48	38

Note: HiSES = high socioeconomic status; LoSES = low socioeconomic status; AveSES = average socioeconomic status.

Source: Data from National Opinion Research Center General Social Survey, 1983–1988 combined.

for social purposes. As the data in Table 11.7 suggest, Catholics would increase the budget in each of the "prosocial" areas.

Readers will note that more Catholic respondents than Protestant ones favored increases in every area. However, it is important, too, to point out that the regions of the proportions were quite different, and in the same ballpark. So there is both similarity and difference.

In my own research, I have created a measure of pro-poor orientation, consisting of four variables: spending on assistance to help the poor (too little, too much, about right), helping the poor (should the government improve the standard of living?), equal

Table 11.7. Similarities and Differences Between Protestants and Catholics, Welfare State/Charity-Related Federal Budget Questions; White Protestants Only (Percent Increase the Budget), Times Mirror/Gallup Survey, 2,936 U.S. Adults.

Budget area	*P*	C	(*P* – C)[a]
Programs for the elderly	71.2	76.0	–4.8
Programs for the homeless	62.4	68.9	–6.5
Improving public schools	66.8	67.6	–0.8
Reducing drug addiction	64.4	70.1	–5.7
Improving nation's health care	67.4	72.8	–10.4
Programs to assist blacks and other minorities	22.2	38.0	–15.8
Scientific research	39.8	52.9	–13.1
Government assistance for unemployed	32.2	45.0	–13.7
Research on AIDS	65.5	72.4	–6.9
Social security	58.0	66.8	–10.8

[a]Protestant minus Catholic.

Source: Data from *The People, the Press, & Politics: A Study of the American Electorate*, April 25–May 10, 1987, Times Mirror Center. Reprinted with permission.

wealth (should the government help to reduce income differences?), and spending less on the poor. The result was a scale running from 4 (pro-poor) to 12 (antipoor). Means are listed in Table 11.8. Note that there is a big difference between white and black Protestants on these measures. Catholics come out more pro-poor than white Protestants, but less so than black Protestants.

Following up this attention to race, religion, and welfare orientation, Table 11.9 looks at the predictive power of different variables in explaining the pro-poor index.

These results are in line with the general thesis of this chapter. While white Protestant background is not the most important variable in predicting an antipoor view, it is number 2. Catholic is almost zero, at .03. Race is negatively associated with predicting these orientations, and "Black Protestant" has no relationship (suggesting the tension between racial orientations and religious orientations that black Protestants must experience). I also want to

Table 11.8. Means, Pro-Poor Index.

Denomination	*Mean*
Protestants (all)	6.71
White	7.21
Black	5.72
Catholic	6.50

Source: Data from National Opinion Research Center General Social Survey, 1983–1988 combined.

emphasize that, even with all these variables, I can still only "account" for 22 percent of the variance in the pro-poor index, something that clearly shows that there are lots of other factors at work.

Conclusion

It is reasonable to conclude, therefore, that there is a Catholic ethic, and that it is likely to involve a "share-itable" orientation. There are spiritually based cultures and they have an impact on thinking about need. Obviously, more research is needed to explore these ideas further.

Assuming that there is a Catholic ethic, what might it mean for philanthropy? Religions may differ in the way they talk about need, about those in need, and about what to do when need presents itself. There is little question in my mind that religious background is an important factor in shaping these perspectives.

I do not doubt that spiritually based cultures compete with other important cultural determinants (race, most obviously) that shape the individual's thinking. Any attempt to argue that one view only is key would be in error. I have pointed to differences between Protestants (white and black) and Catholics, but there are many other important factors. And the possibility of a "dominance-subdominance" relationship for individuals within any religion is very strong.

Table 11.9. Multiple Regression Results Predicting the Charity Index (ALLDEVAR).

Rank of importance (by beta)	B	*Beta*	*Significance*
1. Political views	.34	.24	.000
11. White Protestant	.64	.16	.214
2. Education	.39	.14	.000
6. Race	–.49	–.12	.061
8. Prestige	.19	.08	.055
7. Rincome[a]	.20	.07	.064
5. Age	.01	.06	.076
3. Region	.04	.05	.150
13. Catholic	.20	.04	.687
4. Sex	–.11	–.03	.444
10. Jew	.53	.03	.487
19. None	.18	.02	.745
12. Black Protestant	.00	.00	.985

Note: ALLDEVAR is scored with 4 = pro-poor, 12 = antipoor. Multiple R = .470; R square = .221.

[a]Respondents' income.

Source: Data from National Opinion Research Center General Social Survey, 1983–1988 combined.

This possibility forces us to think about a melding of religious views. Perhaps religion more sharply differentiated between people in the past but has less influence today, or a strong influence in smaller groups. It might be that ethnic identities or other factors are becoming more central. Whatever the case, an important part of these or any other cultures has to do with issues of need—the nature of people's needs and ways of allocating resources to meet these needs.

References

Albee, G. W. "The Protestant Ethic, Sex, and Psychotherapy." *American Psychologist*, 1977, *32*, 150–161.

Alwin, D. "Religion and Parental Child Rearing Orientations." Unpublished manuscript, Department of Sociology, University of Michigan, 1985.

Feather, N. T. "The Protestant Ethic, Conservatism, and Values." *Journal of Personality and Social Psychology*, 1984, 46(5), 1132–1141.

Fine, R. "The Protestant Ethic and the Analytic Ideal." *Political Psychology*, 1983, 4(2), 245–264.

Ganster, D. C. "Protestant Ethic and Performance: A Reexamination." *Psychological Reports*, 1981, 48(1), 335–338.

Gonsalves, S., and Goodwin, B. "The Protestant Ethic and Conservatism Scales." *High School Journal*, 1984, 68(4), 247–253.

Greeley, A. M. "The Protestant Ethic: Time for a Moratorium." *Sociological Analysis*, 1964, 24, 20–33.

Greeley, A. M. "Evidence That a Maternal Image of God Correlates with Liberal Politics." *Sociology and Social Research*, 1988, 72(3), 150–154.

Greeley, A. M. *The Catholic Myth: The Behavior and Beliefs of American Catholics*. New York: Charles Scribner's Sons, 1990.

Greeley, A. M. "Who Are the Catholic 'Conservatives'?" *America*, Sept. 21, 1991, pp. 158–162.

Greenberg, J. "The Protestant Ethic and Reactions to the Negative Performance Evaluations on a Laboratory Task." *Journal of Applied Psychology*, 1977, 62(6), 682–690.

Greenberg, J. "Protestant Ethic Endorsement and Attitudes Toward Commuting to Work Among Mass Transit Riders." *Journal of Applied Psychology*, 1978, 63(6), 755–758.

Greenberg, J. "Protestant Ethic Endorsement and the Fairness of Equity Inputs." *Journal of Research in Personality*, 1979, 13(1), 81–90.

Gremillion, J. *The Gospel of Peace and Justice*. Maryknoll, N.Y.: Orbis, 1976.

Heaven, P. C. "The Protestant Ethic Scale in South Africa." *Psychological Reports*, 1980, 47(2), 618.

Inglehart, R. *Culture Shift*. Princeton, N.J.: Princeton University Press, 1990.

Jacobs, M. X. *The Jewish Ethic and the Culture of Obligation*. Ann Arbor: Project STaR, University of Michigan, 1994.

Lachman, S., and Kosmin, B. A. *One Nation Under God*. New York: Harmony, 1993.

Lenski, G. *The Religious Factor*. New York: Doubleday, 1963.

McIntosh, W. A., and Alston, J. P. "Lenski Revisited: The Linkage Role of Religion in Primary and Secondary Groups." *American Journal of Sociology*, 1982, 87, 852–882.

Maddison, A. *Economic Growth in Japan and the U.S.S.R.* London: Allen and Unwin, 1969.

Marshall, G. *In Search of the Spirit of Capitalism: An Essay on Max Weber's Protestant Ethic Thesis*. New York: Columbia University Press, 1982.

Merrens, M., and Garrett, J. B. "The Protestant Ethic Scale as a Predictor of

Repetitive Work Performance." *Journal of Applied Psychology*, 1975, 60(1), 125–127.

Mirels, H., and Darland, D. M. "The Protestant Ethic and Self Characterization." *Personality and Individual Differences*, 1990, *11*(9), 895–898.

Mirels, H. L., and Garret, J. "The Protestant Ethic as a Personality Variable." *Journal of Consulting and Clinical Psychology*, 1971, *36*(1), 40–44.

Misner, P. *Social Catholicism in Europe*. New York: Crossroads, 1991.

Mueller, G. H. "The Protestant and the Catholic Ethic." *American Review for the Scientific Study of Religion*, 1978, *2*, 143–166.

Newman, K. *Falling from Grace: The Experience of Downward Mobility in the American Middle Class*. New York: Free Press, 1988.

Novak, M. *The Catholic Ethic and the Spirit of Capitalism*. New York: Free Press, 1993.

Philbrick, J. L. "The Protestant Ethic in East Africa." *Psychologica Africana*, 1976, *16*(3), 173–175.

Ray, J. J. "The Protestant Ethic in Australia." *Journal of Social Psychology*, 1982, *116*(1), 127–138.

Rosenberg, N., and Birdzill, L. E., Jr. "Science, Technology, and the Western Miracle." *Scientific American*, 1990, *263*(5), 42–54.

Schuman, H. "The Religious Factor in Detroit: Review, Replication, and Reanalysis." *American Sociological Review*, 1971, *36*(1), 30–47.

Segalman, R. "The Protestant Ethic in Social Welfare." *Journal of Social Issues*, 1968, *24*(1), 125–141.

Sombart, W. *The Jews and Modern Capitalism*. London: Unwin, 1913.

Stephens, R., Metz, L., and Craig, J. "The Protestant Ethic Effect in a Multichoice Environment." *Bulletin of the Psychonomic Society*, 1975, 6(2), 137–139.

Tracy, D. *The Analogical Imagination*. New York: Crossroads, 1989.

Tropman, J. E. *American Values and Social Welfare: Cultural Contradictions in the Welfare State*. Englewood Cliffs, N.J.: Prentice Hall, 1989.

Tropman, J. E. "The 'Catholic Ethic' Versus the 'Protestant Ethic': Catholic Social Service and the Welfare State." *Social Thought*, 1986, *12*(1), 13–22.

Tropman, J. E. "Social Exploitation." Unpublished manuscript, School of Social Work, University of Michigan, 1992.

Waters, L. K., Batlis, N., and Waters, C. "Protestant Ethic Attitudes Among College Students." *Educational and Psychological Measurement*, 1975, *35*(2), 447–450.

Weber, M. *The Protestant Ethic and the Spirit of Capitalism* (Talcott Parsons, trans.). New York: Charles Scribner's Sons, 1956. (Originally published 1904–1905.)

Weiner, R. *Judaism: A Learning Culture and Its Impact on the Pillars of the Jewish Ethos*. Ann Arbor: Project STaR, University of Michigan, 1994.
Wilensky, H. "Leftism, Catholicism, and Democratic Corporatism: The Role of Political Parties in Recent Welfare State Development." In P. Flora and A. Heidenheimer (eds.), *The Development of Welfare States in Europe and America*. New Brunswick, N.J.: Transaction Books, 1981.
Woodward, K. "The Rites of Americans." *Newsweek*, Nov. 29, 1993, pp. 80–82.
World Bank. *World Development Report*. Washington, D.C.: World Bank, 1986.

Part Four

Social and Political Environments of Care

Investigating the social causes and consequences of caring requires explicit attention to the institutional environment in which our philanthropic activity takes place and toward which we direct many of our reform efforts. Because the communities of participation can enhance or limit our vocations of care, it is crucial to understand their workings. The five chapters in Part Four address ways the institutional infrastructure advances or undermines how care is implemented and transmitted. The first of these chapters addresses the broad issue of what constitutes a caring organizational framework, while the remaining four critically evaluate just how caring specific social organizations, governments, and societies are. We are never fully subservient to or completely in command of the institutions that surround us. But clearly, becoming aware of how they influence us for better or for worse, figuring out what we might do to make them more benevolent, and pursuing an agenda of change are themselves important expressions of care.

What it means for institutions to promote or inhibit a caring society is the topic of Emmett D. Carson's chapter (Chapter Twelve). According to Carson, a caring society is one whose members are concerned "to improve the socioeconomic well-being of their fellow citizens." How to advance such care, he argues, is the most significant commonality among scholars, nonprofit practitioners, and government officials who deal with the nonprofit sector. Drawing on nonprofit research and anecdotal information, Carson examines how families, religious organizations, schools, businesses, and government shape collective caring behavior in the United States. All these communities of participation, he finds, contribute to advancing care to the extent to which they create relationships that transmit values of caring and to the degree to which they actively work to encourage individuals within their sphere of influence to be responsible toward the larger society. At the same time, a number of inhibiting factors curtail such positive institutional influence. These include a lack of moral leadership by organizational officials; intolerance of others' race, religion, culture, or sexual preference; and blind adherence to tradition, such as relying too exclusively on white males for board positions, staffing, and contributions of time and money.

In Chapter Thirteen, Michael K. Briand and Jennifer Alstad pick up on Carson's theme in their call for a renewed commitment to participatory democratic politics. According to Briand and Alstad, a well-meaning summons to care is no substitute for facing up to the fact that our nation's most pressing problems are becoming more severe and now require nothing less than a reinvigoration of a "healthy participatory democratic political process." Unless wedded to a strategy of empowerment, caring too often leads to a debilitating dependency, lapsing into excessive self-sacrifice, paternalism, and the cult of victimhood. Regrettably, the culture of scientific professionalism, once deemed so promising for creating enlightened social policy, has spawned an antidemocratic ethos that has shifted responsibility to government, created an inadequate network of institutionalized caring, and turned citizens into clients and passive consumers of government initiatives. Ultimately, this elitist strategy crushed the willingness of ordinary citizens to take personal responsibility for solving their own and their country's ills. The solution is not to call for more care, either by government or nonprofit organizations. Rather it is to build an infrastructure of deliberative democratic politics that will encourage citizens to reenter politics, recognize their social responsibilities, and activate their capacity for effective collective action.

Steven L. Paprocki and Robert O. Bothwell argue in Chapter Fourteen that to properly assess the extent to which corporations actually do demonstrate care, we must examine not their motivations but their actions. One such behavioral indicator of corporate caring is the level of grantmaking to racial/ethnic populations. Studying the funding priorities of nineteen of the top twenty-five corporations, the authors found that in 1988 these corporations (and their foundations) contributed over $400 million, about 9 percent of total corporate giving. But only $26 million or 17 percent of corporate funding went to support racial/ethnic populations. Most of the grants were for education and human services, and about half of the funding for racial/ethnic populations went for constituency-controlled programs. Forty-eight percent of grants were to organizations with multiracial beneficiaries, with 37 percent going to benefit African Americans and 12 percent to Hispanic Americans. Forty-two percent of funds were for general/operating support, with the next largest proportions going to program development and student aid. Important questions for future research include how recipient organizations used their grants, which grants were denied, and how to resolve the numerous discrepancies between the authors' findings and those presented by other research organizations.

In Chapter Fifteen, Heidi Hartmann and Roberta Spalter-Roth turn their attention to a topic technically outside the realm of philanthropy—but clearly within the realm of care. This is the assistance for poor families with children carried out by what the authors refer to as the public charity of government through tax-funded redistribution programs. Because citizens make choices about how much of their income to redistribute to the poor, one way to encourage a more caring society is to make sure that the citizenry supports public income-transfer programs. To this end, the authors trace the recent history of antiwelfare, pro-work rhetoric surrounding Aid to Families with Dependent Children (AFDC). They conclude that such rhetoric has led to a series of policies and policy proposals to reduce government assistance without at the same time improving incentives for work. There is simply no basis in research for "the consensus that welfare perpetuates dependence and that paid employment is the ticket out of poverty for single mothers and their children." A true test of this dependency thesis can occur only if we institute a genuine work-plus-welfare wage-subsidy program and a variety of income supplements, educational opportunities, and work incentives to make paid employment for welfare recipients truly a viable path out of poverty. Establishing such work and welfare packaging, the authors conclude, is the most effective way to care for needy members of society. Such an approach will quiet antiwelfare rhetoric and provide a more humanitarian treatment of women and families in poverty.

In Chapter Sixteen, Lester M. Salamon and Helmut K. Anheier take the broadest perspective on the institutional environment affecting a society's level and scope of care. In a cross-national study, the authors question the conventional U.S. notion that the size and visibility of a nonprofit sector reveals how caring a society is. The authors argue that large nonprofit sectors may actually signify the weakness rather than the strength of a caring tradition in other realms of a society. Indeed, the concept of a nonprofit sector does not exist in most parts of the world. Salamon and Anheier base their analysis on comparative data from the United States, United Kingdom, Germany, France, Italy, Japan, Hungary, and a number of developing countries. They find "very little relationship between the presence of a coherent nonprofit sector and the extent of 'caring' in a society." Rather, a variety of other factors affect the level of care—for example, a society's legal framework, its level of development and degree of social differentiation, its centralization of social and political control, and its government policies. Only by examining a nonprofit sector within a society's entire institutional environment can we assess whether the size and scope of a nation's nonprofit sector is evidence of a caring society or an indicator of just the opposite.

Chapter Twelve

How Institutions Shape a Caring Society

Emmett D. Carson

It is probably not an exaggeration to suggest that the phrase "separate but equal" accurately describes the level of interaction that exists between scholars and practitioners in most social science disciplines. Scholars typically convene during annual meetings of their associations to share research findings and critique each others' work in national journals whose readership seldom includes those who are not scholars. Similarly, practitioners gather at annual professional meetings where they share information on recent developments and compare their experiences in meeting current challenges. Scholars who "know everything" lament that practitioners do not "adequately utilize their findings," and practitioners lament that scholars have no understanding of how the "real world" operates. The relatively recent emergence of scholarship and professional associations within the nonprofit sector provides a unique opportunity to avoid the gulf that has occurred between scholars and practitioners in other social science fields (Carson, 1993). Moreover, given the complexity of the nonprofit sector and its important role in American society, the traditional divide between scholarship and practice may lead to inefficiencies and misinformation that would be detrimental to society as a whole.

At least one area of common interest between scholars and practitioners in the nonprofit sector, albeit for different reasons, is

Note: Emmett D. Carson is president of the Minneapolis Foundation. The views presented in this chapter are those of the author and not the Minneapolis Foundation.

how various types of institutions promote or inhibit a caring society. This is also a topic of considerable interest to government officials charged with regulating the nonprofit sector in ways to promote the common good. Scholars are concerned with how institutions affect the lives of people who come into contact with them, and practitioners who run institutions are concerned with how to make them more effective in carrying out their respective missions to be of service in their communities. In particular, both groups are concerned with how future generations are encouraged to give and volunteer in support of charitable causes and organizations. The goal of this chapter is to develop a conceptual framework for understanding how institutions influence our collective caring behavior and to test it by combining the existing nonprofit sector research on giving and volunteering with anecdotal information about nonprofit organizations.

At least three questions must be considered at the outset of any discussion to understand how institutions, broadly defined, shape a caring society. What is the definition of a caring society? Why should we care about how institutions promote or inhibit a caring society? And what kinds of institutions are important in helping to shape a caring society? These and related questions are addressed in the next two sections. In the remaining sections, the definitions and hypotheses that have been developed will be examined with regard to five institutions: families, religious organizations, schools, businesses, and government. Throughout these latter sections, it is essential to remember that institutions, like people, are shaped by the cultural beliefs and values that exist at a given point in time. It is also important to recognize that the age of the institution and the age at which an individual comes into contact with an institution are important variables to consider.

Transmitting Values Through Institutions

If we believe that a caring society is better than an uncaring one, and I think we do, then we need to be concerned about how younger generations learn to become caring individuals so that the value of a caring society will continue to be perpetuated long after we are gone. For our purposes here, the institutions that I will focus on are families, religious organizations, schools, businesses, and government. There are certainly other kinds of institutions, but these five are likely to be among the most important in influencing our own behavior and that of our children.

Defining exactly what is a caring society and how to measure it is somewhat more problematic. For example, we often hear the call for "tough love" with regard to such social issues as welfare and drug addiction, which suggests that caring should not always translate into doing. Notwithstanding this caveat, a caring society is one in which people are concerned or interested in, and generally act to improve, the socioeconomic well-being of their fellow citizens. While there are certainly other definitions of a caring society, this definition is a core tenet of most of the major religions as well as a general concept within human rights doctrines. And at least one measure of a caring society is the extent to which people give and volunteer to help others.

With these operational definitions in mind, how do institutions promote or inhibit a caring society? Two major themes are put forward in this chapter. The first is that different institutions create different types of relationships between people that allow for beliefs and values, including that of a caring society, to be more easily transmitted and shared over a person's lifetime. Stated another way, we relate to our families, congregational members, classmates, co-workers, and fellow citizens differently because of the unique character and the degree of intimacy allowed by the institutions where we meet and interact with others.

The second theme is that institutions promote caring societies in direct proportion to the extent that they acknowledge and accept some responsibility for shaping the attitudes of individuals within their respective sphere of influence toward the larger society. In other words, institutions that recognize a dual obligation to provide for the needs of the individual within the institution as well as to shape that individual's worldview with regard to his or her obligation to the rest of us are more likely to promote a caring society. The inverse is also true. Institutions that accept little or no responsibility for how individuals connected to the institution view their obligations to the rest of us are likely to do little to promote a caring society. There are other ways institutions can inhibit a caring society, and these factors are examined in the next section.

Institutional Characteristics That Inhibit Caring

While the goal of this chapter is to explore how institutions help to shape a caring society, it is important to observe that several characteristics or factors can operate within institutions, regardless of type, to inhibit their efforts in this area. Three of the factors that I have identified are: a lack of moral leadership, intolerance toward people who are different, and blind adherence to tradition.

John Gardner (1990, p. 1) describes leadership as "the process of persuasion or example by which an individual induces a group to pursue objectives held by the leader." Leaders establish the tone and priorities of the institutions that they lead and can send powerful messages that can heighten or reduce our sense of mutual responsibility for each other. For example, President Clinton sent powerful messages when, during the campaign, he and Vice President Gore spent a day working to rehabilitate housing in Georgia (Goss and Greene, 1992, p. 1) and working in a soup kitchen for the homeless on a Thanksgiving holiday. Similarly, religious leaders, high school principals and college presidents, business executives and fathers and mothers of families send important signals to those around them about the value of a caring society. When the leaders of these institutions do not provide encouraging messages, it is not surprising that our concern for one another substantially decreases.

Another inhibiting factor is intolerance toward people who are different. We care if you look like us. We care if you speak like us. And we care if you think like us. If you do not meet these criteria, too often we could care less. As René Dubos remarked in *Celebrations of Life*, "Human diversity makes tolerance more than a virtue, it makes it a requirement for survival" (Carruth and Ehrich, 1988, p. 294).

For institutions to promote caring, they cannot be indifferent, or worse, hostile, to some individuals based on race, religion, culture, sexual preference, or other factors. There are numerous examples of how intolerance within institutions inhibits a caring society. AIDS is a good example. When the disease was first detected, intolerance toward the life-style of gays and lesbians, racism toward Haitians, and, more generally, African Americans, as well as a lack of understanding or compassion for why people become addicted to drugs combined to paralyze our major institutions from confronting this problem.

Our government leaders worry about the propriety of dispensing clean needles to drug addicts or condoms to prisoners. Our religious leaders question whether AIDS is some form of divine retribution. Our educational leaders worry about crossing the line between teaching safe sex and promoting sex and whether and at what age to teach tolerance about gay life-styles. And parents worry whether and what to say about these difficult issues at home.

So, what does all this mean for people who have the HIV/AIDS virus? Let me quote a recent report by the National Research Council, a private agency chartered by the federal government. The report states that the AIDS epidemic will have little impact on American society because those who are affected are a "socially marginalized group with little economic, political, and social power." The report goes on to say that those who are affected with the virus are "socially invisible, beyond sight and attention of the majority population" ("Research Group Says AIDS Epidemic Will Have Little Effect on U.S.," 1993, p. A-12). While most of our major institutions grapple with gridlock due to intolerance of this kind, more lives are lost and still more people are put at risk of contracting this deadly disease.

The third inhibiting factor is blind adherence to tradition. The paradox is that at least part of the reason institutions have such powerful effects on our lives is because we can rely on them for stability and continuity. We remember and respond to tradition. Most of us can recall personal experiences of visiting in-laws or friends' houses during holidays and feeling out of sorts because they didn't do things the "right" way. In truth, we confused the way we were used to doing it with the right way. This kind of relatively inconsequential example has important implications in other settings.

In the past, many national nonprofit organizations have been able to exist and grow based mainly on contributions from white males. However, as people of color—African, Asian, Latino, and Native American—become this nation's majority, nonprofit organizations continue to rely on the old habit of largely relying on white males for board positions and staffing as well as for contributions of time and money (Carson, 1989).

I believe that, in most cases, this has less to do with overt racism or sexism but rather is the result of blind adherence to tradition. The irony is that even though minorities are far less likely than whites to be asked by charitable organizations to give or volunteer, they are far more likely to participate when they are asked (Hodgkinson and Weitzman, 1992a, p. 210). For our institutions to thrive, they must remain open to change. Behaving otherwise will only ensure their stagnation and eventual demise.

Against this background, the following sections examine specific types of institutions. We start with the oldest institution of all—the family.

The Family

Perhaps the most important, overstudied, and least understood of all institutions is the family. Family structure is often credited or blamed for individual success or failure, and most would agree that both family structure and family values have an impact on an individual's socioeconomic status and behavior. For example, we know that children raised in households headed by a single female are far more likely to grow up in poverty, have limited access to health care, and often receive inadequate education. This observation is not to suggest that this is the fault of the single parent, usually the mother, but rather recognizes that children living in single female–headed households face poor odds for socioeconomic advancement compared with children raised in traditional two-parent households (Committee on Ways and Means, U.S. House of Representatives, 1992, pp. 1172–1178).

Family values are even more difficult to discuss. We know that parents are tremendous role models for their children in both negative and positive ways. For instance, we know that children who are abused or molested have a greater likelihood of abusing their own children (Kaufman and Zigler, 1987).

Fortunately, positive traits and values can also be transmitted. In its 1992 report *Volunteering and Giving Among American Teenagers*, the INDEPENDENT SECTOR found that teenagers who could think of someone in the world today who, by example, illustrates what it means to be a caring person represented 70 percent of teen volunteers. The most frequently cited example was a teen's mother, at 13 percent. Further, we know that among teenagers in families where both parents volunteer, 87 percent of the teens volunteered. By contrast, among teenagers in families where neither parent volunteered, only 48 percent of the teens participated in volunteer activities (Hodgkinson and Weitzman, 1992b, pp. 33, 69). Based on these findings, consistent with our hypothesis, parents who demonstrate their concern for larger societal issues by volunteering to help others are more likely to transmit that same value to their children, who, in turn, emulate their parents' behavior.

While I do not want to be accused of reviving the vacuous Dan Quayle–Murphy Brown family values debate, I do think there is general agreement that all families may not equally transmit the same or correct values to their children. This has little to do with family type or structure, but rather with the morals and values transmitted by the parents to the children. From this perspective, Barbara Bush's statement on family values at the height of the 1992 presidential election campaign—"However you define family values, that's how we [Republicans] define family values"—misses the point. Perhaps a better sentiment was expressed in Steve Martin's hit movie *Parenthood*, when one of the characters lamented something to the effect that "you even need a license to get a dog, but they let anybody be a parent." The fear that anybody can be a parent has, over time, encouraged us to consider how other institutions—more specifically, churches, schools, and government—might be used to transmit or reinforce societal norms, including that of a caring society.

Religious Institutions

The link between religious institutions and giving and volunteering is one of the strongest findings to emerge from research on the nonprofit sector. As Robert Wuthnow notes in his wonderful book, *Acts of Compassion* (1991, p. 122), "The world's major religions all encourage their followers to be compassionate. The Hebrew Scriptures teach that men and women are created in the image of God and are for this reason deserving of all the caring and kindness that can be given them. . . . The Koran teaches that those who give charity guard themselves from evil. Buddhist thought . . . elevates compassion above all other virtues. And Christianity has emphasized love of neighbor, deeds of mercy, and charity for the needy."

The strong relationship between religious involvement and giving and volunteering has been consistently documented in a number of studies. People who regularly attend church services are far more likely to make a charitable contribution and to volunteer than people who do not regularly attend church. Moreover, among teens who regularly attended church services, 67 percent were active volunteers and 57 percent were active givers (Hodgkinson and Weitzman, 1992b, pp. 151–152, 68).

Wuthnow also makes the distinction between religious liberals and conservatives and suggests that despite the many things that separate these groups—for example, interpretation of scripture, ideological support of government-sponsored social service programs and abortion—members of both groups, albeit for different reasons, engage in charitable behavior. More specifically, religious conservatives are compassionate because they perceive that is what their religious teachings require of them, whereas religious liberals are compassionate because of their belief that their acts will result in a better society for all of us (Wuthnow, 1991, pp. 132–134). Our hypothesis would suggest that the compassionate individuals of both groups belong to either conservative or liberal religious institutions that accept responsibility for their members' actions vis-à-vis the larger society. Of course, far more research is necessary to confirm this assertion.

Schools

There is widespread agreement that schools are important institutions in shaping the values of young people. Society's belief in the importance of schooling is demonstrated by the fact that every state has enacted minimum compulsory education standards. Compulsory school age requirements range from a minimum of six to fourteen years of age in Mississippi to a maximum of five to eighteen years of age in Arkansas and Virginia (Education Commission of the States, 1992). The role of schools, like other institutions, has changed over time. As schools have broadened their mission from focusing on teaching students the three Rs (reading, writing, and arithmetic) to taking responsibility for teaching socialization and multicultural education, consistent with our hypothesis, schools have begun to promote a more caring society.

For example, a growing number of high schools, colleges, and graduate programs allow students to receive credit toward graduation for participating in community service activities. A total of 55 percent of teens attend schools that simply encourage community service (Hodgkinson and Weitzman, 1992b, p. 65). Some schools go further by requiring that students participate in community service activities as a condition for graduation.

Let's think about this for a moment. A student enrolls in an educational institution for the benefit of enhancing his or her academic skills and, as a condition of graduation, that individual may be required to spend time helping others. The INDEPENDENT SECTOR's survey on youth indicates that among youth who attend schools that simply encourage community service, 75 percent of them were active volunteers (Hodgkinson and Weitzman, 1992b, p. 65). We also know that early involvement in volunteer activities as a youth increases the chances that an individual will give or volunteer as an adult. Among the 43 percent of adults who volunteered as youth, 69 percent are active volunteers and 86 percent are active givers, contributing an average of 2.7 percent of their household income (Hodgkinson and Weitzman, 1992a, p. 227). These are remarkable statistics, which suggest that by just promoting community service without making it compulsory, we can have an enormous impact on the volunteering behavior of our youth.

The Private Sector

As with other institutions, it is difficult to generalize about the private sector. The primary goal of a business is to make a profit. Businesses have long recognized the value of advertising and associating their company name with a worthy cause. While, at some level, such activities certainly promote a caring society, self-interest, and not societal interest, is often the primary motivating factor.

At another level, many businesses have established corporate giving departments and/or foundations. To the extent that these corporations have independent boards and have their own endowments, they are more likely to be motivated by societal interests rather than corporate self-interest in promoting a caring society. In fact, a number of corporate shareholders have begun to question the propriety of using corporate profits for societal good deeds.

The private sector can also promote a caring society in other ways. For example, consider the periodic press reports that describe how businesses have taken up the cause of educational reform. Business leaders are active members of work groups, donate computers and other equipment to schools, and participate in cooperative education programs where students combine an academic program with an apprenticeship in a business. While this type of engagement in social issues is admirable, such efforts also respond to the private sector's concerns that they have a well-educated workforce so that they can remain profitable.

Businesses clearly help to promote a caring society in at least two ways. First, by allowing access to federations of charitable organizations, such as the United Way and the National Black United Fund, and facilitating the collection and distribution of the contributions of their employees (in some cases matching these contributions), some corporations have done a lot to promote a caring society. In fact, some have suggested that corporations do too much in supporting charitable federations, in particular, the United Way. More specifically, a long-standing charge has been that some corporations unduly coerce employees to participate in United Way campaigns (*Special Report on Workplace Giving: The New Era*, 1990). Second, corporate-sponsored programs through which employees and retirees can volunteer their time are also ways businesses acknowledge that their employees can and should be encouraged to engage in activities that benefit others.

Government

Let's now examine whether our government promotes a caring society. The United States has always been characterized by the view that individuals bear the primary, if not sole, responsibility for their socioeconomic status. Recall, for example, President Grover Cleveland's words in vetoing legislation that would have provided seeds to farmers during a severe drought in 1887: "I feel obliged to withhold my approval of the plan to indulge a benevolent and charitable sentiment through the appropriation of public funds for that purpose. I can find no warrant for such an appropriation in the Constitution" (Carruth and Ehrich, 1988, p. 128). Times change, however, and following the aftermath of the Great Depression, President Franklin Roosevelt ushered in a new era of government involvement in accepting responsibility for and improving social conditions through such programs as social security, Aid to Families with Dependent Children, and unemployment insurance.

In addition to promoting a caring society through the direct provision of services, the government can also develop public policies to encourage individuals and institutions to be more caring. These actions can range from increasing the tax deductibility of charitable contributions, to establishing government-financed social service organizations, to facilitating the participation of individuals in programs such as the Peace Corps and Vista. In addition, the National and Community Service Act of 1993, through which the government provides educational scholarships to program participants who volunteer their time and abilities to the public in prescribed ways, was explicitly designed to promote a caring society.

Conclusion

So, where do all of these musings leave us? Obviously, this chapter is intended as a point of reference only. The conceptual framework and operational definitions presented here must be rigorously tested and refined or discarded based on their usefulness in explaining how different institutions either promote or inhibit a caring society. One significant gap in our research knowledge is that we do not have detailed information about whether and how different institutions influence our giving and volunteer behavior to support specific causes and activities. Until we have this knowledge, our institutions will encourage specific types of caring more by accident than by design.

This chapter has presented convincing preliminary evidence that families, religious organizations, schools, businesses, and government have a strong influence on our giving and volunteering behaviors, as well as those of our children. Unlike the uncertainty that characterizes most social science research, there is no mystery, no secret, no puzzle in documenting that institutions do have profound effects in shaping our caring attitudes and behavior throughout our lifetimes. What is in question is our resolve, our willpower, and our collective moral conviction to use our various institutions to more systematically promote a caring society. To be successful, this task will require the collaborative effort of both nonprofit scholars and practitioners.

References

Carruth, G., and Ehrich, E. *The Harper Book of American Quotations*. New York: HarperCollins, 1988.

Carson, E. D. "Black Philanthropy: Shaping Tomorrow's Non-Profit Sector." *The Journal: Contemporary Issues in Fundraising*, summer 1989, pp. 23–31.

Carson, E. D. "On Race, Gender, Culture, and Research on the Voluntary Sector." *Nonprofit Management and Leadership*, 1993, *3*(3), 327–335.

Committee on Ways and Means, U.S. House of Representatives. *1992 Green Book: Overview of Entitlement Programs*. Washington, D.C.: U.S. Government Printing Office, 1992.

Education Commission of the States. *Fact Sheet*. Denver, Colo.: Education Commission of the States, Mar. 1992.

Gardner, J. *On Leadership*. New York: Free Press, 1990.

Goss, K. A., and Greene, E. "A Partner in the White House?" *Chronicle of Philanthropy*, Nov. 17, 1992, p. 1.

Hodgkinson, V. A., and Weitzman, M. S., with Noga, S. M., and Gorski, H. A. *Giving and Volunteering in the United States*. Washington, D.C.: INDEPENDENT SECTOR, 1992a.

Hodgkinson, V. A., and Weitzman, M. S., with Noga, S. M., and Gorski, H. A. *Volunteering and Giving Among American Teenagers*. Washington, D.C.: INDEPENDENT SECTOR, 1992b.

Kaufman, J., and Zigler, E. "Do Abused Children Become Abusive Parents?" *American Journal of OrthoPsychiatry*, 1987, 57(2), 186–192.

National Committee for Responsive Philanthropy. *Special Report on Workplace Giving: The New Era*. Washington, D.C.: National Committee for Responsive Philanthropy, 1990.

"Research Group Says AIDS Epidemic Will Have Little Effect on U.S." *New York Times*, Feb. 5, 1993, p. A-12.

Wuthnow, R. *Acts of Compassion*. Princeton, N.J.: Princeton University Press, 1991.

Chapter Thirteen

Strengthening the Democratic Process

Michael K. Briand, Jennifer Alstad

If by "caring" we mean, among other things, the willingness to give freely of one's time, energy, or personal resources to help others, then an important barrier to creating a better society is, paradoxically, the emphasis on caring itself. In this chapter we argue that "caring" so understood, admirable and necessary though it may be, is no substitute for what we require if we are to respond effectively to our nation's most pressing social problems: the revitalization of our public life through a practice of deliberative, participatory democratic politics.

We begin by noting that many of the social problems that concern the independent sector have not only not been ameliorated during the past two decades, they have actually grown more severe. Indeed, more social problems of a serious nature confront us today than ever before. Consider, for example, that (according to the Congressional Budget Office) between 1970 and 1990 the percentage of single mothers living below the poverty line remained virtually constant, declining only slightly from 45 to 43 percent. Worse, according to the Bureau of the Census, the percentage of children living below the poverty line actually increased during the same period, from 14.90 to 19.9 percent. Moreover, the disparity between white and black children remained unchanged: in 1970, 10.5 percent of the former and 41.5 percent of the latter lived in poverty. Twenty years later, the figures were 15.1 and 44.2 percent, respectively (U.S. Bureau of the Census, 1992a, pp. 4–5).

Or consider these statistics concerning crime: the U.S. Bureau of Justice Statistics reported that the incidence of robbery declined only slightly between 1973 and 1990, from a rate of 6.7 per 1,000 persons to 5.7 (U.S. Bureau of the Census, 1992b, p. 184). Over the thirty-year period from 1960 to 1990, the number of prison inmates serving a sentence of a year or more jumped from 212,953 (a rate of 118.6 per 100,000 population) to 738,894 (294.5 per 100,000) (U.S. Bureau of the Census, 1992b, p. 197).

Discouraging statistics appear everywhere one looks. The Bureau of the Census (1992b, p. 144) reports that in 1991 the percentage of black Americans with a college education (11.5 percent) remains roughly half the percentage of white Americans with four years of college (22.4 percent). In 1970, the ratio was almost identical (11.3 versus 4.4 percent). In 1970 the overall homicide rate was 8.3 per 100,000; in 1989 it was 9.2 (U.S. Bureau of the Census, 1992b, p. 40). Again, however, the disparity between white and black Americans remains great. In 1970, white males were murdered at the rate of 6.8 per 100,000. For black males, the rate was 67.6. In 1990, the rates were 9.0 and 69.2, respectively (U.S. Bureau of the Census, 1992b, p. 183). A similar disparity exists with respect to death from heart disease, liver ailments, diabetes, and accidents. As for the environment, the International Trade Commission reports that, in 1960, every day we generated 87.8 million tons of solid waste (2.7 pounds per person) (U.S. Bureau of the Census, 1994, p. 201). In 1988, the figure was 184.2 million tons (4.1 pounds per person) (U.S. Bureau of the Census, 1994, p. 234).

Equally dispiriting statistics could be presented for virtually every social problem that afflicts our communities and country. Despite our efforts, we appear to have made little headway toward solving these problems. This conclusion suggests that many problems are too deep rooted, too widespread, and too complex to be addressed successfully without a sustained and determined commitment to their solution on the part of society as a whole. Put briefly, these problems are *public* problems. They grow out of deficiencies and distortions in the way of life we live—in our self-conceptions, in our values and priorities, and in the way we see and relate to one another. To achieve commitment of the depth and breadth required to begin solving our problems, we must reconnect the public with the problem-solving process. We cannot achieve this reconnection by emphasizing caring. Rather, we must revive the public's *self-interest in political involvement*. What the independent sector needs to do, therefore, is *not* promote a "caring" society, but rather rebuild the "civil infrastructure" of a healthy participatory democratic political process.

The Problem with "Caring"

The most sympathetic observer of philanthropic efforts would be hard pressed to come up with a single convincing example of a problem that owes its mitigation in substantial measure to the actions of "caring" persons and organizations. A recent example of how even the best-intended, best-supported efforts seem bound to fail is instructive. In 1988 a large family foundation with a national orientation gave a nonprofit organization in a medium-sized Midwestern city $10 million and five years to help ensure that middle school girls would eventually graduate from high school without getting pregnant. An additional $10 million was raised by the organization locally. The grantmaker felt encouraged because civic leaders were eager to join the organization's board. Its staff was persuaded that city officials were committed to the purposes of the project.

Yet despite what appeared to be optimal conditions for its success, the project has been a near-total failure. According to a recent study in the city's daily newspaper, by the grantmaker's own criteria—higher graduation rates, better test scores, and a reduction in pregnancies—the project has had no discernible impact whatsoever. Five years and $20 million later, "[the city's school superintendent wants the program . . . out of business, the social workers who went into [the] schools are losing their jobs . . . , and [the organization's administrators] are engaged in a public relations blitz to keep their jobs and raise money for work that . . . is invisible to much of the . . . community."

Of course, as the newspaper remarked, "there's a limit to what 37 people—the largest number of social workers [the organization] ever employed—can do for the several thousand children and families they were spread among. . . . Three dozen people couldn't, in five years, radically change the behavior of neglected and angry kids and big institutions." But the organization could have employed ten to twenty times that number and still made little progress. Why? Because the problem of teenagers performing poorly in school, dropping out, and getting pregnant is a *public* problem. It originates not in any particular personal or institutional state of affairs, but in several mutually reinforcing ones—schools, families, the economy, the culture of the inner city, and the general ethos of contemporary American society. If the conditions in which urban teenage girls grow up are to be improved, the problem must be attacked at its ultimate, hydra-headed source. To wage such a campaign we need public policies to which we, *as a society*, are strongly and stubbornly committed. In turn, to devise such policies we need a more productive kind of politics, one that brings ordinary citizens into the process of understanding problems, facing up to hard choices, reaching a sound judgment about what trade-offs to accept, and deciding on a course of action that everyone can support.

The alternative to deliberative democratic problem solving—"caring"—is a recipe not only for programmatic failure but for the demoralization and burnout of those who already give so much to their communities and society. Moreover, it is a prescription for the perpetuation of a debilitating dependency among those we wish to care for.

In a thought-provoking article, Eugenie Gatens-Robinson (1991, p. 8) cites the *Code of Professional Ethics for Rehabilitation Counselors*, which reads in part, "Rehabilitation counselors shall endeavor at all times to place their clients' interests above their own." As Gatens-Robinson remarks, "This is surely a code for professional sainthood. . . . Is it reasonable," she asks, "to expect this level of dedication to the interests of strangers even within a professional context?" (p. 10). Clearly, she considers a blanket duty of this severity and absoluteness manifestly unreasonable. This "problem of excessive self-sacrifice" is one of several serious problems that the emphasis on caring presents.

Gatens-Robinson alerts us as well to a second problem having even more significant implications for "transmitting the tradition of a caring society." She writes, "Genuinely beneficent action within the context of a practice of care must have certain characteristics if it is to be distinguishable from paternalism. . . . It is necessary to cultivate a respect for the person's *own* interpretation of *their* individual good" (p. 11; emphasis added). *Whose* good, in other words, is served by caring—the recipient's or the caregiver's? For example, is it for the good of the psychiatrically disadvantaged that they be subject to involuntary treatment, or for the good of mental health care professionals? At the very least, we must acknowledge the *potential* for a conflict of interest between what the professional or volunteer (or the organization on whose behalf he or she acts) believes should be done and what the intended beneficiary believes. This is the "problem of paternalism."

A third problem is what we might call the "problem of 'if you don't succeed, try harder.'" If by acting paternalistically caregivers actually succeeded, if they actually realized their stated aims, we might more readily grant the rightness, on balance, of imposing our own views and wishes on those we care about. But this appears not to be the case. Indeed, the need for care-inspired action seems to be growing, not diminishing. Caregivers are having to work harder—they have to "care more"—just to keep up. Anyone familiar with the plight of many caseworkers employed by city and state child protective services knows how overburdened these professionals are. Not surprisingly, professionals are being asked to "care" even more. Thus, Margaret Nosek has written that "involvement in organizations and activities that seek to remove the societal barriers to independent living . . . *can occupy evenings and weekends and can consume personal financial resources*. . . . While tradition does not recognize this type of involvement as professional behavior, it is this author's belief that independent living service cannot be effectively delivered without it" (Nosek, quoted in Gatens-Robinson, p. 8). Does this represent the lengths to which dedicated caregivers are now being driven in order to achieve their goals? Must we become totally consumed with our efforts to demonstrate that care? Does effectiveness require the saintliness of Mother Teresa?

The historian Christopher Lasch (1992), for one, believes that our faltering ability to keep pace with the mounting problems we confront, and the greater efforts to which we exhort one another in consequence, offer compelling evidence that we have gone down the wrong path altogether. "Is it really necessary," he asks, "to point out, at this late date, that public policies based on a therapeutic model . . . have failed miserably, over and over again? Far from promoting self-respect, they have created a nation of dependents. They have given rise to a cult of the victim in which entitlements are based on the display of accumulated injuries inflicted by an uncaring society" (p. 34). A fourth problem posed by our emphasis on caring, then, is the "problem of victimhood." We have simultaneously fostered dependency on the part of many intended beneficiaries and provoked their resentment of us for having done so.

Where is our "caring tradition" getting us? Not, it would appear, very far.

The Antidemocratic Culture of Professionalism

Our inability to solve our most troubling social problems—a failing compounded by the hazards of excessive self-sacrifice, paternalism, and the cult of victimhood—is a symptom of a society that has lost its public character, and that as a consequence now prescribes for every social problem either a governmental or a privately initiated response. The social scientific/professional/expert outlook that we have come to take for granted has turned citizens into clients. It urges us to look inward to solve our problems, rather than outward to the social world that shapes us. In her book *Revolution from Within: A Book of Self-Esteem* (1992), even Gloria Steinem now emphasizes personal transformation as the key to public change (Lehrman, 1992, pp. 32–33). This phenomenon has led Harry Boyte (1992, p. 77), director of Project Public Life at the Humphrey Institute, to argue that "today, in a culture surfeited with therapeutic intimacy, . . . political themes such as practical work with others one might disagree with or even dislike; the dynamics of power; accountability; and understanding others' self-interests" must be rediscovered and resurrected.

The growth of the independent sector in general, and of grantmaking philanthropic institutions in particular, closely parallels the development of scientific and professional expertise in the nineteenth and early twentieth centuries, and hence the emergence of elites claiming to possess specialized knowledge. (For an excellent and compelling historical account of the ideology of progress that provided the cultural context for professionalism, see Lasch, 1991.) This development was accompanied and reinforced by the efforts of political progressives to professionalize government in the name of eliminating patronage and other forms of corruption on which "machine politics" depended and thrived (Gaebler and Osborne, 1992). In a review of Ellen Lagemann's book *The Politics of Knowledge: The Carnegie Corporation, Philanthropy, and Public Policy*, Sandee Brawarsky (1992) illustrates the sea change that began to sweep over foundations such as the Carnegie Corporation early in this century. Citing Lagemann, Brawarsky observes that

> while Carnegie . . . was funding the [National Bureau of Economic Research, a scientific research institute made up of economists, businessmen, and labor representatives who sought to develop economic knowledge], the decision was made *not* to finance a competing

> model of social science expertise, the social settlements like Jane Addams's Hull House in Chicago. The settlements were locally based, staffed by "*pre*professional" women, and rooted in liberal values; they combined social science research with *practice*. In contrast, NBER was national in orientation, staffed by men, and considered *professional* in approach. . . . Its leaders studied social problems from a *scientific*, *abstract* point of view. By denying funds to the settlements, Lagemann claims, [Carnegie] aided their evolution into institutions that were seen as more important for service delivery than research. "Social work" became the central function of settlements, while "sociology" became a field of university study [p. 9; emphasis added].

This account illustrates a growing split between "scientific" research and experientially based practical knowledge, and hence between professional elites claiming to possess the former and ordinary people who were presumed to lack expertise—that is, "scientific knowledge." The responsibility of citizens for solving social problems has been relinquished to professionals in government and the independent sector.

This theme finds an echo in the writings of John McKnight. McKnight (1987) contends that the "social map" that guides our thinking consists of an oversimplified division between "institutions" (for example, government and not-for-profit social service agencies; the courts, law enforcement agencies, and correctional facilities; foundations; and the health care delivery system), on the one hand, and "individuals," on the other. He criticizes this map for excluding the domain of "the community," which is "the social place used by . . . neighbors, neighborhood associations, clubs, civic groups, local enterprises, churches, ethnic associations, temples, local unions, local government, and local media." McKnight explains this exclusion by asserting that "many institutional leaders [*vide*, "professionals"] . . . simply do not believe in the capacities of communities" (p. 57).

Thus, "our role as citizens and our communities have been traded in for the right to clienthood and consumer status" (p. 58). Yet "many individuals continue to reject their roles as consumers" (pp. 54–55). As a result, McKnight says, we "create crime-making corrections systems, sickness-making health systems, and stupid-making schools." We imagine "that our society has a problem in terms of effective human services [that is, a problem of malfunctioning institutions]." But in reality "our essential problem is weak communities. . . . We have reached the limits of institutional problem-solving" (p. 58). "[An institution] can deliver a service, [but] it cannot deliver care. Care is a special relationship characterized by consent rather than control" (p. 57). Institutions are concerned with control, not consent. They are built on "a vision [of a] structure where things *can be done right*, a kind of orderly perfection achieved . . . [in which] the ablest dominate" (p. 56; emphasis added).

Politics and Citizen Responsibility

What did we do in our country before caring became institutionalized? How did we get by before we turned over the task of addressing social problems to government and nonprofit employees? After his visit to the United States in the 1830s, Alexis de Tocqueville wrote in *Democracy in America* that "when a private individual meditates an undertaking . . . directly connected with the welfare of society, he never thinks of soliciting the cooperation of the government. . . . He courts the assistance of other individuals." There was a time, in other words, when the citizens of our country took responsibility themselves for addressing social problems. Foundations and other nonprofits had not been invented, and people did not look to government for solutions.

Why and how did the change occur? A crucial element of the explanation is the conception of the individual that has dominated Western political thought and practice, especially in the United

States, for the past three centuries. According to this view, only the individual is real. It does not recognize what Gatens-Robinson (1991, p. 9) calls the existence of "standing, but not chosen, relationships of responsibility." This way of looking at human social reality has obscured our awareness of the connections that link us inextricably to one another. It thus renders caring a matter of individual morality or ethics. Our ostensible obligations and duties to community and society fail to remind us of the natural self-interest inherent in caring about others with whom we are locked permanently in relationships, and whose well-being therefore has an important intrinsic connection to our own. Today it is nearly impossible to see in the plight of others the diminishment of our own well-being. In short, we fail to see how it matters to *us* how others fare. Failing to see how it matters, it becomes hard to care.

What is worse, our view of the individual as abstracted and decontextualized has delegitimated self-interest, causing it to be contrasted invidiously with virtues such as caring. The result has been to deprive ourselves as a society of the opportunity to harness the powerful motive of self-interest for the purpose of promoting the common good. Self-interest now seems antithetical to the public interest. By obscuring the connection between the individual's self-interest and his or her stake in the quality of the public world that all of us inhabit, we have stigmatized self-interest as selfishness, and in the process have lost the ability to engage the energies of ordinary citizens in the effort to improve our communities and society.

Radical individualism has undermined our ability and willingness *as a people, as a public* to take responsibility for addressing the social problems that seem to overwhelm private efforts to solve them. It blinds us to the importance of a public context—a flourishing practice of democratic politics—in which the public as a whole can and must take responsibility for addressing those problems. In the public life of our communities today, just as in an economic market, people are preoccupied with the competition to realize their particular interests and desires. They try to satisfy these by "buying" the goods and services they want from the "producer" of these goods and services—in this case, government. Citizens are passive "consumers" of what government can provide. So public life gets reduced to the question of "who gets what, when, and how." The "community" is nothing more than a loose collection of individuals and groups, each with opinions, preferences, and positions that have to be accommodated. The assumption is that there is no *common* or *public* good or interest apart from what emerges from a fair competition among *particular* interests. As in an economic market, the best result is the one that comes closest to satisfying every individual's desires.

The market conception of politics has caused us to forget that the public has to take responsibility for maintaining the rules of the democratic game and for sustaining the proper spirit in which the game should be approached. In a democracy, government is supposed to be not only *for* the people, but *of* them and *by* them as well. The market assumptions that have insinuated themselves into our efforts to address community problems obscure the fact that, in addition to (legitimate) self-interest, we have a shared interest in solving problems that were created by us collectively and that therefore must be solved by us collectively. Institutional decision-making devices such as majority rule can deal only mechanically with the competing interests and desires people have. They can aggregate them—add them up—but they cannot integrate them—they cannot reconcile the things that are important to people without compelling someone to lose or compromise.

Only *people* can integrate conflicting interests. When public problems arise—racial tensions, drug abuse, poverty, crime, economic stagnation, environmental pollution, and so on—simply having the authority or power to influence government decisions does not guarantee that solutions will be effective or widely supported. Problems such as these require citizens to work together —to do the hard work of making choices based on a shared perspective. Public problem solving requires a form of political interaction that encourages the hard work of making tough choices through frank, open, realistic, and civil talk among citizens. Only talk of this sort can build an integrated public perspective out of fragmented partial perspectives, and hence create a basis for decisions that everyone can live with.

But this is not the sort of political interaction that our political system exhibits or encourages today. Having abdicated our responsibility as a public to act as the ultimate responsible agent of change and creator of the sorts of communities and society we wish to inhabit, we are, in Lasch's (1992, p. 34) words, "content to restrict [the general level of competence] to the caring class, which arrogates to itself the job of looking out for everybody else. [But] the professionalization of compassion does not make us a kinder, gentler nation. Instead it institutionalizes inequality, under the pretense that everyone is 'special' in his own way. And since the pretense is transparent, the attempt to make people feel good about themselves only makes them cynical. 'Caring' is no substitute for candor." Nor is it a substitute for deliberative democratic politics. Shelby Steele (1992) explains why it was expedient for elites both in and out of government to abandon the ideal of this sort of political practice in favor of the market (per)version that prevails today. Of those "professional carers" who have made a career and created a power base for themselves through ostensible concern for the disadvantaged, Steele writes that

> what began as an attempt to address the very real grievances [of persons, such as blacks and women, who had been excluded from effective participation in public life] wound up creating newly sovereign fiefdoms. . . . The sovereign fiefdoms are ends in themselves—providing career tracks and bases of power. This power tends to be used now mostly to defend and extend the fiefdom. . . . [The leaders of these fiefdoms] . . . come to embody the movement. Over time, they

> and they alone speak for the aggrieved. . . . It is their vocation now, and their means to status and power. . . . Power is where it's at today—power to set up the organization, attract the following, run the fiefdom [pp. 49–50].

But as Steele shrewdly discerns, "this could not have come to pass without the cooperation of the society at large and its institutions. Why did . . . public and private institutions, the corporations and foundations, end up supporting principles that had the effect of turning causes into sovereign fiefdoms?"

> The answer is that those in charge of America's institutions saw the institutionalization and bureaucratization of the protest movements as ultimately desirable, at least in the short term, and the funding of group entitlements as ultimately a less costly way to redress grievances. The leaders of the newly sovereign fiefdoms were backing off from their earlier demands that America live up to its ideals. . . . The language of entitlements is essentially the old, comforting language of power politics, and in the halls of power it went down well enough. . . . *This satisfied the institutions because entitlements were cheaper in every way than real change* [pp. 53–54; emphasis added].

In effect, elites inside and outside government colluded to defuse the impetus toward genuine democratic empowerment of ordinary Americans by redistributing power within their own tight circle. This is just what we should have expected of persons whose model of politics is fashioned after a market, in which the point is to acquire and wield as much power as possible for one's own ends. The promise of an inclusive, genuinely democratic and deliberative practice of politics was not the only casualty, however. Another was the public's ability—indeed, its willingness—to take real responsibility for solving the country's problems.

"Caring" Through Democratic Politics

As Gatens-Robinson (1991, p. 11) observes, the pressure to "care more" emerges from "the same social and political structures that currently ask too much of parents, too much of the children of the ailing old, and too much of nurses and attendants and teachers. *We as a people* have not taken at full reckoning what it would take to transform our educational, economic, and social institutions, our public life and its environment, in such a way that it would not require a saint to educate and care for those among us who are in need, vulnerable, or immature."

We *as a people*. Gatens-Robinson is dead on: We *the public* have not made an informed, conscious decision about how we should address the problems that confront us as a society. We have abdicated this responsibility to professionals in government and the independent sector. As Gatens-Robinson notes, "we have . . . relegated the *public* practices of care to the arena of expertise and have professionalized our social responses" (p. 1). We have not talked among ourselves, as citizens, about the nature and causes of these problems; we have not identified our concerns and the values they reflect; we have not weighed the consequences for what we value of the different courses of action open to us; we have not made the hard choices between conflicting values that would enable us to establish priorities; and hence we have not settled on a general direction or a range of actions that all of us could go along with, thereby permitting our elected officials to devise solutions that will prove both effective and sustainable because they are widely supported. In short, we have abandoned politics. Citing John McDermott, Gatens-Robinson sums up the task we must set ourselves if we are to create a genuinely "caring society": "We *as a people* . . . must actively come to see what is required of us . . . before really pervasive change can be made" (p. 10).

It is crucial that this point not be misconstrued. The point is *not* that politics as it is currently conceived and practiced—in other words, the institutionalized competition and "aggregation" of interests that constitutes the "market" version of politics—is adequate to the task of solving our country's problems. Manifestly, it is not. But the reason that politics-as-usual fails to achieve progress toward solutions is precisely that it does not enable and encourage people to make connections between their particular interests and the well-being of the communities and society of which they are members. The prevailing practice of politics rests on a conception of society as composed of disconnected individuals, a conception that obscures the *self*-interest that each of us has in the welfare of our fellows. Although the way we usually think of politics permits us to talk about cooperation between individuals and groups, it has no place for the idea of *relationships*. In the quasi-Hobbesian world we inhabit, we tend to lose sight of the fact that we are bound to each other in ways that will endure, for good or for ill, over time.

The fact is, however, we are too interdependent to remain unaffected by what each of us does or fails to do. More and more, citizens, communities, and countries resemble members of an extended family—they cannot choose whether to be related to each other, they cannot escape the relationships in which they find themselves. Today, we require good working relationships with each other to safeguard our *own* interests. Remaining preoccupied *exclusively* with our particular interests and goals weakens or even damages our relationships, thereby making it harder to resolve disputes and protect our interests over the long run. Such preoccupation leads us to view each other as potential obstacles or adversaries rather than as partners in a relationship that affects the ability of each party to advance its vital interests.

Seeing the public as a vast web of relationships in which all of us are inescapably enmeshed, rather than imagining it as a mere aggregate of independent individuals who interact with each other, can help us generate a new sense of possibility that will release previously untapped energy for seeking and constructing solutions. Becoming conscious of our relationships will help us realize our capacity for effective collective action. People do not need a guarantee that whatever they do together will succeed. They will make the necessary effort if they believe that others will work with them. To be persuaded of this, however, it helps if everyone recognizes that, like it or not, they are in a relationship with their fellow citizens, that this relationship can be good or bad, and that each person can accomplish a great deal more when the relationship is in good shape than when it is not.

To say that good relationships are imperative does not mean that we should subordinate our respective concerns, beliefs, and interests just for the sake of agreement, to accommodate each other or to get along better. It means only that we should place these in the context of the inescapable long-term association we will have with each other. Like the proverbial water in which the fish swims, our relationships—though we are oblivious to them most of the time—are indispensable to the quality of life we enjoy. Attending consciously to our relationships can help us think together about what each of us might do to make it easier for *all* of us to promote our respective interests.

Does this seem like too tall an order? Does the call for widespread citizen participation in a practice of deliberative, collaborative problem solving represent just as much of a demand for self-sacrifice as the injunction to care? No, it does not, and for this reason: democratic politics draws on people's natural inclination to be moved to action by their own interests. Politics is inherently less "demanding" for the obvious reason that people are more likely to involve themselves in the effort to solve a problem *if they believe they have a personal stake in doing so*.

Moreover, Americans are prepared to reinsert themselves into—and reassert control over—the process of responding to the problems that beset our communities and country. Research conducted by the Kettering Foundation (Harwood Group, 1991) makes abundantly clear that, while ordinary citizens are angry about being shut out of the process in which they supposedly have the right and responsibility to govern themselves, they remain actively involved in efforts to make their communities better places to live. The Kettering report supports the view expressed by the Bradley Foundation's Michael Joyce. "Americans," Joyce (1992) has observed,

> are sick and tired of being told that they are incompetent to run their own affairs. They're sick and tired of being treated as helpless, pathetic victims of social forces that are beyond their control. They're sick and tired of being treated as passive clients by arrogant, paternalistic social scientists, therapists, professionals, and bureaucrats, who claim exclusive right to minister to the hurts inflicted by hostile social forces. . . . Americans are clearly willing and eager to seize control of their daily lives again—to make critical choices for themselves, based on their own common sense. . . . In short, Americans are ready for what might be called "a new citizenship."

The desire to work toward solving our problems does not have to be manufactured. What we need to do is capitalize on the readiness of the public to embrace a form of politics that will permit people to express and pursue their personal concerns in the context of a pragmatic, productive effort to solve public problems. By working together to find a way forward that recognizes everyone's concerns, people will begin to make the connection between their own interests and the quality of the public relationships they have with their fellow citizens.

Conclusion

Imagine a coastal community whose residents live on houseboats that vary in size, design, and construction. A storm blows up and causes the smaller, less sturdy vessels to take on water. Some go under; others barely stay afloat. Sympathetic neighbors rush to the aid of their fellows who have foundered. They volunteer their time, energy, and personal resources to build new and better boats for the victims of the storm. But the volunteers cannot build enough replacements fast enough. Some of the volunteers point out that it is futile to put resources into designing and building new boats so long as the harbor breakwater remains in poor condition. They urge their community to begin immediate repairs on it. But most of their fellow citizens are too preoccupied with helping victims to heed this advice.

The moral of the story is that any response to a crisis, no matter how heroic, is bound to prove ineffective in the absence of attention to *infrastructure*. In the metaphor, a working breakwater is a precondition for a safe harbor. Like the community in the story, our society is being battered by a great storm. Individuals, groups, and whole communities are foundering. Individuals and organizations in the independent sector are trying to respond. But they do not see that we require a new and sturdy "breakwater"—a robust democratic *political* infrastructure—for their efforts to pay off. Instead of working on the necessary infrastructure, they remain focused on "building boats."

If the organizations that constitute the independent sector in America desire to solve the problems about which they profess concern, they will have to turn their efforts from "building better boats" to encouraging the public to claim responsibility for the quality of our public life. We must care *less* about caring and *more* about the interest-driven process by which problems are identified and taken on as a public responsibility. The combined efforts of grantmakers, social scientists and other experts, social service professionals, nonprofit organizations, and individual volunteers will never be enough to solve the most serious and persistent problems we face today. Philanthropy is no substitute for the most fundamental precondition for responding to social problems. What we require first and foremost is the revitalization of our public life through a healthy practice of democratic decision making. All members of the public should actively involve themselves in the process of understanding those problems and making the hard choices that must be made if we are to move forward together toward a sustainable, effective, widely supported policy.

What nonprofit organizations—foundations in particular—need to do, therefore, is invest, directly and indirectly, in the "civil infrastructure" of a citizen-oriented, deliberative democratic process. It is encouraging to see that steps in this direction are already being taken. The Pew Charitable Trusts, for example, have created a "Partnership for Civic Change" to help medium-sized cities develop their capacity for solving problems through communitywide collaboration. In 1992 the Colorado Trust announced a five-year "Healthy Communities Initiative" in response to their finding that "Coloradans desire local action and participation to address community problems of all types." In Connecticut, the Topsfield Foundation devotes its resources entirely to support of its "Study Circles Resource Center," which it created several years ago to promote democratic, participatory discussion courses on social and political issues.

Such efforts are "political" in the best sense—they are intended to strengthen the ability and willingness of people to take responsibility for governing themselves effectively. They are not the only way that foundations can begin strengthening our country's "civil infrastructure." Foundations need to be creative about how they can continue to fulfill their missions while addressing this urgent need. We should start by rethinking the meaning of *political*. So long as *political* remains a pejorative term connoting competitive, blinkered partisanship, both the quality of life in our country and the reputation of philanthropic institutions will continue to decline.

References

Boyte, H. "Dialogue: Community vs. Public." *Responsive Community*, 1992, *2*(4), 75–77.

Brawarsky, S. "The Politics of Knowledge: Foundations and Public Policy." *Carnegie Quarterly*, 1992, *37*(3), 8–11.

Gaebler, T., and Osborne, D. *Reinventing Government: The Rise of an Entrepreneurial Public Sector*. Reading, Mass.: Addison-Wesley, 1992.

Gatens-Robinson, E. "Beneficence and the Habilitation of People with Disabilities." *Contemporary Philosophy*, 1991, *14*(2), 8–11.

Harwood Group. *Citizens and Politics: A View from Main Street America.* Dayton, Ohio: Kettering Foundation, 1991.

Joyce, M. Speech delivered to the Board of Trustees and Founders of the Heritage Foundation, Washington, D.C., Dec. 1992.

Lasch, C. *The True and Only Heaven: Progress and Its Critics.* New York: Norton, 1991.

Lasch, C. "For Shame." *New Republic*, Aug. 10, 1992, pp. 29–34.

Lehrman, K. "The Feminist Mystique." *New Republic*, Mar. 16, 1992, pp. 30–34.

McKnight, J. "Regenerating Community." *Social Policy*, 1987, *17*, 54–58.

Steele, S. "The New Sovereignty." *Harper's*, July 1992, pp. 47–54.

Steinem, G. *Revolution from Within: A Book of Self-Esteem.* Boston: Little, Brown, 1992.

Tocqueville, A. de. *Democracy in America.* 2 vols. New York: Knopf, 1945. (Originally published 1835.)

U.S. Bureau of the Census. *Poverty in the United States: 1991.* Current Population Reports, series P-660, no. 181. Washington, D.C.: U.S. Government Printing Office, 1992a.

U.S. Bureau of the Census. *Statistical Abstract of the United States.* Washington, D.C.: U.S. Government Printing Office, 1992b.

U.S. Bureau of the Census. *Statistical Abstract of the United States.* Washington, D.C.: U.S. Government Printing Office, 1994.

Chapter Fourteen

Corporate Concern for Racial and Ethnic Populations

Steven L. Paprocki, Robert O. Bothwell

In his collection of essays, *Race Matters*, distinguished scholar Cornel West (1993, pp. 25–26) writes, "Why is this shattering of [black] civil society occurring? What has led to the weakening of cultural institutions in the asphalt jungle? The corporate market institutions have greatly contributed to their collapse. . . . Needless to say, the primary motivation of these institutions is to make profits. . . . The eclipse of hope and the collapse of meaning in much of black America is linked to the structural dynamics of corporate market institutions."

Shifts in corporate compensation structures, human resources planning, and grantmaking are challenging the idea that American corporations reflect the caring values of the society they serve. Three examples stand out:

1. While *Fortune* magazine declares the annual average salary and benefit compensation package for chief executive officers inches closer to the one million dollar mark, corporate grantmaking (adjusted for inflation) has stagnated or decreased for the last five years ("Annual Survey . . . ," May 31, 1989). In addition, according to the Conference Board, the proportion of pretax dollars from America's largest corporations to charity has shrunk from 1.79 to 1.59 percent (Conference Board, 1992).
2. While spending thousands of dollars to make their employees more culturally sensitive, many major profitmaking corporations across the country, at the same time, are laying off employees by the thousands.

3. While more and more corporations feature their grantmaking and employee volunteer programs in advertising and promotional materials, many corporate grantmakers refuse to disclose the recipients and conditions of the grants they make. An estimated two-thirds of corporate grants are claimed as business or charitable deductions, but few are disclosed in such a way that specific grants and grant patterns can be discerned.

Is West's perspective accurate? Are American corporations less caring than many believe? West's comments pertain specifically to the corporate impact on African Americans, but do these shifting corporate budget priorities indicate a decrease in the level of corporate regard for all of America's disadvantaged populations in general and racial and ethnic populations in particular? Are corporations indicating their concern for the disadvantaged through their grantmaking programs? Is the real corporate motivation, as West contends, profits, or, as former Dayton-Hudson chief executive officer Kenneth Dayton contends, the opportunity to serve the community?

Both West's and Dayton's concerns and beliefs about American corporate support for a societal ethic of caring are very real. However, neither those who are supportive nor those who are critical should be satisfied with discerning corporate motives alone. Only after a thorough examination of what corporations actually impart to American society can we begin to diagnose the actual level of corporate caring. For this reason, any such diagnosis must begin with a comprehensive statistical overview. This diagnosis requires, among other things, a clearer view of the statistical landscape of corporate grantmaking that is primarily intended to benefit racial and ethnic populations. (This diagnosis also requires hard data on employee discharges/turnover, subcontracting, and many other factors, but this chapter addresses only corporate grantmaking.)

About the Overall Study

As part of its mission to encourage corporate grantmakers (and other philanthropic institutions) to be more responsive to the needs of disenfranchised communities, the National Committee for Responsive Philanthropy (NCRP) initiated a series of surveys to determine the scope of corporate support for racial and ethnic population issues, activities, and organizations (racial and ethnic populations include any of four targeted populations: African Americans, Native Americans, Asian and Pacific Islander Americans, and Hispanics). This initial research effort, combined with subsequent phases of the study, will contribute to an understanding of the complex interrelationship between race, ethnicity, and corporate grantmaking in three ways:

1. By determining the scope and extent of surveyed corporations' domestic grantmaking for racial and ethnic populations' organizations, issues, and activities.
2. By examining a specific pool of funding within the full scope of corporate grantmaking programs (that is, "unencumbered" domestic cash grants). This excludes matching grants, in-kind contributions, grants to nondomestic organizations, donated employee service time, grants to individuals, and grants to redistribution programs that may have multiple purposes or mixed benefits for the donor corporation.
3. By examining the grants within a number of key variables, such as interest area, type of support, racial and ethnic beneficiaries, geographical focus, auspices/sector, and governance of recipient organization.

Of particular concern to racial and ethnic leaders and, consequently, to funders is the complex issue of the relationship between *who controls* the recipient organization and *who are* the primary beneficiaries of the recipient organization. Many racial and ethnic leaders do not consider grants to recipients that are not specifically controlled by racial and ethnic populations (such as symphony orchestras or public libraries) as substantially benefiting racial and ethnic populations. On the other hand, many funders insist that all grants benefit some of the targeted populations. This is a critical issue that threatens the credibility of almost all current racial and ethnic grantmaking research and inhibits the ability to discuss the larger issue of whether racial and ethnic populations are receiving a sufficient, or at least fair, proportion of corporate grantmaking dollars.

Any survey of grantmaking for racial and ethnic populations, therefore, must account for the question of governance. This study addresses this problem and distinguishes itself from other studies by developing a classification system that relates the racial and ethnic composition of the recipient's governing board to the racial and ethnic composition of the recipient's primary beneficiaries and/or grant beneficiaries. (See the section on "Racial and Ethnic Composition of Recipient's Board in Relation to Recipient's Beneficiaries).")

About the First Phase

In the first phase of this study, NCRP analyzed how much of the grantmaking of the top 1988 U.S. profitmaking corporations during 1988 was primarily intended to benefit the four previously mentioned racial and ethnic populations.[1]

NCRP recognized the instability of the profitability indicator. After all, as many as half of the corporations that make *Forbes* magazine's top profitmakers list in any given year fail to make the list the following year. Nonetheless, the 1988 list blends many of America's leading corporate grantmakers with many new corporate giving programs, as well as many older but less notable corporate contribution programs. Collectively, these twenty-five corporations reported contributing over $600 million in 1988, one-eighth of all the funding by U.S. corporations in 1988 as determined by *Giving USA* ("Forbes 500," 1989). Beyond the dollars they allocate, many of the surveyed corporations are leaders in the American corporate grantmaking community and exert a very positive influence on the giving policies and practices of other corporations, both nationally and internationally.

The results of Phase One were published as *Corporate Grantmaking: Giving to Racial/Ethnic Populations—Phase One* (Paprocki and Bothwell, 1994). This original 500-page report and subsequent reports on racial and ethnic grantmaking by industry are available in subscription form from NCRP.[2]

Methods

The first phase of the study focuses on the domestic cash grantmaking patterns of the twenty-five most profitable publicly held corporations in 1988 (as detailed in the May 1, 1989, issue of *Forbes* magazine; see "Forbes 500," 1989). Within this universe, researchers identified and analyzed domestic cash grants primarily intended to benefit racial and ethnic populations. The classification and methods used to accomplish this analysis were adapted from methods and classification systems used by the Foundation Center (1992) and the National Center for Charitable Statistics at INDEPENDENT SECTOR (Hodgkinson, Weitzman, Toppe, and Noga, 1992).[3] Along with information about the corporate grantmaking program, the essential information requested from each corporation included the corporation's 1988 corporate, foundation, and subsidiaries' grants list (including grantee names, dollar amounts, dates, and grant purposes); corporate giving guidelines; and a delineation of the corporation's general giving categories. When not directly available from the corporation, this information was gathered from public tax records (Form IRS 990-PF). Either voluntarily or by providing public tax records, a total of nineteen corporations furnished the minimum information required for inclusion in the survey.[4] After a minimum of five telephone and/or written requests, the following six corporations either refused to participate or did not provide sufficient detail to be included in this survey: American International Group, E. I. du Pont de Nemours, Dow Chemical, GTE, IBM, and Phillip Morris Companies.

After the data were gathered and classified, the findings were analyzed within ten major variables: giving by corporation, giving by interest area, racial/ethnic composition of intended beneficiaries, racial/ethnic composition of the recipient board in relation to the racial/ethnic composition of its primary beneficiaries, geographical focus of the recipient organization, grant range and size by corporation and interest area, giving to special population groups (such as gender, age, or income), auspices/sector of the recipient, giving to specific recipient organizations, and type of support. This report focuses on the first five variables. Data and analyses of the latter five variables are in the full report *Corporate Grantmaking: Giving to Racial/Ethnic Populations—Phase One*, available from NCRP. When appropriate, grants were classified by multiple interest areas, types of support, and racial and ethnic beneficiary groups.

Whenever possible, researchers verified all grant and recipient information with the recipient organization. This level of verification was particularly necessary to determine both the racial and ethnic composition of the board and the beneficiaries of grants and recipient organizations. As a follow-up to the first phase of the study, researchers mailed 600 summaries of the survey to racial and ethnic leaders, surveyed by telephone over 100 racial and ethnic community leaders, and conducted two feedback meetings with advisory committee members, philanthropic researchers, corporate grantmakers, and racial and ethnic leaders from across the United States. Although this subjective aspect of the study is not intended to be a scientific polling, the feedback from these efforts provided invaluable insight and analysis on both the results of the first phase and recommendations for subsequent phases of the study.

Summary of Statistical Findings from Phase One

We touch on various types of findings in this section.

Overall Summary

The nineteen corporations that provided sufficient information to participate in this survey reported contributing $414,000,000 in 1988. However, the participating corporations only provided sufficient detail to review and analyze 15,000 grants totaling $153,000,000. Of this amount, 17 percent ($26,197,624) was awarded in 1,653 grants that were primarily intended to benefit the four target populations.

Giving by Individual Corporation

Overall: Three corporations—ARCO, Amoco, and Exxon—together awarded $12.8 million, almost half of the total giving in this survey. Six other corporations awarded between $1 million and $2 million, and three corporations granted between $500,000 and $1 million primarily to benefit racial and ethnic populations. The remaining seven corporations awarded between $472,500 and $133,500.

Corporate home region: Nine of the participating corporations have headquarters in the Northeast states; five have headquarters in the Midwest, three in the West, and one each in the Mid-Atlantic and Southeastern states. Three of the top five donors to racial and ethnic populations were located in the Midwest.

Racial and ethnic grantmaking specifications: Two of the participating corporations published affirmative action policies that guide their funding for racial and ethnic populations. Five corporations published grantmaking nondiscrimination policies, and eleven publicly indicated grantmaking areas (such as higher education, sciences, and so on) that reflect the corporation's specific interests in funding organizations that benefit racial and ethnic populations.

By industry: The nineteen corporations in this survey represent seven different industries. The six gas and oil companies awarded the most overall and averaged the highest total amount to racial and ethnic populations. The two transportation equipment companies and the two consumer goods manufacturers also ranked near the top in both total giving and average giving by industry. The five telecommunications companies, all regional operating companies ("Baby Bells"), awarded the smallest amounts, which can be partially explained by the fact that all the corporate foundations had been incorporated in the four years prior to the survey.

By governance: More than half of the surveyed corporations (eleven of nineteen) awarded more funding to constituency-controlled groups than to non-constituency-controlled recipients. Six of the eleven awarded at least 60 percent of their racial/ethnic-specific funding to constituency-controlled recipients.

Giving by Interest Area

While consideration of the corporate community's commitment to care must begin with a general sense of the total funding picture for racial and ethnic populations, this study offers new insights when giving to specific interest areas is examined.

Well-Funded Interest Areas. Almost $15 million (57 percent of all funding in this survey) was education related. Of the education funding, 80 percent ($12 million) was awarded for higher education, 13 percent ($2 million) for primary/secondary schools, and 6 percent ($900,000) for community and other types of education, such as literacy programs and public libraries. Within this field, the most common recipients were engineering-related education efforts ($4.5 million), general population colleges and universities ($3.5 million), historically black colleges/universities

($2.6 million), college scholarship programs ($2.5 million), job training programs ($2.3 million), and culture-specific college funds ($1.6 million).

The breakdown of funding within the education interest areas shows that the highest single area of education funding was designated for engineering-related education. Many of the racial and ethnic leaders who responded to NCRP's request for feedback on the first phase of this study indicated great concern that the substantial commitment to this specific area of professional development may have advanced at the cost of other, more generally needed education programs such as primary/secondary education, community literacy programs, bilingual education, and job training programs.

Along with racial and ethnic funding for education, nearly one-third ($8.2 million) of the total surveyed funding was awarded for human services (such as housing, job training, food/hunger, and recreation), and nearly one-fourth of the total funding was awarded each for sciences ($6.4 million) and public benefit grants ($6 million). The remaining 10 percent ($2.6 million) of the funding was awarded for health, arts, and energy/environment.

Least-Funded Interest Areas. The interest areas receiving the smallest amounts of funding in this survey were food and hunger ($39,500), recreation ($162,500), energy/environment ($280,000), philanthropy and volunteerism ($306,500), crime prevention and legal services ($342,500), and social sciences ($507,500). There was no funding awarded for religious propagation, emergency services, health research, or membership benefit organizations.

Racial and Ethnic Composition of Beneficiaries

While most corporate giving programs treat race/ethnic-specific funding as a monolithic category, this study accounted for trends and distinct distribution patterns within the more general category.

For example, the participating corporations directed 48 percent of the funding in this survey to organizations with multiracial beneficiaries (three or more of the target populations). Organizations primarily intending to benefit African Americans received the second highest proportion (37 percent), while those primarily intending to benefit Hispanics received substantially less (12 percent). The surveyed corporations gave significantly less to benefit Native Americans and Asian and Pacific Islander Americans. Nine corporations awarded no grants primarily intended to benefit Native Americans, and eleven awarded no grants to benefit Asian and Pacific Islander Americans.

Racial and Ethnic Composition of Recipient's Board in Relation to Recipient's Beneficiaries

One of the reasons NCRP chose to undertake this study is the lack of data available about any kind of philanthropic giving to racial and ethnic populations, especially corporate giving. It is extremely difficult to ascertain to what extent a given grant actually benefits the racial and ethnic populations it purports to benefit. Pragmatically, how should grants awarded to general population recipients (such as state universities) for special population groups (such as Hispanic college students) be blended with grants awarded to organizations that are primarily for and controlled by racial and ethnic populations (such as the NAACP)? No previous national research efforts have accounted for these distinct types of recipient organizations. However, NCRP has developed such a categorization system with three distinct elements that factor in the racial and ethnic composition of the governing boards in relation to the racial and ethnic composition of the intended beneficiaries.

This methodological innovation permits a side-by-side comparison of (1) grants awarded to organizations controlled by racial and ethnic populations with (2) grants awarded to organizations that primarily benefit, but are not controlled by, racial and ethnic populations, and (3) "special grants" to general-population institutions awarded primarily to benefit racial and ethnic populations. To simplify communication, grants in the first category were defined as grants to "constituency-controlled" organizations and those in the second and third categories as grants to "non-constituency-controlled" organizations. For this study, NCRP determined that an organization was "constituency controlled" when 51 percent of the board of directors (or, alternatively, 33 percent of the board of directors and the chief executive officer) are of the same racial and ethnic population(s) as the primary intended beneficiaries.[5]

Overall: The funding reviewed in this survey was divided almost evenly between constituency-controlled organizations (49 percent) and non-constituency-controlled organizations (51 percent).

By interest area: The proportion of overall corporate funding to constituency-controlled organizations within interest areas ranged greatly from 13 percent for environment/energy projects to 88 percent for civil rights projects.

By racial and ethnic composition: Only 17 percent of the funding awarded to organizations with multiracial beneficiaries was awarded to constituency-controlled groups, while 78 percent of the funding to benefit specific racial and ethnic populations was awarded to constituency-controlled recipients.

The racial and ethnic composition of recipients' governing boards is a particularly critical issue for many racial and ethnic community leaders. Many such leaders assert that only grants awarded to organizations *controlled by* racial and ethnic populations should be counted as grants benefiting racial and ethnic populations. But many funders say that almost all grants benefit some people in the targeted population groups and thus almost all funding should be considered beneficial to racial and ethnic populations. Louis Nuñez, president of the National Puerto Rican Coalition (1991, p. iv), argues that constituency control goes beyond the question of organizational authority: "Corporations can play a constructive role in advancing and strengthening minority [controlled] organizations. . . . The empowerment of such organizations incorporates minorities as active participants in addressing increasingly convergent social concerns and promotes self-sufficiency in the constituencies they serve."

If this study used the "constituency-controlled recipients only" measurement, only $13 million of the funding in this study would be considered. This $13 million constitutes only 9 percent of the $153 million surveyed and falls well below the 24 percent figure of racial and ethnic populations in the United States.

Geographical Parameters of Recipient Organizations

Recipient geographical parameters are not commonly tracked by philanthropic surveys. However, for some racial and ethnic leaders, the distinctions between national and local organizations are very important. In the telephone sampling that followed the release of the survey, many local racial and ethnic leaders voiced concerns about the relationship between national racial and ethnic organizations and corporate donors. Others expressed concern over the relatively small amounts awarded to neighborhood and rural-based organizations (primarily reservation-based recipients). Still others were skeptical about the ability of organizations that are not located in major metropolitan areas or nonheadquarters cities to secure funding from major corporations.

Overall: National and metropolitan organizations each received one-third of the surveyed funding, while state/regional organizations received 18 percent, and organizations without a specific geographical focus (primarily private colleges such as Howard or Harvard universities) received nearly 10 percent of the funding. Neighborhood and rural organizations together were awarded 6 percent of the total funding in this survey.

Cities: Racial/ethnic-specific grants were awarded to organizations in 243 U.S. cities and towns. Two-thirds of this funding was awarded to recipients in New York City, Washington, D.C.,

Chicago, Los Angeles, San Francisco–Oakland, Detroit, Atlanta, Philadelphia, Rochester (New York), Baltimore, and Houston, and over half of the funding was awarded to organizations located in the first five metropolitan areas.

Corporate headquarters: The percent of total funding awarded to organizations in the headquarters communities of the corporate donor ranged from BellSouth's awarding 67 percent of its funding to organizations in Atlanta, to Ameritech's awarding no racial and ethnic grants in its headquarters in the city of Chicago. The five metropolitan areas that received the most funding (noted above) are headquarters for or adjacent to the headquarters of ten of the nineteen corporations.

Additional Highlights from Phase One

Almost half of the grants (743 of 1,653 grants) in this survey were $5,000 or less. Two-thirds were under $10,000, and 87 percent were $25,000 or less. Twenty-four of the 1,653 grants awarded were larger than $100,000.

Type of support: In this survey, 42 percent of the funding was awarded for general/operating support, compared with 11 percent in a Foundation Center survey of foundation giving to diverse minority populations. Nearly 30 percent was awarded for program development and 20 percent for student aid. The remaining 8 percent was awarded for research, capital campaigns, and technical assistance.

Auspices/sector: Almost three-fourths of the funding in this survey was awarded to conventional nonprofit organizations. Private and religion-affiliated colleges/universities received 11 percent of the funding, and public colleges/universities were awarded 13 percent. Primary/secondary schools, government, and religion-affiliated service agencies combined received the remaining 4 percent.

Giving to women of color: Less than 3 percent of the total funding was designated specifically to benefit women and girls. Of these sixty-six grants (averaging less than $11,000 per grant, compared with nearly $16,000 for the average grant in the overall survey), twenty-three grants were awarded to organizations controlled by and primarily for women of color (such as the National Council of Negro Women). The remaining forty-three grants were awarded to organizations that are not controlled by women of color but were primarily intended to benefit this population group. Grants to the recipients controlled by women of color averaged $4,587, while the others averaged $12,826.

Giving to other special populations: Three-fourths of the funding in this survey targeted special population groups. Young adults (primarily college-age students) were targeted for nearly one-third of the funding, economically disadvantaged people were the intended beneficiaries of one-fifth of the funding, and children, youth, and adolescents were targeted for 17 percent.

Recipients: The corporations in this survey awarded grants to 999 organizations. Four recipients and their affiliates received multiple grants totaling $500,000 or more: United Negro College Fund ($1,251,450), National Action Council for Minorities in Engineering ($1,195,500), National Urban League and its affiliates ($910,834), and Opportunities Industrialization Center and its affiliates ($504,350). Apart from these organizations, the following twelve national groups and their affiliates each received a combined total of $100,000 or more: Aspira, Neighborhood Housing Services, NAACP, YMCA, INROADS, Urban Coalition, National Council of La Raza, Boy Scouts, SER Jobs for Progress, Summer Jobs for Youth, LULAC, and Covenant House.

Conclusion

What information does this survey of corporate grantmaking for racial and ethnic populations provide in response to our original questions: Are corporations indicating their concern for the disadvantaged through their grantmaking programs? Do shifting corporate budget priorities indicate a decrease in the level of corporate commitment to racial and ethnic populations in particular?

Clearly, the $26.2 million awarded for racial and ethnic populations is a major financial commitment. In addition to this amount, other corporate grants, scholarships, and in-kind contributions were awarded, at least partially, with the intent of benefiting racial and ethnic population groups. In the final analysis, the top U.S. profit-making companies have indicated a significant concern for racial and ethnic populations. Whether this amount is adequate to meet the needs of racial and ethnic communities, whether this amount is sufficient given all the resources of these corporations, and whether this amount was distributed in the most effective and equitable manner are questions that must be addressed by the corporations, their recipients, and the communities that the recipients benefit. Whether shifting corporate budget priorities indicate a decrease in the level of corporate caring for racial and ethnic populations is a question that additional study may be able to clarify. Certainly, additional research is required to comprehensively answer both of these key questions.

Suggested Areas for Further Study

Areas for further study can be broken down into two categories.

Areas for Further Study Resulting from Findings in This Research. This initial phase of NCRP's multiphase study of corporate grantmaking for racial and ethnic populations reveals aspects of grantmaking that have, as yet, gone relatively unnoticed. However, the significance of Phase One findings stresses the need for continued study in this important area. For example, this study underscores the value of concentrating not just on the corporation making the grant, but on the recipient organizations themselves. This study further suggests that useful and potentially surprising findings may result from determining what organizations inquired about, applied for, or were denied requests for grants. Similarly, reviewing the sizes of such requests or the internal corporate circumstances affecting the approval or denial of funding could provide even more insight into the unexplored dimensions of corporate grantmaking.

Furthermore, the wealth of data uncovered in this initial study of the nineteen top profitmaking companies of 1988 argues strongly for an expanded list of participating corporations. A broader range of corporations, a more substantial breadth of corporations within a given industry, and a more detailed examination of all the funding pools within a specific corporate grantmaking program would undoubtedly provide a more detailed portrait of corporate caring for racial and ethnic populations. In addition, more up-to-date information would provide essential information for both grantseekers and grantmakers, while also providing a record of changes in corporate responsiveness to racial and ethnic community needs and corporate grantmaking priorities.

Areas for Further Study Resulting from Differences Between Findings in This and Related Research. There were numerous differences between the findings in the first two phases of this research and those in related studies of grantmaking to either minority or general-population groups. The following are the most notable:

1. According to the Foundation Center, 11 percent of foundation funding awarded for minority populations (including gays, lesbians, immigrants, and refugees) was designated for general/operating support. However, this study finds that 43 percent of the funding surveyed for roughly the same beneficiary group was earmarked for general/operating expenses.
2. For 1992, the Council for Aid to Education (CAFE) reports that 70 percent of all corporate funding for education was

awarded for higher education and only 15 percent for primary/secondary education. Preliminary findings from Phase Two of the NCRP study, however, indicate that in the same year a sampling of the top gas/oil and telecommunications companies gave only 60 percent of their combined education funding for racial and ethnic populations for higher education and 26 percent for primary/secondary education.

3. Furthermore, according to CAFE, 60 percent of 1992 higher education funding was awarded for research and capital support, while the preliminary findings of this study's second phase indicate that only 10 percent of higher education funding was awarded in these areas primarily for racial and ethnic populations.
4. The Foundation Center only reports on grants of $10,000 or more because they find that less than 5 percent of reported grants are less than $10,000. However, this study shows that two-thirds of the grants awarded to racial and ethnic populations were under the $10,000 mark.
5. Phase One of the NCRP study indicated that less than 2 percent of corporate grantmaking for racial and ethnic populations was awarded for health-related projects. However, in the Foundation Center's study of foundation grantmaking to diverse minority populations, 9 percent of funding was awarded for health. NCRP's research also indicated that 24 percent of the surveyed funding was awarded for physical and social sciences, while only 66.5 percent of the funding in the Foundation Center survey was awarded for these projects. There were also notable differences in the proportion of funding awarded for human services and the parts.

Are these differences a result of methodological differences, differences in the survey universes, or differences in definitions, or are corporate grantmaking patterns to racial and ethnic populations significantly different from other foundation and corporate grant-making patterns? Although we can offer educated speculation on the reasons why the research differs, undoubtedly a new wealth of information could be obtained by determining precisely why these differences have occurred.

Does Cornel West's bleak assessment of the level of corporate caring for African Americans extend to other racial and ethnic population groups as well, and is his perspective accurate within the area of corporate grantmaking? What will future generations think about the level of corporate concern for racial and ethnic populations? One study cannot adequately answer these critical questions. However, this study provides questions, methodology, and benchmarks allowing future studies to continue the important work begun in the first phase of this research and to come closer to the answers than we have ever come before.

Notes

1. Subsequent phases of the study will analyze giving by corporations within six major American industries during 1992–1993.
2. The six industries to be surveyed are telecommunications, gas/oil, banking, automotive, food/beverage, and retailing.
3. Before the development of the methodology, NCRP designated a Project Advisory Committee composed of leaders of racial and ethnic organizations, corporate grantmakers, and philanthropic researchers, whose suggestions were incorporated into the revised methodology. After input from the Advisory Committee, Foundation Center, INDEPENDENT SECTOR, and Council on Foundations, the National Taxonomy of Exempt Entities (NTEE) and the Foundation Center's *Grants Classification System* were selected as the primary classification formations. However, to provide a more detailed examination of the data, NCRP expanded the *Grants Classification System*'s racial and ethnic population categories and

added primarily culture-specific classification categories to the classification scheme.

4. These companies were Ameritech, Amoco, ARCO, Bell Atlantic, BellSouth, Chevron, Citicorp, Digital Equipment, Eastman Kodak, Exxon, Ford Motor Company, General Electric, General Motors, Merck and Company, Mobil Oil, NYNEX, Pacific Telesis, Texaco, and 3M.
5. Although the basic premise remained constant, there were some minor adaptations in the definition for some types of recipients, such as school boards and state-controlled historically black colleges/universities.

References

"Annual Survey on CEO Salaries." *Fortune*, May 31, 1989.

Conference Board. *Corporate Contributions, 1991*. Research report no. 1014. New York: Conference Board, 1992.

"Forbes 500." *Forbes*, May 1, 1989.

Foundation Center. *Grants for Minorities*. New York: Foundation Center, 1992.

Garonzik, E. (ed.). *Guide to the Foundation Center's Grants Classification System*. New York: Foundation Center, 1991.

Hodgkinson, V. A., Weitzman, M. S., Toppe, C. M., and Noga, S. M. (eds.). *Nonprofit Almanac 1992–93: Dimensions of the Independent Sector*. San Francisco: Jossey-Bass, 1992.

Moore, J. "Corporate Giving to Charities Dropped in 1992, First Decrease in 20 Years." *Chronicle of Philanthropy*, Sept. 21, 1993, pp. 8, 10.

National Puerto Rican Coalition. *The Responsiveness of Major U.S. Foundations to Puerto Rican Needs and Concerns*. Washington, D.C.: National Puerto Rican Coalition, 1991.

Paprocki, S. L., and Bothwell, R. O. *Corporate Grantmaking: Giving to Racial/Ethnic Populations—Phase One*. Washington, D.C.: National Committee for Responsive Philanthropy, 1994.

Renz, L., and Lawrence, S. "A Primer on Foundation Science Support." *Science*, 1992, *257*, 1750–1753.

Sommerfeld, M. "Corporate Gifts to K-12 Education Up 13% in 1992." *Chronicle of Higher Education*, Sept. 29, 1993, p. 10.

Weber, N. (ed.). "Giving by Corporations." *Giving USA: The Annual Report on Philanthropy for the Year 1988*, 1988, pp. 68–77.

West, C. *Race Matters*. New York: Vintage Books, 1993.

Chapter Fifteen

Improving Welfare: The Public Role in Caring for Poor Families with Children

Heidi Hartmann, Roberta Spalter-Roth

Philanthropy could be defined as the haves giving to the have-nots; by custom and usage, philanthropy refers to acts that are private and voluntary. Through our tax dollars we also give to others, but through public, government methods generally not considered philanthropic.[1]

The public methods of philanthropy, though resulting from a democratic political process, are, at the individual level and at any point in time, essentially coercive; unless we pursue civil disobedience, we must pay our taxes whether we agree with the uses to which they are put or not. Yet, in the long run, the success of the public sector depends on having the willing support of the citizenry. Public, tax-supported programs for the poor, like private philanthropy, redistribute income from the haves to the have-nots, and redistribute far more income than is redistributed through private charity. Since it is through public charity that most of the poor are supported, it is important to examine out antipoverty programs and inquire how well they meet humanitarian goals and how much they contribute to the development of a caring society.

How well does the public support these tax-funded redistribution programs and why? Through the political process, citizens have an opportunity to redirect tax dollars and to control the amount of taxes levied. One of the ways we can encourage a more caring society is to ensure that our citizenry understand and support our public income-transfer programs. Ideally, our public programs would be seen as being effective and efficient; our citizenry would have the satisfaction of knowing their tax dollars are being used well; and the programs would be seen as benefiting the public as a whole, as well as the particular recipients of the aid. In this chapter we seek to explore how one particular program for the poor, Aid to Families with Dependent Children (AFDC), cares for its clients and contributes to the development of a caring society. Based on our recent and ongoing research, we propose reforms of welfare policy that we believe would better accomplish these goals.

Deteriorating Public Support for the Poor

Until recently, Odendahl (1990, pp. 43–68) argues, the social safety net or support for the poor has been seen in the United States primarily as a responsibility of government.[2] In 1987, when private giving totaled $94 billion—the vast majority of which did not go to the poor, according to Odendahl—government social welfare spending for families and the elderly totaled approximately $260 billion. Of this $260 billion, $40 billion was targeted to the poor and much of the rest (approximately $135 billion or 64 percent of the approximately $210 billion in social security payments) also went to persons who otherwise would have been poor (Albelda and Tilly, 1990).

During the Reagan-Bush era, as part of a generalized attack on the role of government, public leaders sought to shift more of the responsibility of taking care of the needy onto the private sector. The poor were stigmatized while the flames of voter discontent were fanned by provocative rhetoric about an increasingly problematic cycle of dependency *caused* by government handouts.

Government support for the poor fell, but private giving did not compensate for the decline. The dollar value of AFDC benefits and food stamps combined fell by 26 percent in real terms between 1972 and 1991 (Committee on Ways and Means, U.S. House of Representatives, 1992, p. 643). Looking at the income sources of nonprofits that provide social services, many of whom carry out the government's social welfare agenda, Hodgkinson and Weitzman (cited in Odendahl, 1990, p. 60) find that government support of nonprofits fell from 54 percent of their total revenues to 44 percent of their revenues between 1977 and 1984. Abramson and Salamon (1986, p. 84) find that private philanthropy did not make up the shortfall from federal cutbacks and could not be expected to do so given the budget cuts in the 1980s (for example, between 1982 and 1984, increased private giving compensated for only 7 percent of the government spending reductions).

These data suggest that in the United States (and most other industrialized countries), despite attempts to privatize basic care of the needy, having a caring society requires adequately funded public programs. This in turn requires having strong public support that values the government's role in redistributing income. Yet public attitudes, fueled by provocative antidependency rhetoric, seem to have been moving away from public support for AFDC. For example, on several indicators of attitudes toward the poor, the proportion of the population expressing pro-welfare sentiment fell substantially between 1969 and 1980: more people believe we are spending too much on welfare and fewer people believe able-bodied welfare recipients try to find work (Kleugel and Smith, 1986, p. 153). Sawhill (1992) argues that public attitudes toward enabling poor women to stay home to take care of children changed as middle-class mothers of young children increasingly went to work. Welfare policy must conform to new values, Sawhill believes, because the public has the right to express its values through the political system. Public support for work programs is strong, including support for a government role in providing work: in 1980, while 82 percent of people believed "we are spending too much money on welfare," 61 percent believed "the federal government should guarantee a job to every person who wants to work."

Currently, we are faced with a fresh furor to get single mothers "off the welfare rolls." States are developing increasingly moralistic and punitive policies, requiring work outside the home by mothers whose children are as young as one, reducing benefits to families if children fail to attend school, denying benefits to children born while their mothers are receiving AFDC, providing financial incentives for marriage, and encouraging the use of long-term contraceptives such as Norplant. These policies seem to be inspired by an ideology that equates receipt of AFDC with moral bankruptcy and psychological dependency; the poor seem to be singled out for special treatment because they are thought not to have mainstream values. Yet Sawhill (1992) notes that if a new paternalism is to be enacted in welfare policy, it should be applied universally. Thus, if tax policies are tending to reduce tax burdens for larger families for the working poor and middle class, then denying benefits for larger families on welfare would be patently unfair. Similarly, if welfare mothers are required to ensure that their children attend school to receive full benefits, then middle-class college students who cut classes should lose college financial aid.

What are some of the factors contributing to the development of negative attitudes toward welfare, and how can they be altered? How can ideology be informed by knowledge?

The Recent History of Welfare

During the 1980s, under the Reagan and Bush administrations, AFDC was increasingly portrayed by policy makers and the media as a program that "allowed women to live without a husband or a job" (Amott, 1990, p. 290) and as a program that perpetuated the American underclass and reinforced its "dependence on government handouts" (Shirley-Reynolds and Walke, 1986, p. B2). Because welfare was portrayed as inhibiting work effort and rewarding "bad" behavior—specifically laziness, irresponsible reproduction, and pathological dependence—those receiving welfare were stigmatized. The rhetoric of dependency was used to promote a political and ideological consensus in which conservatives and liberals came together to pass the Family Support Act (FSA) of 1988. The FSA strives to transfer responsibility for the support of poor minor children from the state (via AFDC) to the market (by requiring "able-bodied" mothers to find paid employment or to participate in the JOBS program) and to biological fathers (via increased child support enforcement). An underlying assumption of the FSA was that women who participated in the AFDC program did not work at paid employment, and that work and welfare are mutually exclusive alternatives for poor women. The FSA was designed to increase work efforts by mandating participation in job training programs and by facilitating transition between work and welfare, through the continuation of Medicaid and subsidized child care for one year after leaving the welfare rolls. Mothers' ability to survive without welfare would be enhanced by improved child support enforcement from the absent fathers. The FSA, and the substantial effort it envisaged in job training, work readiness preparation, and additional supports for a one-year transition period, capitalized on the public's approval of work as a means of self-support.

Since the passage of the FSA, the feasibility of transferring women from welfare to work through job training and child support has become increasingly questioned, and states, responsible for administering the program, have applied for a variety of waivers that allow them to experiment with alternative models. Given the current slow economic and employment growth and the lack of state funds, most states have not provided their share of matching funds to implement the JOBS program. In addition, lack of jobs for recipients who have finished JOBS training, especially jobs that pay a "family" wage that can support a woman and her children, make transition to work all but impossible except for the lucky few. Finally, providing even the minimal support services mandated in the FSA—child care and Medicaid for one year—is expensive.

These economic realities, however, have not dampened the political rhetoric about the necessity to reform welfare. President Clinton's campaign called for "ending welfare as we know it" and replacing it with two years of job training and education, after which all recipients would be required to work. His administration is currently developing time-limited welfare programs.

All such proposals are based on the assumption that "welfare mothers" are not currently working. Yet our previous research (Institute for Women's Policy Research, 1989) showed that a substantial portion of single mothers employed in low-wage work participated in means-tested government programs (such as AFDC and food stamps) as a supplement to their wages. Other studies, especially a case study by Kathryn Edin (1991) of welfare recipients in one metropolitan area now being replicated elsewhere, also found that recipients supplement their scant benefits with earnings from work, which are also meager. It simply takes both sources of income to survive. Yet, as currently structured, AFDC actually discourages work efforts, because, if reported, all earnings after certain work-related expenses are subtracted lead to a dollar-for-dollar reduction in benefits. These draconian policies, first implemented in 1981 and modified only slightly since, force welfare mothers to cheat—to not report their earnings (and welfare workers to look the other way)—to keep their families together and out of shelters for the homeless.

Research on Welfare and Work

Based on our previous research on low-wage workers, and in the face of the increasingly vitriolic attacks on AFDC participants, we are conducting additional research to provide evidence about how poor families headed by women actually survive. Our research, we hope, can correct prevailing assumptions about welfare recipients.

The purpose of our new study is to examine the survival strategies—including employment activities, participation in government programs, and other income sources—of a nationally representative sample of women who participated in the AFDC program for at least two months during a two-year period. The principal research questions are:

1. How do women participating in AFDC put together their family's income package? What proportion obtain enough money to move their family out of poverty?
2. What factors increase their ability to combine paid employment and participation in AFDC and to use these income packages to move their family out of poverty?
3. What policy alterations can lead to an increase in packaging and an increase in family incomes to above-poverty levels?

Unlike many policy research studies that examine work-to-welfare transitions (see, for example, Gueron and Pauly, 1991; Michalopoulos and Garfinkel, 1991), the study by the Institute for Women's Policy Research (IWPR) defines success as moving out of poverty rather than moving off the welfare rolls.

The results of the first phase of our study can be found in *Combining Work and Welfare* (Spalter-Roth and Hartmann, 1992). The first-phase findings are based on a sample of 585 single mothers, drawn from the 1986 and 1987 panels of the U.S. Bureau of the Census' Survey of Income and Program Participation (SIPP). The SIPP is a panel survey that interviews members of a stratified sample of households over a two and one-half year period. The SIPP is designed to provide longitudinal information on the changing economic circumstances of individuals and families and is particularly useful for studying transitions in family composition, employment, participation in government programs, and income. During the second phase, currently under way, we are extending the study sample to AFDC recipients in the 1984 and 1988 SIPP panels.

The findings that resulted from the first phase of this study challenge the consensus that welfare perpetuates dependence and that paid employment is the ticket out of poverty for single mothers and their children.

These women, referred to as income packagers, *increased* their family income and *decreased* their burden on the taxpayer by combining work and welfare (Figure 15.1). Despite their substantial work effort, the average family income remained below the poverty threshold (at about 95 percent of the poverty threshold for families of their size). The average hourly wages were only slightly above the minimum wage, despite the fact that they had six years of work experience, on the average.

Even those recipients we labeled as "more welfare reliant" (because they received AFDC for an average of twenty-three out of twenty-four months and were employed for fewer than 300 hours per year), received about 40 percent of their income package from sources other than means-tested welfare benefits (usually from the paid employment of other family members; see Figure 15.1). In fact, the three major sources of income for all welfare recipients are means-tested benefits, their own earnings, and the earnings of other family members. Virtually no income is obtained from non-means-tested benefits (such as unemployment insurance), from child support, or from private charity.

Women whom we identified as more reliant on welfare were also more likely to be disabled, had slightly more children (2.2 as opposed to 1.8, on the average), and were less likely to be high school graduates (Figure 15.2). Despite the income from other family members' employment and their lack of total dependence on "government handouts," these women suffered the most poverty (Figure 15.3).

We found that approximately four out of ten women who participated in the AFDC program were also employed for a substantial number of hours over a two-year period (approximately 1,000 hours per year—about half-time employment, the average amount worked by mothers with young children). They either combined paid employment and AFDC participation simultaneously or cycled between them. Thus, despite stereotypes of the lazy, dependent poor, so prominent in the current political climate of "welfare bashing," a substantial portion (40 percent) of single mothers add work to welfare, working about half time; they display the same work behavior as the average mother of young children.

Figure 15.1. Income Packagers Receive Less Public Assistance But Have Higher Family Income Than More Welfare-Reliant Recipients.

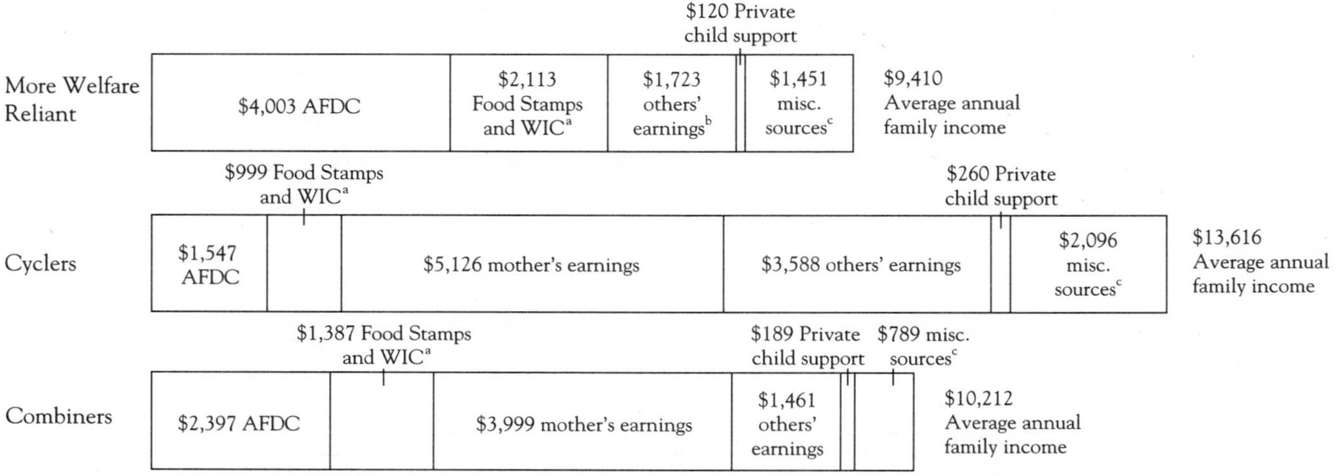

[a]Includes other welfare.

[b]Includes mother's earnings, $124 annually on average.

[c]Includes other public and private benefits and informal resources, including unaccounted-for income.

Source: Institute for Women's Policy Research calculations based on the 1986 and 1988 panels of the Survey of Income and Program Participation.

Figure 15.2. Selected Characteristics of Three Types of Single Mothers Receiving AFDC.

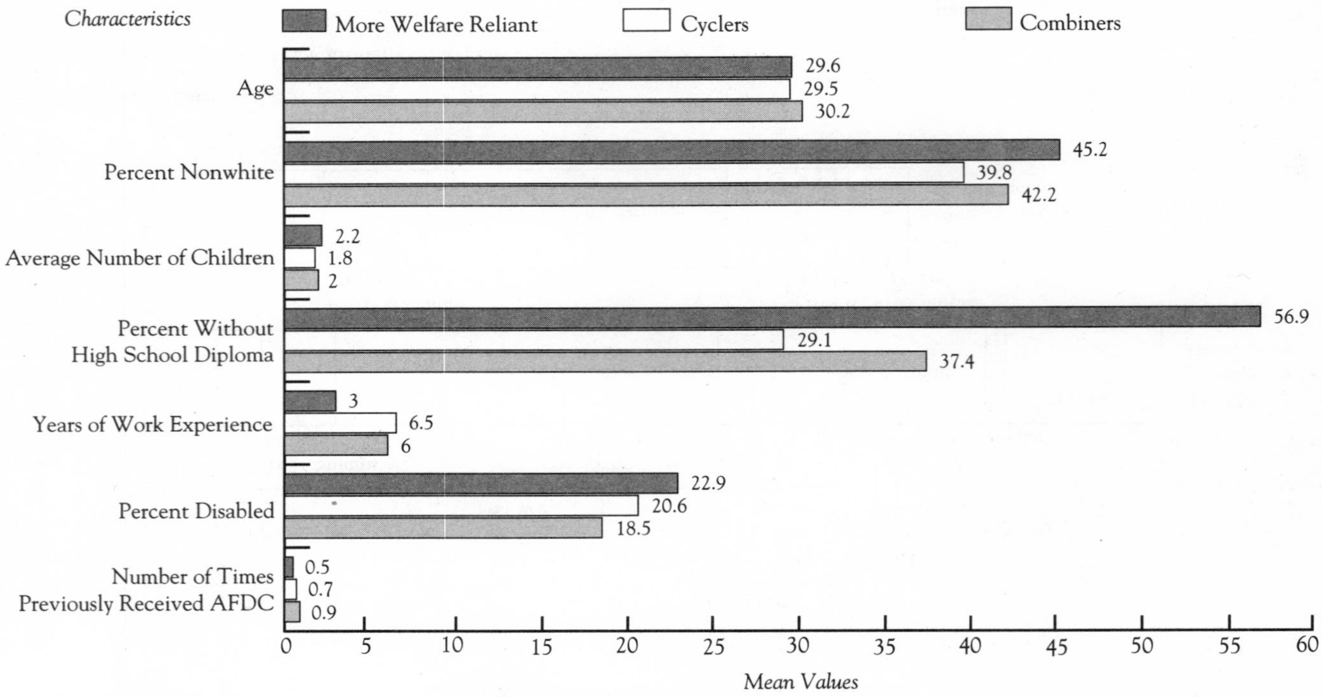

Source: Institute for Women's Policy Research calculations from 1986 and 1987 SIPP panels.

Figure 15.3. Single Mothers on AFDC: Months in Poverty and Health Insurance.

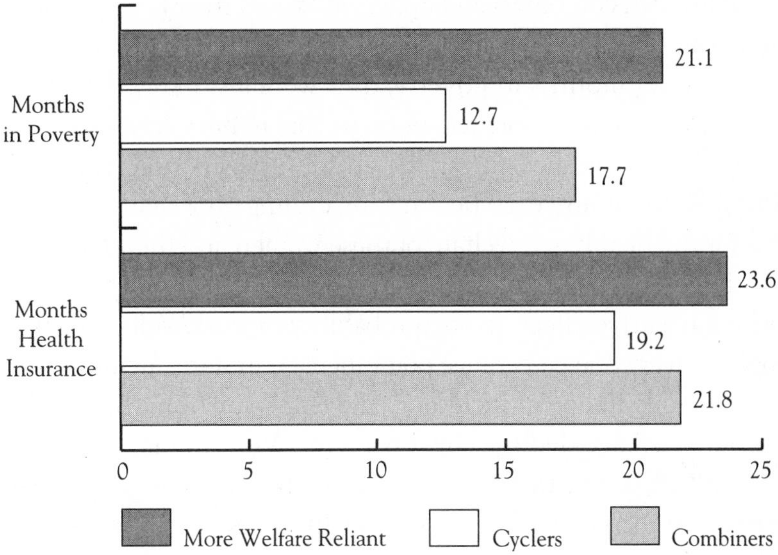

Source: Institute for Women's Policy Research calculations based on 1986 and 1987 SIPP panels.

We found no significant differences, however, between the "more reliant" and the "income packagers" in terms of their race or ethnicity, or their previous marital history (see Figure 15.2). These factors had no independent effect on the probability that a single mother will be primarily reliant on welfare or will add paid employment to AFDC benefits to make up her income package. This finding counters the stereotype that long-term recipients are pathologically dependent on welfare, black, and unmarried. Black, unmarried welfare recipients are as likely to work as others, and we believe (but cannot show conclusively with this data set) that many of the long-term recipients are longtime combiners of work and welfare. Far from sitting on their duffs, they are actively seeking all income sources in a too-often futile attempt to get above poverty. Whether a woman has a high school diploma is by far the most important personal determinant of whether she can package work with welfare.

Although combiners and cyclers increased their family incomes more than the more welfare-reliant, and cyclers in particular experience fewer months in poverty, they were less likely than those recipients who were more reliant on welfare to have access to health care for their families during the entire survey period (see Figure 15.3). Without universal health care, cycling off welfare is dangerous for the health and welfare of these women and their families.

The study also found that high state-level unemployment rates have a negative effect on the probability of work/welfare packaging. For every one percentage point increase in state unemployment rates, the likelihood of including paid employment in the mother's income package declines by 9 percent. Work in manufacturing industries was statistically significant and positively associated with having an income package that brought the family above poverty, perhaps because manufacturing jobs often provide higher wages for the relatively unskilled than do jobs in the service sector. These findings indicate the importance of examining the economic context in which AFDC participants develop their survival strategies.

Conclusion

Our research leads to several conclusions and recommendations.

1. *Combining work and welfare*. The current system of regulations does not enable AFDC participants who are doing paid work to move their families out of poverty. Combining work and welfare, along with income from other sources, should be made legitimate because, at current levels, neither earnings nor means-tested benefits alone can provide a minimally sufficient income for single mothers and their families. Half-time employment or somewhat more, but probably not full-time employment, can reasonably be expected of single mothers, many of whom do not have assistance with parenting. They can only earn minimum wage or somewhat

more, when hampered by low skills and a lack of jobs in other than the low-wage labor market (which is highly unstable as well as low paying). Given these circumstances, substantial, continuing subsidies are needed to bring these families above poverty.

These subsidies could come from AFDC, legitimately, if the earnings disregards were restored and increased (to even larger than their pre-1981 levels)—that is, if what one earns is not automatically deducted from one's award. Using AFDC to supplement wages has several advantages. Payments are made frequently (on a monthly basis) and the AFDC system (the location of the office and so on) is known to this group of women. Yet given current public attitudes, for receipt of AFDC not to be stigmatizing, it would have to be reconceptualized as a wage-subsidy program. Such a reconceptualization may be too difficult if the word *welfare*, or the official title of *AFDC*, is retained. A one-time, permanent transition from welfare to work is unrealistic. Rather we need work plus welfare, even if welfare by another name.

2. *Additional supplements*. Additional wage or income supplements should also be developed and expanded. Larger and more reliable *child support* payments from absent parents to custodial parents would certainly help, assuming fathers have available income. But in the absence of true government responsibility for making the system work (using the tax system, for example, to withhold men's earnings and deliver them to women, or, for another example, providing child support assurance, in which the government will guarantee a minimum benefit level), this system is not likely to increase women's incomes substantially. Child support has the advantage of not being means tested—that is, regardless of one's own earnings, child support payments will continue.

An expanded *earned income credit* (EIC), a means-tested benefit, can also help.[3]

This mechanism, however, requires that even people who owe no taxes (because their earnings are low) file with the IRS, and currently the IRS provides only annual payments, which are not frequent enough to keep families going.[4] At present, the maximum benefit level occurs for approximately 85 percent of full-time work at the minimum wage and provides less than the typical AFDC benefit. Thus, single mothers who work less than full time are not likely to receive enough from the EIC to sustain themselves and their families in the absence of welfare benefits. Likewise the current *dependent care tax credit* for working parents with child-care expenditures could be expanded and made refundable; currently, parents too poor to pay taxes receive no benefit.

The current *unemployment insurance* program needs to be reformed to be more inclusive of low-wage, part-time, and intermittent workers. Currently unemployment insurance is not reaching the typical working welfare mother, because even though she works half time on average she does not earn enough to be covered in most states. If unemployment insurance were more available, welfare would be less needed as the unemployment program for low-income women.

New benefits that could be considered include free (or sliding-scale) *child care* and *child allowances*. These have the advantage of being universal, available to all regardless of income, and thus, like social security, would likely draw broad support. These policies are common in Europe. In the United States, consideration is being given to converting the current tax exemption for children to a refundable tax credit; this would function similarly to a child allowance, increasing the cash income of all those with children through public subsidy, but would likely be small at the outset (for example, $700 per year per child).

Finally, in this category, *universal national health insurance* that is accessible and affordable to all—for example a Canadian-style program financed out of general public revenues—would increase the likelihood that families could make ends meet with low-wage and intermittent jobs; they would not be forced back on welfare simply to obtain medical care.

3. *Policies that "make work pay."* Alternatively, or in addition,

policies that "make work pay," such as eliminating race- and wage-based discrimination in the labor market (through *stronger enforcement of equal employment opportunity laws and regulations* and through new initiatives like *pay equity*), encouraging unionization, strengthening *collective bargaining*, and increasing the *minimum wage* are needed to increase the incomes of the working poor. Making work pay better without government subsidies is a cost-effective strategy for raising the incomes of the less skilled. These policies are also universal ones, not limited to the target poor population; several are under consideration in Congress and the Clinton administration.

4. *Increasing human capital*. Policies that increase women's earning ability through improving their job skills—such as *increased training and education*—are, of course, important. Our research shows that having a high school diploma is generally more important than having some job training in overall earning ability. The Clinton administration and Congress are likely to make improved training and education a priority.

5. *Increasing employment*. If the economy is not generating enough jobs to employ all who seek them, no amount of job training and education or financial inducement to work will succeed. Macroeconomic policy will be needed to stimulate the economy and/or public service employment programs—"job creation" will be necessary to provide employment.

6. *Increased welfare assistance*. Finally, we conclude that not all single mothers can be expected to participate in paid employment. In particular, AFDC participants with an above-average number of children, little work experience, and education well below high school equivalency, disabling conditions, limited access to other income sources, and living in areas with high unemployment rates are less likely to be able to do so. *Higher benefit levels* are a necessary poverty-reduction strategy for these women. There must be provisions to exempt some women in any program designed to make welfare transitional and move everyone into the world of work.

We believe that legitimating work/welfare packaging is a more humane alternative to the current "off-the-rolls" policy. By recasting welfare as a work supplement, for those who are able to work, work/welfare packaging reduces the stigma attached to AFDC recipiency, while it simultaneously encourages paid work. By *validating* the efforts these women make to attempt to bring their families out of poverty, and by reducing the prevalence of "welfare cheating," our proposed policy reforms can create the basis for greater understanding across race and income categories. All families income package; we must not stigmatize those whose packages include AFDC.

Allowing women who work, but have low earnings, to stay on the welfare rolls, however, does *increase* the number of people on the rolls. As we have seen, it also reduces the average benefit paid, while simultaneously increasing family incomes. We believe the American public would probably find such a welfare program more acceptable, rather than less acceptable. Because of the support that the public expresses for work behavior and the current belief that welfare recipients are not working, we think a program that emphasizes work efforts and full employment will meet with greater public support. We believe U.S. taxpayers would rather pay a little to a larger number of families who are perceived as helping themselves through work than pay a lot to a smaller number of people perceived as totally dependent on welfare and living from one month's handout to the next.

Legitimating the combination of work and welfare, as well as developing the additional, more universal strategies listed above, would contribute toward eliminating the antiwelfare rhetoric of moral bankruptcy and psychological dependence from our public discourse, legitimating receipt of AFDC (or its new substitute), and basing public policies on the real-life packaging strategies of AFDC recipients rather than on myths and stereotypes. Providing AFDC and low-income women with access to the same benefits others enjoy—child support, unemployment insurance, child care, health care, tax credits—will both reduce the need for AFDC and increase commonalities among people across class and race lines. Moreover, implementing such policies can increase public support for income-transfer programs (perhaps even to the popularity of the much-loved social security program—the largest income-transfer program of all) and help to stop the erosion of the ties that bind. In short, they can help us build a more caring society through the development of an effective and humanitarian public sector.

Notes

1. The distinction between private and government philanthropy is probably overdrawn, however. Salamon (1987, p. 99) argues that government is now "the single most important source of income for most types of nonprofit agencies, outdistancing private charity by roughly two to one." In addition, a substantial amount of individuals' charitable giving and volunteer service is directed at government agencies. In 1989 some 12 percent of all charitable contributions were given to government, while some 26 percent of all volunteer hours were donated to government agencies (Hodgkinson, Weitzman, Toppe, and Noga, 1992, Table 2.5, p. 7).
2. Salamon (1987, p. 100) shows that by the turn of the twentieth century, many local governments were spending considerable sums on poor support and, then as now, channeling much of it through private charities, so that for many charities government funds provided the majority of support. With the development of the federal social security and Aid to Dependent Children programs from the 1930s through the 1960s, the role of the government in providing income support increased further (Abramson and Salamon, 1986, Chapter Four).
3. The EIC provides about $7 billion to low-income working parents annually. It provides a tax credit (and, for those too poor to owe taxes, a cash payment equal to the credit in an

annual payment from the IRS). The size of the program was substantially increased in 1990 and a small adjustment for family size was implemented. In 1993 the maximum basic benefit was $1,400 per year; benefits tapered to 0 at incomes of about $23,000 annually. As President Clinton's campaign program called for increasing the EIC, Congress was expected to consider further expansion in the 103rd session.

4. Currently, employers can determine that employees are eligible for the EIC, calculate their reduced tax burden or tax credit, and adjust their employees' paychecks accordingly. Only a very small proportion of those who participate in the EIC program receive the credits in their paychecks; most participants receive an annual credit.

References

Abramson, A. J., and Salamon, L. M. *The Non-Profit Sector and the New Federal Budget*. Washington, D.C.: Urban Institute Press, 1986.

Albelda, R., and Tilly, C. "All in the Family: Family Types, Access to Income, and Implications for Family Income Policies." Boston: Department of Economics, University of Massachusetts at Boston, 1990.

Amott, T. "Black Women and AFDC: Making Entitlement Out of Necessity." In L. Gordon (ed.), *Women, the State, and Welfare*. Madison: University of Wisconsin Press, 1990.

Committee on Ways and Means, U.S. House of Representatives. *1990 Green Book*. Washington, D.C.: U.S. Government Printing Office, 1992.

Edin, K. "Surviving the Welfare System: How AFDC Recipients Make Ends Meet in Chicago." *Social Problems*, 1991, *38*(4), 462–474.

Gueron, J., and Pauly, E. *From Welfare to Work*. New York: Russell Sage Foundation, 1991.

Hodgkinson, V. A., Weitzman, M. S., Toppe, C. M., and Noga, S. M. (eds.). *Nonprofit Almanac, 1992–93: Dimensions of the Independent Sector*. San Francisco: Jossey-Bass, 1992.

Institute for Women's Policy Research. *Low Wage Jobs and Workers: Trends and Options for Change*. Washington, D.C.: Institute for Women's Policy Research, 1989.

Kleugel, J. R., and Smith, E. R. *Beliefs About Inequality*. New York: Aldine De Gruyter, 1986.

Michalopoulos, C., and Garfinkel, I. "Reducing Welfare Dependence." Madison: Institute for Research on Poverty, University of Wisconsin, 1991.

Odendahl, T. J. *Charity Begins at Home: Generosity and Self-Interest Among the Philanthropic Elite*. New York: Basic Books, 1990.

Salamon, L. M. "Partners in Public Service: The Scope and Theory of Government-Nonprofit Relations." In W. W. Powell (ed.), *The Non-Profit Sector: A Research Handbook* (pp. 99–117). New Haven, Conn.: Yale University Press, 1987.

Sawhill, I. V. "The New Paternalism: Earned Welfare." *Responsive Community*, 1992, *2*(2), 26–35.

Shirley-Reynolds, S., and Walke, R. "New Ideas on Welfare." *Albuquerque Journal*, Nov. 9, 1986, p. B2.

Spalter-Roth, R. M., and Hartmann, H. I. *Combining Work and Welfare: An Alternative Anti-Poverty Strategy*. Washington, D.C.: Institute for Women's Policy Research, 1992.

Chapter Sixteen

Caring Sector or Caring Society: Discovering the Nonprofit Sector Cross-Nationally

Lester M. Salamon, Helmut K. Anheier

This chapter challenges the conventional rhetoric of voluntarism, which equates the size and visibility of the nonprofit sector, and the level and breadth of private charitable giving, with the presence of a "caring tradition" in a society. We argue instead that large nonprofit sectors may actually signify the weakness rather than the strength of a caring tradition in a society. At the very least, it is important to recognize that the nonprofit sector is only one possible embodiment of a society's "caring tradition," and by no means necessarily the most significant one. In some places, the state has taken on the function of caring for those in need, while in others, business enterprises have assumed major caring responsibilities. In such cases, the caring function may be performed far more effectively than in places where primary reliance is placed on private, voluntary action. The presence of a strong voluntary sector may therefore signify not the presence, but the relative absence, or weakness, of a caring tradition elsewhere in society or the successful resistance to other, more effective, expressions of caring.

This, at any rate, is a thesis that finds considerable support in cross-national analysis of the character and role of the nonprofit sector. What such analysis shows is that the concept of the nonprofit sector does not even exist in coherent form in a great many countries, but this does not seem to bear any relation to the extent of "caring" evident in the society. Rather, a variety of other factors seem to be involved, including the legal framework in use, the level of development, the degree of social differentiation, and the extent of centralization of social and political control. These factors help explain under what conditions and in what form the nonprofit sector may supplement "caring," and when it compensates for the lack of such a tradition.

To illustrate these points, this chapter explores the position of the nonprofit sector in the legal and institutional framework of the twelve countries examined as part of the *Johns Hopkins Comparative Nonprofit Sector Project*. These countries were chosen to represent a broad cross section of national experiences with respect to level of development, culture, religion, geographical region, political structure, and reliance on nonprofit organizations, as opposed to the state, to meet human needs (Salamon and Anheier, 1992, 1994). The chapter draws on the responses of a network of field associates to a project "field guide" seeking information on the terminology and concepts used in the twelve project countries to depict what in the United States is referred to as the *nonprofit sector* (see Amenomori, 1993; Anheier and Seibel, 1993; Archambault, 1993; Atingdui, 1994; Barbetta, 1993; Kandil, 1993; Kendall and Knapp, 1993; Kuti, 1993; Landim, 1993; Pongsapich, 1993; Sen, 1994). By examining how the nonprofit sector is treated in these countries, it should be possible to identify the factors that explain the existence or nonexistence of a distinct nonprofit sphere, the kind of role that organizations in this sphere perform, and the relation this bears to the promotion of a "caring tradition."

Twelve Realities in Search of a Concept

Cross-national research has long recognized fundamental differences in the scope and structure of the nonprofit sector and in the way it is constituted and defined from place to place (James, 1989; Anheier and Seibel, 1990; Gidron, Kramer, and Salamon, 1992). But the true nature of the conceptual challenge facing students of this field has only recently become clear. In point of fact, few societies have anything approaching a coherent notion of a distinct private nonprofit sector, and those that do often include entities that would be unrecognizable to American students of the subject. To a significant extent, therefore, the search for a nonprofit sector is a voyage of discovery in conceptual as well as empirical terms.

United States

Of all the countries examined here, the United States is probably the one with the clearest concept of a distinguishable nonprofit sector. As reflected in Figure 16.1, however, it is also the developed country with possibly the lowest level of public social welfare spending as a share of gross national product, a situation that raises important questions about the relation between the presence of a nonprofit sector and the operation of an effective caring tradition. It is important to note that the disparity between the United States and other countries in terms of public social welfare expenditures—which represents only 19 percent of the U.S. gross national product—is not made up by private giving, which at 2.2 percent of the U.S. gross national product is only about 1 percent above the level in the United Kingdom.

While far from simple or homogeneous, the concept of the nonprofit sector at least has a coherent place in American law and usage. Indeed, there are those who believe that the "nonprofit sector" is a distinctively American concept, invented in response to America's distinctive tradition of individualism and hostility to statism, and its long-standing practice of organized action outside the confines of the state (Tocqueville, [1835] 1945; Hall, 1992).

U.S. law thus recognizes a distinct sphere of private organizations serving public purposes and not organized principally to earn a profit. Such organizations are permitted to incorporate under state laws and to secure exemption from federal income taxes and most state and local taxes. No fewer than twenty-six different subsections of the tax law are available under which such tax-exempt status can be secured. Broadly, however, they fall into two groups—one covering essentially member-serving organizations such as business

Figure 16.1. Government Social Welfare Spending as a Share of Gross Domestic Product, United States Versus Western Europe.

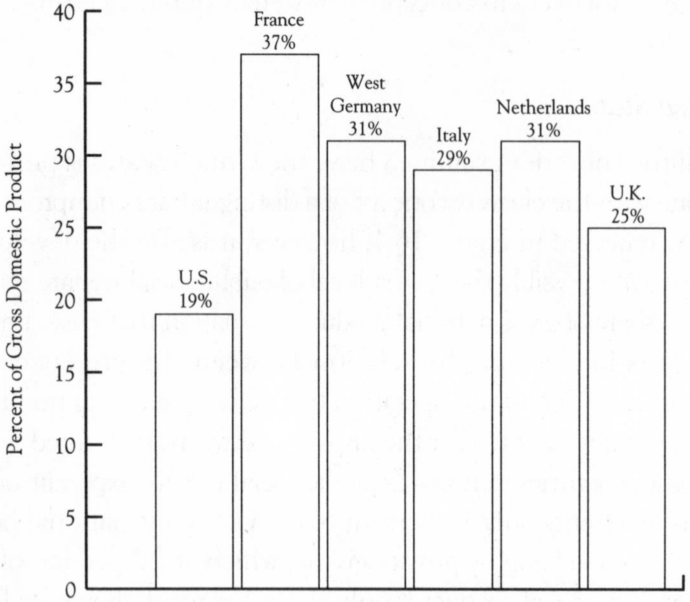

Source: Salamon, 1992, p. 36. Reprinted by permission of the publisher from *Nonprofit Sector: A Primer* by Lester M. Salamon. Copyright © 1992 by Lester M. Salamon. Published by the Foundation Center, 79 Fifth Ave., New York, NY 10003.

associations, social clubs, and labor unions, and the other covering organizations that operate principally to serve the needs of the public more broadly. The latter group, defined by section 501(c)(3) of the tax code, form the core of what is generally regarded as the charitable nonprofit sector. This group not only enjoys exemption from federal income taxes, but also the privilege of receiving charitable gifts on which donors can claim a deduction on their own income taxes. Included here are organizations serving "religious, charitable, scientific, literary, or educational purposes," each of these a term of art defined through the English common law traditions over some 300 years. The term *charitable* in particular is quite broad in its interpretation, embracing organizations that promote the general welfare in any of a variety of ways, from providing child care to promoting health, from guaranteeing free expression to offering family counseling (Hopkins, 1987, pp. 55–71). While the legal treatment of different types of organizations is far from simple, the U.S. nonprofit sector is perhaps unique in the extent to which popular conceptions of the sector correspond with basic distinctions in the law.

United Kingdom

The United Kingdom shares with the United States a reasonably clear concept of a nonprofit sector ("voluntary sector" in U.K. usage), but the legal boundaries of this sector are nowhere near as neatly demarcated. No single body of tax or other law embraces this set of institutions. One reason for this is that different legal systems exist in the United Kingdom—one covering England and Wales, another Scotland, and a third Northern Ireland. Beyond this, however, the common law tradition, which puts a premium on flexibility and evolution rather than precise delineation of organizational types, has had a stronger hold in the United Kingdom than in the United States, preventing even the kind of codification that the tax laws have achieved in the United States. The result is a reasonably prominent notion of an organizational space outside the state and the market, but a far more complicated one than in the American setting.

The center of gravity of the U.K. nonprofit sector are so-called "public charities" (see Kendall and Knapp, 1993). These are organizations formally registered as "charities" by the U.K. Charity Commission and thereby accorded the protection of the Crown, the Courts, and the Charity Commission for their activities, including protection from taxation. The requirements for such classification have never been clearly and definitively specified, however. The listing provided in the Preamble to the Statute of Charitable Uses of 1601 has been a start, but it has been successively revised.

Perhaps the most definitive ruling was in Pemsel's case in 1891, which approved four different classes of charities: those for relief of poverty, those for the advancement of education, those for the advancement of religion, and those for other purposes "beneficial to the community."

While they share a common set of basic purposes, charities can take any of a number of legal forms—trusts, unincorporated associations, companies limited by guarantee. But other types of voluntary organizations not recognized as "charities" by the Charity Commission can also take the same legal forms. This includes such entities as "friendly societies," "industrial and benevolent societies," building societies, universities, private schools, and cooperatives. It has been estimated that at least half the U.K. voluntary sector falls into these categories.

Defined in legal terms, therefore, the U.K. nonprofit sector is a bewilderingly confused set of institutions with poorly defined boundaries. For the most part, social science research has tended to focus on the registered charities (Posnett, 1987), but this overlooks a significant range of organizations. While the concept of a voluntary sector seems easy to identify in British usage, therefore, its applicability to particular organizations is far from simple.

The European Continent: Germany, France, and Italy

Despite their differences, both the United States and the United Kingdom share a basic notion of an organizational universe distinct from the state and the market. In the continental countries of Europe, by contrast, such a notion is far less developed. There the right to form private organizations is more tightly defined by law, and the concept of a public-serving nonprofit sector is complicated by the notion that the state is considered the truest embodiment of the public good.

Germany. In Germany, for example, a rather rigid and well-defined system exists for defining the status and rights of organizations. However, this system is not particularly designed to clarify the existence of a set of organizations that fit common notions of a private, nonprofit sector. To the contrary, they actually blur such a classification.

At the heart of the German system are two distinct systems of law, one of which (civil law) applies to private individuals and organizations, and the other of which (public law) applies to public institutions. Organizations must find a legal home in either civil law or public law. The problem, however, is that nonprofit organizations are private organizations that often serve essentially public purposes. They are thus civil law in form and public law in function, posing a challenge to the neat symmetry of the German legal order.

To cope with this challenge, a variety of special provisions have been made (Anheier and Seibel, 1993). In the first place, civil law acknowledges the existence of various types of civil law organizations that serve essentially public purposes. This includes: (1) so-called "ideal associations," or *Vereine*, which are essentially membership organizations serving other than commercial purposes (for example, political and civic organizations, local voters' groups, sports clubs); (2) certain limited-liability companies and other forms of corporations considered to have a public mission, such as hospitals; and (3) foundations. Under German tax law, these civil law organizations are tax exempt and eligible to receive tax deductible gifts to the extent that they are *gemeinnützige*, or public-benefit, organizations serving certain specified public purposes (such as public health, youth and youth welfare, life saving, prisoners' welfare).

These features of German usage are not far from the patterns evident in the United States and the United Kingdom. The problem, however, is that not all of what would normally be considered part of the nonprofit sector in the United States and the United Kingdom falls under civil law in Germany. A significant portion also falls under public law. Although theoretically reserved for public agencies, the public law category has been broadened to include a wide variety of organizations that are public in purpose but essentially private in structure, such as public television stations, the Bavarian Red

Cross, the Jewish Welfare Agency, most universities, and even the Roman Catholic and Protestant churches. Germany has thus included within the domain of public law corporations (which applies mainly to government agencies) many types of organizations that would be classified as private, nonprofit organizations in other societies. Yet not all public law corporations fit this criterion.

In the German setting, therefore, no clear line can be drawn between public and private institutions in defining the nonprofit sector. By law, some are public and some private. What is more, particular types of organizations can end up on both sides of this amorphous line, depending on peculiar historical circumstances. Thus, some German charitable foundations are chartered under civil law and some under public law. Similarly, the church, commonly regarded as a preeminently private institution, is covered by the public law in Germany. Nor does the tax structure clarify what the legal structure leaves confused. While German law permits tax exemptions for private donations to public-benefit organizations, this category includes government agencies, civil law organizations, and functionally independent public law organizations.

In short, although Germany contains a rather rigid and formal legal structure and a sizable and well-developed set of nonprofit organizations, including some of the largest private social welfare organizations in the world—the so-called "free welfare associations"—no coherent concept of a nonprofit sector exists. Rather, this sector is thoroughly mixed up with both the governmental and private, for-profit spheres. The search for a nonprofit sector in Germany thus requires exceptional diligence and patience as well as a high tolerance for ambivalence.

France. In France, the nonprofit sphere is more clearly specified, but it embraces a far wider range of organizations. The central organizing concept in the French setting is the concept of "solidarity"—the need to join together to pursue common objectives. Although historically the state has been viewed as the highest expression of solidarity, since 1901 the law has acknowledged the legitimacy of a variety of other institutions that encourage the same goal. These organizations are embraced within what is known as *économie sociale*, or the social economy. Included here are three broad sets of organizations—cooperatives, mutuals, and associations—each with its own set of laws, its own structures, and its own pattern of development (Archambault, 1993).

The cooperative sector includes member-oriented nonprofit organizations engaged in some form of commercial activity, such as agricultural and consumer cooperatives and cooperative banks. Mutual associations include insurance funds and related schemes to provide for family, health, and other social emergencies and risks, usually as an additional coverage to the public social security system. In recent years, many mutuals have moved closer to the for-profit sector, particularly in the insurance brokerage area, and would likely not be regarded as nonprofit organizations from a U.S. perspective.

Finally, associations form the third part of the French social economy sector. Included here are some 600,000 to 700,000 declared associations regulated by the Law of 1901 as well as an unknown number of undeclared associations with no legal status. These associations perform a wide variety of social welfare and representational functions, particularly in the areas of sports, recreation, health, and welfare. Also included are some 2,000 public utility associations, which, unlike other associations, may own real estate and receive tax-deductible gifts. These and other privileges are granted by the *Conseil d'Etat*, the highest administrative office in the Republic.

Italy. Italy in a way stands between the freewheeling and open world of nonprofit action in the United States and the United Kingdom on the one hand and the more tightly regulated and structured situation of Germany and France on the other. On paper, Italy shares much of the formal structure of the French and German systems, including the strong presence of cooperatives and mutuals, as well as key aspects of the legal system. But a long tradition of informality and the special position of the Catholic Church introduce a much more amorphous pattern in reality. Three rather distinct spheres thus exist in Italy: a public sphere, a secular private world, and the semiautonomous realm of the Catholic Church, with its own body of law (see Barbetta, 1993). Nonprofit organizations operate in each of these spheres, albeit without a great deal of clarity. Thus, some organizations, such as *Opere Pie* or Catholic social welfare agencies, began as private institutions under the auspices of the Catholic Church. Separate and partially contradictory legislative enactments since then "assigned" them to either the private, public, or ecclesiastical sector.

Formally, organizations functioning for other-than-business purposes are supposed to secure legal status as incorporated entities under public or civil law. Few such organizations become officially incorporated, however. Incorporated is time consuming and requires a Presidential Decree. Incorporation is thus considered a privilege to be granted by the state, not a right inherent in the organization. Although it carries certain privileges and increases the potential array of business activities an organization can engage in, the high transaction costs keep most associations from seeking incorporation.

Most associations consequently remain in an unincorporated status, giving rise to *associazionismo*, a large world of informal associations through which citizens join together to pursue common interests in such fields as culture, sport, recreation, social welfare, and religion. The act of establishing an unincorporated association requires only the drafting of a charter to be lodged at a notary office. The great majority of Italy's secular nonprofit sector consists of such unincorporated associations and foundations, while Catholic organizations enjoy a separate legal status under ecclesiastical law.

Recent policies in social services and banking are aimed at reducing the constraints many nonprofit organizations face as unincorporated associations. For example, in the field of social services, a 1991 law addressed the problems of the many unincorporated associations that operated as *voluntariato*, or voluntary philanthropic institutions, and made it easier for them to administer grants, own real estate, and receive donations. While these provisions have begun to systematize the nonprofit sphere in Italy, for the most part this sphere continues to operate in a largely inadequate legal environment that forces founders of nonprofit organizations to remain personally liable or to adopt legal forms typical for the business world that may be ill-suited for the type of activities carried out by nonprofits.

Japan

In Japan, the nonprofit sphere is, if anything, even more restricted than in the European setting. A rather fully developed "welfare state," Japan has no general law authorizing the formation of nonprofit organizations or granting them tax or other concessions. Although the status of *koeki hojin*, or charitable organization, is established under the Uniform Civil Code of 1896, such organizations are entitled to tax benefits only if they are specifically authorized under other legal provisions (in health, welfare, scientific research, and the like), and even then only if the responsible ministry judges that the organization serves a valid public purpose as defined by the ministry (Amenomori, 1993). As a result, next to *koeki hojin*, eight other major types of nonprofit organizations exist under laws establishing "nonprofit" social welfare corporations, private school corporations, religious organizations, health-related organizations, and research organizations. What is more, the narrow interpretation of public benefit has increased the requirements for the establishment of nonprofit organizations. The status of *koeki hojin* is granted by the state, and significant assets are required for incorporation. The amount required may vary from case to case, and in the absence of general procedural rules, registration forms the de facto equivalent of a state licensing system for nonprofit organizations. The one major exception to this are the numerous *jichikai* and *chonaikai*—informal and formal multipurpose associations at the local level. But these organizations generally operate on a voluntary basis, with little legal structure or protection. For the most part, the nonprofit sector hardly functions as a distinguishable sector in Japan. Its borderlines are often unclear, with no strict distinction in place to set apart nonprofit organizations on the one hand and the public, for-profit, and household sectors on the other. What exist, rather, are a variety of separate institutional types in particular policy spheres, each governed by the laws and practices of that sphere with little general policy or conceptualization.

Developing Countries

This general lack of a distinguishable nonprofit sector is also characteristic of the developing countries. Although a rich array of institutions often exist in these countries outside the formal boundaries of the state, these institutions are rarely considered to be part of a single entity called the nonprofit sector. Rather they represent the institutional manifestations of a variety of often discontinuous social and political developments stretching over centuries of history. In popular parlance, the closest one comes to the concept of a nonprofit sector in these countries is the range of organizations commonly associated with the term *nongovernmental organizations*, or NGOs. But the range of entities masquerading under this label has evolved over time and is now quite broad, including the membership organizations represented at the League of Nations and later the United Nations, Northern-based voluntary relief and development agencies operating in the developing world, indigenous umbrella groups providing technical assistance to local grassroots organizations, and the local grassroots organizations themselves.

India, in many respects, comes closest to a nonprofit sector in the sense in which the term is used in the West. Equipped with a British-inspired legal system that has generally facilitated the formation of nonprofit institutions, a set of Hindu, Buddhist, and Islamic religious traditions generally supportive of charitable activity, and popular political leaders in the Gandhian tradition who valued grassroots organizing and action, India has provided fertile soil for the growth of nonprofit-type institutions (Sen, 1994). Indeed, a rich organizational tapestry exists on which can be read much of the history of this subcontinent. Included are Christian missionary and charitable organizations that entered the country under colonial rule, formal caste associations that formed early in the twentieth century, Gandhian organizations that emerged during the independence period at the village level, professional associations of various sorts, international NGOs, development-oriented technical assistance organizations, empowerment groups formed largely in the 1980s, indigenous foundations and corporate philanthropy programs, and grassroots development organizations. Although these various organizational survivals hardly comprise a self-conscious sector, they nevertheless represent a significant "third sector" that exists with some meaningful degree of independence from the state and the corporate sector.

In most other parts of the developing world, the opportunities for nonprofit development are considerably more constrained. In Egypt, for example, six types of nonprofit organizations exist: associations and foundations, professional groups, business associations, foreign foundations, advocacy organizations, and religious organizations like the Islamic Brotherhood, Islamic charitable trusts, *wakf*, and the Christian Coptic charities (Kandil, 1993). However, each of these is governed by a specific body of law that defines its rights and responsibilities. The broadest of these, Law 32 of 1964, allows for the establishment of a wide array of associations and foundations for social, cultural, religious, and charitable purposes, yet it imposes significant restrictions on the organizations, including the right to investigate the internal affairs of the association, to appoint board members, and to suspend and dissolve the organization if deemed necessary.

A similar situation exists in Brazil (see Landim, 1993), where a subset of associations and foundations is permitted to form "public-utility organizations," but only "under the discretionary jurisdiction of the President of the Republic, and the proper presentation of requests does not give the right to their approval" (Federal Ministry of Justice, 1990, p. 7). Faced with these restrictions, people wanting to form organizations often have had to do so on a purely informal basis, outside the prevailing laws. The result in Brazil is a profusion of informal or semiformal organizations, an *associativismo* movement seeking to create a "civil society," frequently under the protective auspices of the church. Even staid professional organizations have often found themselves functioning as hotbeds of civil-society protest as a consequence, politicizing what in other parts of the world are often dismissed as narrow, member-oriented institutions.

Similarly in Thailand, a complex set of registration requirements has led groups with any political or advocacy objectives to remain unregistered and to function as "forums," "units," or "working groups" (Pongsapich, 1993). What show up on official records as formally constituted nonprofit organizations, therefore, tend to be "safe" commercial organizations such as chambers of commerce and import-export groups, cremation societies, and employers' organizations, thus obscuring the diverse institutional universe that in fact exists. Slowly, the autocratic stance of the Thai government toward the nonprofit sector is giving way to a more cooperative relationship. Joint coordinating councils between government and the NGO community have been formed, and the current development plan acknowledges the role of nonprofit organizations, particularly in rural development.

In Ghana, nonprofit organizations include local self-help groups, village associations, women's societies, agricultural development groups, hospitals, local community groups, missionary societies, and traditional ethnic associations (Atingdui, 1994). As part of its colonial past, Ghana inherited the British legal system, and with it the laws on incorporation and charitable trusts. Because of restrictions to incorporate independently and separately in the colonies, the British system of charities and voluntary associations could not take hold in Ghana, although charitable organizations and missionary societies had been present in the country since the early nineteenth century. After independence, the government followed the common law tradition in introducing numerous acts and ordinances to regulate particular segments of the nonprofit sector. The successive legal development came to a halt in 1982, when the new military government required nonprofit organizations, in particular religious bodies, to reapply for charitable status, which was now granted by the government. In recent years, the status of nonprofit organizations has improved. As the country's economy and political system were consolidated, its political leadership came to acknowledge the contribution such organizations could make and overseas assistance became available to finance both international and local NGOs.

Hungary

Finally, in Hungary we find the situation of a country in the midst of a transition from a largely informal to a more formal nonprofit sector, but in a situation in which the borders between the state and the business sector are also very much in flux and where the concept of a for-profit sector is also very much a novelty. That a clear concept of a nonprofit sector has yet to emerge in Hungary or elsewhere in the former Soviet bloc should therefore come as no surprise. Indeed, the very concept of a voluntary sector encounters suspicion in this part of the world because of the use made of such institutions as instruments of social control under the communist regime. As pressures emerged to allow the flowering of a true "civil society" in Hungary during the 1980s, laws on the formation of foundations and associations were liberalized, leading to a rapid upsurge of such organizations. In many cases, however, these bear little relationship to their Western counterparts (Kuti, 1993). In some cases, ministry officials fearful of being thrown from power transferred significant resources to supposedly independent "foundations" and then moved over to operate these foundations. In other instances, entrepreneurs utilized the foundation form as a way to avoid taxation. As a consequence, the nonprofit sector quickly acquired a hybrid status that continues to haunt its development as a truly distinctive sector of national life.

Searching for Patterns

Several conclusions flow from this Cook's tour of the world of nonprofit organizations in twelve countries. In the first place, it should be clear that the term *nonprofit sector* (or any comparable term) disguises as much as it reveals when applied cross-nationally. In point of fact, few countries have a coherent notion of an identifiable nonprofit sector. What exists in fact is a wild assortment of institutional types that vary greatly in basic composition from place to place. Under these circumstances, efforts to make cross-national comparisons using local definitions of this sector are destined to be seriously misleading at best.

In the second place, however, while no single "nonprofit sector" exists throughout the world, there are still striking similarities in the types of institutions that do exist outside the confines of the state. An explorer from outer space charged with locating "third sector"–type institutions in different societies throughout the world would thus have no trouble coming up with significant examples in virtually every country and region.

How are we to make sense of this mixture of diversity and commonality? What accounts for the presence or absence of a more-or-less distinct nonprofit sector in different societies? And how is this set of institutions likely to evolve in the years ahead?

Clearly, it is impossible to answer these questions fully here. But it may be possible to suggest at least some potentially fruitful lines of thought for future exploration. In particular, while the character and role of the nonprofit sector in any country are ultimately shaped by the entire pattern of social, economic, and political development of that country, at least three more general factors also seem to play a significant role: first, the type of legal system that exists; second, the level of development; and third, the degree of centralization in political and social terms. Let us examine each in turn.

Type of Legal System

The legal system in place in a country can significantly affect the organizational universe that exists by making it easier or more difficult to establish certain kinds of institutions. The fact that a nonprofit sector seems to have a more vibrant and coherent existence in the United Kingdom and the United States than on the European continent or in Japan may be traceable at least in part to this factor.

What differentiates these two sets of societies is the presence of a common law legal system in the United Kingdom and the United States as opposed to a civil law system in France, Germany, Italy, Hungary, and Japan. In civil law countries, the rights and obligations of individuals and organizations are explicitly spelled out in codified laws. If a particular type of institution is not explicitly provided for in the law in such countries, it does not have a legal right to exist. What is more, the state in such countries is assumed to act in the public, or common, good and is covered by public law. For an organization to function in a public capacity in such societies, it must therefore be given this right by a public institution. This can be done by creating a "public law corporation"—that is, a quasi-private organization that nevertheless functions within the bounds of public law, by designating certain private institutions as "public utilities," or by specifying certain permissible activities the performance of which qualifies a private organization as a public-benefit entity.

In common law countries, by contrast, private institutions can claim the privilege of operating in the public interest as a matter of right. Instead of carefully codified laws on what constitutes a permissible private action for the public good, common law countries have built up much more ambivalent systems of case law that define what the community means by the public good. The result is a far more open field for the formation of nonprofit organizations claiming public-benefit status.

Level of Development

A second crucial factor that seems to affect the shape and character of the nonprofit sector in a society is the level of development it has achieved. "Development" is, of course, an ambiguous concept, embracing a wide assortment of possible dimensions. For our purposes here, however, several key features of development seem particularly important. The first is the degree of social differentiation that economic growth brings with it. As economic growth proceeds, the number and scope of social roles increase substantially, creating new and varied bases for social organization. Instead of a vast peasantry and a small landed elite, new occupations and professions emerge and hence new bases for forming organizations. The greater the degree of differentiation of social roles, therefore, the more highly defined the nonprofit sector is likely to be.

Of special importance in this regard is a second factor often associated with economic development: the rise of an urban middle class, particularly an educated urban middle class. In a real sense, the creation of nonprofit organizations is the work of the middle class. While it may be an overstatement to assert "no middle class, no nonprofit sector," this equation has a certain degree of historical validity (Moore, 1967). At the very least, middle-class professionals have played a prominent role in the emergence of third sector organizations in much of the developing world, and the stronger the middle classes the stronger the nonprofit sector is likely to be. This point finds confirmation in the contrast between the relatively well-developed nonprofit sectors in Brazil and India as contrasted with countries such as Ghana and perhaps Egypt.

Finally, development is important to the emergence of the nonprofit sector because of its implications for communications (Salamon, 1994). Organizations live on communications much as armies live on their beliefs. As economic development opens new communications links, rural peasants and the urban poor gain new sources of information not tied to traditional powers-that-be. In the process, they become available for new forms of mobilization and organization. Even middle-class professionals require effective communications to develop organizationally. The invention of the fax and other high-speed communications technology has thus been credited with contributing in important measure to the rapid democratization of Central and Eastern Europe in the late 1980s, and with the spread of democratic regimes elsewhere in the world as well (Huntington, 1991).

These features may help to explain some of the peculiar characteristics of the nonprofit sector in the developing countries noted earlier—the politicization of even the most mainstream business and professional associations as new social forces take advantage of the nonprofit form to exert their influence, the importance of grassroots NGOs functioning as agents of social change and not simply vendors of particular services, and the general sense of tension between the nonprofit sector and the state as new ways of interacting are worked out between rising and established social and economic groups.

Degree of Centralization

A final factor affecting the structure of the nonprofit sector in different countries is the degree of centralization the citizens are willing (or required) to tolerate in the country's basic political and institutional structures. Generally speaking, the more centralized the structure, the less room for a coherent nonprofit sector. By contrast, the less centralized the structure, the greater the opportunity for the operation of extensive nonprofit organizations. Thus,

Germany, which has a federal administrative structure, has a vibrant nonprofit sector, whereas France, a more centralized government, has had a much more limited nonprofit sphere historically.

What shapes the degree of centralization that exists in a particular society is, of course, complex. The presence historically of landed elites able to resist the control of a powerful monarch is one such consideration, as reflected in the history of England. So, too, is the presence of distinct ethnic or religious groups determined to maintain their own way of life within an overall national structure, which characterizes the situation in India, the United States, and to a lesser extent, Germany. Similarly, the degree of centralization is affected by the relationship that exists between political and religious authorities. Where church and state are essentially one, the opportunities for third sector development are generally limited. Where a sharp separation exists between church and state, the social space left open for the flowering of a third sector is much more extensive. Thus, the historically close relationship between state and church in Italy has probably played a role in limiting the development of a coherent nonprofit sector in that country, while the sharp separation has helped to foster third sector growth in the United States. Similarly, the rise of liberation theology and the break between at least segments of the Catholic Church and the state in Brazil in recent years have helped to stimulate the emergence of a nonprofit sphere in that country.

Summary

To be sure, no one of these factors by itself will determine the contours of the nonprofit sector in a country. What is important is the interaction among them. Thus the presence of a common law tradition is no guarantee of an open posture toward the formation of nonprofit organizations if the level of development and the historic structure of government authority work against it. This is evident, for example, in the case of Ghana, which has a common law legal code but a political structure that until recently was hostile to the formation of an independent nonprofit sphere. By contrast, the nonprofit sector has made much headway in Germany despite its civil law system, thanks to a tradition of decentralization and the hold of the Catholic doctrine of "subsidiarity," which places a premium on solving problems through private institutions first and permits reliance on government only as a last resort.

While far from comprising a complete "theory" of organizational patterns, the three dimensions identified here—type of legal system, level of development, and degree of centralization—provide at least a framework for identifying differences and similarities in the character and structure of the nonprofit sector in different locales and a vocabulary for clarifying certain fundamental differences. As reflected in Figure 16.2, this set of factors defines an eightfold division of societies. The first dimension sets developed countries apart from developing countries; the second separates civil law from common law traditions. The third divides each of the resulting four cells into two depending on whether the administrative structure is centralized or decentralized.

Using this schema, it is possible to describe more precisely some of the differences and similarities among societies that are relevant to the character and structure of the nonprofit sector. Thus, for example, the United States and the United Kingdom are both developed countries that share a common law tradition and are both generally congenial to the development of the nonprofit sector. But in terms of the degree of centralization, England evolved a far more centralized political and institutional structure than the United States, and this has limited the space available for the development of the nonprofit sector.

Similarly, both Germany and Japan are civil law countries. While this creates a potential for tight limitation of the nonprofit sector, this limitation has materialized much more heavily in Japan than in Germany. One plausible reason for this is the much higher degree of political centralization in Japan, reflecting the

Figure 16.2. Types of Nonprofit Sectors.

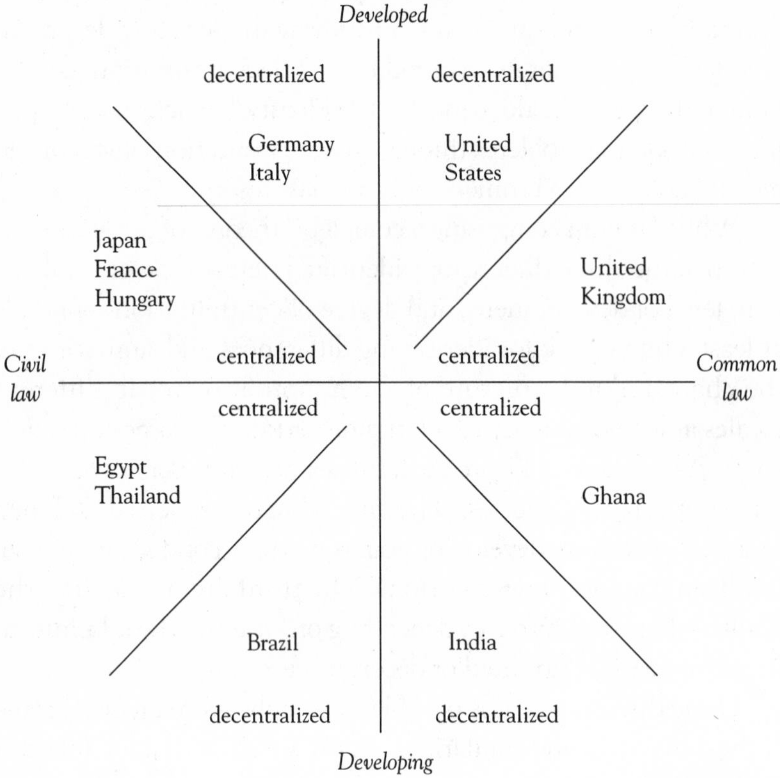

homogeneity of the society and the power of the centralizing regimes that took power at the end of the feudal era. In Germany, by contrast, the survival of a tradition of federalism from feudal days, and the principle of subsidiarity borrowed from Catholic doctrine, have helped to preserve a much larger space for the development of nonprofit institutions.

Conclusion

This chapter challenges the conventional rhetoric of voluntarism, which tends to equate the scope of a "caring tradition" in a society with the size and visibility of the nonprofit sector it contains. The preservation, transmission, and implementation of a "caring tradition" are by no means vested exclusively, or even chiefly, in the nonprofit sector around the world. To the contrary, no coherent concept of a nonprofit sector exists in most parts of the world. Based on cross-national analysis, we find very little relationship between the presence of a coherent nonprofit sector and the extent of "caring" in a society. Rather, government is more often viewed as the appropriate agent of the caring tradition. Indeed, even an autocratic state can often function as a potent instrument of caring. This is exemplified perhaps best by Bismarck's Germany, which was in an important way also a "caring" state as expressed in the term "*fürsorglicher Staat*," both literally and practically, that the state is explicitly obliged to care for its subjects, even though notions of democracy and civil liberty may have had little room. In contrast, the liberal state, represented by the United States and the United Kingdom, has historically been, if not "uncaring," at least not as concerned about notions of equity and social welfare, while at the same time willing to tolerate higher degrees of income inequality. Indeed, in these cases, reliance on the nonprofit sector (as opposed to the state) has become an excuse for disregarding serious social and economic problems (Lubove, 1968). In this sense, the nonprofit sector can function as more of a barrier to the effective operation of a caring tradition than an asset.

Fortunately, this notion of a trade-off between state action and nonprofit action has itself come into question in recent years (Salamon, 1987; Gidron, Kramer, and Salamon, 1992). Although the nonprofit sector differs widely from place to place, as reflected above, significant questions have been raised in recent years about the capacity of government, by itself, to solve the interrelated crises of the welfare state, development, socialism, and the environment that now confront the world. The result has been a widespread "associational revolution" that has begun to narrow significantly the vast differences in the role and character of the nonprofit sector around the world (Salamon, 1994).

Where this trend will lead is anyone's guess. What seems clear, however, is that no single pattern will evolve. As we have seen, a variety of factors seem to determine the scope and function of the nonprofit sector in a society. These factors include the legal framework in use, the level of development and degree of social differentiation, and the extent of centralization of social and political control. While sharing certain common features, the future shape and contours of the nonprofit sector from place to place will therefore continue to reflect peculiar patterns of cultural and historical development. To understand the shape of the nonprofit sector, and the contributions it makes to caring in any society, it is important to begin with a clear understanding of where this sector has come from, and how it fits into the broader pattern of social and political life. It is in this sense that the kind of basic definitional and conceptual work presented here is crucial.

References

Amenomori, T. "Defining the Nonprofit Sector: Japan." In L. M. Salamon and H. K. Anheier (eds.), *Working Papers of the Johns Hopkins Comparative Nonprofit Sector Project*, no. 15. Baltimore, Md.: Johns Hopkins Institute for Policy Studies, 1993.

Anheier, H. K., and Seibel, W. (eds.). *The Third Sector: Comparative Studies of Nonprofit Organizations*. Berlin: De Gruyter, 1990.

Anheier, H. K., and Seibel, W. "Defining the Nonprofit Sector: Germany." In L. M. Salamon and H. K. Anheier (eds.), *Working Papers of the Johns Hopkins Comparative Nonprofit Sector Project*, no. 6. Baltimore, Md.: Johns Hopkins Institute for Policy Studies, 1993.

Archambault, E. "Defining the Nonprofit Sector: France." In L. M. Salamon and H. K. Anheier (eds.), *Working Papers of the Johns Hopkins Comparative Nonprofit Sector Project*, no. 7. Baltimore, Md.: Johns Hopkins Institute for Policy Studies, 1993.

Atingdui, L. "Defining the Nonprofit Sector: Ghana." In L. M. Salamon and H. K. Anheier (eds.), *Working Papers of the Johns Hopkins Comparative Nonprofit Sector Project*, no. 14. Baltimore, Md.: Johns Hopkins Institute for Policy Studies, 1994.

Barbetta, G. P. "Defining the Nonprofit Sector: Italy." In L. M. Salamon and H. K. Anheier (eds.), *Working Papers of the Johns Hopkins Comparative Nonprofit Sector Project*, no. 8. Baltimore, Md.: Johns Hopkins Institute for Policy Studies, 1993.

Federal Ministry of Justice (Brazil). *Entidade de Utilidade Publica Federal: Manual para Requerimento* (Federal public utility: A requirements manual). Brasília, Brazil: Federal Ministry of Justice, 1990.

Gidron, B., Kramer, R. M., and Salamon, L. M. (eds.). *Government and the Third Sector: Emerging Relationships in Welfare States*. San Francisco: Jossey-Bass, 1992.

Hall, P. *Inventing the Nonprofit Sector*. Baltimore, Md.: Johns Hopkins University Press, 1992.

Hopkins, B. R. *The Law of Tax-Exempt Organizations*. (5th ed.) New York: Wiley, 1987.

Huntington, S. *The Third Wave: Democratization in the Late Twentieth Century*. Norman: Oklahoma University Press, 1991.

James, E. (ed.). *The Nonprofit Sector in International Perspective: Studies in Comparative Culture and Policy*. Oxford, England: Oxford University Press, 1989.

Kandil, A. "Defining the Nonprofit Sector: Egypt." In L. M. Salamon and H. K. Anheier (eds.), *Working Papers of the Johns Hopkins Comparative Nonprofit Sector Project*, no. 10. Baltimore, Md.: Johns Hopkins Institute for Policy Studies, 1993.

Kendall, J., and Knapp, M. "Defining the Nonprofit Sector: United Kingdom." In L. M. Salamon and H. K. Anheier (eds.), *Working Papers of the Johns Hopkins Comparative Nonprofit Sector Project*, no. 5. Baltimore, Md.: Institute for Policy Studies, Johns Hopkins University, 1993.

Kuti, É. "Defining the Nonprofit Sector: Hungary." In L. M. Salamon and H. K. Anheier (eds.), *Working Papers of the Johns Hopkins Comparative Nonprofit Sector Project*, no. 13. Baltimore, Md.: Johns Hopkins Institute for Policy Studies, 1993.

Landim, L. "Defining the Nonprofit Sector: Brazil." In L. M. Salamon and H. K. Anheier (eds.), *Working Papers of the Johns Hopkins Comparative Nonprofit Sector Project*, no. 9. Baltimore, Md.: Johns Hopkins Institute for Policy Studies, 1993.

Lubove, R. *The Struggle for Social Security*. Cambridge, Mass.: Harvard University Press, 1968.

Moore, B. *The Social Origins of Dictatorship and Democracy*. Boston: Beacon Press, 1967.

Pongsapich, A. "Defining the Nonprofit Sector: Thailand." In L. M. Salamon and H. K. Anheier (eds.), *Working Papers of the Johns Hopkins Comparative Nonprofit Sector Project*, no. 11. Baltimore, Md.: Johns Hopkins Institute for Policy Studies, 1993.

Posnett, J. "Trends in the Income of Registered Charities." *Charity Trends*, 1987, *10*, 6–8.

Salamon, L. M. "Partners in Public Service: The Scope and Theory of Government—Nonprofit Relations." In W. W. Powell (ed.), *The Nonprofit*

Sector: A Research Handbook (pp. 99–117). New Haven, Conn.: Yale University Press, 1987.

Salamon, L. M. *The Nonprofit Sector: A Primer.* New York: Foundation Center, 1992.

Salamon, L. M. "The Rise of the Nonprofit Sector on the World Scene." *Foreign Affairs*, 1994, *74*(3), 111–124.

Salamon, L. M., and Anheier, H. K. "Toward an Understanding of the International Nonprofit Sector." *Nonprofit Management and Leadership*, 1992, *2*(3), 311–324.

Salamon, L. M., and Anheier, H. K. *The Emerging Sector: Nonprofit Organizations in Comparative Perspective—An Overview.* Baltimore, Md.: Johns Hopkins Institute for Policy Studies, 1994.

Sen, S. "Defining the Nonprofit Sector: India." In L. M. Salamon and H. K. Anheier (eds.), *Working Papers of the Johns Hopkins Comparative Nonprofit Sector Project*, no. 12. Baltimore, Md.: Johns Hopkins Institute for Policy Studies, 1994.

Tocqueville, A. de. *Democracy in America.* Henry Reeve text. New York: Knopf, 1945. (Originally published 1835.)

Part Five

Mobilizing Care Through Mutual Self-Interest

For both Thomas Aquinas and Alexis de Tocqueville, the identification of interests by diverse individuals provides a positive and even necessary aperture rather than a barrier to authentic public virtue. It is the enlargement of that rudimentary familial feeling of mutuality—not its elimination—that properly motivates a sustainable devotion to the welfare of others. Whether framed by Aquinas as the identification of love of self and love of neighbor or by Tocqueville as self-interest properly understood, the point is the same: the intersection of care for self and care for others ideally governs the realm of practical morality. This is not to deny that self-interest may be wrongly understood as readily as it is rightly understood. Linking what I need to what I perceive others need can be a temptation fraught with self-deception as much as an opportunity inspiring insight and commitment. The first three selections in Part Five explore how identification of one's interests with those in need is a powerful incentive for a devoted and even sacrificial discharge of duty. The fourth selection, however, suggests a potential shortcoming of commitments mobilized by mutual self-interest, namely, the propensity to limit the scope of our mutuality to our neighborhoods and local community organizations.

One place where mutual self-interest has a positive effect is in self-help groups, which Thomasina Borkman and Maria Parisi define (in Chapter Seventeen) as voluntary associations run by individuals utilizing their own experiential knowledge to resolve a common problem. Borkman and Parisi focus on self-help groups directed at grassroots empowerment rather than at therapeutic recovery from addiction. The authors cite six ways self-help organizations contribute to building a caring society. They advance pluralism by creating "communities of acceptance," strengthen family and other personal relationships by providing support groups for dealing with problems, encourage closer ties with members of the wider community, teach skills that help their members to act effectively in other spheres of daily life, transform victims into empowered agents, and encourage members to become politically active. According to Borkman and Parisi, there is as yet little research on the negative repercussions of such political self-help groups. But in the meantime we can learn much from studying the distinctive mechanisms by which self-help groups engender a humanistic ethos and fashion participative organizational forms.

For Anica Mikuš Kos in Chapter Eighteen, the mobilizing power of self-interest shows up in the way refugees from Bosnia and Herzegovina come to assist each other within the broader context of Slovenian relief efforts. In the past, Yugoslavia depended on government rather than civic participation to advance social welfare. With the dissolution of socialism and the onslaught of civil war, Slovenians, including the author, joined international volunteers in providing material and psychosocial assistance to the beleaguered refugees, who often faced additional hardships in the bleak resettlement camps. Among the most significant "networks of solidarity" designed to assist children and overcome depression-induced inactivity was the development of schools for refugee children. In addition to providing education, the schools offered mental health care for children and parents and gave refugees an opportunity to become active contributors as teachers. In these schools as well as in the array of other initiatives, it turns out that "the most important source of help for the distress of refugees has been the refugee community itself." In addition to generating a voluntary sector and improving forms of psychosocial intervention, the presence of the refugees has provided the impetus for creating patterns of mutual assistance. One positive note in an otherwise appalling situation of death, displacement, and depression has been the activities of the refugees themselves to neutralize the harsh effects on children and adults of what Mikuš Kos starkly calls the "war evil."

In Chapter Nineteen, John Bell approaches the issue of self-interest properly understood by analyzing how self-help or mutual aid (rather than altruism) motivates people to volunteer in their local communities. Drawing on his unique data from Belgium, Greece, Iceland, The Netherlands, Portugal, Spain, and the United Kingdom, Bell finds that along with a small group of "altruists," the most engaged members in a community are the "self-interested"—those who participate from the incentive of self-help. Of course, there are always some who enter community service as a productive way to use their leisure time. However, the fact that parents with child-care responsibilities and mothers working full time actively participate in community projects from which they or their families benefit demonstrates the strength of self-interest to mobilize busy people. Indeed, Bell's research challenges the notion that people facing adverse conditions are necessarily less involved. On the contrary, Bell concludes, there is every reason to believe that we can generate higher levels of involvement by emphasizing "the participative rather than the volunteering dimension of community activity."

The final chapter in Part Five—Chapter Twenty—is more cautionary about the effects of mutual self-interest. According to Julian Wolpert, there are several realms where grounding commitment in mutual self-interest turns out to be a barrier to fuller care. It is not surprising that nonprofits devote a large proportion of their resources to benefiting their donor constituencies, not least because this increases people's willingness to contribute. However, the upshot is that about 85 to 90 percent of charitable dollars end up supporting community, cultural, educational, and health care amenities that are used by the donors themselves rather than targeted to the poor. Wolpert argues that giving priority to local preferences would not be so detrimental if communities remained diverse mixtures of rich and poor. But given today's high degree of community homogeneity, the nonprofit sector needs a new strategy to ensure that an adequate level of support gets transferred to people in need. To counteract the tendency for nonprofits to provide such a large proportion of their services to their contributors, says Wolpert, the nonprofit sector should begin to set and administer its agenda from a more centralized vantage point.

Chapter Seventeen

The Role of Self-Help Groups in Fostering a Caring Society

Thomasina Borkman, Maria Parisi

The goal of this book is to explore the role that the generations, institutions, and public policy play in promoting or inhibiting the development of a caring society. The purpose of this chapter is to address these questions: (1) What roles do mutual-aid self-help groups play in our society to promote and inhibit a caring society? (2) What common cultural characteristics and structures have these groups evolved to promote a caring society?

The awkward phrase "mutual-aid self-help group" is used to refer to its dual characteristics of mutual aid (free reciprocal help in a collective context) and self-help (mobilizing internal resources of personal responsibility, experiential understanding, self-determination, and self-empowerment). Hereafter these groups will be referred to as *self-help groups* or *SHGs*. SHGs are defined as voluntary associations for persons with a common problem that are oriented to resolving the common problem utilizing their own experiential knowledge of it; they are owned and controlled by the members. Support groups controlled by professionals are excluded here.

SHGs have expanded dramatically in the last twenty years, both in number and in the kinds of illnesses and personal troubles they address. As many people attend these groups as are seen by psychotherapists and counselors for mental health problems, according to the estimates. Mutual-aid SHGs are a contemporary social invention that have diffused so widely in American society that many people have the knowledge and competency to initiate and sustain them. This capability was demonstrated in 1991 when thousands of groups sprang up within a few weeks to support the military, their families, and friends as a response to the Persian Gulf War.

A preliminary issue is the question of what a caring society is. Logically, a caring society could have different qualities than a caring individual because of the differing levels of analysis. In a literature search we found few references and no definition of a caring society. Instead, we found a broader literature on civil society that occasionally referred to a caring society as one form of civil society (for example, Joseph, 1990).

The concept of a civil society has a long history; it was widely used in the nineteenth century but fell into disuse until recently. The breakup of communist countries in Eastern Europe has been the occasion for the resurrection of the concept. Scholars in the United States have recently reclaimed the term and applied it to contemporary Western democracies.

Cohen and Arato (1992, p. ix) define civil society as "a sphere of social interaction between economy and state, composed above all of the intimate sphere (especially the family), the sphere of associations (especially voluntary associations), social movements, and forms of public communication." A major point they make is that there are many kinds of civil societies, some of which would not fit anyone's definition of caring society.

Many analysts view the United States as a mixed picture of civil society but certainly not a caring society. "While civil society in Havel's Czechoslovakia is rebounding from four decades of pulverization, civil society in the US is eroding from a far higher plane" (Gitlin, 1990, p. 46). Against the backdrop of social disorganization in the United States, "civil society looks more like a necessary achievement than a comfortable reality" (Walzer, 1991, p. 293). The increasingly individualistic values of selfishness, lack of concern for the common good, and greed reduce the spirit of civility, producing the so-called "elbow society" in which universal, indiscriminate aggression prevails. Bellah and associates in *Habits of the*

Heart (1985) show how contemporary individualism has reduced community spirit and civil actions.

In developing a definition of a caring society, we examined the themes and values emphasized in the conference at which the paper forming the basis of this chapter was presented as well as the literature on civil society. Using these values as well as our own, a caring society is defined here as a civil society that includes:

1. Pluralism
2. A healthy intimate sphere, including the family
3. A widened community
4. The ability to form voluntary associations
5. Civic values
6. Activism and social movements

The question arises as to how the decline of civil society can be reversed in order to develop a more caring society. Social movements are seen as one possible route to increasing civility and humanizing society, especially the "new social movements"—such as feminism, ecology, peace, and local-autonomy movements (Gitlin, 1990).

SHGs have been mentioned as a countertendency to the declining civility. Gitlin (1990) mentions them as groups organized around single issues taking citizenship seriously and functioning vigorously outside the marketplace. But he does not elaborate on these points. The literature on self-help groups has characterized them as social movements (Back and Taylor, 1976; Katz, 1981; Katz and Bender, 1990), but their tendency to identify with their common disease or condition (such as addiction, gay rights, or sickle cell anemia) rather than with other similar SHGs has stymied the in-depth analysis of them as a collective social movement. This is the first publication to our knowledge that analyzes how SHGs contribute to a civil society.

The first question about the role SHGs play in promoting and inhibiting a caring society is answered in the findings section. The second question about cultural and structural characteristics follows. The implications of the findings on SHGs for the third sector and a caring society are presented in the conclusion to the chapter.

Methodology

This chapter is based on a review of empirical research on mutual-aid SHGs from several sources. The senior author (Borkman) has conducted a number of research studies and supervised graduate student research on SHGs over the past twenty years. These have included twelve-step programs such as Alcoholics Anonymous (AA) and Adult Children of Alcoholics, medical groups such as ostomy groups, women's consciousness-raising groups, groups for disabilities such as stuttering or parents of learning-disabled children, self-help agencies of recovering alcoholics or ex-mental patients, and groups for battered women. In addition, a library search of the major data bases from psychology, social work, sociological abstracts, and Educational Resources Information Center (ERIC) was done for the 1990s through the summer of 1992 (National Project for Self-Help Groups, 1992). The criteria used to select some 200 relevant articles were those containing systematic empirical research rather than programmatic statements about one group or opinion essays by a practitioner.

The review of articles on SHGs focused on those in the health and human services; self-help activities in housing, economics, or community development are not included. We chose not to review findings about SHGs' effectiveness in resolving focal problems for members. Instead we looked at aspects of the groups that are related to the concept of a caring society; aspects such as developing leadership skills are often side benefits of participation rather than deliberately planned benefits of belonging.

Research on self-help groups can be described as being in its infancy. Research began relatively recently (since the 1970s); it is more descriptive than experimental or predictive and is limited in a number of ways. The research disproportionately focuses on one or a few groups of a specific type (for example, ex-mental patients), and the samples of members in a group studied are also small. Quantitative studies often use simple descriptive statistics rather than multivariate analyses. There are many case studies of a few groups and cross-sectional studies of members and groups at one point in time. Measurements are often inappropriately borrowed from research on professional group therapy. However, despite these and other inadequacies, the research findings across a wide variety of types of groups present a consistent picture on a general level. The information reported in this chapter is representative of the consistent findings found in the research literature.

Findings

Findings on the ways that SHGs both promote and inhibit a caring society will be discussed.

Promoting a Civil Society

The findings are organized in terms of the six characteristics of a caring society that we identified. The body of findings from a wide variety of SHGs pertaining to each area is so extensive that it cannot be described in detail here. Instead, we summarize the literature in each area and illustrate each area with findings from two or more SHGs.

1. *Pluralism*. Pluralism as a facet of a caring society includes tolerance and mutual respect for all members and collectivities in it. Although pluralism is most likely to be connected now with multiculturalism, there is also great diversity in stigmatized diseases, disabilities, and social and family conditions that separate people from

full participation in mainstream society. SHGs are valuable to a caring society by creating and maintaining alternative ideologies that "normalize" individuals and help them become contributing members of the community rather than dependent victims.

By creating "communities of acceptance" that help destigmatize conditions, SHGs promote a caring society (Clark and Hughes, 1992; Droge, Arntson, and Norton, 1986; Henry and Robinson, 1978; Robinson and Henry, 1977; Borkman, 1984; Browning, Thorin, and Rhoades, 1984; Chesler, 1984; Chesler and Chesney, 1988; Katz, 1986; Rosecrance, 1988). Successful SHGs for people who stutter adopt the "nonavoidance approach," in which they stutter freely rather than avoid it to reduce stigma. Paradoxically, the nonavoiders are more accepting and less ashamed of their stuttering than those who follow an avoidance approach by trying to hide it in public (Borkman and Zappola, 1972; Borkman, 1975).

Faulkner, Britt-Moholt, and Kliman-Simone (1977) present research on three SHGs for women in racially mixed families demonstrating how group members come together to help each other deal with a shared problem and provide each other with emotional and practical support. In coming together, they see the similarities in their situations and stop feeling like "isolated freaks."

Another example of how SHGs create safe havens for people who are stigmatized, even by association, are groups for families of persons with AIDS. The greatest fear they reported was that others would not be understanding and would isolate them. By failing to share the news with those close to them, however, they isolated themselves. They had almost no one outside the group to turn to for support: "Perhaps the greatest need the support group served was in providing a place to admit to others, without fear of being ostracized or judged, that a family member had AIDS" (Kelly and Sykes, 1989, p. 241).

2. A *healthy intimate sphere, including the family*. Strong vital families are another important aspect of a caring society. Many SHGs are composed of persons who are family members of persons with

problematic conditions or illnesses, such as groups for women in racially mixed families (Faulkner, Britt-Moholt, and Kliman-Simone, 1977), families of the mentally ill (Biegel and Yamatani, 1987), bereaved parents after the death of a child (Klass, 1984–85), adolescents, parents, and adults with sickle cell disease (Clark and Hughes, 1992), parents of children with cancer, parents of murdered children, and adolescent children of alcoholics (Gidron, Chesler, and Chesney, 1991), to name a few.

Specific objectives of these SHGs include strengthening families by supporting persons who are dealing with a condition of a family member, as demonstrated in the following examples. Through his study on members of Toughlove, a self-help organization of parents of disruptive and/or defiant adolescents, Klug (1990) concludes that the SHG offers the experience of learning assertiveness within a supportive community in which participants regain stability and control in their family lives. Additionally, Kelly and Sykes (1989) studied support groups for family members of persons with AIDS who may need help not only in dealing with AIDS, but also with their feelings about homosexuality and drug abuse. The authors reported that often adults are so caught up in caring for someone with AIDS or in their own grief that children are kept in ignorance about what is happening around them, sometimes deliberately in efforts to "protect" them. As a result, young family members suffer the loss of a family member without really knowing why. In helping each other deal with the situation and related issues, adult SHG members may better attend to their children.

3. A *widened community*. While SHGs can provide safe communities, the ability to develop alternative expanded communities is a common feature of them (see Clark and Hughes, 1992; Emerick, 1989; Faulkner, Britt-Moholt, and Kliman-Simone, 1977). Data on AA, one of the most frequently studied SHGs, illustrate that groups often become expanded communities for their members and members' families and friends. Two studies found that a majority of AA members developed new friends and socialized with members

outside of meetings (Henry and Robinson, 1978; Kleist, 1990). In addition, Kleist (1990) found that AA members preferred turning to other members for tasks traditionally appropriate for family and former (non-AA) friends such as grieving the death of a partner or marital problems. For depression, AA members were just as likely to prefer getting help from another member as from professionals. The network of informal friendships ensures that the AA program continues beyond the meetings into everyday life and fosters a feeling that help is always available.

Similarly, leaders in SHGs for families and persons with sickle cell disease reported that more than half the groups engaged in visiting members at their homes during respite care (Clark and Hughes, 1992).

A study of over thirty SHGs for people who stutter (Borkman, Shaw, Shaw, and Hickey, 1985) showed great variability in their attitudes and behavior about creating a community outside of meetings. Interestingly, groups that had social functions and encouraged members to become friends and socialize outside of meetings were likely to survive longer than groups that discouraged such aspects of community.

4. *The ability to form voluntary associations*. "By assuming various tasks and roles, members develop their own leadership skills and learn valuable techniques that will help them in their daily lives," Clark and Hughes (1992, p. 51) note. Peer-group leaders in Recovery, Inc., an SHG for people with psychiatric problems, are selected after they have been members for a long time. They receive formal training from the movement's leadership and follow official guidelines based on the founder's framework (Galanter, 1988). In Recovery, Inc., a comparison of persons who were new members or long-standing peer leaders of Recovery, Inc., and a community control sample revealed that members who were peer leaders appeared to stabilize a symptom-free existence through their roles. Prior to joining, about half the members had been hospitalized for psychiatric treatment. After joining, however, less than 10 percent had

been hospitalized over the course of their membership. Leaders in particular moved toward relinquishing their need for both professional psychotherapy and somatic treatments. Participants apparently substituted their involvement in the movement for their role of therapy patient (Galanter, 1988).

Self-helpers become empowered to start their own SHGs for their own distinctive needs. For example, a woman with an ileostomy refused to join a group for people with an ostomy; rather, she started an ileostomy group that met her own needs. At a later time she left as the group's needs became broader than her own (Kerson, 1990). By choosing their own SHGs, individuals define their needs in ways outsiders do not understand.

In addition to teaching transferable organizational skills, SHG members learn to become discerning consumers (Silverman and Murrow, 1976; Rosecrance, 1988). Members of an SHG for breast cancer patients became knowledgeable medical consumers. They were able to get insurance companies to discontinue classifying breast reconstruction as cosmetic surgery and start covering the procedure (Miller, 1987).

5. *Civic values*. SHGs promote a caring society by transforming participants from "victims" into self-respecting altruistic helpers (see Droge, Arntson, and Norton, 1986; Faulkner, Britt-Moholt, and Kliman-Simone, 1977; Galanter, Castaneda, and Salamon, 1987; Galanter, Talbott, Gallegos, and Rubenstone, 1990; Grimsmo, Helgesen, and Borchgrevink, 1981). A new volunteer helper role referred to as *prosumer* (Toffler, 1980) has been developed in many groups. Prosumers who both voluntarily help others and receive help from peers are variously called sponsors, buddies, peer helpers, or visitors.

Clark and Hughes (1992) studied groups for adults and adolescents with sickle cell disease as well as groups of parents whose children suffer from the disease. Over 80 percent of the members indicated that they attended meetings to give support to other members. In addition, leaders in more than half of fifty-two groups indicated that members visit others while they are hospitalized and that they establish a buddy system for group members.

The visitor role in an SHG for ostomy patients provides another example of prosumers. Ostomy visitors are persons with an ostomy who visit other ostomates in the hospital and afterward at home in a helping role. Benefits to the visitors included increasing their level of acceptance of their ostomy, which was significantly greater than nonvisitors' levels of acceptance. Serving in the helper role may encourage the visitors to be less dependent and allow them to feel useful (that is, by sharing their experiential knowledge, which is useful to new ostomates), thus reducing exaggerated preoccupation with their ostomates. Trainor (1981) suggested that the helping role enables visitors to accept the radical change in bodily function and image resulting from the ostomy.

Another example of the development of the prosumer involves a cohort of alcohol-impaired physicians who were successfully treated in a voluntary program that combined hospitalization, professionally directed psychotherapeutic treatment, a halfway house, and AA. The physicians indicated that AA was the most potent element in their recovery. Two aspects of their new caregiver role evolved with time: helping new AA members as experiential peers, and serving as professionals in addiction treatment (Galanter, Talbott, Gallegos, and Rubenstone, 1990).

6. *Activism and social movements*. SHGs empower people to become activist citizens and to join social movements that influence public policy. Empowerment operates at personal, interpersonal, social, and political levels. At the personal and interpersonal levels, many researchers have focused on the empowering aspects of people defining their own problems in a manner meaningful to them (Borkman, 1990a; Browning, Thorin, and Rhoades, 1984; Galanter, 1988; Hicks and Borkman, 1988; Kelly and Sykes, 1989; Klass, 1984–85; Neighbors, Elliott, and Gant, 1990; Rosecrance, 1988; Silverman and Murrow, 1976; Wright, Green, and Gibson, 1984). Widows' groups, for example, allow members to grieve for

years or as long as necessary rather than succumb to the pressure of family and friends who want to short-cut their grieving (Silverman and Cooperband, 1975).

SHGs further facilitate empowerment at the personal and interpersonal levels in that individuals may often choose from a variety of different groups with different ideologies or definitions of the problem for the same issue. Weight Watchers, TOPS, and Overeaters Anonymous, for example, have different definitions of weight problems (Kerson, 1990). Emerick (1989) found a variety of political philosophies from radical separatist groups to conservative partnership groups among 104 mental patient movement groups.

The social level of empowerment is seen in SHG influences on the formal human service agencies and professionals to humanize their services (Borkman, 1990b; Chesler, 1991; Galanter, Castaneda, and Salamon, 1987; Katz, 1981; Kelly and Sykes, 1989; Miller, 1987; Hicks and Borkman, 1988). Chesler (1991) studied Candlelighters, groups for parents whose children had cancer. They varied in their activism toward the health care system. He found that activist groups pressured the medical system to change clinic schedules for visitors, staffing patterns, and rules (for example, allowing parents to hold their children during some procedures).

La Leche League, an SHG for women that recommends breastfeeding and aids the transition to motherhood, encourages nursing as early as possible after childbirth. Members often make their first calls to group leaders during the first day or so in the hospital when unanticipated problems arise. They reported their most common problem as being that their newborns were not brought to them within the first twelve hours. The League offers support, encouragement, and information new mothers can use with medical "authorities" to stand up for their rights (Silverman and Murrow, 1976).

Zola (1987) identified aspects of empowerment on the political level. Following demystification and encouragement for personal advocacy, some members and groups may participate in collective advocacy. He describes the development of the disability rights movement along these lines. Prior to the 1970s, various groups were organized separately around specific disabilities—for example, blindness or cerebral palsy. Over time they moved toward a more action-oriented organization. Lobbying together, they were able to, among other things, secure passage of the Americans with Disabilities Act, the most far-reaching legislation to prohibit discrimination against the disabled.

Inhibiting a Caring Society

While SHGs help facilitate a caring society in the positive ways we have discussed, the next question is, "How do SHGs inhibit a caring society?" The ideas about how SHGs function in a positive manner represent ideals to some extent that are not always realized in practice. There are organizational deficiencies, barriers erected to exclude eligible persons, cases of intolerance or inequitable treatment of others, and so forth. There is no way of knowing how often these problems occur since relatively little research has been conducted on the issue of how SHGs actually function. Thus, the extent of the inhibitors of a caring society among SHGs is unknown.

Organizational problems may be relatively frequent, especially among new SHGs (Powell, 1990; Borkman, 1975). These groups are often initiated from the grassroots by committed people facing a pressing situation. However, these initiators do not necessarily have any experience in constructing and leading a voluntary association. In addition, the typical issues facing all voluntary associations (and all organizations, in fact)—such as people who monopolize conversations or control or manipulate the group for personal gain—are found in these groups. Self-help clearinghouses often provide training and consultation to SHG leaders struggling with organizational issues as a technical assistance function, but many states and areas do not have clearinghouses available (Wollert, 1990). To the extent that organizational difficulties detract from the effectiveness for the SHGs, they inhibit a caring society.

The literature suggests that minority groups such as African Americans, Hispanics, Asians, and others are underrepresented in SHGs (Powell, 1987). However, there are almost no empirical data to indicate to what extent minority underrepresentation results from self-selection (in that they do not seek out groups) versus barriers that have been created to exclude them. African Americans and Hispanics have adapted SHGs to fit their cultural preferences; for example, in AA there are Spanish-speaking groups in large cities. Anecdotal accounts suggest that patterns of racial, gender, life-style, and religious discrimination found in society at large do occur in SHGs, but the groups' well-known compassion for people sharing the common problem and their ethos and norms of inclusiveness suggest that such patterns of discrimination may be less exaggerated and common than in society at large.

More research is needed on how SHGs function to determine the ways and extent to which organizational deficiencies and discrimination occur. In addition, research can identify other factors associated with SHG functioning that inhibit a caring society.

We now turn to the second major issue considered in the chapter —the distinctive organizational structures and cultural ethos by which SHGs promote a caring society.

Structures and Cultural Characteristics of SHGs

The mechanisms by which groups accomplish these roles for civil society (engender community, teach leadership skills, strengthen families, and so on) are found in their cultural characteristics and organizational structures. Although SHGs are extremely diverse in many ways, analysts point to a distinctive ethos, values, and ideas that comprise key aspects of their culture and to similarities in structure that cut across these differences.

The distinctive self-help ethos or spirit embodies a number of values along with a zest, dedication, and enthusiasm about resolving the common problem and helping peers (Riessman, 1982, 1990). The values include self-and-other empowerment, reciprocal mutual helping or altruism, egalitarianism, interdependence instead of competition or dependency, respect for knowledge and wisdom based on personal experience, and a respectful humanizing attitude toward the person with the problem irrespective of how stigmatized the condition is. Established SHGs have developed a respectful destigmatized frame of reference about how they define their common problem in addition to a desirable, constructive, and possible resolution to the problem (Antze, 1976; Borkman, 1990a; Suler, 1984). Part of their frame of reference is a common language about the problem and its resolution. Relationships in the group are based on mutuality of need; interdependence is valued (Kurtz, 1981). Norms are developed about minimizing external status differences that detract from egalitarianism and mutuality.

A potentially key ingredient of their success in promoting a caring society is that the structures of leadership, communication, and status correspond to and reinforce the cultural values and beliefs, at least in many groups. The parallels between the cultural aspects and the reinforcing structures are easy to see in a twelve-step anonymous group like AA; the twelve traditions are suggested rules about group structures (Kurtz, 1990). A twelve-step anonymous group like AA or its imitators (such as Gamblers Anonymous, Al Anon, Co-Dependents Anonymous) is one organizational form of SHG that needs to be distinguished from others. The others exhibit a wide range of organizational structures from small local informal groups to legally incorporated national nonprofit organizations. For example, in twelve-step groups the egalitarian values are manifested by practices and norms about rotating leadership, a flat hierarchy, absence of formal leadership positions, and the concept of "anonymity." Anonymity is interpreted to mean using first names only and minimizing external status differences such as discussing occupational prestige, awards, income, residential location, and so on that separate people. The practice of rotating leadership and encouraging members to help the group means that many people learn organizational skills, including leadership.

Many large, complex groups have multiple structures to meet the needs of members at different phases of problem resolution. For example, there are small sharing groups for newcomers or those in anguish about some aspects of their problem. In addition, there may be a large informational meeting in a lecture format in which professionals are invited to discuss some aspect of the disease and members ask questions.

The mutual-aid self-help phenomena is being replicated in more and more places and for more and more problems as people learn to use SHGs for problem solving. More groups are continually being formed. For example, the fall 1992 *Touching Bases: A Newsletter of the Westchester Self-Help Clearinghouse* describes five SHGs new to the authors: Adults Who Lost a Parent in Childhood, Adults Without Families, Career Changers, Celiac Sprue Support Group, and Co-Dependents of Sex Addicts (COSA). The groups, however, usually develop in isolation from groups with other problems (for example, diabetes groups do not talk to parents of children with cancer groups). There is generally no awareness of being part of a larger movement of people with the same self-help approach or mutual-aid process of problem solving. The tendency for people to identify with the problem rather than the process of solving it limits the extent to which a coherent, self-conscious, organized social movement can occur.

Conclusion

As shown in the findings, SHGs offer a "commons" in which individuals work mutually with their peers to problem-solve their common issues, which in turn promotes a caring society. Members are able to start, find, or act within an alternative framework that helps them strengthen families and become contributing members of an expanded community. In addition, members learn leadership and transferable organizational skills and become empowered, discerning consumers and self-respecting altruistic helpers. Members may become activist citizens and join social movements that influence public policy. SHGs help counter the trend toward an "elbow society" with greatly reduced civility, which some analysts see us moving toward.

What are the implications of these findings about SHGs for the third sector? The analysis has suggested that SHGs can and do contribute extensively to a caring society, a largely unfamiliar idea because of the paucity of direct research about the topic. Before additional research is suggested to fill the gaps, however, SHGs need to be integrated conceptually with nonprofit organizations, voluntary associations, and other third sector phenomena. Mutual-aid groups hold an uneasy, ambiguous, and not well-defined place in conceptual maps of the third sector. As Lohmann says in his book *The Commons: New Perspectives on Nonprofit Organizations and Voluntary Action* (1992, p. 230), "Self-help groups have seldom figured very significantly in recent discussions of nonprofit and voluntary action because of the absence of theory and because a large proportion of them are unincorporated associations that fall outside the established counting and classifying filters." Lohmann's framework conceptually integrates SHGs and other membership organizations with other kinds of voluntary associations and nonprofit organizations. He defines them in broad terms that encompass various degrees of formality of organization and diverse structural forms such as networks, communities, groups, and unincorporated and incorporated organizations.

To date, SHGs have been researched from an individualistic psychological framework for the most part; analysts tend to compare them with professional therapy or services. Consequently, there is little in the literature on the broader issues related to the role that SHGs play in civil society. The multiple benefits of participation, such as learning leadership skills or the capacity to form voluntary associations or being an active spokesperson in the public sphere for one's group, have not been studied, except incidentally. Systematic research needs to be done on the topics related to a civil society that have been identified in this chapter as a beginning. This research should include an analysis of SHGs as a "new social movement" (Habermas, 1981; Melucci, 1985) with values and goals similar to the feminist, peace, and ecology movements, to better understand their role in creating a more caring society (Cohen and Arato, 1992). In addition, the negative aspects of SHGs that detract from a civil society need to be systematically researched. To date the research on SHGs is so limited that data are not available to ask how extensive their benefits or liabilities are. Another interesting set of research questions would involve comparisons of the conventional nonprofit organizations in health and human services with SHGs in terms of benefits and liabilities to a civil society. Finally, there are hybrids—self-help agencies that possess characteristics of SHGs (in terms of culture and problem-solving ethos) within a conventional nonprofit organizational structure (see Shaw and Borkman, 1990). But these hybrids have never been adequately researched because of a lack of conceptual linking between them and SHGs.

In conclusion, when SHGs are theoretically more integrated with other third sector organizations, fruitful comparative research can be done among them. Findings on SHGs can then be more easily applied to both nonprofit and private organizations in the health and human service fields.

References

Antze, P. "The Role of Ideologies in Peer Psychotherapy Groups." *Journal of Applied Behavioral Science*, 1976, *12*, 323–346.

Back, K. W., and Taylor, R. C. "Self-Help Groups: Tool or Symbol?" *Journal of Applied Behavioral Science*, 1976, *12*, 295–308.

Bellah, R. N., and others. *Habits of the Heart*. New York: HarperCollins, 1985.

Biegel, D. E., and Yamatani, H. "Help-Giving in Self-Help Groups." *Hospital and Community Psychiatry,* 1987, *38*(11), 1195–1197.

Borkman, T. "Stutterers' Self-Help Organizations: Emergence of Group Life Among the Stigmatized." *Sociological Research Symposium V.* Richmond: Virginia Commonwealth University, 1975.

Borkman, T. "Mutual Self-Help Groups: Strengthening the Selectively Unsupportive Personal and Community Networks of Their Members." In A. Gartner and F. Riessman (eds.), *The Self-Help Revolution.* New York: Human Sciences Press, 1984.

Borkman, T. "Experiential, Professional, and Lay Frames of Reference." In T. J. Powell (ed.), *Working with Self-Help* (pp. 3–30). Silver Spring, Md.: National Association of Social Workers Press, 1990a.

Borkman, T. "Self-Help Groups at the Turning Point: Emerging Egalitarian Alliances with the Formal Health Care System." *American Journal of Community Psychology,* 1990b, *18*(2), 321–331.

Borkman, T., Shaw, M., Shaw, R., and Hickey, A. "Survivability of Self-Help Groups for Persons Who Stutter: A Discriminant Analysis." Paper presented at the 16th annual meeting of the Association of Voluntary Action Scholars, Blacksburg, Va., Oct. 1985.

Borkman, T., and Zappola, A. "A Sociological Survey of the Council of Adult Stutterers, Washington, D.C.: Members' Attitudes Toward Stuttering and Their Self-Help Organization." Unpublished paper, Department of Sociology, Catholic University of America, 1972.

Browning, P., Thorin, E., and Rhoades, C. "A National Profile of Self-Help/Self-Advocacy Groups of People with Mental Retardation." *Mental Retardation,* 1984, *22*(5), 226–230.

Chesler, M. "Support Systems for Parents of Children with Cancer." *Proceedings of the American Cancer Society Fourth National Conference on Human Values and Cancer.* New York: American Cancer Society, 1984.

Chesler, M. "Mobilizing Consumer Activism in Health Care: The Role of Self-Help Groups." In *Research in Social Movements, Conflicts, and Change,* 1991, *13,* 275–305.

Chesler, M., and Chesney, B. "Self-Help Groups: Empowerment Attitudes and Behaviors of Disabled or Chronically Ill Persons." In H. Yuker (ed.), *Attitudes Toward Persons with Disabilities.* New York: Springer, 1988.

Clark, T., and Hughes, M. *Sickle Cell Mutual Help Groups, a Five Year Study: Information, Findings, and Resources.* Chapel Hill, N.C.: Psychosocial Research Division, University of North Carolina, 1992.

Cohen, J., and Arato, A. *Civil Society and Political Theory.* Cambridge, Mass.: MIT Press, 1992.

Droge, D., Arntson, P., and Norton, R. "The Social Support Function in Epilepsy Self-Help Groups." *Small Group Behavior,* 1986, *17*(2), 139–163.

Emerick, R. E. "Group Demographics in the Mental Patient Movement: Group

Location, Age, and Size as Structural Factors." *Community Mental Health Journal*, 1989, *25*(4), 277–299.

Faulkner, J., Britt-Moholt, C., and Kliman-Simone, J. "Self-Help and Individual Change." *Wright Institute Report*, 1977, 6–7.

Galanter, M. "Zealous Self-Help Groups as Adjuncts to Psychiatric Treatment: A Study of Recovery." *American Journal of Psychiatry*, 1988, *145*(10), 1248–1253.

Galanter, M., Castaneda, R., and Salamon, I. "Institutional Self-Help Therapy for Alcoholism: Clinical Outcome." *Alcoholism: Clinical and Experimental Research*, 1987, *11*(5), 424–429.

Galanter, M., Talbott, D., Gallegos, K., and Rubenstone, E. "Combined Alcoholics Anonymous and Professional Care for Addicted Physicians." *American Journal of Psychiatry*, 1990, *147*(1), 64–68.

Gidron, B., Chesler, M., and Chesney, B. "Cross-Cultural Perspectives on Self-Help Groups: Comparison Between Participants and Nonparticipants in Israel and the United States." *American Journal of Community Psychology*, 1991, *19*(5), 667–681.

Gitlin, T. "The Uncivil Society." *New Perspectives Quarterly*, 1990, *7*, 46–49.

Grimsmo, A., Helgesen, G., and Borchgrevink, C. "Short-Term and Long-Term Effects of Lay Groups on Weight Reduction." *British Medical Journal*, 1981, *283*(4), 1093–1095.

Habermas, J. "New Social Movements." *Telos*, 1981, *49*, 33–37.

Henry, S., and Robinson, D. "Understanding Alcoholics Anonymous." *Lancet*, 1978, *18*, 372–375.

Hicks, F. M., and Borkman, T. "Self-Help Groups and Political Empowerment." Paper presented at the 84th annual meeting of the American Political Science Association, Washington, D.C., Sept. 1988.

Joseph, J. A. "The Genesis of Community." *Vital Speeches of the Day*, 1990, *56*, 748–751.

Katz, A. H. "Self-Help and Mutual Aid: An Emerging Movement?" *Annual Review of Sociology*, 1981, *7*, 129–155.

Katz, A. H. "Fellowship, Helping, and Healing: The Emergence of Self-Help Groups." *Journal of Voluntary Action Research*, 1986, *15*(2), 4–13.

Katz, A. H., and Bender, E. I. *Helping One Another: Self-Help Groups in a Changing World*. Oakland, Calif.: Third Party Publishing, 1990.

Kelly, J., and Sykes, P. "Helping the Helpers: A Support Group for Family Members of Persons with AIDS." *Social Work*, 1989, *34*(3), 239–242.

Kerson, T. S. "Lending Vision: Ways in Which Self-Help and Voluntary Efforts Promote Creativity." In H. Weissman (ed.), *Serious Play*, 1990, pp. 211–220.

Klass, D. "Bereaved Parents and the Compassionate Friends: Affiliation and Healing." *Omega*, 1984–85, *15*(4), 353–373.

Kleist, J. "Network Resource Utilization Patterns of Members of Alcoholics

Anonymous." Unpublished doctoral dissertation, Department of Psychology, University of Akron, 1990.
Klug, W. "A Preliminary Investigation of Toughlove: Assertiveness and Support in a Parent's Self-Help Group." Unpublished manuscript, Boston, 1990.
Kurtz, E. "Why A.A. Works." *Journal of Studies on Alcohol*, 1981, *43*(1), 38–80.
Kurtz, L. F. "Twelve-Step Programs." In T. J. Powell (ed.), *Working with Self-Help* (pp. 93–119). Silver Spring, Md.: National Association of Social Workers Press, 1990.
Lohmann, R. A. *The Commons: New Perspectives on Nonprofit Organizations and Voluntary Action*. San Francisco: Jossey-Bass, 1992.
Melucci, A. "The Symbolic Challenge of Contemporary Movements." *Social Research*, 1985, *52*, 789–816.
Miller, L. "What Health Professionals Can Learn from Breast Cancer Patients." In *The Surgeon General's Workshop on Self-Help and Public Health*. U.S. Department of Health and Human Services. Washington, D.C.: U.S. Government Printing Office, 1987.
National Project for Self-Help Groups. *Selected Bibliography for Self-Help Groups, Social Support, and Peer Counseling*. Fairfax, Va.: Department of Sociology and Anthropology, George Mason University, 1992.
Neighbors, H. W., Elliott, K. A., and Gant, L. M. "Self-Help and Black Americans: A Strategy for Empowerment." In T. J. Powell (ed.), *Working with Self-Help*. Silver Spring, Md.: National Association of Social Workers Press, 1990.
Powell, T. J. *Self-Help Organizations and Professional Practice*. Silver Spring, Md.: National Association of Social Workers Press, 1987.
Powell, T. J. "Differences Between National Self-Help Organizations and Local Self-Help Groups: Implications for Members and Professionals." In T. J. Powell (ed.), *Working with Self-Help*. Silver Spring, Md.: National Association of Social Workers Press, 1990.
Riessman, F. "The Self-Help Ethos." *Social Policy*, 1982, *12*, 42–43.
Riessman, F. "Restructuring Help: A Human Services Paradigm for the 1990's." *American Journal of Community Psychology*, 1990, *18*(2), 221–230.
Robinson, D., and Henry, S. *Self-Help and Health: Mutual Aid for Modern Problems*. London: Martin Robertson, 1977.
Rosecrance, J. "Active Gamblers as Peer Counselors." *International Journal of the Addictions*, 1988, *23*(7), 751–766.
Shaw, S., and Borkman, T. *Social Model Alcohol Recovery: An Environmental Approach*. Burbank, Calif.: Bridge Focus, 1990.
Silverman, P., and Cooperband, A. "On Widowhood: Mutual Help and the Elderly Widow." *Journal of Geriatric Psychiatry*, 1975, *8*(1), 9–27.
Silverman, P., and Murrow, H. G. "Mutual Help During Critical Role Transitions." *Journal of Applied Behavioral Science*, 1976, *12*(3), 410–418.

Suler, J. "The Role of Ideology in Self-Help Groups." *Social Policy*, 1984, *14*(3), 29–36.

Toffler, A. *The Third Wave*. New York: Morrow, 1980.

Trainor, M. A. "Acceptance of Ostomy and the Visitor Role in a Self-Help Group for Ostomy Patients." *Nursing Research*, 1981, *7*, 102–106.

Walzer, M. "The Idea of Civil Society: A Path to Social Reconstruction." *Dissent*, 1991, *38*, 293–304.

Westchester Self-Help Clearinghouse. *Touching Bases: A Newsletter of the Westchester Self-Help Clearinghouse*. White Plains, N.Y.: Westchester Jewish Community Services, 1992.

Wollert, R. "Self-Help Clearinghouse Concept: An Overview of an Emergent System for Promoting Mutual Aid." In T. J. Powell (ed.), *Working with Self-Help*. Silver Spring, Md.: National Association for Social Workers Press, 1990.

Wright, H. H., Green, R. L., and Gibson, M. "The Role of the Self-Help Group in the Delivery of Health Services to Underserved Populations in the 1980's." *Psychiatric Forum*, 1984, 42–47.

Zola, I. K. "The Politicization of the Self-Help Movement." *Social Policy*, 1987, *18*, 32–33.

Chapter Eighteen

How Volunteers Help Bosnian Refugees in Slovenia

Anica Mikuš Kos

The war in the former Yugoslavia, a country that had twenty-four million inhabitants, has produced about three million refugees. About 70,000 refugees from Bosnia and Herzegovina fled in the spring of 1992 to Slovenia. Half were children. Their arrival necessitated different mechanisms for helping people who had lost their homes and all their personal property and generally found themselves in great distress.

In this chapter, I will try to sketch the role of volunteers providing psychosocial help for young refugees in Slovenia—a good example of mobilization of care through mutual aid. Their contribution is only one element in the social processes important for improving the quality of the refugees' life. It is not possible to understand what is happening to the refugee children and adolescents without understanding the psychosocial processes in the family and in the refugee community. Therefore, I will focus on the volunteers' activities and their impact on the refugees' situation within the larger context of the refugees' lives.

I feel obligated to explain that I am deeply engaged myself in the relief activities as a volunteer and as a mental health professional. I have not performed my duties in the role of researcher. The methodology of action research would be the most appropriate for an analysis of the processes I am concerned with (Bogdan and Taylor, 1975). But the events linked to the war in Bosnia and Herzegovina—especially the arrival of the refugees in Slovenia—happened so fast and the need for relief was so urgent that there was no time to undertake a well-run project. However, even limited insight into the relief processes and their interaction with government policy in the war and refugee crisis situation can probably facilitate the development of more efficient mechanisms for providing help to refugees.

Among displaced persons living as war refugees in Slovenia, there are about 70,000 people who have the formal status of temporary refugees. In August 1992 the Slovene government closed the borders, and further refugees were not accepted. But many nevertheless managed to enter Slovenia; they are the so-called illegal refugees. About 20,000 persons are illegal refugees, which means that they generally do not have the rights of legal refugees but are tolerated by the Slovene government. Illegal refugees have some rights, however; these include the right of children to attend the primary school that Slovenia has organized for refugees. About 15,000 legal refugees reside in the refugee centers, which are mainly military barracks of the former Yugoslav army. The rest live mostly with Bosnian families and friends who migrated to Slovenia from Bosnia and Herzegovina in the former Yugoslavia. These people found work in Slovenia, where they performed mainly unskilled or semiskilled jobs. Their social situation, which was often unsatisfactory even before the war, deteriorated significantly with the arrival of numerous refugee family members and friends. Sometimes as many as seventeen persons may live in a space of thirty-five square meters. The illegal refugees also live with their families or friends who had migrated to Slovenia before the war.

For a better understanding of the whole situation and its dynamic, it must be stated that the Republic of Slovenia has about two million inhabitants. Given the current unfavorable economic situation of Slovenia, an influx of about 90,000 refugees presents a considerable financial burden to the state.

"Networks of Solidarity" to Help Refugees

When the war in Bosnia and Herzegovina began in the spring of 1992, Slovenia was not at all prepared for the arrival of refugees, although it had already had some experience with refugees from Croatia, who came to Slovenia earlier in considerably smaller numbers. However, the Slovene government reacted immediately and efficiently by providing shelters and food to refugees and by creating "networks of solidarity" to assist them in other ways. Various services, such as health and social services, provide help to refugees within the scope of their regular activities. Additional special health and social services were established in refugee camps. Later the Refugee Bureau was established as the administrative agency of the government of Slovenia and was empowered to organize and regulate the refugees' living conditions.

Besides the help to refugees provided on the state level, the Slovene humanitarian organizations and nongovernmental organizations—the Red Cross and Caritas—have played a very important role in collecting and distributing clothes, food, and other vitally necessary items.

The generosity of the Slovene people and their desire to help the refugees have been reflected in a high level of individual giving. People have brought clothes, food, toys, dishes, and electronic devices to refugee camps. Among the latter, television sets have been the most appreciated. They have been the only means of acquiring current information about the situation in Bosnia and Herzegovina, since telephone service and other communications have been disrupted and newspapers in the Croatian language have not usually been available in refugee camps. Employees of some companies have collected money and goods for refugees. People have been particularly willing to provide goods for refugee children.

Schools, kindergartens, and voluntary organizations have encouraged children to offer their toys and school-related items to refugee children. Such incentives should be expanded and cultivated, because the presence of refugees in Slovenia with the accompanying helping activities can be a great lesson in solidarity and philanthropy for Slovene children.

A few of the existing voluntary organizations began to recruit volunteers to help refugees. Most of the giving has involved donations of material goods or activities of a practical nature rather than providing psychosocial help to refugees such as visiting or befriending them or offering emotional support. This can be partly attributed to the Slovene national character, which has traits such as uneasiness in establishing social contacts with strangers, reserve in communication with people, and emotional coolness.

To shed more light on the situation of the volunteers, it should be explained that in the former socialist countries, there were few civic incentives for engaging in helping activities for people in need. The principle of the system—solidarity—meant that the state collected financial revenues and allocated them according to the needs of the population. Another feature of socialist society was the wide network of state health and social welfare services, which were supposed to cover all the needs of the people. These precepts and practices were inherent in the socialist order. But they also to some degree reflected the tendency of the state to control the resources and activities in the field of social welfare through state institutions. Such circumstances were not favorable to the development of a broad spectrum of volunteer organizations, self-help organizations, and other nongovernmental organizations.

However, in the last decade of the socialist regime, more voluntary organizations were established in Slovenia. They were dedicated to helping disabled children or adults and others in need. But their number was rather limited. It can be stated that at the beginning of the war in the former Yugoslavia, no important networks of volunteer organizations existed in Slovenia. The value of voluntarism was not adequately appreciated, nor were people encouraged to engage in philanthropic activities (Kohn, 1990; Rosenhan, 1970; Smith, 1981).

After the refugees had been in Slovenia for a short time, some volunteers—mainly students—started to visit the camps and to engage in various occupational and social activities with children and adolescents. Volunteers also arrived from other European countries and have worked together with Slovene volunteers and refugee volunteers in camps. They have been teaching different activities, such as sports, theater, music, foreign language courses, and sewing, as well as taking care of children in kindergartens. Hundreds of volunteers have participated so far in various helping activities.

But the presence of volunteers in the camps is unpredictable. It depends on numerous circumstances. For instance, in Ljubljana—the capital of Slovenia and a university town with many students—a large number of volunteers are active, while in smaller towns there are no Slovene or foreign volunteers, but only refugee volunteers. However, the presence of nonrefugee volunteers is very important. If they are Slovene, they make refugee children, adolescents, and adults feel that they are welcome in Slovenia. On the other hand, through direct contact the Slovene volunteers have the opportunity to become acquainted with refugees, to perceive them as human beings with names and faces, with their sorrows and needs, and they acquire insight into their human and cultural richness. So, besides being helpful by befriending children and youth and conducting various activities, volunteers fulfill the important role of promoting a positive image of the refugees and contributing to positive attitudes toward the refugees in the Slovene population. Volunteers from other countries introduce a lot of activities in the camps, and their efforts are greatly appreciated. Surprisingly, the language barrier has not been much of a problem, and some young people from Bosnia and Herzegovina have learned English through befriending foreign volunteers.

The most important source of help for the problems of the refugees has been the refugee community itself. The help provided in this framework has not been material, because the refugees have only a few goods to share. It has been manifested by emotional support, especially in crisis situations such as the death of a family member, through care for children or elderly, sick, disabled, and injured persons, and by transmitting information. Children and youth are on the receiving end but also on the giving side. For example, they carry wounded young soldiers, bring food for elderly people, and take care of children in kindergartens.

Other countries have offered their help either at the government level or through philanthropic organizations (Caritas, Red Cross, International Relief Organization), through various foundations (Open Society Fund and so on), and through individual donations. They have made it possible for groups of refugee children to visit other parts of Europe, which has had beneficial effects on the mental health of these children. The foreign Islamic organizations have contributed large sums of money—for instance, for the organization of the primary school for refugee children.

United Nations organizations like UNICEF have been providing food and medical supplies for children and have also become involved in funding mental health projects for children. Besides carrying out other functions, the UN High Commissioner for Refugees has advocated the refugees' rights and has been very active in fundraising for different projects that provide psychosocial help.

The Developmental Dynamics of Conviviality with Refugees

Refugees who arrived in Slovenia from Bosnia and Herzegovina in the spring of 1992 had faced many war atrocities. They had been humiliated, had suffered severe adversity during the escape from their countries, had been deprived of all their property, and were frightened and coping with intense stress. These tragic events evoked tremendous sympathy among Slovenes and a considerable amount of willingness to help the displaced persons. The refugees were happy to be received by Slovenia and often expressed their gratitude both in private and in public. During the first weeks the host country and its guests experienced a honeymoon of conviviality.

But after some weeks it became increasingly evident that the refugees, whom Slovenia called "temporary refugees," would not leave Slovenia soon. Voices claiming that the economic situation of Slovenia was bad enough without expenditures for refugees began to make themselves heard. They pointed at the fact that many Slovene families lived at the margin of poverty or already in poverty and that unemployment was increasing. Some political parties objected to Slovene hospitality toward the refugees. The Slovene public was disappointed by the initial unreadiness to help and lack of engagement of European countries much richer than Slovenia. They asked why Slovenia, which was no longer formally connected with Bosnia and Herzegovina, should suffer nearly all the economic and organizational burden of helping the refugees.

On the other hand, the moral and emotional situation of the refugees deteriorated. Their psychological resistance and coping capacities decreased. They were more and more desperate regarding the possibility of repatriation. They had lived for weeks in bad material circumstances in crowded rooms without any privacy and in refugee centers with severe restrictions on free movement. They had received more and more news about deaths of family members, about destroyed homes. Besides experiencing the hospitality of Slovenia, they became aware of less favorable attitudes toward them. They became increasingly disappointed by the world community, which made limited efforts to end the war in Bosnia and Herzegovina and to protect its inhabitants from massacres, loss, displacement, deprivation, and humiliation. Dissatisfaction, despair, disappointment, hopelessness, helplessness, irritability, and tension were growing. The refugees became less capable of tolerating frustration. Disputes appeared in their own community. In some camps, there were also conflicts between refugees and administrators. But taking into account the number of displaced persons from Bosnia and Herzegovina, the enormity of the stresses to which they have been exposed, and their present situation, the number of incidents has been astonishingly small.

Of course the atmosphere described affected children. Many

parents were depressed that they were not able to help their children in distress, and so the help of relatives, friends, and volunteers became very important for these children.

In the fall of 1992 as well as later, the efforts of the Slovene government to meet the basic needs of the refugees were efficient enough. But the government attitudes toward the refugees were not clearly expressed. It was not evident how much hospitality toward the displaced persons was appropriate. In December 1992 there were elections in Slovenia. During the election campaign, neither the government nor the political parties—even the left-oriented parties—were willing to risk encouraging people to demonstrate friendship toward persons who "eat from Slovene money" and who were citizens of a country that was previously part of the former Yugoslavia. The antirefugee attitudes of some people reflected xenophobia as well as an aversion toward the former Yugoslav state, in which Slovenia felt exploited by southern republics—one of which was Bosnia and Herzegovina. The prevailing impression was that the voices of those who warned Slovenes about the economic consequences of the support to refugees were much louder than the voices of citizens who believed that Slovenia was acting correctly by assuming the costs and providing the care for the displaced persons and that a friendly hand should be extended to them. But some public opinion surveys indicated that those who objected to the Slovene hospitality toward refugees were in a minority.

After some months, Slovenia succeeded in taking care of the basic material needs of the refugees, partly with its own resources and partly with foreign aid. So, the refugees acquired adequate clothing. The food was provided for people in centers, and central heating was installed in the barracks. The elementary needs of the residents of the refugee camps were covered. But the situation is still extremely unsatisfactory for the refugees living outside the camps with families, though their problems remain somewhat hidden.

In both populations—the population living in the camps and the population living with families—the psychosocial problems became more and more pronounced and evident.

Emerging Psychosocial Problems and Needs

The duration of exile, the war situation, the disappointment, and the confinement in overcrowded spaces contributed to the increase in psychosocial problems, which were different from the symptoms of acute distress in the first weeks of exile. The refugees became more and more depressed and inactive. The autumn rains and winter frost aggravated the situation. People from Bosnia and Herzegovina could easily describe their feelings and state of mind. But they had difficulty overcoming the adversity created by their life in exile in the refugee community.

The inactivity of refugees is a well-known phenomenon. It is due to their depression and to their total dependence on events they cannot control, like war or the behavior of the host country. Slovenes have adopted a paternalistic attitude toward the refugees, treating them as helpless people who are incapable of carrying out basic organizational tasks, which probably also contributed to their inactivity. The prevailing philosophy and practice was that something must be done for the refugees instead of working with them to encourage and push them to articulate and negotiate their own interests and realize them with resources from their own community. The volunteer organizations were also permeated with such attitudes. This situation certainly has not encouraged the refugees to take charge of their own situation. One consequence was that sometimes helping activities were conceived within the framework of a different culture and did not adequately meet the needs of the refugees or were not particularly acceptable to them.

Economic and Political Determinants of the Quality of Life

Obviously the psychosocial situation of refugees depends first of all on political decisions. It could be improved above all by such measures as giving the refugees a chance to earn some money, allowing freedom of movement for people in centers, and trying to arrange reunions in Slovenia of the separated family members now dispersed in different countries.

The most important barrier to change at the legal and organizational level is the uncertainty regarding the duration and the development of the war situation and the resulting possibilities of repatriation. This uncertain situation inhibits to some extent the Slovene incentives for helping the refugees become integrated into the new environment, learn the language of the host country, and acquire at least minimal economic independence—the most important measures for improving their psychosocial conditions. On the Slovene side, such measures are obstructed, too, by economic and political tendencies that do not favor the integration of refugees into Slovene society. The uncertainty has also prevented many refugees from actively working toward important positive changes in their everyday life and from searching for long-term solutions.

School for Refugee Children: A Good Example of Cooperative Efforts

One of the most important achievements in normalizing the life of the refugees and in reducing psychosocial distress in the children was the creation of the compulsory elementary school for all refugee children age seven to fifteen years, living in Slovenia either legally or illegally. The school is one of the rare organizations for refugees in which a partnership with the government of Slovenia has been realized. The school is organized and managed by the joint efforts of the Ministry of Education of the Republic of Slovenia and by the representative of the Ministry of Education of Bosnia and Herzegovina. Teachers are with rare exceptions refugees: half are professional educators; the rest are highly qualified professionals in other fields—for example, doctors, lawyers, university students, and others. They received special training for their future teaching activities as well as training in how to recognize and provide help for emotional distress in children. These mental health training activities started as a volunteer activity of the Counseling Center for Children, Adolescents, and Parents in Ljubljana. The teachers can be considered volunteers, since they receive only modest compensation. The school for refugee children is supported by foreign funds. The children of Slovenia are encouraged to collect school equipment for their refugee peers. The functioning of the school is a good illustration of how the whole enterprise of helping the refugees survive physically and mentally includes and integrates political actions, philanthropic donations, volunteer work, and public goodwill.

The existence of the school system for refugee children also shows that among the projects aimed at improving the psychosocial situation of the refugee community, absolute priority should be given to those that are comprehensive and embrace the totality of the refugee population—for instance, all schoolchildren. It is rational to first direct the available financial resources and energy to comprehensive organizational projects embracing most of the population. Many optional activities undertaken by volunteers can be integrated into such projects.

The care for the psychosocial well-being of adolescents illustrates the differences between comprehensive and sporadic helping interventions, which include those delivered by volunteers. The latter reach only the small part of the population willing to participate in activities offered like sports, cultural activities, and educational courses. The next problem is that the adolescents most at risk do not take part in such activities. This is characteristic of adolescents who are depressed or lonely, have difficulty establishing contact, lack assertiveness, or are inclined to engage in disruptive behavior. Including adolescents in schools would be a measure that would benefit all adolescents, or at least the great majority. Among the most beneficial effects of introducing secondary schooling would be the prevention of psychosocial disorders in the adolescent refugee population. Here it must be stressed that adolescents can be considered to be the population most at risk in the current situation, and few protective mechanisms are provided for them.

Role of Philanthropy in Reducing Distress

The relief efforts, in the first instance, are of an organizational, social, and economic nature. But the question is, how much emotional and moral help could be offered to refugees through individual human assistance and through the involvement of organized volunteers.

There have been some favorable changes in the refugee scene in Slovenia. After the elections in Slovenia in December 1992, the political situation has seemed to be more favorable for the refugees. Friendly attitudes toward the refugees have been more openly expressed, and incentives for face-to-face contacts between Slovenes and refugees have been offered. At Christmas, the Catholic Church, which is influential in Slovenia, transmitted messages encouraging Slovenes to offer friendly help and support to refugees—for example, by inviting children to their homes and presenting Christmas or New Year's gifts to them. Slovenia also became increasingly aware of the need to find ways of improving the psychosocial situation of the refugees. Various projects have been conceived at the level of the Ministry of Health, of the Ministry of Education, and in the framework of the civil society. Fundraising efforts have been undertaken. At the same time, it has become more and more evident that it is easier to provide material help than psychosocial help.

The process of reducing the social distance between Slovenes and refugees has had an important impact. It happens spontaneously in smaller localities where refugees live in families outside the camps. Usually refugee children first begin to establish friendly relations with the Slovene children. It also happens in schools for refugee children when they are located in the same building as the Slovene school. Refugee teachers are helped by Slovene schools and their Slovene colleagues. The individual contacts between refugees and Slovenes can be encouraged by different organizations like the church and volunteer organizations. Such contacts diminish feelings of isolation, increase feelings of security, and significantly improve the psychosocial situation of the refugees. The influence of face-to-face contacts on the image of refugees in Slovenia has already been described. Direct contacts are often the source of incentives and pressures for more general actions aimed at improving the life of refugees. Volunteers are specially active in child advocacy.

Individual helping behavior on the part of Slovenes has often had the function of softening or correcting government decisions. Their readiness to provide assistance to the refugees was obvious from the discrepancy between the official directives and everyday practice. For instance, for some time refugee adolescents were not supposed to enter Slovene high schools. However, many were included in schools where there was room for an additional student due to the decision of the school principal.

We can also speak about the complementary function of volunteers' activities in relation to the functions of big systems (Ilsley, 1990). Volunteers detect individual needs that cannot be fulfilled by the big organizations like the Red Cross. So Slovene volunteers and friendly families can provide a needed or desired special object that cannot be obtained from the Red Cross supplies. They can take a child with special interests to a certain place. Briefly, they individualize the care and helping opportunities, which is of great importance, especially for the well-being of refugee children and adolescents.

An important and interesting question is how the particular

networks of solidarity interlace—how they interact and what the productive and counterproductive effects of these interactions are. Some examples of these interactions have already been given.

The relation between the natural helping network of the refugee community and the Slovene activities is of special importance. It seems that Slovenes who are willing to offer psychosocial help are often not sensitized enough to the already-existing networks, sources, and strategies of mutual help, social construction of reality, and other concepts and value systems within the Muslim population. Too little attention is paid to the recognition of these resources; their potential is not utilized enough and integrated into the helping efforts of Slovenes.

I will illustrate the above reflections with my personal experience. As a child psychiatrist who tried to introduce mental health work in the refugee centers, I faced the problems just described. Only a small number of children and parents accepted the Slovene model of psychological help offered to them, which involved visits to the outpatient clinics. To reach children and their parents I had to introduce myself to the community of refugees, sitting on the stone stairs of the barracks or on a bench under a tree in the yard and establishing first human, then professional contacts with them. My principal function in the group work with parents was to discover and activate supportive and healing forces in refugees. It was very important for my work to recognize their protective strategies and principles of mutual help. For instance, I had to deal with the fact that mothers were not willing to inform a child about a father's or brother's death, and the secret was kept by the whole community. So I had to find persons within the community who could help the mother and the child with the discovery of the death of a close relative. The population coming from underdeveloped rural areas was not prone to accept antidepressive drugs or sleeping pills, even in case of serious disorders, but they were willing to take herbal medicine to which they were accustomed in their villages. At the beginning I made many mistakes in counseling. I used inappropriate words or gave advice that proved unacceptable to the refugees. I had much to learn in order to be able to integrate my knowledge in their special life experiences and ways of thinking.

In the field of children's mental health, the network of volunteers could be better used in providing help to children with special emotional needs (Eisenbruch, 1988). This approach would be crucial in situations where there are many emotionally disturbed children without available professional mental health helpers. But to fulfill this role, the volunteers should be aware of the cultural and social characteristics of the population being served. They should also be familiar with the resources within the refugee community and be trained to link them with their own resources and activities.

Conclusion

The refugees' situation in Slovenia reflects the interactions among public attitudes, government policies, laws, and regulations on the one hand and the nonprofit sector on the other—interactions that can promote or inhibit caring activities and solidarity in a time of crisis. The situation of the refugees also involves interactions between two cultures. Additional research on the interface of two or more cultures and their relation in caring actions would be of great interest.

An important question is how the caring actions they experience or witness influence the vision of the world of refugee children and youth and whether they at least partly neutralize the effects of the war evil experienced by the children. A related question is what impact the help provided will have on the future caring behavior of the refugee children and youth.

The presence of the refugees in Slovenia has inspired the development of various philanthropic and volunteer activities and created an opportunity to promote them among Slovene children and youth. What is the impact of this situation on the caring behavior of Slovene youth now and in the future?

The picture presented is not a scientifically valid analysis based on research. Such research would be of interest, because the war situation, the refugee situation, and the consequent caring actions are a sad natural experiment from which many important findings could be derived.

References

Bogdan, R., and Taylor, S. J. *Introduction to Qualitative Research Methods: A Phenomenological Approach to the Social Sciences*. New York: Wiley, 1975.

Eisenbruch, M. "The Mental Health of Refugee Children and Their Cultural Development." *International Migration Review*, 1988, *22*, 282–300.

Ilsley, P. J. *Enhancing the Volunteer Experience: New Insights on Strengthening Volunteer Participation, Learning, and Commitment*. San Francisco: Jossey-Bass, 1990.

Kohn, A. *The Brighter Side of Human Nature: Altruism and Empathy in Everyday Life*. New York: Basic Books, 1990.

Rosenhan, D. "The Natural Socialization of Altruistic Autonomy." In J. Macauley and L. Berkowitz (eds.), *Altruism and Helping Behavior*. New York: Academic Press, 1970.

Smith, D. H. "Altruism, Volunteers and Volunteering." *Journal of Voluntary Action Research*, 1981, *10*(1), 21–36.

Chapter Nineteen

The Activist and the Alienated: Participation Trends in Community Service

John Bell

The *community sector* is increasingly recognized as a distinct and important phenomenon. It has been defined as "all autonomous or largely self governing citizens' and residents' activity which maintains and improves collective life and conditions for people in their own localities and networks" (Chanan, 1992, p. 42). This helps us to focus on activity and outcomes and to avoid the usual concentration on institutional form. To date, most work in the United Kingdom on the community sector has concentrated on how local organizations coexist, cooperate, and compete, and how they interact "upward" with statutory organizations and with the private sector. There has been relatively little examination of the factors that predispose individuals to become active in community organizations, nor of the characteristics that define them. Gabriel Chanan (1992) has argued for a more sophisticated understanding of different types of involvement, and I have identified the "special" nature of most community activists (Bell, 1992a), but much of this work is based on impressionistic and anecdotal evidence or on methodology. Halfpenny (1990) has argued that variations in volunteering described in much of the literature tend to be determined by the definition used rather than involving substantive difference.

A crucial distinction is the difference between traditional forms of volunteering and what can be called *participation*. The former conjures images of altruism, of motivation based on the desire to help others, of retired solicitors driving to the legal advice center

Note: The research described here has been supported by the European Foundation for the Improvement of Living and Working Conditions, Dublin.

in the housing estate, there to give the benefit of their experience to those in need. My thesis is that community participation is much wider and more complex than this, and that it is in large part motivated by self-help or mutual aid rather than altruism. In this chapter, I use a large, cross-national survey to distinguish between the altruistic volunteer and the self-interested participant, and then examine the demographic, economic, and social factors that underlie these groups. If we can assume that the community sector has intrinsic value and fulfills important functions of social care, community cohesion, and interaction, then it is essential to begin to understand who plays the active and organizing roles that enable it to function.

My basic hypothesis is that community participation is not a randomly distributed phenomenon. The types of people who participate in their localities, the reasons they do so, and the constraints on what they are able to do will make some people much more likely to get involved than others. Additionally, the degree of participation will vary. I explore these issues in relation to two factors that I believe will make a difference to participation: the presence of children in the household and other care responsibilities; and the degree of concern for issues in the locality. Does the need to solve child-care and other care problems lead to higher levels of participation, or do these problems act as constraints on the ability to participate? Does a high level of concern for locally relevant issues lead to higher levels of participation, and does this vary depending on the impact local issues have on the household?

Data Source

The data used in this chapter come from what is thought to be the first cross-national statistical analysis of participation in the community sector. The research formed part of a larger study that examined the concept of the community sector at the national level, and then sought to demonstrate empirically its existence and nature in similar peripheral urban areas. The data used are taken from seven parallel household surveys, each of around 250 respondents, undertaken in particular localities in Belgium, Greece, Ireland, The Netherlands, Portugal, Spain, and the United Kingdom. The localities examined, while differing in many ways, were chosen according to specific criteria. They all

- Are geographically peripheral to a large urban center
- Display a range of indicators to social and economic deprivation, particularly unemployment and poor housing conditions
- Have some inward investment, or at least show some signs of activity to improve local socioeconomic conditions
- Are known to have a diversity of identifiable, active, local community groups and other voluntary organizations

An important issue to keep in mind is that while the countries from which the data come are diverse, the areas studied show impressive similarities of community participation and activity. It is clear that the socioeconomic mix described does tend to produce similar levels of participation and overall community activity. Whether the pattern would be similar in other contexts—for example in different areas in Europe, or in different countries altogether—is open to question, although my feeling is that similar patterns would emerge.

Data were collected on a range of local concerns, from issues confronting each area, to knowledge and use of different local groups and organizations, and the use of various approaches to solving problems. Strenuous efforts were taken to ensure that the questions and response codings were parallel across all seven localities. Full technical details can be found in Bell (1992b).

In Search of the Activist

The first task is to isolate "true" community activists, people who are seriously involved in local-group activities. The data were transformed and clustered, in relation to:

- Knowledge of local groups and organizations
- Overall involvement in local groups and organizations
- Absolute number of groups used
- Absolute number of groups given direct help with organizational tasks

The cluster procedure used was a single-solution model based on nearest centroid sorting. A case is assigned to the cluster for which the distance between the case and the center of the cluster (centroid) is smallest. In this procedure, the number of cluster centers is predetermined by the analyst. The procedure was run using three-, four-, and five-center models. In each case a four-center model provided the most satisfactory distribution. Analysis was performed using SPSS/PC+ version 4 running on an IBM PS/2 Model L40 SX.

Since there were variations in opportunities to be active and knowledgeable in the different localities, the clustering procedure was performed for each individual locality. The localities were then recombined, using consistent definitions, to leave us with three distinct groups (Table 19.1).

Moderate is defined by a "helping with" score of around .7, together with comparatively high levels of general involvement or knowledge of the local community sector (20 percent or more). The highly active are defined as helping with an average of at least one local group, with additionally high levels of overall activity (10 percent or more) and good knowledge of local groups (40 percent or

Table 19.1. Degrees of Activism.

	Percent	*Number*
Highly active	5.1	81
Moderately active	8.9	142
Not very active	86.0	1368

more). Overall, I conclude that some one in seven members of the community in deprived urban areas are closely involved in local community activity, with one in twenty playing significant and regular organizing roles. I believe this 14 percent to be the lynchpin of organized community activity, and an understanding of their characteristics and motives to be essential for those wishing to understand the community sector. What then does analysis in terms of social and economic factors tell us? The key results are summarized in Table 19.2.

The first conclusion is that there is no typical type of person who gets involved in local-group activity. The analysis has suggested a large number of factors that appear to have a strong influence on likelihood of participation. But overall, at least some people of all types are highly active in the community groups in their localities, and some are totally uninvolved. More or less equal numbers of men and women are active overall, with a slightly greater number of women highly active. Peak ages of activity are between forty and sixty-nine. Marital status makes little difference in level of activity—what matters much more is the structure of the household and the distribution of responsibilities within it. Of particular importance is the limiting effect of children in the household, especially younger children. Those with homemaking and general care responsibilities, however, have proportionately much higher than average levels of activism. The absolute size of the household does not make a great difference, except where there are more than six people present, when rates of activism are higher. Overcrowding, however, does reduce the proportion of activists.

Both short- and long-term residence in the locality is associated with lower rates of activism than medium length, around ten to twenty years. Residents in privately owned accommodations have the highest rates of activism, while those renting privately have an exceptionally low rate. Unemployed people show high rates of local activism, particularly when no one in the household has paid employment. The retired and those not looking for work have

Table 19.2. Summary of Demographic, Social, and Economic Factors.

	Highly active	*Moderately active*
Age		
<30	4.6	9.8
30–39	5.2	12.2
40–49	10.8	16.1
50–59	10.5	11.2
60–69	9.3	18.2
70–79	0.0	9.8
80+	0.0	6.4
Gender		
Male	6.5	13.5
Female	8.6	11.8
Marital status		
Single	8.1	
Married or living as though married	7.8	
Divorced	7.0	
Widowed	2.0	
Housekeeping		
Yes	10.3	
No	7.3	
Caring		
Yes	18.0	25.9
No	9.1	14.1
Child care		
Yes	9.5	14.2
No	9.6	15.0
Children in household		
Living alone	10.1	
Couple only	14.1	
With children	8.1	
Other	2.1	
Crowding—persons per room		
Up to 1	7.4	
1–1½	7.7	
1½+	6.4	

Table 19.2. Cont.

	Highly active	*Moderately active*
Number in household		
Alone	8.6	
2 people	10.6	
3–5	8.4	
6+	12.3	
Residence in locality		
<5 years	7.6	
5–9	8.1	
10–19	11.0	
20–29	9.4	
30+	5.1	
Housing tenure		
Social housing	7.5	
Private rent	2.9	
Private own	11.2	
Other	1.2	
Employment status of respondent		
Full-time employed	10.8	10.0
Part-time employed	11.1	10.9
Not looking	6.5	12.3
Unemployed	13.8	12.6
Retired	7.1	10.0
Employment of main household earner		
Employer/manager	14.9	11.9
White collar	13.8	14.5
Skilled manual	4.1	8.7
Unskilled manual	8.5	11.2

Note: All results are percentages of category.

rather low rates. Among men, part-time workers are much more likely to be active than full-timers—a position reversed for women. "Higher"-status occupations by the main earner are associated with high rates of activity, while skilled manual work by the main earner is associated with the lowest. The highly active are much more likely to use local groups and influential people than others in the community for problem solving, and are somewhat more likely to use official authorities. The above compresses an enormous amount into a short space but is essential as context for discussion of two particular items: children and other care responsibilities in the household, and engagement with local issues.

Child and Other Care Responsibilities

Only a relatively small number of people (7 percent) said they had non-child-related care responsibilities in the household (see Table 19.3). This includes in particular care for elderly, sick, or disabled relatives. However, within this group a surprisingly large proportion—18 percent—were also highly active. I suggest that such people find the support and encouragement in their local groups that they need to be able to manage their caring tasks. There is also a high level of moderate activity by carers (table not shown), lending support to this suggestion.

Given what is known about the heavy time commitments involved in care responsibilities, it would be valuable to know more about this situation. If this result is borne out, it would have important implications for our understanding of the needs and desires of carers, and the role of local groups in meeting these. Noncarers were

Table 19.3. Highly Active by Caring.

Count *Column percent*	*Caring?* *Yes*	 *No*	*Row total*
Not very active	29 82.0	423 90.9	451 90.2
Highly active	6 18.0	42 9.1	49 9.8
Column total	35 7.0	465 93.0	500 100.0

Note: Figures may not precisely add up because of rounding.

Table 19.4. Highly Active by Child Care.

Count *Column percent*	*Caring?* *Yes*	 *No*	*Row total*
Not very active	126 90.5	334 90.4	461 90.4
Highly active	13 9.5	35 9.6	49 9.6
Column total	140 27.4	370 72.6	509 100.0

Note: Figures may not precisely add up because of rounding.

little different from the average figure for main or moderate activism. Contrasting this picture with the importance of child care for activity, we see in Table 19.4 little apparent influence on the highly active as a result of doing child-care tasks, while the likelihood of doing moderate activity is a little reduced where child responsibilities exist (table not shown).

Unlike other household responsibilities, child care does not act as any kind of spur for community activity, even though the presence of children inevitably necessitates greater contact with the locality. It may be that any desire for greater involvement is tempered by the time required for looking after children. Table 19.5 shows the greatest levels of high activity in households of a married (or equivalent) couple alone, at 14 percent. Ten percent of people alone are highly active, as are 8 percent of people in families with children.

Analysis of this material to take age into account shows interesting results. In the under-thirty-five age group, only 5 percent of respondents in families with (presumably young) children were highly active, compared with 9 percent of couples without children and 26 percent of single people. In the thirty-five- to forty-nine-year-old group, there were no highly active single people,

Table 19.5. Highly Active by Presence of Children in Household.

Count *Column percent*	*Living alone*	*Couple only*	*With children*	*Other type*	*Row total*
Not very active	72 89.9	96 85.6	182 91.9	107 97.9	457 91.4
Highly active	8 10.1	16 14.4	16 8.1	2 2.1	43 8.6
Column total	80 15.9	113 22.5	199 39.7	109 21.8	500 100.0

Note: Figures may not precisely add up because of rounding.

12 percent of couples without children, and 13 percent of households with children—more than double the rate for younger families. These results suggest that single younger people are highly active locally, perhaps in order to meet others, while those with small children are the least able to be active. Younger children clearly require more time, both before school age and in the early years there, while older children are more independent.

Engagement with Local Issues

Engagement with issues in the locality has similar complexities to that of involvement in local-group activity. "Issues" in this case were defined by spontaneously mentioned factors strongly affecting the locality, as well as agreement with statements attributing preselected issues to the locality. The variables used covered

- Level of interest in local issues, defined as proportion of opportunities taken to mention issues
- Whether the issues mentioned affected any members of the household

- Whether the respondent had taken any significant action to tackle issues raised

I believed there would be different groups of people in relation to their degree of interest in issues, the taking of action, and the connection between interest, action, and effect in the household.

Table 19.6 shows four distinct groups. The largest, the "unengaged," reflect a high level of concern with issues affecting the locality but a low level of activity in relation to them. The likelihood of the household being affected by the issues was fairly low, but still nearly one in four issues for the locality affected the household.

The second largest are the "alienated." They show little interest in issues that affect the locality. When they do mention something, it is almost always when it affects the household. This group does almost nothing to tackle the few issues that do concern them. The size of this group is disturbing. The responses suggest an almost total lack of engagement with conditions in the locality—localities known from other evidence to display a wide range of adverse conditions, with a large number of groups attempting to do something about them.

The third group are the "self-interested." They display a concern for local issues and show the highest level of any group for activity in relation to them. Their important distinguishing feature is the high level to which local issues affect the household, suggesting that the action taken is largely for the purpose of self-help. Attempts to bring new people into local participation might be best served by appealing to the possible personal benefits rather than altruistic benefits for the community as a whole.

The final, smallest group are "altruists," characterized by concern for local issues and a high level of activity in relation to them, but their households are almost completely unaffected by the issues raised. While a small group, these people may have more time available to spend on local action, if we assume that the failure to be

Table 19.6 Clustering by Concern for Local Issues and Involvement in Associated Activity.

Unengaged	723	45.4%
Alienated	675	42.4%
Self-interested	110	7.0%
Altruists	84	5.3%

Note: Figures may not precisely add up because of rounding.

affected by locality issues indicates a lack of serious problems overall. Table 19.7 analyzes these clusters in relation to activity in local groups.

This table is particularly interesting. The highest level of serious local activity is seen among the altruists, who show a rate of activism of 16 percent. Not surprisingly, the next largest proportion is shown by the "self-interested" group (at 13 percent), these being the people actively concerned about local issues, where the issues also affect the household. However, the rate of high activism among the "alienated" and "unengaged" groups is not as low as might be expected, at around 6 percent. Although these people are not interested in issues affecting the locality in a general sense, activity in a local group may for some bring immediate relief or support for issues that seem pressing to the household. This is supportive evidence for the assertion that self-help is a major motive for local activity. Among the moderate activists (table not shown), the level of activity among the "altruists" drops to little more than the average of 12 percent, while that of the "self-interested" is much larger—31 percent. A possible reason is that if an "altruist" does get involved in local activity, he or she is likely to be strongly involved. The self-interested seem for some reason to be prepared to be active but cannot get involved as closely. The fact that the local issues affect the household may cause these individuals to spend time dealing with them.

Table 19.7. Activity by Relationship to Issues in Locality.

Count *Column percent*	*Alienated*	*Unengaged*	*Altruist*	*Self-interested*	*Row total*
Not very active	517 93.3	509 93.9	62 83.8	68 86.9	1157 92.6
Highly active	37 6.7	33 6.1	12 16.2	10 13.1	93 7.4
Column total	555 44.4	543 43.4	74 5.9	79 6.3	1250 100.0

Note: Figures may not precisely add up because of rounding.

Underlying Factors?

What are we to make of this disparate picture? First, there is a connection with sheer physical or circumstantial ability to participate. Older people, those with children in the household needing care, and those employed full time show lower rates than others. When people do overcome barriers to participation of this nature, it may be because the advantages to them are a sufficient incentive for the effort to be worthwhile. This is behind some of the more surprising results in the analysis, particularly those relating to care responsibilities and women in full-time employment. In both these cases, the proportion of people both highly and moderately active was much larger than expected, since both conditions were assumed to cause considerable restraints on activism. Could the reason then be the self-help functions of groups? Carers in particular have difficulty participating in any form of community activity. The need for respite and burden sharing is often met for carers by local community activity. There would seem to be no other satisfactory explanation for this finding.

Other aspects of the analysis support the self-help thesis, in particular the association of a high level of activism with the perception of many adverse issues in the locality, and with unemployment. Strong support also comes from the greater use of local groups for problem solving by the already highly active. We should remember that the highly active are primarily defined by their help with the running and organization of local groups, not simply by making use of what they have to offer. Many if not most of the groups covered by the survey offered "services" of one kind or another to people in the locality, including to those not officially "members" of the group. They were thus available to all in the community as a problem-solving mechanism.

From the point of view of groups, then, there are issues here of the extent to which people are aware of them at all, and of the services they may have to offer. One of the recognized benefits of community activity for individuals is the widening of social networks, partly because most local community groups are also in contact with others in the locality. People highly active in one group are likely to be aware of other groups to which they could turn in times of adversity. The networking argument is strengthened if we bring the use of influential local people for problem solving into the picture. The much greater use of them by the highly active demonstrates their greater connection with informal sources of support and influence.

This brings us to the issue of marginalization, which in some recent work has been in part defined as the absence of informal sources of information (Shanks, Bell, and Chanan, 1991). Chanan (1992, p. 77) emphasizes that, beyond the concentric rings of core activists, regular helpers, and occasional users lies a hinterland of the marginal and socially excluded. He puts forward a number of factors involved: "'Everything that disadvantages a person . . . also makes it harder for him or her to participate in group activities: poor transport, lack of money, lack of safety, depressing environment, lack of facilities, being stuck at home.' To this must be added age, illness, fear of racial or sexual harassment, sheer lack of information on what is available, being tied down by care responsibilities. Many of these factors particularly affect women."

Taken as individual factors, our analysis does not give total support to the argument that people experiencing adverse conditions do not get involved in local action. Households with unemployment and no secure income display a rather high level of local activity, as do some in older age groups and those with care responsibilities. Also, if the factors are particularly concentrated for women, how are we to explain their equal numbers with men for local activity, and the greater extent of high-level activity on the part of women? On the other hand, those with child-care responsibilities may well be "stuck at home," and we have already indicated a probable information gap as a factor in the use of groups as a problem-solving mechanism.

To address some of these dilemmas, we must shift our focus and consider not the relative levels of local activity, but the actual numbers of people involved. Thus, the numbers of people engaged in any significant amount of local activity is around one in five, while the proportion of those with a high level of activity is not much more than one in twenty. The types of people most inclined to be highly active still only represent fairly small absolute numbers. Only one in ten people in their forties are highly active, one in six carers, one in six of the female unemployed, one in seven of the "altruists" about locality issues.

Being in any of the situations or life stages used in this analysis cannot then be said to create a disposition to be locally active. Instead, a limited number of people of any sort seem to be disposed toward this rather unusual activity. Certain events or circumstances may make them more likely to get involved, be it a need for support with caring, or a desire to do something active while unemployed. Similarly, other commitments of time and energy such as child care or full-time work may act as disincentives. Overall, however, we must conclude that the motivations for activity are not obviously connected to the descriptive factors analyzed here. The factors do of course play an important role in whether people are or are not able to get involved, and as such are worthy of both analysis and policy attention. But they are not sufficient as an explanation of the "inner mystery" of the local activist.

Conclusion

While preliminary and tentative, the results of my analysis appear to have important implications for policy toward communities and stimulation of philanthropy. First, the factors around participation, concern, and "voluntarism" are highly complex and currently little understood at the population level; there is a clear need for more quantitative (as well as qualitative) research.

Second, there is significant untapped potential in the community that could be harnessed by local groups and organizations. If between one in ten and one in five local people are locally active, there must be more such people available, and overcoming barriers to participation is especially important in tapping these resources.

Third, self-help as a motive for local action is very important. While there are some altruists around, far more people are currently unengaged or alienated but may be encouraged to become involved in community activity if they perceive a potential advantage to themselves or their household. In the same way that disinterest and barriers to participation lead to a vicious circle of alienation from the locality, so encouragement of participation and self-help can bring cumulative benefits to both individuals and communities. We should recognize the convergence of interests between individuals, the groups in which they are active, and society more widely. This is not to say that a precise balance sheet could be drawn up to itemize who is getting what, or that interests always will converge. The benefits can be seen in a longer and wider context. Motivated individuals who are being supported by group involvement have a greater incentive for continued involvement, and to behave altruistically toward others in their time of need—a kind of delayed reciprocity. At the same time, strong and self-confident local organizations help maintain the fabric of local communities, which are themselves the bedrock of society.

I believe the message to policy makers in this field is clear. They must see philanthropy by individuals in this context, and must try to support local community activity to a greater extent than previously. In this way I believe more philanthropic behavior will ultimately be generated. Policy needs to involve people by recognizing and embracing their needs and problems and showing how, by getting involved locally, these needs and problems can be addressed. I believe the emphasis should be put on the participative rather than the volunteering dimension of community activity. My analysis also shows the different levels of involvement that people have. I believe that, tracked over time, we would observe a progression by individuals through the levels to the point where many become centrally involved for a period, before withdrawing once more. Policies should be followed that encourage the alienated and uninterested to become involved at a relatively shallow level if necessary, but with encouragement for closer engagement over time, if desired. More community activists will be found by recognizing this than by looking for the atypical altruists. But there must also be understanding and respect for those not willing to become involved in community activity—the accusations of apathy directed by community activists against other people in the locality become tiresome. Not only are many unable to participate, many are socially isolated and likely to be deeply uncomfortable with demands for new relationships.

Fourth, the disincentive to local activism attributed to child-care responsibilities poses a challenge for the transmission of caring attitudes across the generations. I have no sociopsychological element in this research, but I believe that engagement with the local community and understanding of caring attitudes may be influenced by the experience of the family during its early, formative years. Confrontation by a society that organizes itself so as to create barriers to participation by, for example, inflexible arrangements, lack of child-care facilities, and exclusion of single parents must act against the integration of young families into the locality. Such inflexibility is, I believe, often just as much a feature of local groups as of more formal organizations and must be addressed—young families are in effect discriminated against by many local community groups. Finally, the spread of different types of people in local groups is wide and diverse. Therefore, local authorities and others wishing to engage with the community more extensively could make more use of local groups, both as a generally representative sample of the community and as a means of reaching other people in the community. Regeneration initiatives, planning proposals, and other policy issues that will affect communities are increasingly required to have input from communities. This analysis suggests that local groups contain a wide enough cross section for them to be a useful surrogate of wide community perspectives. Additionally, by working with local groups—for instance, making information available—institutions would have a way of reaching households in many different circumstances, and via them, of reaching still other groups in society.

References

Bell, J. *Community Development Teamwork: Measuring the Impact*. London: Community Development Foundation, 1992a.

Bell, J. *The Components of Community Action*. Dublin: European Foundation for the Improvement of Living and Working Conditions, 1992b.

Chanan, G. *Out of the Shadows: Strategies for Local Community Action in Europe*. Dublin: European Foundation for the Improvement of Living and Working Conditions, 1992.

Halfpenny, P. "Volunteering in Britain." In *Charity Trends*. (13th ed.) London: Charities Aid Foundation, 1990.

Shanks, K., Bell, J., and Chanan, G. *Social Change and Local Action in an Urban Area*. London: Community Development Foundation, 1991.

Chapter Twenty

Fragmentation in America's Nonprofit Sector

Julian Wolpert

New statistical evidence shows that some places in the United States are generous and others are parsimonious, so Americans face wide disparities in services and income transfers depending on where they happen to live. These disparities are evident in both public and nonprofit sectors and cannot be explained away by differences in community wealth or distress. The "new federalism" of the 1980s aggravated the equity problems by decentralizing funding responsibility to state and local government and nonprofits, thereby helping to legitimize local standards of generosity and their disparities.

Lessons from observing our severely decentralized and fragmented nonprofit sector help to inform public sector efforts about the impacts of relying on local communities to "take care of their own." Study findings point to the need for some selective recentralization of service responsibility, especially for programs targeted for maintaining safety nets.

Greater disclosure about who we are and what we do in the nonprofit sector provides both greater opportunities and responsibilities. We are improving our ability to measure the nonprofit sector with some degree of comprehensiveness and rigor. Nonprofits have been harmed and also have benefited from the lack of good information in the past. Good news and the remaining deficiencies will be revealed and we had better be ready.

Note: The research discussed in this paper is part of a larger study being conducted with support from the Twentieth Century Fund and the Nonprofit Research Fund at the Aspen Institute.

On the one hand, we will be better able to document the vital niche of nonprofits in America's service structure and economy, their growth, their diversified bases of support, their often precarious efforts to find sufficient support to maintain service levels, and their need for fair and balanced treatment by government. On the other hand, the improved data may just possibly reveal that the autonomy that nonprofits enjoy creates important service disparities that can probably be addressed only through some restructuring of the nonprofit sector.

Qualifying the Conventional Wisdom

Some early findings from a preliminary review of the recent literature and my own analyses can be examined alongside the conventional wisdom to illustrate the dilemmas of greater disclosure. For example, included among the conventional wisdom is that Americans are very generous and that nonprofits are very effective in delivering services to those who need them most. The common threads in recent findings suggest that the conventional wisdom needs to be qualified somewhat and that improved data yield both research and policy imperatives. My argument is that preparations can now be made with our better data for improved self-study. A list of preliminary findings for which we must be prepared includes the following items:

1. American generosity varies significantly within income, social, and demographic groups and from place to place in both levels and targeting of contributions.

2. Differences in giving levels have been declining but principally due to the harsher economic environment in the more generous places rather than greater generosity in the more parsimonious places.

3. Giving rates are higher where per capita income is higher,

where the political and cultural ideology is liberal rather than conservative, and where distress levels and population numbers are lower.

4. Higher giving rates are associated with greater targeting for nonprofit educational, cultural, and health organizations rather than truly charitable services.

5. Little is still known about recipients of nonprofit services, who they are, why they have turned to nonprofits for aid, their satisfaction with the services received, and those who have not been served.

6. The increased sorting of Americans into socially homogeneous communities has reproduced a nonprofit service infrastructure in the suburbs often at the expense of support for center-city and rural institutions—that is, the sector's real growth as a service provider is quite small.

7. Our severely fragmented and atomized nonprofit sector is not structured to address disparities between service sectors and regions of the country.

These preliminary findings are not surprising, but they are suggestive of what improved data are likely to reveal and of the policy attention that may be required to these and similar issues within the nonprofit sector. Let us look at some of these issues and data findings in more detail and explore their possible policy implications.

Fragmented Structure of the Nonprofit Sector

Improved information is becoming available about the structure of the American nonprofit sector. The data indicate that the nonprofit sector is even more fragmented than either local government or the private sector (see Wolpert, 1992, for a discussion of decentralization and equity in public and nonprofit sectors). Local autonomy in the nonprofit sector enables charitable agencies to effectively match local preferences for services with revenues for their provision. Yet nonprofits in contrast to government can be decentralized and fragmented because of their modest and specialized niche in our three-sector national, regional, and local service economy, where responsibility for maintaining safety nets and funding many health and social services still resides primarily with national (and secondarily with state) government. The nominal role of nonprofits as agents of redistributive transfers has largely been ceded to a federated welfare state that takes more or less responsibility for maintaining safety nets, depending on national and state political climates and mandates. Even though the federal government is now more reluctant to act as an agent of redistribution, the nonprofit sector lacks both the resources and the infrastructure to respond at a sufficient intercommunity level.

Even before the Great Depression of the 1930s, philanthropists and nonprofit leadership recognized that structural problems of poverty at the national level or even highly localized poverty concentrations could not be addressed sufficiently through their decentralized and fragmented structure. Federal and state government acceptance of their more prominent redistributive role at that time gave nonprofits greater liberty to pursue activities more suited to their localized bases of support. Local autonomy permits donations to be channeled primarily into civic and community services and amenities that enhance the variety and quality of life.

The U.S. nonprofit sector has never been centralized or even highly integrated nationally. Management decisions are fragmented and atomized among the hundreds of thousands of separate nonprofit organizations. Allocation decisions within the limits of the tax code are prerogatives of boards of trustees and professional management of the separate agencies. Most of the sector has neither a hierarchical structure nor distinctive regional tiers with discretion over allocation of contributions. The nonprofit sector is voluntary, noncoercive, does not issue entitlements or guarantee safety nets, and has no formal obligations to other localities or the national society. The nonprofit sector has remained decentralized to serve its local donor base and is not structured to make transfers between communities.

Local control by nonprofits in increasingly income-segregated communities requires them to compete for gifts and member fees by offering good value (that is, direct benefit) to contributors in services per donated dollar. Communities that are generous in their cross-subsidies and transfers must sooner or later yield to the standards of the more frugal localities or face a potential magnet effect in attracting the service dependent to their midst. Presumably, communities pay a high price by persisting with either public or nonprofit services targeted more to the poor than to cultural, educational, and health care amenities used by the donors themselves.

Effects of Fragmentation

The decentralized structure of the nonprofit sector and its effects are not difficult to demonstrate. The nonprofit sector is overwhelmingly community based. In general, locally raised funds are not systematically allocated on the basis of charitable needs. Furthermore, communities are largely on their own to raise funds for services preferred by donors without being able to count on contributions by outsiders. Revenues are substantially raised and spent in the same communities or metropolitan areas. Generally, little leakage occurs between these areas except when localized natural disasters lead to national, albeit temporary, relief efforts.

Some important exceptions to local autonomy do occur. Community foundations, donors' forums, and federated agencies like the United Way often assume the function of negotiating allocations, at least among human service providers. Many of the largest philanthropic foundations and corporations have an opportunity to target their contributions nationally. A number of the relief, health, and disease campaigns are nationally integrated, although most operate through state and local chapters. Some of the church groups and charities also conduct national fundraising campaigns based on prior agreements covering the division of proceeds between local groups and national or international charitable functions.

No precise measures are available yet about the proportion of donations that are both raised and spent locally, but estimates range from 85 to 90 percent. The national health and overseas relief campaigns alone raise only about 6 percent of the $130 billion of total annual donations. In effect, this means that local autonomy in allocation decisions is effectively able to give highest priority to local preferences rather than disparities between communities.

Decentralized autonomy in fundraising and allocation had a more redistributive effect when communities were a blend of rich and poor. However, decades of urban flight and suburbanization have produced a high degree of income and wealth segregation and distinctive agendas for nonprofit services. The focus of fundraising in affluent communities can be targeted to pluralistic tastes through serving thin markets for amenities not provided by private or public sectors. In the needier large cities, the share allocated for charitable purposes is greater but at the expense of amenity services. Of course, local resources and the magnitude of nonprofit efforts in the poorest large cities cannot be large enough alone to address structural or deep-seated social problems. Nonprofits can play only a minor role in these cities, largely through providing the infrastructure and advocacy for publicly supported human service programs.

One can argue that decentralized autonomy in the nonprofit sector is a mechanism for maximizing the rate of donations. A more centralized scheme even at a regional tier could reduce donation levels, because many donors would realize less direct benefits from their gifts. Greater centralization would jeopardize support for many highly valued local cultural, education, and health organizations whose claims for support may not be able to compete with preferences and priorities at metropolitan, state, or national levels.

Local autonomy in the nonprofit sector means that the level and variety of services available to community residents are affected by the resources and generosity of donors in that community. Evidence is presented here to show that American communities differ not only by level of fiscal resources and distress but also by their rates and types of generosity. In addition, the analysis is intended to test whether the variations in generosity levels are stable or declining (as a result of magnet effects) for charitable (that is, redistributive) donations as opposed to amenity-supporting contributions.

Preliminary Data Analysis

A satisfactory data set on American generosity for examining place-to-place differences would include information on donations targeted to specific service sectors in each community, along with data on income distribution and public sector service support in the same communities. However, few data on contributions are disaggregated by place. To examine differences in donations, United Way (UW) contributions per employee in America's eighty-five largest metropolitan areas are used here for the years 1972, 1986, and 1989 (Table 20.1).

These data show an extreme range in donations per employee (an eighteenfold difference from the most to the least generous places in 1972 and a thirteenfold difference in 1986 and 1989). Donation levels were highest in the smaller areas with a half to one million population. The analyses indicate a significant negative relationship between 1972 contribution levels and their changes from 1972 to 1986 (Table 20.2). Strong and consistent differences in contribution rates between the places persisted over the entire period but were diminished over time by a relative decline in generosity in the most generous places. UW donations per employee were initially greater in lower-income areas but increased with per capita income growth and declined with changes in metro poverty levels during the 1972–1989 period. These results at least partly

Table 20.1. **Private Generosity Measures for Metropolitan Areas.**

Metro	*UW89*	*UW72*	*UW72-89*	*FED90*	*FED81*	*FED81–90*	*NPSUPP*	*Human*	*Kidney*	*AIDS*	*Conserv*
Akron	41	30	1.35	272	195	1.39	0.22	0.25	0.006	0.25	11
Albany	22	16	1.41	NA	111	NA	0.85	0.04	0.017	0.51	46
Allentown	32	NA	NA	306	228	1.34	0.26	0.14	0.011	0.25	55
Anaheim	16	8	1.83	18	18	1.00	0.14	0.23	0.013	0.64	92
Atlanta	38	14	2.69	161	107	1.50	0.47	0.10	0.006	0.53	52
Austin	19	8	2.28	81	62	1.31	0.20	0.25	0.011	0.58	47
Baltimore	33	11	2.93	228	131	1.74	0.29	0.18	0.015	0.35	34
Bergen	13	4	2.99	139	88	1.58	0.15	0.24	0.016	0.71	29
Birmingham	41	16	2.62	466	304	1.53	0.18	0.15	0.004	0.19	57
Boston	38	11	3.32	120	80	1.50	1.15	0.08	0.008	0.62	9
Buffalo	38	18	2.09	162	129	1.41	0.29	0.23	0.012	0.36	38
Charlotte	44	13	3.40	311	148	2.10	0.30	0.12	0.006	0.54	55
Chicago	33	12	2.65	218	140	1.55	0.43	0.14	0.013	0.55	36
Cincinnati	60	21	2.90	241	163	1.48	0.32	0.19	0.008	0.34	58
Cleveland	69	24	2.83	387	272	1.42	0.44	0.16	0.010	0.36	10
Columbus	59	14	4.09	417	214	1.95	0.37	0.22	0.009	0.37	85
Dallas	38	13	2.84	177	241	0.73	0.37	0.12	0.007	0.48	60
Dayton	49	21	2.35	330	214	1.54	0.20	0.14	0.007	0.45	70
Denver	37	13	2.87	112	131	0.85	0.31	0.13	0.007	0.50	55
Detroit	36	22	1.67	284	268	1.06	0.27	0.17	0.008	0.28	21
Fort Lauderdale	13	6	2.03	69	60	1.14	0.10	NA	0.002	0.34	39
Fort Worth	39	15	2.69	169	209	0.81	0.16	0.30	0.007	0.26	67
Fresno	6	6	0.93	NA	NA	NA	0.23	0.37	0.007	0.18	33
Gary	27	15	1.73	322	304	1.06	0.14	0.37	0.006	0.14	15

Table 20.1. (cont.)

Metro	*UW89*	*UW72*	*UW72-89*	*FED90*	*FED81*	*FED81–90*	*NPSUPP*	*Human*	*Kidney*	*AIDS*	*Conserv*
Grand Rapids	41	13	3.19	304	256	1.19	0.42	0.21	0.014	0.42	74
Grnsbro/W-S	56	15	3.72	372	322	1.16	0.16	0.19	0.007	0.18	48
Grnvl/Spartb	35	11	3.24	NA	NA	NA	0.26	NA	0.008	NA	44
Harrisburg	45	14	3.20	302	225	1.34	0.26	0.44	0.015	0.48	94
Hartford	71	NA	NA	263	180	1.46	0.44	0.20	0.008	0.57	18
Honolulu	45	17	2.66	48	NA	NA	0.31	0.22	0.023	0.70	54
Houston	38	12	3.27	170	170	1.00	0.24	NA	0.006	0.24	51
Indianapolis	44	14	3.06	417	263	1.59	0.29	0.21	0.008	0.31	57
Jacksonville	31	13	2.37	151	156	0.97	0.24	0.32	0.006	0.33	60
Jersey City	10	NA	NA	NA	66	NA	0.57	0.27	0.050	2.91	13
Kansas City K	39	13	2.99	213	156	1.37	0.28	0.25	0.008	NA	45
Kansas City M	43	16	2.65	213	156	1.37	0.00	NA	0.008	NA	40
Knoxville	36	13	2.75	243	140	1.74	0.22	0.11	0.007	0.19	72
Los Angeles	22	9	2.37	101	75	1.35	0.36	NA	0.001	2.22	35
Louisville	38	NA	NA	250	224	1.12	0.31	0.13	0.010	0.36	38
Memphis	39	16	2.45	263	156	1.69	0.33	0.13	0.005	0.29	35
Miami	24	13	1.93	80	76	1.05	0.33	0.16	0.014	0.82	21
Middlesex	41	6	6.95	87	46	1.88	0.14	0.28	0.011	0.47	48
Milwaukee	37	19	1.96	322	300	1.07	0.31	0.38	0.013	0.32	38
Minneapolis	51	25	2.04	436	324	1.35	0.35	0.22	0.009	NA	26
Monmouth	7	2	2.74	54	31	1.75	0.11	0.18	0.014	0.51	41
Nashville	41	16	2.59	510	338	1.51	0.33	0.15	0.005	0.20	40
Nassau Co	7	4	1.75	NA	101	NA	0.20	0.28	0.018	NA	24
New Haven	28	18	1.54	131	94	1.39	0.69	0.15	0.021	1.19	25
New Orleans	32	13	2.51	200	182	1.10	0.16	0.30	0.005	0.28	57

Table 20.1. (cont.)

Metro	*UW89*	*UW72*	*UW72-89*	*FED90*	*FED81*	*FED81–90*	*NPSUPP*	*Human*	*Kidney*	*AIDS*	*Conserv*
New York City	26	NA	NA	73	56	1.31	0.97	0.12	0.020	NA	10
Newark	38	NA	NA	258	105	2.45	0.12	0.19	0.002	0.10	34
Norfolk	39	13	2.92	145	132	1.10	0.25	0.04	0.008	0.42	56
Oakland	28	NA	NA	93	70	1.33	0.21	0.29	0.009	0.95	4
Oklahoma City	29	NA	NA	199	382	0.52	0.26	0.13	0.004	0.26	59
Omaha	44	16	2.80	382	289	1.32	0.28	0.17	0.007	0.35	61
Orlando	18	NA	NA	108	142	0.76	0.22	0.25	0.012	0.51	66
Oxnard	16	NA	NA	NA	NA	NA	0.19	0.38	0.009	0.82	92
Philadelphia	35	16	2.11	119	86	1.38	0.38	0.15	0.010	0.51	28
Phoenix	23	8	2.80	84	61	1.38	0.19	NA	0.006	0.34	65
Pittsburgh	42	NA	NA	211	175	1.21	0.40	0.13	0.013	0.27	23
Portland	28	14	1.96	233	177	1.32	0.26	0.16	0.008	0.41	30
Providence	27	20	1.38	269	195	1.38	0.71	0.20	0.011	0.57	25
Raleigh	32	10	3.19	55	28	1.97	0.87	0.09	0.010	0.52	32
Richmond	40	9	4.49	338	227	1.49	0.38	0.42	0.015	0.39	75
Riverside	17	13	1.36	NA	NA	NA	0.07	0.25	0.003	0.16	57
Rochester	74	36	2.05	155	134	1.16	0.39	0.15	0.012	0.34	38
Sacramento	19	8	2.25	93	65	1.43	0.15	0.31	0.007	0.36	32
Salt Lake City	14	8	1.67	123	164	0.75	0.10	0.29	0.003	0.21	62
San Antonio	41	11	3.63	152	198	0.77	0.20	0.22	0.006	0.41	41
San Diego	25	12	2.10	143	106	1.35	0.21	0.27	0.006	0.68	61
San Francisco	28	12	2.31	137	155	0.88	1.16	0.11	0.016	3.15	18
San Jose	30	9	3.49	52	48	1.06	0.21	0.45	0.005	0.48	23
Scranton	27	13	2.07	392	301	1.30	0.15	0.16	0.005	0.14	54

Table 20.1. (cont.)

Metro	*UW89*	*UW72*	*UW72-89*	*FED90*	*FED81*	*FED81–90*	*NPSUPP*	*Human*	*Kidney*	*AIDS*	*Conserv*
Seattle	44	NA	NA	235	127	1.85	0.27	0.24	0.004	0.44	25
Springfield	42	NA	NA	173	152	1.14	0.46	0.36	0.008	0.61	13
St. Louis	47	23	2.09	191	126	1.52	0.30	0.13	0.010	0.32	36
Syracuse	37	18	2.07	159	128	1.24	0.34	0.23	0.010	0.32	42
Tampa	19	11	1.78	100	82	1.22	0.18	0.08	0.004	0.18	67
Toledo	41	27	1.56	268	226	1.19	0.27	0.17	0.010	0.22	41
Tucson	45	17	2.72	115	86	1.34	0.22	0.24	0.011	0.41	33
Tulsa	55	NA	NA	808	1294	0.62	0.43	0.10	0.006	0.24	48
West Palm Beach	23	NA	NA	179	66	2.72	0.20	NA	0.024	0.91	58
Washington	34	11	3.14	123	82	1.50	1.01	NA	0.025	1.21	52
Wilmington	62	28	2.24	136	100	1.36	0.22	0.38	0.011	0.32	23
Youngstown	30	16	1.92	369	279	1.32	0.12	0.30	0.003	0.13	21

Where:

UW89, UW86 & UW72 = United Way contributions per employee in 1989, 1986, and 1972 and UW72–89 = their relative changes between 1972 and 1989. Source: United Way of America.

FED90, FED81 & FED81–90 = Contributions per Jewish resident to Federation in 1990, 1981 and the relative changes between 1981 and 1990. Source: Council of Jewish Federations.

NPSUPP = Gifts and grants to metro nonprofits per capita, 1989. Source: INDEPENDENT SECTOR.

HUMAN = Share of gifts and grants to nonprofits accounted for by human service agencies, 1989. Source: INDEPENDENT SECTOR.

KIDNEY = Donations per capita to the American Kidney Foundation, 1990.

AIDS = Donors per capita to the American Foundation for AIDS Research, 1990.

CONSERV = American Conservative Union rating of district House members, 1990.

confirm the assumption that donations rise with affluence and decline with distress.

UW data, of course, are not ideal indicators of community generosity because of the variations in how campaigns are organized (Brilliant, 1990). Additional data series are needed to corroborate the UW patterns. Comparable data were available on donations to Jewish Federated Campaigns (that have a similarly local structure for fundraising) in the same metropolitan areas for 1981, 1986, and 1990. These are total contributions to local Federations divided by the estimated Jewish population in the metropolitan region. The analysis indicates that donation levels were highly correlated (.48) with UW contributions in the same places (Table 20.2). The data also indicate similar extreme ranges from the most to the least generous places (a forty-five-fold difference) and the same significant trend toward smoothing of differences. Similar findings were found for the Catholic Campaign for Human Development.

Data on giving levels for the American Kidney Foundation and the American Foundation for AIDS Research tell a similar story. Donations for kidney research average only one cent per capita across the eighty-five metropolitan areas, but their range is fifty times between the least and most generous places. The range is forty times for donors for AIDS research. Furthermore, places generous in UW and Federation donations (that is, smaller cities) are less generous donors to kidney and AIDS research, which have higher participation rates in the largest West and East Coast metro areas.

The correspondence of findings for these quite distinct data series provides additional confirmation for the hypotheses concerning extreme place-to-place differences in nonprofit generosity levels, the positive relationship of donations to per capita income changes, and the smoothing trend in rates of giving. Data available at the state level only, including per capita contributions to the American Diabetes, Cancer, Heart, AIDS Research, and Planned Parenthood Associations and for Public TV and Radio, show similar close associations in donation levels among the states and wide vari-

Table 20.2. Correlation of Generosity Measures in the Eighty-Five Largest Metropolitan Areas.

Variables	*UW89*	*UW86*	*UW72*	*UW 72–89*	*FED90*	*FED81*	*FED 81–90*	*NP SUPP*	*Human*	*Kidney*	*AIDS*	*Health Variables*
UW89	*	0.95	0.73	0.21	0.48	8.43	0.36	0.08	−0.16	−0.17	−0.26	−0.14 UW89
UW86		*	0.73	0.14	0.44	0.39	0.30	0.05	−0.12	−0.19	−0.28	−0.14 UW86
UW72			*	−0.30	0.38	0.41	0.41	0.09	−0.14	0.00	−0.17	−0.30 UW72
UW72–89				*	−0.05	−0.19	−0.19	−0.02	0.10	0.11	0.03	0.47 UW72–89
FED90					*	0.84	0.04	−0.06	−0.09	−0.24	−0.32	−0.34 FED90
FED81						*	−0.34	−0.13	−0.03	−0.29	−0.33	−0.46 FED81
FED81–90							*	−0.05	−0.10	−0.21	−0.23	−0.33 FED81–90
NPSUPP								*	−0.41	0.41	0.52	0.26 NPSUPP
Human									*	0.04	−0.03	0.00 Human
Kidney										*	0.60	0.30 Kidney
AIDS											*	0.41 AIDS
Wealth												* Wealth

Note: Coefficients >0.19 are significant at 90% level, >0.25 are significant at 95%, >0.29 are significant at 99%.

Where:

UW89, UW86 & UW72 = United Way contributions per employee in 1989, 1986, and 1972 and UW72–89 = their relative changes between 1972 and 1989. Source: United Way of America.

FED90, FED81 & FED81–90 = Contributions per Jewish resident to Federation in 1990, 1981 and the relative changes between 1981 and 1990. Source: Council of Jewish Federations.

NPSUPP = Gifts and grants to metro nonprofits per capita, 1989. Source: INDEPENDENT SECTOR.

HUMAN = Share of gifts and grants to nonprofits accounted for by human service agencies, 1989. Source: INDEPENDENT SECTOR.

KIDNEY = Donations per capita to the American Kidney Foundation, 1990.

AIDS = Donors per capita to the American Foundation for AIDS Research, 1990.

WEALTH = Woodes and Poole wealth index, 1990.

ations between the most and least generous states (Table 20.3). Giving rates are higher in the less populous states and where per capita income is higher and distress levels are lower. Furthermore, except for Heart Association donations, giving levels are significantly higher in the more progressive than in the more traditional states.

These findings provide at least partial evidence for arguing that decentralization of contributions for human services makes recipients of such services vulnerable to wide differences in local generosity that supports such services. The analysis cannot, however, confirm the notion that the most generous communities are forced to cut back generosity levels because of a magnet effect. Clearly, needy people are unlikely to make migration decisions solely on the basis of UW, Jewish Federation, or Catholic support for human services. Their relative consistency over the range of metro areas suggests, however, that local autonomy can be highly prejudicial to low-income people in the less generous places.

Charitable Versus Amenity-Supporting Generosity

Local autonomy in fundraising and allocations has other implications as well. Theory would lead us to expect that the proportion of household contributions targeted to charity (that is, redistributive purposes) is quite small relative to the share devoted to support for amenities or for church membership. The assumption here is that sustained charitable transfers are prompted more by altruistic motives than by expectations of direct or indirect benefit. In contrast, membership fees and support for amenity activities, even though allowable as tax-deductible contributions, often represent the purchase of valued services. The fact that these services are purchased from nonprofit organizations rather than in the market economy has some relevance because the fees often include cross-subsidies for lower-income users. However, charitable donations are more likely than contributions for amenities to target beneficiaries with incomes lower than those of the donors.

Table 20.3. State Measures of Generosity (Thirty-Six States).

State	*Diabetes*	*Heart*	*Cancer*	*Public TV*	*Public Radio*	*Planned Parent*	*AIDS*	*Moral*	*Indiv*	*Trad*
Alabama	0.38	6.66	65.50	0.25	0.03	0.01	42.19	0	1	1
Arizona	1.15	4.78	137.20	1.24	0.05	0.06	155.22	1	0	1
California	0.81	3.76	95.10	1.61	0.01	0.15	NA	1	1	0
Colorado	0.67	2.63	98.40	1.25	0.13	0.09	101.61	1	0	0
Connecticut	0.90	5.79	160.10	0.88	0.11	0.09	428.68	1	1	0
Delaware	0.77	7.69	200.10	NA	NA	0.13	122.03	0	1	1
District	1.34	13.47	120.30	13.00	6.38	0.54	501.28	NA	NA	NA
Florida	0.32	4.40	120.20	0.72	0.01	0.05	381.98	0	1	1
Georgia	0.57	5.16	135.80	0.08	0.01	0.03	106.80	0	1	1
Hawaii	0.50	11.50	196.20	0.63	0.30	0.15	136.88	0	1	1
Illinois	0.59	3.45	89.00	1.25	0.01	0.06	439.00	1	1	0
Indiana	0.77	4.45	69.90	0.55	0.02	0.03	96.38	0	1	0
Kansas	0.83	6.11	112.30	0.64	0.10	0.05	253.01	1	1	0
Kentucky	0.31	4.07	51.70	0.73	0.05	0.02	72.07	0	1	1
Louisiana	0.36	2.66	24.50	0.53	0.04	0.01	89.69	0	1	1
Maryland	1.46	5.32	120.30	0.64	0.04	0.33	222.28	0	1	1
Massachusetts	0.31	4.21	106.40	2.35	0.09	0.30	185.31	1	1	0
Michigan	0.70	2.30	61.60	1.14	0.03	0.05	486.98	1	0	0
Minnesota	1.48	5.35	143.20	1.39	0.19	0.07	334.65	1	0	0
Missouri	1.14	4.49	106.00	0.96	0.02	0.03	82.31	0	1	1
Nebraska	1.07	5.06	74.20	0.84	0.09	0.03	71.40	1	1	0
New Jersey	0.65	2.74	86.30	0.16	0.01	0.17	494.60	0	1	0

Table 20.3. (cont.)

State	*Diabetes*	*Heart*	*Cancer*	*Public TV*	*Public Radio*	*Planned Parent*	AIDS	*Moral*	*Indiv*	*Trad*
New York	1.35	2.72	124.20	2.08	0.01	0.24	NA	1	1	0
North Carolina	0.34	3.53	54.70	0.64	0.03	0.04	73.57	1	0	1
Ohio	0.49	4.80	122.50	0.87	0.02	0.11	155.69	1	1	0
Oklahoma	0.98	5.71	57.20	0.65	0.04	0.02	75.25	0	1	1
Oregon	0.60	3.66	70.70	1.19	0.15	0.10	81.48	1	0	0
Pennsylvania	0.56	5.02	98.50	1.26	0.03	0.07	173.42	0	1	0
Rhode Island	1.02	5.81	102.40	0.24	0.00	0.08	75.13	1	1	0
South Carolina	0.75	3.29	89.60	0.00	0.00	0.02	49.58	0	0	1
Tennessee	0.49	6.01	69.50	0.50	0.03	0.03	442.29	0	0	1
Texas	0.68	5.22	87.30	0.61	0.01	0.03	163.10	0	1	1
Utah	0.64	4.95	83.00	0.80	0.15	0.03	25.46	1	0	0
Virginia	0.76	6.70	114.60	0.49	0.02	0.08	79.62	0	0	1
Washington	1.02	4.12	91.10	1.74	0.05	0.11	65.17	1	1	0
Wisconsin	NA	5.02	90.90	1.06	0.06	0.05	156.37	1	0	0

Where:

Diabetes, Heart, Cancer, Public TV & Radio, Planned Parenthood & AIDS = Contributions per Capita (or relative to effective buying income) to the respective campaigns; Moral, Indiv & Trad = Daniel Elazar scoring of states according to moral, individualistic, and traditional orientations (see Elazar, 1972).

A satisfactory data set would allow us to distinguish charitable gifts from membership fees and support for amenities. The data series used to examine the composition of contributions were derived from the IRS 990 forms filed by nonprofit organizations in the late 1980s and classified according to the National Taxonomy of Exempt Entities (NTEE) code of agency specialization by the National Center for Charitable Statistics. The classification does not provide precise distinctions between charitable as opposed to other functional service categories. Instead, a rough proxy measure is used based on the share of total nonprofit expenditures, assets, and support of organizations in the "human service" category in each of the eighty-five metro areas. Human services are assumed to be somewhat more charitable and redistributive than any of the other service categories (Salamon, 1992). However, this proxy measure is not fully adequate because few nonprofit human service organizations target their activities exclusively to low-income clients (Gronbjerg and others, 1992).

The analyses indicate considerable variation between metro areas in the human service share of total nonprofit support and expenditures (see Table 20.1). The shares are smallest in the largest metro areas and where poverty is most pronounced. Furthermore, the shares are smaller where total per capita gifts and grants to nonprofit agencies are largest (refer to the correlation between NPSUPP and Human in Table 20.2). The findings indicate that places not only vary significantly in the human service component of their generosity, but higher levels of generosity are reflected by greater relative support for purposes other than human services. The analysis also shows that nonprofits have a very modest share of human service support in both the largest and the poorest cities relative to their role in supporting cultural, health, and educational services and relative to public sector local, state, and federal aid.

The nonprofits can also be classified by center-city and suburban locations. Nonprofits in center cities are about three times as prominent as in suburban areas in terms of gifts and grants received, expenditures, and assets (and are about five times as prominent on a per capita basis). Per capita support for AIDS and kidney research are, respectively, two times and 30 percent higher in center-city than in suburban portions of metropolitan areas. Higher poverty rates in center cities also imply that considerable assistance is needed from suburban residents to sustain the nonprofit institutions concentrated in the center city. City nonprofits will be even harder pressed financially if suburbanization leads to greater loosening of ties to these institutions.

The analyses also reveal that 25 percent of support for the center-city nonprofits is targeted to human service organizations relative to 18 percent in the suburbs. Suburbanites can spend more of their donations for civic purposes and to support arts, educational, and health facilities. The data also indicate only a modest (but not significant) relationship between the shares of nonprofit support for human services in center cities relative to their own suburbs. Growing stratification and homogenization have helped to produce different nonprofit agendas in center cities and suburban fringes.

The examination of generosity differences between communities and states does not include analysis of direct and pass-through public sector transfers and service programs at federal, state, or local levels and their effects on private giving. The analysis of these complex interdependencies warrants separate treatment in a subsequent publication.

Conclusion

This chapter has argued that decentralization and fragmentation of support, whether by government or nonprofits, implies a reduced emphasis on equity. The nonprofit sector, as an example of an almost completely decentralized system, largely provides services and amenities to its own local donor base and is not organized to retarget support between service sectors and from places of affluence to places of distress. Greater giving and volunteering does not necessarily trickle down to address equity problems.

These and other findings from the growing data resources provide nonprofit leadership with some important policy alternatives. One option is to develop a better inventory of nonprofit efforts and impacts at national, regional, and service subsector levels to assess the distributional issues. The inventory stage could be followed up with proposals of national and local remedies for the major service gaps and disparities. Another option, of course, is to highlight the contributions nonprofits make to the variety and diversity of American life as a necessary and sufficient rationale for their independent status, rather than as an agent for charitable services. These and other options merit review and discussion within the nonprofit community.

References

Brilliant, E. L. *The United Way*. New York: Columbia University Press, 1990.

Elazar, D. *American Federalism: A View from the States*. New York: Crowell, 1972.

Gronbjerg, K. A., with Nagle, A., Garvin, L., and Wingate, L. *Nonprofit Human Service Facilities in Illinois: Structure, Adequacy, and Management*. Report prepared for the Illinois Facilities Fund, Chicago, 1992.

Salamon, L. M. "The Charitable Behavior of the Charitable Sector: The Case of Social Services." In C. T. Clotfelter (ed.), *Who Benefits from the Nonprofit Sector?* Chicago: University of Chicago Press, 1992.

Wolpert, J. "Decentralization and Equity in Public and Nonprofit Sectors." Paper presented at the annual conference of the Association for Research on Nonprofit Organizations and Voluntary Action (ARNOVA), Yale University, Oct. 1992.

Conclusion: Reflections on Caring and Community

Margaret Gates

This book will have special meaning to practitioners like myself in education and youth service due to the responsibility we feel to instill in children a sense of community and caring. For some readers it will fulfill its promise, while others might find the diversity of themes and approaches confusing and the more technical research reports daunting. For many, it will provide a new web of findings and conclusions on which they can hang what they have already learned through study and experience.

The latter group is the true constituency of the INDEPENDENT SECTOR's own research and its efforts, such as the biennial research forum, to encourage and disseminate the work of academic investigators. These are the practitioners whose personal qualities and professional positions allow them to think broadly and to place their own work in the larger context of the sector. I believe that these are also the individuals who are or will become leaders in the nonprofit world and who will have important roles to play in the formulation of public policy. They are the "big-picture" people and the ones with the "vision thing," as former President Bush would say.

Competing Themes

For such an audience, I would like to conclude this book by emphasizing some of its competing themes and some of my own contrarian views. To begin, there is no consensus with respect to the definition of a *caring society* or whether one exists in the United States today. To some, philanthropy and the nonprofit sector may be the embodiment of our "caring society"; for others, they are but adjuncts to government's role and imperfect ones at that. While religion remains a predominant source of charity, in this pluralistic nation different religious communities require different approaches. What then do we transmit to our children and how do we do it?

The question "What is meant by the concept 'caring society'?" was raised by several authors, including Thomasina Borkman and Maria Parisi in Chapter Seventeen. In a bibliographic search they found few references to that term but did note the increasing use by U.S. scholars of the term *civil society* to describe Western democracies. According to the authors, "Many analysts view the United States as a mixed picture of civil society but certainly not a caring society." For their discussion of self-help groups they constructed their own broad definition of a caring society without saying whether as a nation we meet its standards. While to some this may be dismissed as a problem or semantics, to practitioners who view themselves as caregivers and part of a caring community, it is at the heart of the matter.

In his introduction to the volume, Paul G. Schervish identifies the word *care* as a derivative of the Latin *caritas* and discusses the philosophical arguments as to whether caring must be entirely selfless. Concluding that it does not, he relates this fact to Tocqueville's definition of philanthropy as "self-interest rightly understood." And he reminds us that neither philanthropy nor the nonprofit sector has a corner on virtue "because the charitable sector must rely on the moral sensitivity of those in command of resources."

This issue is also addressed by Lester Salamon and Helmut K. Anheier, who in their cross-national study of nonprofits conclude that while we may be a caring *sector*, we are not a caring *society*. Their chapter—Chapter Sixteen—argues that a large nonprofit sector "may actually signify the weakness rather than the strength of a caring tradition in a society." This follows from the fact that in most nations government is viewed as the appropriate agent of the caring tradition. Salamon and Anheier points out that historically the United States has been less concerned about social equity and welfare than other countries, while at the same time willing to tolerate higher degrees of income inequality.

These authors have raised what I consider to be the paramount public policy issue: What should be the respective roles of government and the so-called third sector? While one might presume that nonprofit practitioners have an interest in claiming as much territory as possible, I find the opposite to be the case. Those I respect the most in this sector have been the strongest voices in resisting the federal government's suggestions that increased human service needs should be met by ever-increasing efforts in the voluntary sector.

In fact, notwithstanding the suggestion of several authors that the INDEPENDENT SECTOR itself has irresponsibly propagated a significant portion of the rhetoric about the power of voluntarism and philanthropy, one of the sanest statements I have seen on the capability of the sector is Brian O'Connell's "What Voluntary Activity Can and Cannot Do for America" (1989). He warned President Bush in 1989: "Voluntary organizations provide wonderful elements of spirit, participation, personal service, influence, and the freedom to do one's own thing, but if we overload them with the basic responsibilities for services, undercut their income, and limit their roles for advocacy and criticism, they will fail us and we will be at another point of national breakdown when people will demand that government do it all" (p. 491).

The fact that Americans actually do most of their caring for each other through government programs rather than through philanthropy is made clearly by Heidi Hartmann and Roberta Spalter-Roth in their chapter on improving welfare (Chapter Fifteen). They are sensitive to the fact that tax-funded income-redistribution programs are vulnerable to attacks such as they suffered during the Reagan-Bush years, when it was suggested that the programs actually caused dependency by the poor. When public opinion turns in this direction, not only are the poor stigmatized but taxpayer support for the programs erodes, jeopardizing their future and our claim to a society that cares for poor families.

For all practitioners who focus on children, particularly those from low-income families, it is vital that we be prepared to enter the public debate on welfare reform. To do so, research and analysis such as is contained in Chapter Fifteen is needed. Dissemination of such information to nonprofit practitioners by a nonprofit research group exemplifies the symbiosis within the sector at its best.

On the issue of the respective roles of the nonprofit and government sectors in caring for people, Michael K. Briand and Jennifer Alstad put forward a third alternative. In Chapter Thirteen, they argue that "caring [defined as the willingness to give freely of one's time, energy, or personal resources to help others], admirable and necessary though it may be, is no substitute for what we require if we are to respond effectively to our nation's most pressing social problems: the revitalization of our public life through a practice of deliberative, participatory democratic politics." The authors challenge us to name a single social problem the mitigation of which is owed in substantial measure to a "caring" person or organization. They also decry the "caring professions," which they say have paternalistically turned citizens into clients while creating "fiefdoms" for themselves. Further, the alternative they see is not government, which in their view bears considerable responsibility for the current state of affairs, but a new infrastructure of interest-driven public discourse.

While such solutions are not within the frame of reference of many practitioners, the arguments against the therapeutic model and for community consensus with respect to individual responsibility may sound familiar, since they had considerable political currency during the 1980s. Surely no professional in the human service field should remain ignorant of this school of thought.

Practitioners will identify with and learn from other critiques of the sector in this book. Julian Wolpert's contribution in Chapter Twenty, anticipating new data from the National Center for

Charitable Statistics that will fly in the face of conventional wisdom, discusses structural problems within the sector. Chief among these is the fact that most philanthropic money is raised and spent in the same location, an arrangement that worked better when communities were a blend of rich and poor. But urban flight and suburbanization have resulted in the segregation of wealth. Poor communities have greater human service needs and a smaller donor base, while rich communities can afford more "amenities" (cultural, health, and educational organizations). Those of us who have worked in national human service agencies whose local affiliates depend on the United Way and other community fundraising sources are painfully aware of this phenomenon. Whatever can be learned from new data bases that will suggest how to ameliorate this situation will be welcomed.

Another chapter that promises new data of interest to those of us working with racial and ethnic minorities is Chapter Fourteen, by Steven L. Paprocki and Robert O. Bothwell. They are with the National Committee for Responsive Philanthropy (NCRP), whose mission is to make philanthropy more responsive to the socially, economically, and politically disenfranchised. This organization is little known to most local practitioners but has attracted the support of many national nonprofit leaders over its nearly twenty-year history. It has been a vehement critic of the United Way's grip on workplace solicitation, among other things, and therefore could be considered a foe of the large national human service agencies that are the prime beneficiaries of the United Way campaigns. However, for organizations serving racial and ethnic minorities and women, NCRP can be an ally and a source of information about how organized philanthropy is responding to those populations.

As a former social service agency executive, I was especially interested in historian Peter Dobkin Hall's chapter (Chapter Eight). He describes the alternating ascendencies of religion and politics as the leading voices in public discourse from the beginning of our national history. By doing so he creates a context for contemporary events that is especially valuable to those working in youth-serving agencies, some of which played major roles in the historical developments he records.

For example, he tells us that from the roots of the YMCA movement, founded in the 1850s to counter politically radical young men's organizations, sprang the Boys Clubs, Boy Scouts, and Girl Scouts as "character-building" groups. Gradually the involvement of teachers and social workers redefined character education from a set of moral concerns to a set of criteria for psychological and social adjustment. He also reports that the "suburbanization" of America resulted in these organizations, as well as churches, affirming their sense of themselves as a privileged class.

Because organizations often fail to recognize such interpretations of their own histories, it is extremely important that others do so. We cannot envision the future of our sector without understanding the societal forces that have shaped and will continue to shape its directions.

Hall's chapter also focuses our attention on a strong theme of the volume: religion. The author traces the important but diminishing role of church leaders in framing public discussion generally and particularly with respect to the education of youth. He notes, for example, that although President Clinton attributes religious roots to the community service movement, the movement itself makes no such claims and has adopted instead the therapeutic language of personal development. In his conclusion, Hall projects "an increasing willingness to justify educating the young for community and national service in explicitly religious and political terms."

I am not among the practitioners who would like to see a greater role for religion in the work of mainstream youth-serving agencies. Therefore, I would encourage Hall or others to look carefully at the varying positions these agencies take on recognizing God in their membership pledges, denying membership to young people deemed immoral because of their sexual orientation, taking positions on issues such as abortion rights on religious or moral grounds, and so on. The issues are similar to those faced by schools, except that public schools are considered an extension of government and therefore affected by the principle of separation of church and state. Nonprofit organizations, while not always bound by that principle, often prefer to play by the same rules on the grounds that they are publicly supported and because they wish to maximize pluralism.

Another chapter in which we hear a strong religious theme is Chapter One. Its author is Virginia A. Hodgkinson, who as vice president for research for the INDEPENDENT SECTOR was instrumental in setting the agenda for the research forum that generated this publication. Under her stewardship, surveys have been done to gather data on patterns of giving and volunteering. From the point of view of practitioners, the value of this information cannot be overestimated. In her chapter she analyzes data from various surveys to learn how caring traditions are passed on.

Perhaps the most consistent and least surprising finding of her analyses is that "membership in religious institutions and particularly frequency of attendance at religious services is a strong predictor of giving and volunteering." Part of the reason for this is, as Hodgkinson says, "that churches are voluntary institutions and must be totally supported by the membership. . . . They are in essence the first shared community beyond the family." I would add that since a principal tenet of Christianity, and I believe of the world's other major religions, is charity, followers of those faiths would be more likely than others to practice charity.

What was not so obvious to me was that with respect to caring for others, "Religions may differ in the way they think about need and the way that they provide aid," as John E. Tropman points out in Chapter Eleven. His concept of the "Catholic ethic" as contrasted with the Protestant ethic is that the former relies less on charity and more on "share-ity," which implies "that all have access to some portion of resources, and that, when need occurs, they should be shared." He suggests further that the Protestant ethic embodies the notion of the unworthy poor who may not deserve assistance.

In Chapter Nine, Eliezer Jaffe explains still another approach to charity, *gemiluth chasadim*—an act of benevolence toward one's fellow human beings or, in practice, an interest-free loan. In most large Jewish communities in America, Europe, and Israel, wealthy Orthodox families lend money without interest to needy members of the community. Important in this tradition is the belief that making a loan rather than a gift preserves the recipient's sense of self-respect.

Amani Kandil tells us that in the Islamic philanthropic tradition in Egypt, *Zakat* or charitable tithing is obligatory for individuals and corporations. Much of the money and goods given reach the poor through mosques. Unfortunately, it is difficult to study or document giving patterns because a principle of Islam is that "the left hand must not know what the right hand is giving"—the admonition of the prophet Mohammed that Muslims must give in secret.

Such traditions tell us that while the idea of charity is common to most major religions, the way it is offered varies. In teaching the young to be giving, the spirit in which they are asked to do this is important. Several authors have cited their concern that children will become proud of their good works or develop an attitude of noblesse oblige.

How then in a pluralistic society do practitioners in secular settings instill the will and ability in our children to care for others? With my practitioner's eye I moved through the chapters of the book that deal specifically with children. In Ervin Staub's chapter on the origins of caring—Chapter Two—I found the psychologist's interesting discussion of child development preceded by this daunting statement: "We cannot teach children caring values without experiences that predispose them to care. A child who experiences rejection and hostility and develops negative feelings about people is not going to learn through instruction to care about others. Caring about people is rooted in experiences of interaction with other human beings."

Staub's research and analysis led him to the concept of the "prosocial value orientation," which he believes is more important in governing caring behavior than is empathy or morality. He then constructed four "worldviews": (1) a caring worldview (prosocial orientation), associated with the largest number of kinds of helping; (2) a religious worldview, strongly associated with charitable donations and helping one's own community; (3) a liberal worldview, associated with creating social change; and (4) a materialistic worldview, associated with acquiring power and wealth rather than helping others. I find this analysis insightful because it teases apart three different caring orientations. This framework enables practitioners to develop clearer strategies for encouraging in children the desired behaviors.

Another appealing aspect of Staub's chapter is his reach beyond the definition of *caring* used in Hodgkinson's chapter, explicitly accepted in Carson's, and implicitly adopted by others. That definition is weighted toward direct personal help, volunteering, or giving money. While it is consistent with the INDEPENDENT SECTOR survey definition and is perhaps useful as a means of creating parameters for our discussion, I found it limiting. So I was pleased that Staub extended his discussion (as did others) to behavior in the public domain and even to national policy. Questions must be raised and answered about the extent of our caring: Do we care collectively for everyone equally regardless of race, nationality, economic status? Do we care more about Americans than about Bosnians or Somalis or Haitians? As parents, teachers, or mentors we must expect that at some point in their moral development children will ask such questions.

In light of Hodgkinson's important conclusion that the earlier children become members of religious or voluntary organizations the better in terms of their projected rates of giving and volunteering, practitioners may want to examine what opportunities they make available to elementary school–aged children. In that regard, I was dismayed that Virginia A. Walter—author of Chapter Six—had difficulty locating a Los Angeles organization sponsoring a community service program for children under twelve. I know that a number of major youth-serving agencies such as the Girl Scouts and the Boy Scouts have for decades specialized in giving their young members opportunities to help others—to contribute to their communities and to support their own organizations.

Fortunately, Boys and Girls Clubs of America have shared with us their instructive experience in public housing. Steven Schinke and Roxanne Spillett's evaluation research shows that the establishment of a Boys and Girls Club in a housing project creates a more caring community, but as they point out in Chapter Seven, "A research question still to be answered is to what extent a Boys and Girls Club or similar organization creates more caring children and adolescents."

I would like to see one of the university-based nonprofit research centers tackle that question in collaboration with several national youth-serving organizations. Most national agencies have statements of purpose and curricular material from decades ago as well as lists of past members who could be surveyed. While I recognize the considerable methodological problems that such research raises, the project could provide the answer to whether (and how) the well-established youth organizations are agents for creating more caring young people.

Silvia Blitzer Golombek's chapter, "Children as Philanthropists: The Younger, the Better" (Chapter Five), asks for a new paradigm. She would have us stop thinking of young children as "human becomings" and instead see them as complete human beings with skills and experience to contribute to society. She points out that authors like Jonathan Kozol and Robert Coles have long looked at and listened to children in this way. She also cites the youth service school of thought that holds that by taking responsibility for someone else or for a social cause, a child internalizes a new self-image—that of problem solver or change maker. Finally, she offers us the service-learning model where the teacher, student, and community become partners in a project integrated into the curriculum. The student is involved from the design stage through the evaluation. These ideas have gained substantial support in education and youth work, as well as in the White House, which through the Commission on National and Community Service recently developed the Americorp program incorporating this model.

While commenting on the work of authors Walter, Golombek, and Staub, I would like to note that all acknowledged but did not explore gender issues in their chapters. Because of my background in the field of social service and informal education for girls and young women, I naturally feel that this was a lost opportunity. The volunteering and giving patterns of women and men are different, and we need to know why if we expect to work with girls and boys to increase these caring behaviors. Survey data published by the INDEPENDENT SECTOR hopefully will be analyzed by researchers for this purpose. Hodgkinson used these data to explain why the rate of volunteering among African Americans and Hispanics was lower than among non-Hispanic whites. She perceived that the rate of volunteering was the same among all people who were asked to volunteer, but that the minority groups were asked less often. Gender issues need the same exploration and analysis.

Two authors report to us on extensive interviews they have done to determine how caring values are transmitted from parents to children. In Chapter Four, Paul G. Schervish notes that in twenty years there will literally be millions of millionaires and asks what is likely to ensure that they will give back some of their wealth to the community through philanthropy. By interviewing philanthropists and their children, he has begun to identify variables that with further study could become indicators of whether the intergenerational transmission of philanthropy will occur in a family.

Reading about these families, I cannot help recalling that there have been well-publicized statements by people who have earned substantial wealth who argue that their children as well as society would be better served if tax policy prevented great wealth from being passed between generations. I would like to know what the long-term public policy implications are of our having to count on wealthy parents being successful in raising their children to care about others.

In Chapter Three, Martin Halpern has contributed the life stories of children of the left-wing movement, asking what the consequences are when a caring subculture is out of sync with the larger society. Can it survive and pass on its traditions to the next generation? Halpern concludes that despite the attacks on the left by our government in the 1950s, and the cold-war excoriation of communism, many children of the left have carried their caring values into other social action, such as the civil rights and peace movements. No doubt the left as a subculture is weakened, but the will toward social justice, while more diffuse, exists and can still be rallied among children of the left-wing movement.

In digesting the work of Schervish and Halpern, Staub's four worldviews came to mind, and I asked myself what the chances are that Schervish's second- or third-generation wealthy will become social activists rather than philanthropists, or that Halpern's children of the left-wing will become volunteers in soup kitchens. In other words, if as Staub suggests, there are several distinct attitudes toward caring for others that an individual might have and different ways of manifesting them, is it important which of these ways parents, churches, teachers, and youth workers transmit? After all, even considering the question strictly from the point of view of the INDEPENDENT SECTOR, we not only need philanthropists and volunteers. We also need advocates for social change and professionals as well as volunteers with what Staub calls a "prosocial" worldview. I would like to know more about how each of us develops our particular worldview. Is it our temperament, role models, skills, philosophy?

Conclusion

Like any good book of its kind, this volume raises more questions than it answers. Nevertheless, in addition to food for thought, the volume contains abundant information that will advance both research and practice.

Reference

O'Connell, G. "What Voluntary Activity Can and Cannot Do for America." *Public Administration Review*, Sept.-Oct. 1989, pp. 486–491.

Name Index

H

I

J

K

U

V

W

Y

Z

Subject Index

D

E

V

W

Y

Z